A Storied Sage

Buddhism and Modernity

A SERIES EDITED BY DONALD S. LOPEZ JR.

RECENT BOOKS IN THE SERIES

Rescued from the Nation

BY STEVEN KEMPER (2015)

Grains of Gold

BY GENDUN CHOPEL (2014)

The Birth of Insight

BY ERIK BRAUN (2013)

Religious Bodies Politic

BY ANYA BERNSTEIN (2013)

From Stone to Flesh

BY DONALD S. LOPEZ JR. (2013)

The Museum on the Roof of the World

BY CLARE E. HARRIS (2012)

A Storied Sage

Canon and Creation in the Making of a Japanese Buddha

MICAH L. AUERBACK

The University of Chicago Press Chicago and London

The University of Chicago Press, Chicago 60637
The University of Chicago Press, Ltd., London

Printed in the United States of America
25 24 23 22 21 20 19 18 17 16 1 2 3 4 5

ISBN-13: 978-0-226-28638-9 (cloth)
ISBN-13: 978-0-226-28641-9 (e-book)
DOI: 10.7208/chicago/9780226286419.001.0001

The University of Chicago Press gratefully acknowledges the generous support of the University of Michigan toward the publication of this book.

Library of Congress Cataloging-in-Publication Data
Names: Auerback, Micah L., 1974– author.
Title: A storied sage : canon and creation in the making of a Japanese Buddha / Micah L. Auerback.
Other titles: Buddhism and modernity.
Description: Chicago ; London : The University of Chicago Press, 2016. | Series: Buddhism and modernity
Identifiers: LCCN 2016001192| ISBN 9780226286389 (cloth : alk. paper) | ISBN 9780226286419 (e-book)
Subjects: LCSH: Gautama Buddha. | Buddhism—Japan.
Classification: LCC BQ882 .A94 2016 | DDC 294.3/63—dc23
LC record available at http://lccn.loc.gov/2016001192

♾ This paper meets the requirements of ANSI/NISO Z39.48–1992 (Permanence of Paper).

Contents

Illustrations

Acknowledgments

This book has represented both a new intellectual departure in my life and a return to a personal curiosity about the Buddha from childhood onward. Donald S. Lopez Jr., my faculty mentor and the chair of my academic department through the period of the conception and composition of this book, must receive the lion's share of the credit for its execution. I also owe particular debts of gratitude to other senior colleagues at the University of Michigan who helped me start the project and who followed through to its completion, notably Hitomi Tonomura and David M. Halperin.

This project began in earnest while I was a visiting researcher at the International Research Center for Japanese Studies (Nichibunken) in Kyoto, Japan, courtesy of the Japan Foundation's postdoctoral fellowship (2010–2011). Scholars of particular assistance to me there include my faculty host, Sueki Fumihiko, as well as Araki Hiroshi, John Breen, Patricia Fister, and Inaga Shigemi. My friend Yamaguchi Makoto, while still a professor at Kansai University in Osaka, arranged for me to return to Japan as a visiting scholar for eight weeks in the summer of 2014. I am indebted to him, to his wife, Sayaka, and to their son, Keigo, for their hospitality and care. The Center for Japanese Studies at the University of Michigan also generously funded my research in Japan.

A number of other colleagues and friends, many far away, have provided critical help as I struggled to find and interpret primary sources. Matthew Fraleigh, Maki Fukuoka, Orion Klautau, Dylan Luers, Aaron Proffitt, and

Tomoyuki Sasaki each went to a great deal of trouble to secure books or to make scans or copies that I requested, often for rather obscure materials. Matthew Fraleigh deserves special credit for his willingness to help me with the interpretation of *kanbun*. My colleagues Ben Brose and Kevin Carr have patiently listened to my questions and ideas, and offered valuable feedback. During the course of the research, I received precious guidance and suggestions from Komine Kazuaki, Jacqueline I. Stone, Kathleen Staggs, and Watanabe Mariko, among others. Nathaniel (Nate) Gallant not only discussed many aspects of the research with me, but also provided a valuable occasion and inspiration for visiting sites associated with Jiun Onkō and his disciple, Kōgetsu Sōgi. I am further grateful to the various clerics and specialists affiliated with temples connected to these figures.

Parts of the work in this study were previously presented at the Midwest Japan Forum; at a joint meeting of the East Asia: Transregional Histories Workshop and the Visual and Material Perspectives on East Asia Workshop at the University of Chicago; at the Early Modern Japan Network held in association with the Association of Asian Studies Annual Meeting; and at Western Michigan University. I am indebted to the hosts and to the audiences on those occasions, particularly for their comments and questions. I am particularly grateful to Anne Walthall, who not only shared her expertise concerning Hirata Atsutane, but also graciously read a draft of the fourth chapter and returned it with detailed comments. Hank Glassman read through a draft of the first chapter and returned it with detailed comments as well.

My immediate family provided me with the critical support that I needed in order to complete this project. I thank my mother, Samye Miller; my stepfather, Darryl Stith; and my brother, Benjamin Auerbach, for their unflagging trust in me.

Conventions

East Asian names given in this text mostly follow the standard practice, in which the family name precedes the given name. Exceptions are made for individuals when they write in European languages. A number of individuals discussed in this text used multiple names in different periods of their lives, or, when writing, used pen names (Jpn., *gō* or *gagō*). In other cases, the pronunciation of the characters used to record their name is a matter of dispute. In all such cases, this text arbitrarily (and anachronistically) unifies individuals under one name and one pronunciation. Some individuals—particularly artists, writers, and intellectuals—are best known in Japanese not by their family names, but by their pen names, or less commonly, by one of their other personal names. In these cases, this text generally follows the Japanese practice and refers to such individuals by their pen names or personal names. Just as Natsume Sōseki is typically referred to as "Sōseki," not "Natsume," in this text Hirata Atsutane—who was born Ōwada Shōkichi, but later used the personal name Hanbei, and after his marriage and adoption in his twenties took on the surname Hirata, and who also styled himself "Daigaku," "Ibukinoya," and "Masuganoya," among other names—will be known as he conventionally is in Japanese, as "Atsutane." Okakura Kakuzō, best known by his pen name, Tenshin, is one exception to this use of pen names; here, he is simply "Okakura."

Gregorian years are given for all periods; the year as calculated by traditional East Asian calendrical practice is added when needed. For dates preceding the synchronization of the Japanese national calendar with the Gregorian calendar in 1873, month and date refer to the unit in the Japanese calendrical system, not to the month and date by the Gregorian (or Julian) calculation. The ages of individuals are calculated in the European manner, and not using the traditional East Asian count, by which a newborn baby is already considered to be one year old.

In a book featuring many different tellings of the same story, it is easy to confuse different versions with one another. This text therefore generally cites East Asian literary and artistic works mentioned for the first time in the following format: *Title Translated into English (Title in romanization*, date). After that point, the translated English title then becomes the basic way to refer to any given work. Also, in the interest of helping a nonspecialist readership, this text keeps abbreviations to a minimum. The only one used consistently refers to the *Taishō shinshū Daizōkyō (The Newly Revised Tripiṭaka of the Taishō Era [1912–1926])*, the standard edition of the Buddhist sacred canon in East Asia, in the form "*T* text number: page number, column, line number" (e.g., *T* 189:623c23). Sūtra titles preceded by an asterisk (*) indicate the reconstructions of titles no longer extant in a language of South Asia.

INTRODUCTION

A Buddha without Buddhism

In Japan, the Buddha is poised to outlive Buddhism. Long-established Japanese Buddhist denominations continue to hemorrhage parishioners, and even the new religious groups descended from Buddhist antecedents, so vigorous in the twentieth century, have begun to contract in number. Paradoxically, the Buddha retains a high profile among the Japanese public. Developments over recent years suggest that his stature might even be growing: In 2011, Japan's public educational broadcaster, NHK, included "The Words of the Buddha" in an ongoing television series introducing edifying "great books," ranking them alongside such classics in the global canon of letters as Machiavelli's *The Prince*, Kafka's *Metamorphosis*, and Nietzsche's *Thus Spake Zarathustra*. Meanwhile, critics lauded the bestselling manga series Saint Young Men (2006–), which reimagines the Buddha and Jesus as impecunious twentysomething roommates in present-day Tokyo. And in January 2014, the second film in a Japanese anime trilogy about the life of the Buddha had its gala premiere not in Japan, but at the Louvre in Paris—complete with celebrity appearances by the voice actors and the reigning pop diva Hamasaki Ayumi (1978–). No representative of the Buddhist clergy was in evidence.

Japanese Buddhist clerics and laity traditionally have not focused devotion exclusively, or even principally, on the historical Buddha—that is, the Buddha of our era, as calculated by the Buddhist cosmology, a figure known in

East Asia by such honorifics as "the sage of the Śākya clan," or Śākyamuni. For more than a century, clerics and secular observers alike have noted his relative obscurity as an object of worship in Japan, an observation that has evidently unsettled them to the point of euphemism. "Among the Buddhists of our land," wrote one scholar-cleric in a popular mass-circulation magazine in 1897, "there appear to be awfully cool feelings toward the Master of their Teachings."[1] In 1984, the introduction to the catalog for an exhibit of art depicting the Buddha concluded wistfully: "It is regrettable that faith in Śākyamuni did not take root among the masses in our land, nor later become a dominant force in its Buddhist world."[2] As recently as 2012, a typically inexpensive and glossy popular introduction to the Buddha could note, with understatement: "In Japanese Buddhism, the founders and patriarchs of the denominations seem to be venerated more highly than the Buddha."[3]

Indeed, scholars of Japanese Buddhism in its late, fully developed form often consider the "veneration of denominational founders" (*soshi shinkō*) a defining characteristic, distinguishing it from forms of Buddhism on the Asian continent.[4] Temples built in the Chinese and Korean traditions typically center upon a "[Treasure] Hall of the Great Hero" (Ch. *Daxiong [bao]dian*, Kor. *Taeŭng [po]jŏn*), an honorific for Śākyamuni. On the other hand, it is utterly typical to find images of the founders of Japanese Buddhist denominations or institutions venerated in Japanese temples alongside other deities, even when no image of Śākyamuni is immediately evident. Nor does Śākyamuni necessarily displace Japan's denominational founders: at the main gate of the temple Seiryōji (famed for its tenth-century standing image of Śākyamuni and still an active center of its cult), the contemporary visitor is first greeted by a modern bronze image of a young Hōnen (a.k.a. Genkū, 1133–1212), revered as the founder of Japan's Pure Land denomination (Jōdoshū), to which the temple has been affiliated since the late nineteenth century. Further, it is uncommon for a Japanese Buddhist institution to reverence images depicting events from the life of the Buddha, particularly images preceding the twentieth century. Any recent interest in the Buddha thus not only contrasts with the long and slow decline of institutional Japanese Buddhism, but also breaks with his generally marginal place in the devotional life of Japanese Buddhism.

The present study approaches this paradox of a "Buddha without Buddhism" through a diachronic analysis of narrative and its transformation. Narratives recounting the life of the Buddha—typically to be found in written texts, but also including material culture and ritual practice—have both preceded and outlived other genres in which he appears.[5] Starting from ancient Japan (eighth to sixteenth centuries) and extending into the early 1910s, around the end of Japan's Meiji period (1868–1912), this study shows that stories of the life of the Buddha acquired their resonance in part because they fell outside of the control of Buddhist organizations. Beginning around the turn of the seventeenth century, nonclerical authors began to narrate the Buddha's life story in growing numbers.

After treating the ancient and medieval hagiographic tradition of the life of the Buddha, *A Storied Sage* turns to chart the rise of a "vernacular Buddha" in the popular literary imagination of Japan's seventeenth century. It then considers the appearance of text-critical scholarship about the life of the Buddha in the first decades of the nineteenth century. It concludes by illuminating the activities of elite Meiji-period makers of culture—both lay intellectuals and lay artists in paint, few of whom expressed any commitment to any religious organization—who recast the Buddha as a human being and historical figure. These men inducted the Buddha into the distinctly modern, universal cult of great men of the past. In its brief afterword, the book revisits the questions of hagiography, authority, and emulation, reflecting on what might still constitute a life sacred in modern Japan, and how such sacred lives remain relevant in a "post-Buddhist" society. *A Storied Sage* thus argues that for Japan's Buddhist heritage, modernity meant not only secularization, but also new acts of narrative apotheosis.

Today we find it generally uncontroversial that the Buddha was a historically verifiable prince-turned-sage from ancient India who achieved a cosmic awakening and made his insight available in our world. We still commonly deem his teachings "Buddhism"—that is, "Buddha-ism," cousin to such other world religions as "Christianity" ("Christ-ism") and the now obsolete "Mohammedanism." Such "common sense," though, would only have perplexed the bulk of Buddhist devotees in premodern Japan. Knowing no "world religions," they would have seen the historical Buddha not as the founder and central figure of a global faith, but rather as an illusion, a pale reflection of his true, transcendent, and eternal self. This was, in fact, the very conception of the Buddha advanced in the scripture most influential in medieval Japanese religion, the *Lotus Sutra*.

For succor, Buddhist devotees in medieval Japan would often have supplicated not the distant historical Śākyamuni, but rather a pantheon of other savior deities and saintly figures of old. The savior deities typically had roots in the Buddhist traditions brought to Japan from the Asian continent, but the saints from the past were overwhelmingly native sons, typically understood to be able to help Japanese people more easily than could the distant and long-departed Buddha. The combined pantheon of savior deities and native saints—including a number of other, transcendent buddhas—long since supplanted Śākyamuni as the main objects of worship (*honzon*) in Japanese Buddhist temples (if, indeed, he had ever been the main *honzon*). In 1926, a would-be reformer of Buddhism, the recently laicized Zen Buddhist cleric Kawaguchi Ekai (1866–1945), itemized some of the major rivals to Śākyamuni in Japan:

> In some denominations, the Buddha Amitābha is the object of worship; in others, it is the Buddha Mahāvairocana, and in others, it is the title of a scripture. Again, in temples exclusively devoted to the receipt of benefits (*riyaku*), bodhisattvas like Avalokiteśvara, Mañjuśrī, and Samantabhadra are venerated as the main objects of worship. Again, as the objects of worship in individual halls, some venerate such monks as the Great Masters Kōbō [a.k.a. Kūkai, 774–835], Kenshin [a.k.a. Shinran, 1173–1262], or Risshō [a.k.a. Nichiren, 1222–1282]. And in extreme cases, some temples gather donations from superstitious worshippers, taking as their main image the gods Acalanātha, or Gaṇeśa, or Sarasvatī, or Indra, or Mahākalā, or Vaiśravaṇa, or even Hārītī, or Katō Kiyomasa [1562–1611], or foxes and badgers and the like.[6]

Kawaguchi recounted these details to illustrate the absurdity and disorder resulting from the lack of any single, unifying focus of devotion in Japanese Buddhism. His enumeration begins with deities inherited from India: transcendent, "cosmic" buddhas, and bodhisattvas, "wisdom-beings" who serve as compassionate saviors. The "Great Masters" whom he mentions each stand as the font of a different Buddhist denomination; in each case, the extraordinary life and works of the founder earned him a place as an object of devotion in his own right. The remaining "extreme cases" include a celebrated warrior of medieval Japan, along with lowly trickster animals, among a legion of Indian deities brought to Japan as part of the broader Buddhist pantheon.

To be sure, Śākyamuni also appears in Japanese temples among this welter of gods, but his historical manifestation tends to be downplayed or rendered invisible. In his specifically biographical aspect, for instance, he does appear in the iconography of the Womb World Mandala (Taizōkai) venerated in the Japanese tradition of esoteric Buddhism. Here he makes the "gesture of turning the Wheel of the Dharma" (Skt. *dharmacakra pravartana mudrā*). This is one of many mudras, or stylized gestures, to be found in Buddhist art and practice; the particular gesture here alludes to his preaching activity as a human being. But within the mandala, Śākyamuni's Hall or Cloister (*in*) is displaced from the center. At the heart of the mandala sits a different, transcendent buddha, Mahāvairocana (Jpn. Dainichi), from whom Śākyamuni derives, or whom he represents. Thus arranged, this iconography, highly influential in the Japanese context, communicates the subordinate position of the historical Śākyamuni. More often, though, Śākyamuni as object of veneration typically manifests in a transcendent form, unrelated to any specific moment in his life history. Such iconographic choices distinguish Japanese paintings or sculptures of the Buddha from their counterparts elsewhere in the greater Buddhist world. Images of Śākyamuni in other regions of Buddhist Asia—particularly those made in the Himalayas and in Southeast Asia—often depict him seated, his left hand facing up in his lap, and his right hand reaching down to touch the ground. This gesture alludes to a different moment in the Buddha's life history: his victory over the forces of delusion, or his awakening. This iconography is only very rarely employed in Japanese Buddhist art—even during its earliest period, when Japan's connections to the continent were the strongest.[7]

Whatever else "Buddhism" was in premodern Japan, then, it was explicitly not a "Buddha-ism" dominated by the figure of the human, historical Śākyamuni. Nor did that situation change dramatically with Japan's entry into modernity, typically located in the latter half of the nineteenth century. Like Takada Dōken (1858–1923), also of Zen background, Kawaguchi Ekai stands as an exceptional religious reformer who promoted a place for the Buddha Śākyamuni as the sole object of worship in novel, lay-centered forms of Japanese Buddhist practice.[8] Efforts to launch and sustain such new institutions, conducted from the Meiji years onward, have all faltered; for their part, established Buddhist denominations in Japan have proven reluctant to tamper with their basic ritual and doctrinal frameworks in order to elevate the figure of the Buddha.[9]

More often, established denominations of Japanese Buddhism have, instead, continued to stress the line of descent linking their distinctive teachings to orthodox lineages of transmission, which typically originate with or include Śākyamuni, reaching the Japanese lineage founder only after transmission through India and China. This relationship was strongly emphasized in the special exhibit celebrating the opening in April 2011 of the Ryukoku Museum in Kyoto, Japan, affiliated with Ryukoku University, the flagship educational institution for the Honganji subdenomination of True Pure Land Buddhism. Titled "Śākyamuni and Shinran," the special exhibit ran in conjunction with the commemoration of the seven-hundred-fiftieth anniversary of the death of the founder of Japanese Pure Land Buddhism, Shinran.[10] Occupying multiple floors of the museum, this highly polished exhibition began with artifacts and displays explaining the life of Śākyamuni, the development of Buddhist teaching and practice in India after his death, and Pure Land Buddhist practice in India and China. Continuing on the next floor, the second part of the exhibit shifted to Japan, tracing the distinctive development of Pure Land Buddhist practice there. Here, the focus turned squarely to the life and works of Shinran, and the later advance of his teachings. Of course, Japanese True Pure Land Buddhism has long portrayed Shinran's teaching as a natural inheritance from Śākyamuni, but this exhibit—which represents the edifice of Japanese True Pure Land Buddhism as resting directly upon the foundation laid in Śākyamuni's life, and in no metaphorical sense—stands out as an exceedingly concrete depiction of that relationship. At the same time, it typifies the way in which the figure of the historical Buddha has been subordinated to the histories and self-identities of Japanese Buddhist denominations.

The historical Buddha, then, still communicates to early twenty-first century Japanese society, but typically as mediated by institutions not distinctly Buddhist in character or intent. He has not been a central object of devotion in traditional Japanese Buddhism, nor has he occupied a prominent role in its doctrine, ritual, or narrative, in spite of sporadic efforts by twentieth-century clerical reformers. Even for institutions affiliated with Japanese Buddhist groups, like the Ryukoku Museum, his life may be represented in a mode unmistakably derived from nineteenth-century European academic practice. Needless to say, however, such modern modes of narration have little in common with the accounts of the Buddha's life told and retold in premodern Japan.

The Life of the Buddha as Transmitted to Japan

The vast body of Buddhist literature disseminated in Chinese to Japan from the Asian continent included a range of varied sources relating the life of the Buddha. For a summary of a typical and prominent life of the Buddha as transmitted to ancient Japan, we will look to the *Sutra of Past and Present Cause and Effect* (Chinese: *Guoqu xianzai yinguo jing*, *T* 189), esteemed in no small part for its literary qualities. Like not a few other accounts of the life of the Buddha in the Chinese-language corpus, this sutra (here, a document purporting to record the teachings of the Buddha in his words) has no single antecedent in the literature surviving in Indic or Central Asian languages, though it does echo other texts translated into Chinese.[11] The text's translator, Guṇabhadra (Ch. Qiunabatuoluo, 394–468), also translated from the Āgamas, a body of scriptures with close parallels in all Buddhist traditions. In mid-ninth-century Japan, this text was the basis for at least four illustrated scrolls. As the earliest illustrated handscroll extant in Japan, the *Illustrated Sutra of Past and Present Cause and Effect* was the font of a long-lived and influential artistic genre in Japan. Notably, though, few of those later illustrated scrolls told the life story of the Buddha.

Although the *Sutra of Past and Present Cause and Effect* is not an entirely representative example of Chinese-language biographies of the Buddha, it may still serve as a basis of comparison for later Japanese reworkings of that biography. To establish that comparison for this study, and to suggest a few of the problems in its form and content, it is worthwhile to summarize the text in some detail. The *Sutra of Past and Present Cause and Effect* begins not with the life of the Buddha proper, but rather with a framing narrative. In the Buddha's monastery in the Jetavana park, near the ancient Indian town of Śrāvastī, the Buddha's disciples assemble to ask him to tell them of the past "causes and conditions," the events of their former existences which brought them all to their present state. In response, the Buddha expounds the tale of his own former existence in the unfathomably distant past as an ascetic named Sumedha, who sets off on his journey to Buddhahood by making an offering to the Buddha named Dīpaṣkara (whose name is here translated into Chinese as Pugwang, "Universal Radiance").[12] Sumedha buys flowers to offer him from a woman, accepting her condition that she be reborn as his wife during his future rebirths. After Sumedha offers the flowers, Dīpaṃkara makes a prophecy of Sumedha's rebirth in the distant future as the Buddha Śākyamuni; when Sumedha lays down his hair and deerskin raiment to keep the Buddha's feet dry, he receives permission to become a renunciant, and the vast crowds around him vow to be his followers at that future time.

After his death, Sumedha is reborn countless times, in countless varied lives, in his role as a bodhisattva, a "wisdom being" seeking awakening to save all sentient beings. Finally, he becomes a god in the Tuṣita heaven, only one of many in the Buddhist cosmos. Having accumulated sufficient karmic merit, the bodhisattva decides that the time has come for him to become a buddha. He chooses to be born at the very center point of our world, in the North Indian kingdom of Kapilavastu, as the son of the Śākya clan's king Śuddhodana and his consort, Māyā. The bodhisattva is aware of Māyā's karmic lot, recognizing that she has only a short time left to live, and that she will in any case die seven days after his birth in the human realm. At this stage, the Buddha-to-be announces a blueprint for his later career to his fellow deities in heaven:

> I will descend to be born in Jambudvīpa, in the house of King Śuddhodana of Kapilavastu, of the Śākya clan, scion of [King] Ikṣvāku. Born there, I will leave my parents and relations, abandon wife and child and my rank as a wheel-turning king, renounce the world and study the Way, practice austerities, subjugate Māra, attain perfect wisdom, and turn the wheel of the Dharma. . . . In the manner of the actions of the Buddhas of the past, I will universally benefit gods and men. I will raise the banner of the great Dharma, topple the banner of Māra, and empty the ocean of delusion.[13]

True to his word, the bodhisattva descends into Māyā's body. Even while a fetus, he preaches the dharma to countless numbers of gods and spirits, who visit him in Māyā's womb. Māyā is due to give birth but shows no signs of imminent delivery, and goes with her retinue on an outing to the garden at Lumbinī. When she reaches up to pick a blossom from the "tree of no sadness," the bodhisattva emerges from her left side, causing her no pain. Seven lotus blossoms sprout from the ground; unassisted, the newborn prince takes seven steps upon these, raises his left hand, and declares, "Among all men and gods, I am the most venerable and the most superior. I will put an end to the endless cycle of samsara. In this lifetime, I will benefit all gods and men."[14] The prince is bathed and feted by heavenly beings, taken home, and inspected by the soothsayer Asita, who points out thirty-two characteristic marks on the body of the prince. On the basis of that observation, Asita predicts that the prince will grow up to be either a wheel-turning king—a universal monarch, in ancient Indian conception—or, if he should renounce the world, a sage who attains unexcelled, perfect awakening.

Fearful that the prince might renounce the world and leave him bereft of a successor, his father Śuddhodana attempts to prevent him from absconding, building him a lavishly appointed palace for each of the three seasons, complete with hundreds of female attendants and endless sensual pleasures. Māyā, overwhelmed by the strain of giving birth to a future Buddha, dies, as predicted, seven days later and is reborn as a deity in the Trāyastriṃśa heaven. The infant is given over to the care of her sister, Mahāprajāpatī.

The boy excels in learning (at the age of seven) and sporting competition (at the age of ten): to the astonishment of his teacher, he already knows the contents of all the books in India, and he singlehandedly picks up and flings away an elephant that was incited by his evil cousin, Devadatta, before defeating Devadatta and another cousin, Nanda, in both archery and wrestling. King Śuddhodana ritually recognizes the prince as his successor. On a royal outing with his father, the prince sits under a tree and watches a plowing ritual. A god from the Heaven of the Pure Abode manifests himself as a worm, which is eaten by a bird. At this sight, the prince gives rise to pity for all sentient beings, who are doomed to kill and eat one another; he enters into a deep state of meditation under the tree. When his father later finds the prince there and listens to his explanation, he recalls Asita's prophecy and weeps. When the prince reaches the age of seventeen, his father arranges his marriage to a relative named Yaśodharā, but after the wedding festivities, the prince refuses to sleep with her, preferring instead to meditate. When Śuddhodana learns from the prince's female attendants that they have never seen him have sex with Yaśodharā, he even suspects that the prince might be impotent.

The prince's palace complex has four gates, each opening onto a different garden in a different cardinal direction. The prince receives his father's permission to make four excursions through these gates, one to each of the gardens. In each encounter, despite the king's best efforts to police what the prince will see, Śākyamuni nonetheless discovers something he has never seen before. For each excursion, the god from the Heaven of the Pure Abode transforms himself, taking in succession the forms of an old man, a sick man, a corpse, and a renunciant. The prince thus learns of the inevitability of impermanence and suffering, and the possibility of their redemption. In the latter two encounters, a friend sent by the king, his loyal servant Udāyin, accompanies the prince.

Moved by these encounters, at the age of nineteen, Śākyamuni resolves to leave the palace to seek awakening and an escape from the cycle of birth and death, or samsara. Though he defies his father's wishes by leaving, he nonetheless fulfills his responsibility to produce an heir: he impregnates Yaśodharā—forewarned of his departure by three prophetic nightmares, in which the moon falls from the sky, her teeth fall out, and she loses her left arm—simply by pointing his finger at her belly. When everyone in the palace is asleep, the prince is aided by his groom Channa and the gods, and rides his horse Kaṇṭhaka over the palace fortifications to escape into the forest of ascetic practice.

He removes his ornaments, cuts off his hair, exchanges his clothing with that of a passing hunter (another manifestation of a helpful god), and sends these items home with his groom and horse. In the forest, Śākyamuni meets a group of ascetics attempting to free themselves from the suffering of existence through the mortification of the flesh. Śākyamuni rejects their methods, and is advised to seek out the guidance of two ascetic masters, named Ārāḍa and Kālāma.[15] In the meantime, Channa returns to the palace, where his report is greeted by mourning. The king sends messengers to the forest to bring the prince home, but Śākyamuni rebuffs them. On his way to meet the two ascetic masters, the prince comes to the land of Rājagṛha, whose king, Bimbisāra, offers him co-rule over his kingdom, but the prince again refuses. He finds the two ascetic masters, only to best them in debate and thus earn their admiration and loyalty.

The prince begins six years of harsh austerities with five ascetic companions, seated on the bank of the river Nairañjanā. Horrified at a report of his extreme self-mortification, Śuddhodana, Mahāprajāpatī, and Yaśodharā dispatch Channa with one thousand carts laden with supplies for Śākyamuni. The prince has by this point starved himself until he is skin and bone, but he again refuses. Eventually, he concludes that extreme asceticism will not advance his awakening, either. He bathes in the river, though he is too weak to get out of the water without the aid of the gods. The god of the Heaven of the Pure Abode instructs a cowherd girl named Nandabalā to succor Śākyamuni with food. Her offering of milk gruel gives the prince strength to continue, though his five companions abandon him as a traitor.

The prince sits under a peepul tree, vowing not to move until he has attained awakening. A serpent deity, remembering that this is what previous Buddhas have done before their awakening, comes to praise Śākyamuni with *gāthās*, a poetic form common in Buddhist texts. Transforming himself into a man, the god Indra presents the prince with grass to spread upon his seat, securing a promise to be the first to receive teaching from the Buddha-to-be.

The demon king Māra, lord of the heaven of desire, is alarmed that a Buddha might manifest in the world and frustrate his rule. He sends his army of demons and his three beautiful daughters against the bodhisattva, but neither force nor seduction can break his resolve. Defeated, Māra retreats to his heaven. Meditating through the night, Śākyamuni gains insight into the conditions of beings trapped in the five realms, or paths: hell, animal, hungry ghost, human, and divine. The first three are evil paths, but he finds that even the highest gods are bound by the law of causality and must suffer accordingly. "In the three worlds," he concludes, "there is no ease."[16] In the final watch of the night, the bodhisattva gains insight into the twelvefold chain of causal relation through which ignorance inevitably leads to old age, suffering, and death. Now a fully awakened Buddha, he realizes again that ignorance may be eliminated, and that there is a Noble Eightfold Path leading to the state of *parinirvāṇa*, a term transcribed into this sutra with no explicit definition. All the gods, with the exception of Māra, are overwhelmed with joy and shower the new Buddha with offerings and praise.

The gods Brahmā and Indra beg the Buddha to turn the wheel of dharma, a request to which he accedes after seven days in meditation. Omniscient, he scans the entire universe for two weeks, only to discover that both Ārāḍa and Kālāma have passed away. However, he does note that his former five companions are still alive, residing in the Deer Park at Vārāṇasī. On his way there, the Buddha receives offerings from two merchants, the first people to take refuge in him; he converts an unbeliever; and he is sheltered by the divine serpent king Mucilinda while he meditates for seven days. Reaching the Deer Park, the Buddha preaches the "Four Sublime Verities" [17] and the Noble Eightfold Path to the five ascetics. At the Buddha's summons, their hair and beards fall out of their own accord, and monastic robes spontaneously appear to clad their bodies. They attain awakening as arhats, "worthy ones" who have exhausted their karmic afflictions. Their awakening restores to the world the complete "Three Treasures": the Buddha; his teaching, or dharma; and his monastic followers, the sangha. Although the narration of the sutra does not explicate the point directly, it presumes that readers are aware that these treasures are subject to cosmically long, recurring periods of absence.

The rest of the sutra narrates further conversions to the Buddha's cause: the wealthy layman Yaśas and his fifty relatives, who all also attain the state of the arhat; the three Kāśyapa brothers and their followers, who discard their worship of a sacred flame when the Buddha uses his superhuman powers to achieve such wonders as igniting and extinguishing their flame at will; and King Bimbisāra, who now accepts the Buddha's teaching, in place of his worldly rule. In these sections, the Buddha also converts some of the disciples most important in the Buddhist world as a whole: the friends Śāriputra and Maudgalyāyana, and the Buddha's later successor Mahākāśyapa, who like the Buddha was adorned with the "thirty-two marks" of an awakened being.

The sutra closes by returning to the framing narrative, during which the Buddha has been telling the story of his own life. Here, the Buddha discloses the karmic connections between the characters in the tale of Sumedha and his own time. Sumedha, of course, is none other than the Buddha himself; the various heretics and onlookers whom he encountered as Sumedha have now become the Kāśyapa brothers and their followers; the woman who sold Sumedha the flowers to offer to Dīpaṃkara later became his wife Yaśodharā, and so on. In the Buddha's final words of the text, which may be taken to summarize its key message: "You must all know that the karmic seeds of the past do not perish, even though countless cosmic eons may pass, but I . . . have achieved omniscient knowledge. You should all practice the Way assiduously, without neglect."[18]

Complications in the Tales of the Life of the Buddha

As this short summary shows, even historically influential versions of the life of the Buddha may vary considerably from the versions familiar in the contemporary Anglophone world. The *Sutra of Past and Present Cause and Effect* neither begins nor ends where we might expect: in addition to the framing story, its narrative proper begins countless eons before the birth of the Buddha, and it ends abruptly, while the Buddha is still engaged in his preaching career. The use of a frame story to set off an account of events in past lives to explain events in the narrative present, prominent in this text, is less definitively characteristic of Chinese-language biographies of the Buddha than of a vast genre of "birth" (Skt. *jātaka*) stories (Jpn. *honjōtan*, "tales of root births") in a range of Buddhist scriptural languages. Although this sutra is typically classified in Anglophone scholarship as a biography, or hagiography—labels that will appear in this work as well—there is a strong sense in which it is not the life story of a single individual, nor even the story of a single being who passes through various roles in various lifetimes. After all, at multiple points in the narrative, the Buddha-to-be or other characters discuss in broad terms how a Buddha is made, by following what John Strong called a "bio-blueprint," which the life story of the Buddha both describes and prescribes.[19] That feature of the text announces that the biography of Śākyamuni is, in one sense, not at all the biography of any specific individual, but rather, just one enactment of an unchanging, cosmic formula. In these and other senses, narratives such as the one in this sutra confound our expectations when we consider them biographies or hagiographies.

The content of the sutra proves no less challenging than its form. The Buddha now so well known in the Anglophone world, "today regarded as the founder of a global humanist religion of science," is nowhere evident in this narrative.[20] Nor does this Buddha prove to be a philosopher first of all, for he wins over disciples as much through displays of wonder as through his argumentation. Even before his awakening, the prince is here described not as a human being really suffering from existential doubts, but as an exalted figure who actually has no traffic with sex, death, or impurity. He fulfills his filial duty to impregnate his wife and therefore to produce an heir merely by pointing his finger at her belly, and his youthful encounters with loss and transience on his various outings all turn out to be mere displays engineered by the gods. Such Buddhist texts as the *Lotus Sutra* press these implications further, representing the Buddha Śākyamuni as in no sense a truly existent human being, but rather as an illusory projection of his true, transcendent form. Indeed, by the time Buddhism reached Japan, there was already a well-elaborated theory of the different "bodies" of the Buddha. The most influential articulation of this theory associated the Buddha with "three bodies" (Skt. *trikāya*, Jpn. *sanjin*): his eternal *dharmakāya*, or "body of truth"; his *saṃbhodgakāya*, or "body of reward," a body visible only to advanced students of the Buddhist path; and his transitory *nirmāṇakāya*, or "body of transformation," the body visible to ordinary, unawakened beings.

If this vision of the Buddha—as wonderworker or emanation—conflicts with later humanistic interpretations of his importance, then other details of the text conflict with elements elsewhere in the biographical literature. From the first through the tenth centuries CE, some sixteen translations of varying biographical texts into Chinese are recorded. All but three of these survived to reach Japan, and even lost texts could be transmitted in alternate versions.[21] There is also a much larger quantity of Buddhist texts describing episodes from the life of the Buddha episodically. Among these various biographical sources—none of which has ever definitively displaced the others—the prince has other wives, or his wife has a different name; Yaśodharā bears him at least one son, named Rāhula; the Buddha's age at the events of his life vary by as many as ten years; he seeks out not two ascetic sages, named Ārāḍa and Kālāma, but a single sage named Ārāḍa Kālāma; at the end of his asceticism, he is succored not by a single cowherd girl named Nandabalā, but by two girls, one named Nanda and one Nandabalā, or by one named Sujātā; and he sees not five paths of rebirth, but six. These are just a few elements in this text to contradict others. A different kind of problem concerns the parts of the Buddha's career left unelaborated in the *Sutra of Past and Present Cause and Effect*: In what order did the Buddha preach his various teachings? How did he die? How were his teachings transmitted and preserved after his death?

Chinese Buddhist intellectuals thus faced an excess of contradictory accounts of some events of the life of the Buddha, on the one hand, and a paucity of complete accounts of the life of the Buddha, on the other. From the early sixth century onward, Chinese monks began to select and combine material from the various incomplete accounts of the Buddha's life into anthologies, which aimed to relate the complete biography. These anthologies appeared sometimes as independent works, and sometimes as part of larger encyclopedias or collections of biographies. Also by the sixth century, Chinese Buddhist exegetes began to develop hermeneutic techniques by which to adjudicate among various—apparently conflicting—scriptural teachings. Only in Japan during the Edo period (1603–1868) did lay scholars, unbeholden to Buddhist institutions, begin to scrutinize the multiplicity of, and contradiction among, various Buddhist scriptures—including accounts of the life of the Buddha. For the first time, they understood such contradictions not as evidence of the Buddha's "skillful means" in preaching different messages, each suited to the spiritual capacities of different listeners, but rather as grounds for considering these different versions to be in contradiction, and not all equally valid.

Determining the generic classification of the canonical biographies of the Buddha, inquiring into the nature of their protagonist, and tracing the development and ramifications of various narratives of his life through the study of textual variants are all worthy projects, but settling them is not an aim of the present study. Rather, this study reveals how such questions were treated across centuries of retelling the life of the Buddha in multiple forms in Japan. It is, therefore, concerned less with the "actual" life of the Buddha itself than with the myriad transformations undergone by the accounts of that life in the Japanese context. Nor is the pursuit of those transformations, however fascinating and diverse, an end in its own right. Rather, by reading and rereading the "same" story—and by "trespassing" (i.e., reading) across different periods, textual genres, and material media—this study not only exposes the conditions of knowledge implicit in Japanese retellings of the life, but also reveals why that life has remained meaningful and worthy of study, both for Buddhist intellectuals and for their opponents.

The Scope and Position of This Study

Despite the relative marginality of tales of the life of the Buddha in the mature Japanese Buddhist tradition, the study of Japanese retellings poses difficulties arising from the quantity and variety of sources still available. As noted by the art historian Donohashi Akio, "no tale or legend coming to Japan from foreign lands has had such great influence on Japanese painting" as that of the Buddha, an observation which might be applied to textual biographies as well.[22] Elements of his biography not only stimulated the hagiography of such indigenous heroes of Japanese history and religion as Prince Shōtoku; they also influenced even Japan's early monumental work of fiction, the *Tale of Genji*, itself.[23] A list prepared by Komine Kazuaki, a leading investigator of the biographies of the Buddha in premodern Japan, identifies some thirty principal premodern texts and images, created in Japan from the seventh century through the middle of the nineteenth. These too have their own variants: one family of texts, known collectively as the *Original Ground of Śākyamuni* (*Shaka no honji*), is extant in no fewer than six handscroll editions (some incomplete) and ten illustrated codices, not counting manuscript and print editions produced without illustration.[24] This list excludes many key representations of scenes from the life of Śākyamuni in painting or sculpture, both extant and lost.

A Storied Sage makes no effort to treat the biographical tradition comprehensively; in this study, the selection of sources has been driven principally by the need to show where and how the biographical tradition changed. Thus *A Storied Sage* highlights not so much continuity within the biographical tradition—although that is not to be underestimated—but rather, moments of tension, rupture, or reorientation in the epistemic foundations of the depictions of the Buddha. Some genres of material production, such as the vast proliferation of images of the Buddha's final extinction, or *parinirvāṇa*, receive only scant treatment as a result.

The study of hagiography—in its broadest sense, referring to any representation of a sacred life—retains a prominent role in the Anglophone study of a variety of religious traditions. Within the vast literature about the saints of European Christianity, however, scholarship concerning the production of hagiographies after the medieval period, or their adaptation by later authors, remains relatively scant.[25] Likewise, the English-language monographs comprising the recent outpouring of scholarship concerning hagiography in Japanese Buddhism all focus on the ancient and medieval periods.[26] While recent Anglophone monographs concerning South Asia have begun to treat the tales of premodern sacred figures in the modern world, similar studies have yet to be carried out for any figures within the world of Japanese Buddhism.[27] (There is, however, an excellent Japanese-language study of the various doctrinal, literary, and historiographic reframings of Shinran in the modern period.[28])

Within Anglophone scholarship on Japanese Buddhism, the study closest to *A Storied Sage* might be Michael Radich's 2011 *How Ajātaśatru Was Reformed: The Domestication of "Ajase" and Stories in Buddhist History*.[29] This research treats the complex of legends concerning the prince Ajātaśatru, contemporary to the Buddha and an "anti-saint" of sorts. A parricide and a regicide, the prince developed into a symbol of repentance in Buddhist literature produced in ancient India, of healing in medieval China, and of implacable evil in medieval Japan. In the twentieth century, his tale was appropriated among Japanese psychoanalytic circles as a challenge to the universality of Freud's Oedipus complex. Despite its basic similarities, this study does not share the emphasis in *A Storied Sage* upon the problem of historical knowledge. Again, unlike Ajātaśatru—who was hardly a moral exemplar, even for Shinran—the historical Buddha has traditionally been an object of longing and devotion. Even the most adventurous reworkings of his life story in Japan maintain that disposition to the object of the narrative. By contrast, this study focuses on the tensions that developed between the historical Buddha as an object of devotion, on the one hand, and as an object of historical study, on the other. Precisely because the Buddha Śākyamuni's life was—and is still—considered to be a kind of "historical fact," the investigation of its development in Japan requires a different approach.

The Structure of This Study

After a brief consideration of continental literature and material culture treating the life of the Buddha, chapter 1, "The Buddha as Preceptor," surveys the depictions of the Buddha's life story in Japanese Buddhism from its ancient to medieval periods. It touches on monuments (the five-story pagoda at the temple Hōryūji, early eighth century), homiletic texts (*Tōdaiji Notes for Sermons*, early ninth century), and texts written for beginning students of Buddhism.

Taking its inspiration from the Buddha's common epithet as "teacher of gods and humans," this chapter considers this heterogeneous body of tales as products and instruments of pedagogy. These works "learned from" the Chinese-language hagiographies that were translated, or compiled anew, on the Asian continent. The chief innovation in these tales occurred in their accounts of the Buddha's own teaching career, an area in which otherwise influential scriptures (typified by the *Sutra of Past and Present Cause and Effect*) were particularly lacking in detail. Elaboration of the types of the Buddha's teachings and the order in which they were produced allowed early Japanese intellectuals to assert the priority of their particular school, particularly in the Tendai tradition of Buddhism. Such accounts of the lives of the Buddha themselves served pedagogical purposes, as textbooks for novice students of Buddhism. In the early medieval period, some reformist clerics even sought to revive the religious centrality of the historical Buddha. As this chapter shows, early hagiographers of the Buddha in Japan were, on the whole, faithful pupils of their teachers in China and Korea.

Having explained the assimilation of continental hagiographies in Japan, chapter 2, "The Buddha as Local Hero," moves to the turn of the seventeenth century, a period when over a century of civil war finally ended and Buddhist temples began to lose their preeminence in learning, publication, and entertainment. This chapter pursues the early modern reinvention of the tale of the historical Buddha as an entertaining romance, stressing its role as a commodity, peddled by authors outside temple walls who cared less for orthodoxy than for profit. Adapted by anonymous commercial writers and the master dramatist Chikamatsu Monzaemon (1653–1725) alike, tales about the Buddha grew increasingly unconstrained by the strictures of received orthodoxy. Chikamatsu's Buddha narrowly escapes from the dastardly schemes of his wicked stepmother through the heroism of his loyal retainer, and he attains awakening not through his own meditative skill, but when his guru strikes him with his staff. Chikamatsu stocks the drama with acts of derring-do and graphic violence, possible on stage because he wrote not for human actors, but for puppets. Yet this play is no arbitrary act of anachronism: like Vittore Carpaccio's sixteenth-century painting of Saint Augustine, which brings the Church Father into the studio of a Renaissance scholar, Chikamatsu's play transports a venerable saint into the world of its own creation. In this way, the timeless Indian sage metamorphosed into a vernacular figure, easily understood by early modern Japanese. Although the Buddha was vernacularized, he was not necessarily demoted to human status or secularized, for these tales continued to revel in the Buddha's superhuman powers. A second, mid-nineteenth-century wave of popular literature about the Buddha inherited the innovations of the seventeenth century, transposing his story into the new registers of kabuki, the epic serial adventure story, and even woodblock illustration by Katsushika Hokusai (1760–1849). Like their predecessors, these nineteenth-century retellings lived on in commercial reprints and in theatrical production, dominating popular perceptions of the Buddha into the twentieth century.

Sheltered from commercial pressures and increasingly inward looking, the established Buddhist institutions of the early modern era seem not to have disputed these retellings. Sporadically, though, individual clerical intellectuals did attempt to revive orthodox visions of the life of the Buddha. Chapter 3, "The Buddha as Exemplar," shows how these revivals elevated the historical Buddha not just as an object of devotion, but also as an exemplar for proper conduct. It focuses upon a specialist in monastic discipline, Kōgetsu Sōgi (1756–1833), who produced her own written version of the life of the historical Buddha. A nun and disciple of the influential monastic reformer Jiun Onkō (1718–1805), Kōgetsu wrote of her dismay at the circulation of "distorted" popular tales of the Buddha. In response, she composed her own orthodox life of the Buddha, *Light of the Three Ages*, in elegant neoclassical Japanese prose. A traditionalist but not a hostage to tradition, Kōgetsu based her retelling on Jiun's teachings and her own investigation of canonical texts, infusing her book with acerbic observations about the Buddhist clerics of her day. *Light of the Three Ages* represents one of the few prose works by early modern women to enter print in their own era. Half a century after Kōgetsu's death, reformist male Buddhist clerics rediscovered her book and republished it, enlisting Kōgetsu as an ally in their project of reviving the pure practice of the monastic discipline.

Chapter 4, "The Buddha as Fraud," takes up the study of the life of the Buddha by Hirata Atsutane (1776–1843), a giant of Japanese "National Learning," and also a virulent adversary of Buddhism. Ironically, this avowed opponent of the Buddha became his most important premodern critical biographer. Atsutane was the first scholar in Japan to use text-critical scrutiny of Buddhist texts themselves to produce a demythologized account of the Buddha as a mere human being who lived in a historical past.

Based on this scholarship, Atsutane composed two critiques of Buddhism: one in an oral, vernacular style, and the other built from annotations of scriptural passages in the Chinese. In each text, the life of the historical Buddha occupies pride of place. This study recognizes Atsutane as the "father" of the historical Buddha, in the sense of distinguishing the study of the Buddha from devotion to him, and of locating the Buddha merely as a figure in history. Atsutane made extensive use of long-neglected scriptures, particularly from a class of texts preserved in the Buddhist canon known as the Āgamas. These he recognized as the oldest Buddhist scriptures available in Japan, though he did not know that they have parallels in Buddhist canons in such languages as Pāli and Tibetan. Unlike his near contemporary Kōgetsu, he studied scriptures not to elevate the Buddha, but to demolish him. Atsutane accused the Buddha of being a cheat and a fraud who shamelessly appropriated and distorted orthodox Brahmanical teachings for his own nefarious ends. However demythologized, though, Atsutane's Buddha is not the humanistic Buddha familiar from later rationalist reworkings—Atsutane believed in the reality of the Buddha's superhuman powers, even as he dismissed them as mere displays of magic.

Atsutane restricted these iconoclastic claims to texts intended to circulate only among the disciples of his private academy. After his death, a rogue disciple acquired Atsutane's vernacular text, *A Mocking Discourse upon Emerging from Meditation* (1811), and printed it in a pirate edition (1849). Atsutane's successors at the academy protested, but too late to prevent the text from circulating widely over the following decades. Leading Buddhist intellectuals of the day reacted to Atsutane's work with shock. On the eve of the Meiji Restoration of 1868, during a time of profound social dislocation, one Zen monk even managed to publish a refutation in print, but he seems to have convinced few readers not already committed to the Buddhist cause. His failure to counter the new historicist scholarship foreshadowed the profound trauma that would be visited on Japanese Buddhists in their transition to modernity.

In the aftermath of the Meiji Restoration of 1868, Buddhist institutions struggled to survive. Chapter 5, "The Buddha as Character," shows how lay intellectuals took the lead in a new wave of scholarly inquiry into the historical Buddha. Following the recently developed European consensus about the historical reality and global stature of the Buddha, Japanese intellectuals "discovered" him as a philosopher and a historical personage. The key recognition here was of the Buddha not merely as a human figure (*jinbutsu*), but also as the human possessor of a moral or ethical character (*jinkaku*) of unique world-historical importance.

That turn to history registered in printed texts as well as in the new artistic style of "Japanese painting," or Nihonga. From the 1890s, young Nihonga artists experimented in decoupling scenes of the life the Buddha from received iconographic conventions. Unimpressed, art critics pilloried their early attempts as inauthentic, neither inheriting the received traditions, nor depicting a truly Indian Buddha. From 1901, members of the nascent Nihonga community began to journey to India, sometimes for protracted sojourns. There they sought authentically "Indian" landscapes, art, and architecture. The works of art to result from these travels set the standard for new, historically informed iconographies of the Buddha in painting and sculpture.

The reinscription of the Buddha as a historical figure did not put a stop to his career as an object of devotion. Instead, late-Meiji-era intellectuals could now apotheosize him within the new European-inspired cult of great men of the past. This chapter foregrounds the role in this process of a coterie of laymen, linked through Tokyo Imperial University's newly founded Department of Philosophy: Inoue Tetsujirō (1856–1944), Takayama Chogyū (1871–1902), and Anesaki Masaharu (1873–1949). Members of this group tried both to universalize the Buddha's prominence through comparison with the global canon of other great men, and to grapple with the Buddha's "Aryan" identity as dictated by European racial theory. They penned the first modern demythologized retelling of the Buddha's life in a book for the edification of young readers. And through careful comparison of the Āgamas in their Pāli and Chinese incarnations, they attempted to trace the historical development of the human character of the Buddha into its later, apotheosized progeny.

Nor did that process of apotheosis end with their investigations. In the first decade of the twentieth century, appeals to "character" became a powerful device through which to secure the place of the historical Buddha in a new global pantheon. Japanese intellectuals concluded that the Buddha was no run-of-the-mill holder of a "great character"; his character was evinced in the sheer level of adoration that he attracted over thousands of years. Reread in this way, the fantastic elements of the lives of the Buddha ceased to mitigate his value, and instead became evidence in support of it. That character, claimed the disciples of modernity, lived on for resuscitation and emulation.

In its afterword, *A Storied Sage* considers hagiographic literature as an entity with a life history in its own right. In Japan, the devotional hagiographies of the Buddha may indeed have "given up the ghost" in the transition to modernity; today, the vast popular literature about the life of the Buddha produced before the twentieth century languishes, now largely forgotten. Yet the Buddha whom we meet today through Japanese television, film, and manga is nonetheless the descendent of that earlier, forgotten figure. For the Buddha to attain relevance in a new era, he had to give up his superhuman powers and become a mere man. It is precisely as a man that he has been able to embody the transcendent values of the modern age.

ONE

The Buddha as Preceptor

Whether written, painted, or sculpted, surprisingly few Japanese portrayals of the life of Śākyamuni predate Japan's turbulent sixteenth century. This chapter focuses upon these early respresentations of the life of the Buddha. It argues that they were largely consonant with versions circulating elsewhere in East Asia; in other words, their authors generally aspired to retell what they perceived to be an "orthodox" version of the life tale, on the basis of teachings authorized by Buddhist or state institutions. Like the Buddha of those continental precedents, the Buddha of ancient and medieval Japan appears principally as a great teacher, and master of an authoritative teaching.[1]

In both form and content, these early Japanese biographies shine as the products of eager and receptive students. Particularly in their early phases, Japanese retellings largely recapitulated the form of continental precedents: when written, they were typically composed in classical Chinese or a highly Siniziced form of Japanese; when painted, they tended to follow continental styles with little evident variation. There was no lack of exemplars to follow. By the seventh century, Buddhist intellectuals in China had already devoted considerable effort to distilling comprehensive accounts of the life of the Buddha from the many conflicting scriptural accounts.

Perhaps this is one reason that Japanese counterparts showed relatively little interest in crafting such long, comprehensive versions. Rather, Japanese Buddhist intellectuals produced narratives and images that drew upon specific, isolated episodes from the life story of Śākyamuni, and they embedded other narratives of the life of the Buddha within the edifices of larger textual or architectural frameworks. Despite the tectonic political shifts marking the advent of Japan's medieval world late in the twelfth century, these patterns of production, content, style, and context remained remarkably consistent until the sixteenth century.

The relative paucity of indigenous biographical narratives about the Buddha did not stem from any more general reluctance to produce hagiography in ancient and medieval Japan. The same period saw an upsurge of interest in the lives of indigenous Japanese Buddhist heroes, including the early prince regent Shōtoku (574–622) and the renegade populist monk Gyōki (668–749). Shōtoku was already the focus of a cult as early as the Heian period (conventionally, 794–1185), and he was later considered a reincarnation of Śākyamuni.[2] Self-contained accounts of Gyōki began to circulate from the issuance of a compact but complete memorial biography of him, recorded by a disciple in 749.[3] By Japan's medieval period, both Gyōki and Shōtoku, among others, were venerated as bodhisattvas in their own right. Also following continental precedents, Japanese authors began to write biographies of Japan's own eminent monks by the late eighth century.[4]

How to account for the relative lack of Japanese biographic interest in Śākyamuni? To be certain, the Buddhist traditions influential in Japan did tend to relegate the historical Śākyamuni to a conspicuously diminished role: the *nirmāṇakāya* (Jpn. *ōjin*), the mere "emanation" or "magical transformation" body, a pale reflection of a much greater cosmic reality. Indeed, an insistence on the provisional and incomplete nature of the man Śākyamuni and of his teaching lies at the heart of the *Lotus Sutra*, which stands as arguably the single most influential text in Japanese Buddhist history. According to the *Lotus Sutra*, the figure who merely manifested as Śākyamuni is actually "a being of almost infinite extent and duration who appears in particular times and places through the expedient device of self-conjuring."[5] This interpretation was taken up within "Heavenly Terrace" or Tiantai (Jpn. Tendai, Kor. Ch'ŏnt'ae), a major movement in East Asian Buddhism that accepted this sutra as its key text for exegesis. In Japan, Tendai Buddhism was arguably the single dominant intellectual tradition through at least the end of the Heian period. Saichō, its Japanese founder, and his successors "redefined Śākyamuni of the *Lotus Sutra*, not as an individual person who had once cultivated bodhisattva practice and achieved Buddhahood, but as an originally inherent Buddha, without beginning or end."[6] Given this particular standpoint, it is not surprising that so much early Buddhist art in Japan focuses not upon the Buddha Śākyamuni, but upon other, cosmic figures who are still available to help supplicants in this world.

The Biography of the Buddha in Imperial China: Elite Monastic Sources

Unlike their continental counterparts, Japanese Buddhist monastics and laity left no records of successful voyages to the medieval homelands of the Buddhist world in South and Southeast Asia; the Japanese archipelago produced no traveler comparable to the celebrated pilgrims Xuanzang (600/602–664), Yijing (635–713), or Hyech'o (c. 704–780). To be sure, some towering figures in Japanese Buddhist history aspired to travel to India, and some devout Japanese Buddhists actually did attempt to travel to India, but it seems that none of them returned safely.[7] Further, virtually all the continental Buddhist masters to reach Japan before the modern period were Korean or Chinese in origin.[8] Thus, until at least their first contact with Europeans in the sixteenth century, Japanese had to rely almost entirely upon sources written in Chinese to learn about India or the Buddha.[9]

Because ancient and medieval Japanese retellings of the life of the Buddha relied so heavily on precedents originating in China, here it will be useful to survey two sets of Chinese biographical texts used extensively in premodern Japan: first, the canonical (translated) accounts of the life of the Buddha, and second, the original Chinese anthologies built from them. Of course, the difference here is not so much between texts that reflect Indian sources and those that were built from such accounts; instead, the difference is between sources that claimed a foreign provenance (typically known in Chinese as a *jing*, "scripture") and those that did not. Biographical accounts of the Buddha began to reach China by the end of the latter Han dynasty (25–220).[10] Most of the biographical accounts ultimately influential in imperial China were established by the Tang period (618–907); needless to say, some are more closely related to extant South Asian sources than others.

Independently circulating accounts of part or all of the life of the Buddha, translated into Chinese by the early Tang period, include the following: the *Avadāna [i.e., Tale] of the Practice [of the Bodhisattva]* (*Xiuxing benqi jing*, *T* 184, date of translation controversial); the *Avadāna of the Auspicious [Deeds] of the Prince [Siddhārtha]* (*Taizi ruiying benqi jing*, *T* 185, translated between 222 and 229); two texts related to the *Ex-*

haustive Narrative of the Play [of the Buddha] (Skt. *Lalitavistara*), the *Sutra of the Display [of the Deeds of the Buddha]* (*Puyao jing*, *T* 186, translated between 265 and 313) and the *Extended Garland [of the Deeds of the Buddha]* (*Fangguang dazhuangyan jing*, *T* 187, translated between 680 and 688); Aśvaghoṣa's *Acts of the Buddha* (*Buddhacarita*), translated into Chinese as *Praise of the Deeds of the Buddha* (*Fo suo xing zan*, *T* 192, translated between 414 and 421); the *Sutra of Past and Present Cause and Effect* (translated between 435 and 443); and the compilation *Sutra of the Collection of Authentic Deeds of the Buddha* (*Fo benxing ji jing*, *T* 190, translated between 560 and 600).[11]

It would be a mistake to regard these texts as uniform efforts to establish faithful correspondence between various Indic "originals" and target texts in Chinese. Like much other Buddhist scriptural literature, the biographies of the Buddha came to zones of Chinese culture haphazardly, and not always intact. For instance, while they are cataloged as distinct scriptures, an early version of the *Avadāna of the Practice* and the *Middle Scripture of the Authentic Deeds* (*Zhong benqi jing*, *T* 196, translated between 196 and 200) actually seem to be related texts; they may have originally formed two parts of a single continuous text.[12] In other cases, Chinese translators dynamically reorganized materials from various scriptures into larger edited textual compendia, employing a process labeled by Funayama Tōru, with a playful nod to the manufacture of electronics, as "*sutras* made in India, [but] assembled in China."[13] The *Sutra of the Collection of Authentic Deeds of the Buddha*, which demonstrably draws on multiple other scriptures, is emblematic of this tendency. Nor would such recombination necessarily have seemed to represent the imposition of a framework alien to the texts in question. The later catalogers of Chinese Buddhist scriptures sometimes treated various biographical scriptures as though they were extracts from a single large text.[14]

Elements of the biography of the Buddha also entered the Chinese language within other vast textual assemblages, including the Chinese versions of the Āgama literature, and a key text of the *vinaya*, or monastic discipline, the enormous *Minor Section of the Monastic Code of the Root Group That Teaches That All Exists* (Skt. *Mūlasarvastivāda vinayakṣudrakavastu*, Ch. *Genben shuo yiqie youbu pinaiye zashi*, *T* 1451, translated into Chinese in the early 700s).[15] The final wave of texts with biographical accounts of Śākyamuni arrived in China at the start of the Northern Song dynasty (960–1127). With texts came the Gupta-era Indian cult of the eight sacred sites (*aṣṭamahāpratihārya*), pilgrimage destinations associated with specific scenes in the Buddha's life, each symbolized by a stupa, or reliquary mound. Such texts in this final wave of premodern textual translation included the *Sutra of the Great Sammata King* (*Zhongxu mohedi jing, T* 191) and the *Sutra of the Titles of the Eight Great Numinous Stupas* (*Bada lingta minghao jing, T* 1685).[16] These newly translated Buddhist texts attracted relatively little attention and interest from the Chinese monastic community, who were at the time actively attempting to distinguish Buddhism in China from its Indian origins.[17]

Therefore, it was the long first wave of translation activities that generally provided Chinese writers with the basic materials that they used in building up their own biographical records. A monk named Sengyou (445–518) is credited with the first extant Chinese effort to narrate a self-contained biography of the Buddha, the *Genealogy of Śākyamuni* (Ch. *Shijia pu, T* 2040, first issued in 502). The *Genealogy* synthesized the various conflicting scriptural descriptions of the life of Śākyamuni as they had been translated in China. Sengyou selected and arranged passages from the sutra and *vinaya* texts available to him—each a fragmentary account from the Buddha's biography in its own right—into an original anthology, so as to tell the complete story of the Buddha's life.

Sengyou aimed for comprehensiveness: he began with the origins of the present world and the Śākya clan, proceeded to narrate the career of Śākyamuni through his awakening and cremation, continued to retell the enshrinement and adoration of his relics, and concluded with the Buddha Śākyamuni's prediction of the demise of his dharma and of the advent of Maitreya, the Buddha of the future. The decision to couch the biography in such broad terms was innovative because at that early date, Sengyou would not have had access to any single canonical source recounting the Buddha's life in its entirety, particularly one that continued beyond his awakening and through his final extinction, or *parinirvāṇa*.[18] His work was critically innovative, too, because it resulted from his conscious decisions to adjudicate between competing accounts of the same events, decisions that Sengyou sometimes explained with his own commentary.

Later independent Chinese biographies of the Buddha largely followed Sengyou's model. The monk Daoxuan (596–667) abridged Sengyou's anthology—which Sengyou had issued in both five- and ten-fascicle editions—into the much shorter, one-volume *Genealogy of the Śākya Clan* (Ch. *Shijia shi pu, T* 2014) of 665. Around the same time, the lay literatus Wang Bo (ca. 649–ca. 676) composed his own *Record of the Attainment of the Way by the Tathāgata Śākyamuni* (Ch. *Shijia rulai chengdao ji, T* 1508). Centuries later, the monk Daocheng (fl. 1019) of the Northern Song dynasty reissued Wang's text with his own detailed commentary, as the *Annotated Record of the Attainment of the Way by the Tathāgata Śākyamuni* (*Shijia rulai chengdao ji zhu, T* 1509), which began to function very much like a scripture in its own right. It eventually circulated widely throughout the region: to Korea, the Ryūkyū kingdom, the Japanese archipelago, and Vietnam, where it could still be dedicated in memorial ritual, just like a conventional sutra, as late as the early twentieth century.[19]

Wang's work also exerted a strong influence on the final great biographical compendium concerning the Buddha to be produced in late imperial China: the *Origins and Transmission of the Śākya Clan* (*Shishi yuanliu*, ca. 1425). First assembled by the monk Baocheng (fl. 1425), early in the Ming dynasty (1368–1644), the text was reissued at imperial behest in 1486, graced with a preface by the reigning emperor himself. In this, its first imperially sponsored edition, the illustrations for the text were substantially elaborated. Late in the eighteenth century, a prince of the Qing dynasty (1644–1911) commissioned another edition, whose illustrations he ordered to be rendered not in an Indian manner, but in the style of contemporary Chinese life, to allow readers to feel more familiarity with the material.[20] As this pocket publication history suggests, the *Origins and Transmission of the Śākya Clan* achieved no little success as a text. Appearing in various editions under various titles, its illustrated editions circulated widely, inspiring wall murals at Buddhist temples in both China and Korea.[21] The *Origins and Transmission* reached Japan as well, though it exerted a much slighter impact there.[22]

The life of the Buddha also reappeared in biographical compendia of Buddhist lineages produced within China, typically to answer a need for the legitimization of particular groups. The biography of the Buddha Śākyamuni features prominently in the *Chronicle of the Bejeweled Forest* (*Baolin zhuan*, compiled in 801), the *Anthology from the Patriarchal Hall* (*Zutang ji*, compiled in 952), the *Record of the Transmission of the Light of the Lamp of the Jingde Era* (*Jingde chuandeng lu, T* 2076, compiled in 1004), the *Orthodox Transmission of the Śākya Clan* (*Shimen zhengtong*, compiled in 1237), and the *Chronicle of the Buddhas and Patriarchs* (*Fozu tongji, T* 2035, compiled in 1269), among others. Produced by rival groups within Chan and Tiantai Buddhism, these compendia naturally differ in many senses, including their presentations of the historical Buddha. Nonetheless, they uniformly express deference to texts recognized as scriptural, whether cited directly or through the medium of preceding anthologies like Sengyou's.

Taken together, these Chinese accounts evince a generally conservative stance toward the biography of the Buddha. To make such an evaluation is not to deny that, as centuries passed, Chinese accounts of the life of Śākyamuni did change in certain ways. They drew on a growing base of sources, increasingly appealing to more specifically Mahāyāna texts and traditions, to more compendia of scriptural material assembled within China, and to more non-Buddhist texts. Ideas about the canonicity of specific events associated with the career of the Buddha developed as well. For instance, Sengyou's pioneering anthology deliberately excluded an *avadāna* that is sometimes considered the tale of the commencement of the bodhisattva's path to eventual Buddhahood as Śākyamuni (the story of the ascetic Sumedha [Ch. Chanhui] and his encounter with the ancient Buddha Dīpaṃkara); yet it was incorporated into one descendant of Baocheng's work.[23] The temporal span covered by these biographic anthologies grew as well. The narrative of Sengyou's work ends with the transmission of dharma after the Buddha's *parinirvāṇa*, and Sengyou expressed little interest in the passage of Buddhism to China. By contrast, Baocheng devoted the second half of his *Origins and Transmission of the Śākya Clan* to the transplantation to China and flourishing of the Buddha's teaching there.

Nonetheless, throughout all these developments, the underlying commitment to the authority of the scriptures survived. Even Baocheng's late imperial compilation relies heavily on scriptures attributed to the Buddha for its first half. Each of its hundreds of short chapters is structured around citation from a particular text, whose title appears in the formulaic first words of each chapter: "The *Sutra of the Collection of Authentic Deeds of the Buddha* says," "The *Sutra of Past and Present Cause and Effect* says," and so on. Indeed, these two sources—both translated before the Tang—together account for the bulk of the chapters describing the life of Śākyamuni in the *Origins and Transmission of the Śākya Clan*.[24]

An enduring expression of deference to the authority of a canon (in this case, a canon that included historical works and Buddhist commentaries) need not imply *doctrinal* conservatism. In one of his scattered comments about his own work as a compiler within the *Genealogy of the Śākya*, Sengyou observed that he had compared two distinct accounts of the Buddha's *parinirvāṇa* available to him, one "Hīnayāna" and the other Mahāyāna.[25] While relying on the account preserved in the Chinese translation of the "Hīnayāna" *Dīrghāgama* for most of the story of the Buddha's final days, he substituted the account of the blacksmith Cunda's gift of food to the aged Buddha, the final donation accepted before the Buddha's *parinirvāṇa*, from the Mahāyāna *Sutra of the Great Decease* (*Mahāparinirvāṇa sūtra*): "I checked these two sutras," noted Sengyou. "There are many differences [between the 'Hīnayāna' version] and the final offering of Cunda as explained in the *Sutra of the Great Decease*. These are the particularities of the manifestations of the Mahāyāna and Hīnayāna sutras."[26] In such passages do we find the germ of text-critical study of the life of the Buddha, but it is only a germ. Even in this earliest extant Chinese compilation of sources for the life of the Buddha, there is no unconditional preference for "more primitive" or "earlier" scriptures as "more accurate," at least in the sense that a monk with leanings toward the Mahāyāna, like Sengyou, would have understood them.[27]

The Biography of the Buddha in Imperial China: Popular and Peripheral Sources

Over the long term, the products of elite monastics within the Buddhist intellectual culture of Imperial China decisively shaped all the retellings of the life story of the Buddha, but they did not wholly dominate those retellings. Other bodies of texts and objects suggest how the Buddha's tale was reshaped in the preaching and ritual practice of China across the second half of the first millennium. Painted or carved in cave temples opened along the ancient Silk Road, the representation of the life of the Buddha has a long if uneven presence; recorded in surviving manuscripts, it makes up part of the vast body of texts discovered in the so-called Library Cave in the Mogao Cave complex at Dunhuang. A comprehensive account of the life of the Buddha as it survives in these cave temple sites remains to be written. Here, it will suffice to note that a lasting deference to the authority of canonical Buddhist scriptures continued to inform even those retellings of the Buddha's life sometimes regarded as particularly "Sinicized." Two relatively comprehensive retellings of the Buddha's life discovered at Dunhuang illustrate this sustained interest in canonicity: a program of murals from the second half of the sixth century, and a body of manuscript literature already extant, in some form, by the start of the seventh.[28]

When the material heritage of the cave temples in Central Asian and Chinese cultural spheres depicts either the past lives of the Buddha or his final life, they employ individual scenes, episodic sequences, and narrative epitomes to tell their stories. However, it is in fact rare to find continuous sequences of paintings or carvings covering all or most of his final life as Prince Siddhartha. Two notable exceptions to the general dearth of continuous narrative treatments of the life of Siddhartha include the program of late-fifth-century reliefs and carved alcove images to be found in Yungang Cave 6, as well as the program of murals depicting the life of the Buddha, dating to the sixth or seventh century, at Kizil Cave 110 (a.k.a. the "Cave of the Steps," *Treppenhöhle*).[29] While each of these unusual caves is largely devoted to the life of the Buddha, neither bears a format easily comparable to any surviving early depictions of the Buddha in Japan.

Here, then, it will be more useful to examine the visual program surviving in Mogao Cave 290 at Dunhuang, because it is more easily comparable to later Japanese painted examples.[30] This cave dates from the latter sixth century; although the life of the Buddha does not dominate the overall iconography of the cave, the topic is treated in a gabled roof and pillar with murals. These murals depict eighty-seven scenes of the Buddha's life, spanning events from his birth to his first preaching. This mural program offers the most detailed visual depiction of the life of the Buddha extant at Dunhuang, but it is nonetheless a selective retelling of that life: while the program lavishes attention upon some events, such as the wonders surrounding the birth of the Buddha (a total of twenty-one panels are devoted to these wonders), it excludes others that we might expect to find even within its limited narrative scope—notably, the Defeat of Māra. It is therefore worthwhile to recall Eugene Wang's warning, concerning the illustrations of a different cave at Mogao, not "to let the textual order govern our perception of the pictorial program."[31] Thus, these murals in Cave 290 do not so much mechanically reflect any fixed text as offer an interpretation of the life of the Buddha in their own right.

Unlike the carvings at Yungang Cave 6, though, the paintings in the Dunhuang cave do appear to respond primarily to a single scriptural account of the Buddha's life, which is still extant in Chinese: the *Avadāna of the Practice*.[32] This is the first clue to the textual anchor of this program of murals. In their overall design, too, they show clear evidence of adaptation from a format indigenous to China, the illustrated handscroll. Divided across the two gables of the roof, these murals are arranged in two parallel sets of three horizontal registers apiece, making the process of following their story similar to reading such a scroll. In addition, the murals in Cave 290 recall textual precedent still more directly through the inclusion of captions, which originally labeled the activity above each panel.[33] Although badly abraded today, the remaining fragments of text seem to match passages from the *Avadāna of the Practice*. This direct juxtaposition of narrative image to scriptural text likely represents an innovation to previous Chinese artistic practice.[34] Such juxtaposition is unmistakeably evident in the various editions of the *Illustrated Sutra of Past and Present Cause and Effect*, which began to be produced in Japan in the mid-eighth century.

Both as fragments and as complete texts, Buddhist scriptures with biographies of the Buddha were also discovered at Dunhuang in some quantity. Although the *Avadāna of the Practice* is evident among these, the greatest bulk of surviving texts seems to belong to the much longer *Sutra of the Collection of Authentic Deeds of the Buddha*.[35] Apart from such orthodox scriptural texts, however, there is another class of texts with tales from the life of the Buddha. Prominent among these is the *Sutra on the Achievement of the Way by the Prince* [i.e., *Siddhartha*] (*Taizi chengdao jing*; henceforth, *Sutra on the Achievement of the Way*), which survives in multiple fragments. Its extant datable manuscript versions date to the late Tang period (early tenth century), though the text itself is clearly older.[36] The text, which incorporates vernacular language and alternates between prose and rhyming poetry, is closely associated with the genre known as *bianwen*, or "transformation texts."[37]

Despite such formal innovations, the story told in *Sutra on the Achievement of the Way* remains largely continuous with the established scriptural tradition of its day.[38] The chief divergences from known scriptural version lie with the fate of Siddhartha's wife, Yaśodharā. In the more familiar accounts of the life of the Buddha, the prince's son Rāhula is born shortly before his father's fateful departure from the palace. However, there is a separate canonical tradition, according to which Rāhula is conceived on the night of his father's departure and remains in his mother's womb until the night of his father's enlightenment, for a period of six years. Drawing on this tradition, multiple late Chinese scriptural accounts of the life of the Buddha describe the practice of the long-pregnant Yaśodharā, abandoned in the royal palace, and align it with Siddhartha's training and eventual enlightenment. After she gives birth to Rāhula, she endures accusations of infidelity and must prove his paternity, in some versions, through trial by fire.

The trials of Yaśodharā receive a dramatic retelling in the *Sutra on the Achievement of the Way*, in which Yaśodharā is saved from the fire pit by her distant husband, whom she alerts by burning a piece of incense that he left behind for her.[39] The pit of fire transforms into a cool lake in which Yaśodharā and little Rāhula are supported on lotus blossoms and saved. Recognizing her fidelity at last, King Śuddhodana grants her request to leave the world to enter ascetic practices beside her husband. It is here, among the last few lines of one version of the text, that the *Sutra on the Achievement of the Way* diverges most dramatically from any scriptural account of the life of the Buddha: "She bade farewell to the great King, went to the Himayalas, and pursued the Way. When the Buddha said to her, 'Welcome,' she became a man forthwith. Following the Buddha, she renounced the world and achieved the state of arhat. Her son was called 'Rāhula of the Mystic Practices.'"[40] These developments unfold during a very compressed space, but they do mark a departure from canonical accounts of Yaśodharā, who is typically said to have joined the Buddha's sangha, if at all, only *after* his awakening. Canonical reworkings of Yaśodharā's pregnancy as a form of Buddhist austerity aside, her departure to practice alongside the Buddha, and her literal transformation into a male ascetic stand out as unique to the Dunhuang corpus.[41]

The text includes some other marked deviations from the canonical corpus, and these center on his life before renunciation, including his various encounters on his trips outside the palace. Here, there are not four encounters, but five: in the first, the prince meets a husband, who is bustling about. When he has his groom ask why, he receives this response: "At home, I have a pregnant wife who is about to give birth, and who is in terrible pain. That is why I am running around."[42] The injection of birth scenes into Japanese visual versions of the prince's encounters shows that this development was not unique to Dunhuang.[43] On his final venture outside the palace, when the prince meets an ascetic, he has his groom ask the ascetic about his master. The ascetic replies, "My master is the great teacher of the Three Realms, the compassionate father of the four classes of beings, the Buddha Śākyamuni."[44] To have the ascetic state that he is a follower of a Buddha who has, technically speaking, not yet manifested himself in the narrative world is slightly perplexing. Nonetheless, it does not undermine the overall tone of reverence and praise for the Buddha Śākyamuni, a tone sustained throughout the *Sutra on the Achievement of the Way*, and related Dunhuang texts. This text also mentions in passing that the prince fathered not just one child (Rāhula) by Yaśodharā, but a total of *eight*.[45] Since the other children never reappear in the narrative, this interjection would seem to be a kind of throwaway reassurance to audiences about the filial character of the prince.

On balance, the *Sutra on the Achievement of the Way* and related Dunhuang texts do not so much deviate from or subvert the message of canonical scriptures as amplify it, albeit at times in clumsy ways. Indeed, this text seems to have been capable of treatment as a sutra in its own right: not only does its title appear in some cases as a *jing* or "scripture," but this text was also evidently copied out and dedicated as a way of making merit for the dead as early as the year 604.[46] The fashioning of the *Sutra on the Achievement of the Way* into a text capable of benefiting sentient beings anticipates the later, similar use of the *Annotated Record of the Attainment of the Way by the Tathāgata Śākyamuni*. Such cases suggest that the boundaries between "apocryphal" and "canonical" Buddhist texts were far more permeable than retroactive judgements may lead us to believe. Such evidence also helps distinguish indigenous Chinese productions—however great the liberties they took with "canonical" literature—from early modern Japanese commercial texts, which for multiple reasons could not be easily mistaken for scripture.

In short, the Chinese production of biographical texts covering the life of Śākyamuni was, like certain other projects of acculturation in Chinese Buddhism, a work of massive scale and considerable rigor. Across a span of over a millennium, Buddhist monastics in China produced translations of many of the key accounts of the life of the Buddha. Even as translation work was still under way, Chinese Buddhist monastics set about trying to reconcile conflicting narratives and giving the life story of the Buddha a single, authoritative chronology, which unfolded in historical time, as they understood it. They further labored to make the biography accessible to those who could not read the canon, who were uninterested in it, or who found it distasteful according to their cultural norms. The Buddha's biography therefore also underwent a degree of reassembly and re-representation, appearing in popular preaching, in widely disseminated print editions, and in the adornment of cave temples and freestanding institutions alike. Citation and commentary remained the dominant narrative modalities, and fidelity to some account considered scriptural the critical norm.

Between the utter volume of work of translation and the vast labor involved in commentary and the assembly of anthologies, Chinese writers supplied virtually all the basic material that would go into the making of new tales of Śākyamuni in Japan.[47] Comparative textual and historical studies of the biographies, of the sort that Sengyou undertook, were absorbed into premodern Japanese monastic scholasticism, but not duplicated there. Perhaps because of these works' sheer comprehensiveness, Japanese scholar-monks did not revisit these issues in any sustained way.[48]

Ancient and Medieval Japanese Material Accounts of the Life of the Buddha

The route by which tales of the Buddha first reached Japan remains unclear. The biography of the Buddha Śākyamuni might have arrived around the time of the "official" reception of Buddhism in Japan. Spurious or not, the official arrival of Buddhism in Japan is conventionally dated to 552 CE, based on a highly problematic record in the *Chronicle of Japan* (*Nihon shoki*, completed in 720 CE). An alternate account of the arrival of Buddhism, preserved in the in the *Records of the Temple Gangōji and Its Accumulated Treasures* (*Gangōji garan engi narabi ni ruki shizai chō*, originally dated to 749, but extant only in an abridged copy of 1165) mentions a "box of scrolls [containing] an explanation of the origin of the Buddha" as part of the collection of Buddhist artifacts sent by a king of the state of Paekche almost fifteen years earlier, in 538 CE. This "explanation of the origin of the Buddha" might well mark the first introduction of the biography of the Buddha to Japan, as an integral part of the arrival of the dharma.[49] Even if the *Records of Gangōji* should prove to be a forgery, at the very least it suggests that a biography of the Buddha was retroactively considered necessary for the transmission of Buddhism to take place at all.

On the whole, biographies of Śākyamuni as independent scriptures and commentative texts were not the most important foci of elite patronage in ancient Japan, but they were dutifully accepted as part of the larger scriptural canon. Along with most other key Chinese Buddhist texts predating the early Tang, they reached Japan by the end of the eighth century. Using the vast corpus of extant official documents from the Shōsōin imperial repository, Miyazaki Kenji documented the first appearance in extant Japanese records—typically, references to the copying of a sutra text—of the titles of almost all the texts in the Chinese *Record of Śākyamuni's Teachings* [*Compiled during*] *the Kaiyuan Era* (*Kaiyuan shijiao lu*, *T* 2154) of 730. With regard to the scriptural biographies of the Buddha, he noted mention of the following texts in documentation from the Nara period (710–794): the *Sutra of Past and Present Cause and Effect*, by 731; the *Sutra of the Collection of Authentic Deeds of the Buddha*, by 737; the version of the *Lalitavistara* as *Extended Garland* [*of the Deeds of the Buddha*], by 737; the *Minor Section of the Monastic Code of the Root Group That Teaches That All Exists*, by 737; the Chinese Āgama literature, between 737 and 742; the *Avadāna of the Practice*, by 741; the version of the *Lalitavistara* as the *Sutra of the Display* [*of the*

Deeds of the Buddha], by 742; Sengyou's *Genealogy of the Śākya*, by 751; the *Avadāna of the Auspicious* [*Deeds*] *of the Prince* [*Siddhārtha*], by 755; and the translation of the *Buddhacarita* as *Praise of the Deeds of the Buddha*, by 768.[50]

Some of these scriptural biographies did attract more attention than others. The best known today are the surviving sections of a manuscript version of the *Sutra of Past and Present Cause and Effect*, the earliest extant illustrated scrolls in Japan. The color illustrations, which line the upper register above the columns of Chinese text, likely have a continental precedent, though it is now lost. With its easily legible script and straightforward illustrations, the overall style of the work is pleasingly simple, even naive. Considering its close correspondence between image and text, art historian Kajitani Ryōji described it as "a work in the style of a textbook."[51] In this regard, the *Illustrated Sutra of Past and Present Cause and Effect* was hardly unique: a didactic quality tints the first eight hundred years or so of depictions of the Buddha created in Japan.

To be sure, reference to this didactic quality neither exhausts nor encompasses all the workings of these many centuries of biographical narration, but it does usefully tie them together under a single rubric—a rubric, moreover, that increasingly ceases to capture biographical production after the sixteenth century. It is also true that didacticism is rarely an end in itself. The texts examined in this section—written and visual—were all, literally as well as figuratively, embedded in larger assemblages of meaning: architectural, intellectual, ritual, and literary. Within these frames, the cult of Śākyamuni in ancient and medieval Japan was quantitatively dwarfed by devotion to a pantheon of other figures, including the celestial Buddha Amitābha (Jpn. Amida), the bodhisattva Avalokiteśvara (Jpn. Kanzeon or Kannon), and the historical figures Prince Shōtoku (sometimes worshipped as an incarnation of Śākyamuni) and the monk Kūkai, worshipped as the Great Master Who Spread the Dharma (Kōbō Daishi).

Despite the wide range of forms, these biographic accounts generally share a common commitment to texts that premodern Japanese Buddhist devotees understood as canonical scripture. To the creators of these accounts, such canonicity would have resided in a relatively restricted body of Chinese texts narrating the life of Śākyamuni: either those understood to be "translations" from Indic languages, or compilations of excerpts from such works made in the Chinese cultural sphere. Such a commitment to canonicity should not be understood to suggest a uniformity of content or style in the biographical accounts produced during these years; nor does it mean that everything in those biographies was, in fact, actually authorized by a scriptural account known then or today.

From at least the time of Sengyou, Buddhist clerics in China had been cognizant that the various biographical accounts available to them often contradict each another, a condition insuring the impossibility of fidelity to the entire corpus. At least for conscientious intellectual clerics, it is difficult to imagine "canonicity" as an equal acceptance of all scriptures. Instead, to note a commitment to canonicity, whether in the writings of Chinese or Japanese Buddhist clergy, is simply to comment on their common orientation toward the biography as an object of knowledge—an orientation inferable from the content of these texts, and directly observable in their frequent reference by name to a limited body of texts. This is the orientation shared by biographical materials predating the late medieval period in Japan—an orientation that unifies them despite the vast differences in genre, era, creator, and purpose.

With a few exceptions, the vast bulk of literary and artistic material in this corpus is anonymous and undated, at least until the seventeenth century. Further, those materials largely do not come down to us in situ, or in their original forms. Not only are the descriptions of the Buddha's life story fragmentary, but the sources recounting those narrative fragments themselves also often survive only as fragments, and sometimes are known only through reports in other documentation. Although these sources may sometimes be linked to particular movements within Japanese Buddhism, in all but a few cases, it is impossible to associate them with specific individuals or institutions, or precise dates of creation and dissemination.

Compared with the other corpora available from the world of premodern Japanese Buddhism, this may seem rather modest. It would not be correct, however, to say that the figure of Śākyamuni was of little concern to monks in medieval Japan. He was, after all, central to the self-identity of the Zen institution, whose arrival in Japan is typically traced to the return from study abroad by the monk Eisai (a.k.a. Yōsai, 1141–1215). Indeed, Śākyamuni remains a central object of worship in the world of Japanese Zen; the Sōtō (Ch. Caodong) denomination of Zen—overwhelmingly Japan's largest Zen movement, and encompassing more temples than either of the two major True Pure Land subdenominations—specifies Śākyamuni as the only figure appropriate for the central place in home Buddhist altars, and other, smaller Zen denominations strongly recommend him.

For a small but influential group of early medieval monks based in the "Southern Capital" of Nara, Śākyamuni was not just a distant object of veneration, but also a living presence whose relics embodied his power and whose precepts could still be observed. Figures remembered as central to this "precept revival" movement—Jōkei (1155–1213), Myōe (1173–1232), and Eizon (a.k.a. Eison, 1201–1290)—recorded intense, though certainly not exclusive, personal devotion to Śākyamuni. Jōkei regarded Śākyamuni as both present in this world, as relics, and capable of saving the dead in the next, as savior.[52] Myōe even planned (as had Eisai) to travel to India to visit the sacred sites of the Buddha's life.[53] As has been demonstrated by Nishimura Ryō, the figure admired by Jōkei, Myōe, Eizon, and others was not principally a historical human being. It was, rather, the Buddha as a cosmic, merciful father, who in the *Compassion Flower Sutra* (Skt. **Karuṇa puṇḍarīka nāma mahāyāna sūtra*, Jpn. *Hikekyō*, *T* 157) consented to be born into our world, known as the Realm That Must Be Endured (Skt. *Sahāloka*, Jpn. *Shaba sekai*) precisely because of its defiled, dire condition.[54] For this reason, it may be natural that no leader in the "precept revival" movement turned his energy to the composition of an extended narrative about the historical Buddha.

Early Japanese interest in the historical Buddha may have been diffuse, but it was also widespread, as the sources under scrutiny in the following pages demonstrate. From the tenth through the sixteenth centuries, the Buddhist clergy dominated Japanese intellectual life, which helps account for the relatively high level of fidelity to canonical texts that we find in these sources. Even in the overwhelmingly frequent cases of unclear authorship and provenance, it seems safe to attribute the creation of these early Japanese accounts to a highly literate, monastic environment. In some cases, we also know something of the nature of the audience intended for the narrative at hand.

From their inception in Japan and through the early sixteenth century, material depictions of the Buddha's life narrative—whether sculpted or painted—communicated didactic messages as well. Like their textual counterparts, their choice of topic, if not their iconographic disposition, derived largely from accounts in Chinese-language scriptures and their later reworkings. To treat these material works as primarily didactic pieces does not, of course, deny that they fulfilled other purposes as well. But taking this didactic quality as its interpretive lens, the present section surveys four related bodies of ancient and medieval material: (1) sculpture; (2) illustrated handscroll depictions of the Buddha's life; (3) paintings of the Buddha's life, typically produced as sets of hanging scrolls; and (4) texts and narrative artwork associated with specific medieval ritual practices.

Before approaching these categories, it will be useful to note that canonical scriptures were not the sole source of material imagery in representing the life of the Buddha, nor were frozen material forms their only product. In the case of the life of the Buddha Śākyamuni, narrative could also gave rise to ritual or liturgical performance as well as art: the pouring of *amacha* over a metal image of the standing newborn in rituals for the Buddha's birthday is a classic example.[55] This ritual reenacts the lustration of the infant prince by celestial dragons spewing hot and cold water, and features an image of a standing newborn Buddha, usually pointing to heaven with his right hand and to the earth with his left. Eighth-century sources claim, however dubiously, that this ritual was practiced in Japan as early as the sixth or early seventh century; in fact, a large number of early newborn Buddha images found in Japan do date from the seventh and eighth centuries, though their production has continued up to contemporary times.[56] A still more important instance of ritual as one consequence of narrative, revisited later in this chapter, is the use of a painting (or, much less commonly, a sculpture) of the Buddha's *parinirvāṇa* scene in the yearly commemoration of his attainment of final liberation, the Nirvana Assembly (*Nehan-e*). Nor were objects and rituals linked to the life of the Buddha mechanically reproduced on the basis of frozen canonical formulae: as this section shows, rituals and narrative art were newly produced in the medieval period in conjunction with oral storytelling.

Of course, it is not possible to distinguish other representations of the Buddha's life narrative from ritual uses, either. Much like their purely textual counterparts, material reworkings of the Buddha's life story in ancient and medieval Japan derived largely from Chinese-language scriptures or the anthologies built from them. Such debt to continental examples is evident, however indirectly, even when the prototypes for the Japanese works were themselves material, not textual. Although the relationship between image and word was never a matter of mechanical correspondence, it is fair to say that ancient through medieval depictions of the life of the Buddha generally maintained their linkage with the biographical corpus of scriptures, though by the fourteenth century, that linkage had gradually begun to loosen.

In Japan, the earliest datable, surviving narratives of the life of the Buddha are visual and sculpted, not written or painted. The five-story pagoda at the temple Hōryūji (the oldest surviving wooden pagoda in Japan) preserves four small groups of clay sculptures, each set into an artificial grotto in one of the four sides of the pagoda's base level. This combination of clay sculpture with painting in diorama-like settings uses a contemporary Chinese technique known as "sculpted wall landscapes" (*su shanshui bi*).[57] Dated to 711, and probably altered around the time of the first renovation of the pagoda (no later than 736), these four narrative tableaux depict scenes important to their early elite patrons. On the east side, there is the debate between the layman Vimalakīrti and the bodhisattva of wisdom, Mañjuśrī, an enactment of the climactic scene from the *Sutra of Vimalakīrti* (Skt. *Vimalakīrtinirdeśa*, Ch. *Weimo jing*, *T* 475 in its most influential Chinese version); on the north, the *parinirvāṇa* of Śākyamuni; on the west, the cremation of Śākyamuni and the division of his relics; and on the south, the advent of the Buddha of the future, Maitreya.[58]

The significance of this unusual combination of scenes—only some of which derive from the life of the Buddha Śākyamuni—remains unclear. Reflecting on the unstable political situation of the early eighth century, the art historian Yamagishi Kōki argued that the combination expressed the preoccupation of the Fujiwara clan patriarch, Fuhito (659–720), with insuring the investiture of his young grandson. Indeed, this boy eventually did become the future emperor and great patron of Buddhism, Shōmu (701–756). In Yamagishi's reading, the three scenes at the pagoda connecting the Buddha of our world with the next Buddha, Maitreya, represent the Fujiwaras' hope for the safe transfer of power to their young scion and intended heir. The tableau of the debate, meanwhile, would have reflected the Fujiwara patronage of the Vimalakīrti Assembly (Jpn. *Yuima-e*), a debate ritual closely associated with the clan's founder and revived by Fuhito.[59] While Yamagishi's case cannot be conclusively proven, its very plausibility is a reminder that even orthodox narratives might tell stories other than the ones they putatively portray.

The life of the Buddha constitutes the subject of the oldest extant illustrated handscrolls in Japan, a body of material today collectively known as the *Illustrated Sutra of Past and Present Cause and Effect* (*Kako genzai einga kyō*) and based on the titular scripture.[60] Individual scrolls and fragments, datable to the mid-eighth through ninth centuries, survive from at least four different sets of this work. While no complete set of these scrolls survives from this early period, the existing pieces all share a common and distinctive format: the length of the scroll divides to present two continuous horizontal spaces, both flowing from right to left, with the text of the scripture in the bottom register, and the corresponding illustrations running parallel to the text in the upper register. As the art historian Naitō Tōichirō noted as early as 1934, the illustrations in the upper register proceed "frame by frame," in a manner "just like a movie film."[61]

The link between text and image here is decidedly robust: scrutinizing one eighth-century version of the *Illustrated Sutra*, Naitō found that all but one of the illustrations closely reflect the content of the corresponding scriptural passage below.[62] (This scene, in which the prince's horse and groom apparently take their leave of him while he sits under a tree in meditation, at the "wrong" time—which is to say, before his renunciation—actually results from conflicts in the sequence *within* the scriptural canon as known in China.[63])

The early versions of these scrolls are thought to approximate continental models closely, though no direct models survive from the continent survive. Nonetheless, the effort to duplicate such models suggests multiple kinds of pedagogical imitation. First, the scripture represents itself as a lesson by the Buddha about the correspondence of effects to the causes that produced them. As the Buddha tells his monastic audience at the very start of the sutra: "Since you have asked to hear the past causes [of later events], hear them clearly! Hear them clearly! Think well upon them, for I shall now explain them to you."[64] Indeed, in the *jātaka*-style framing of the sutra, the Buddha begins by telling his listeners the story of his former life as Sumedha, the ascetic whose receipt of prophecy from the Buddha Dīpaṃkara launched him on his path to awakening. Only after relating that story does he then go on to narrate the account of his birth as the prince Siddhartha. As do many *jātaka* tales, the text ends with a coda set in the narrative present, in which the Buddha matches the characters in his past life with their current identities. Thus, the very framing of the sutra enacts a kind of correspondence.

The material vehicle for this message is yet another epitome of correspondence. The producers of the *Illustrated Sutra* scrolls not only duplicated the text of the sutra, but also followed continental styles for the calligraphy and painting in these scrolls. They succeeded so well that, even late in the nineteenth century, some Japanese connoisseurs still held that the early editions of the scrolls had actually been produced in China. Only in 1896 did the historian and antiquarian Kosugi Sugimura (1834–1910) reveal his discovery of an inscription on one of the scrolls that confirmed its domestic provenance.[65]

The *Illustrated Sutra* format perdured for an unusually long period: even as the style of the illustrations changed, sets of *Illustrated Sutra* scrolls continued to be produced well into the medieval period, the last dated as late as 1516.[66] These later copies preserved the format evident in the eighth-century editions. By that point, of course, the parallel layout of the *Illustrated Sutra* had long since grown archaic, but in this case, form and content would appear to have been fused too tightly to permit much variation. In the meantime, the narrative handscroll as a material form had attained immense success in medieval Japan—a period that left behind a vast body of illustrated scrolls treating a vast range of subjects, including the lives of other figures important to Japanese Buddhism. At a relatively early point, the dominant form for the narrative handscroll in Japan changed, featuring not text and image in parallel rows, but rather, text and image in alternation.

Around 1515—centuries after the alternating form had emerged as the standard for Japanese handscrolls—the artist Kanō Motonobu (1476–1559) employed that new standard format in another important illustrated biography of the Buddha. This illustrated biography comprised the first part of the *Origin Tale of the Hall of Śākyamuni* (*Shakadō engi*, a.k.a. *Seiryōji engi*), a narrative scroll complete in six fascicles.[67] Despite the title by which it is known now, this scroll wholly neglects the origins of the temple Seiryōji, popularly known as the "Hall of Śākyamuni."[68] Instead, it tells the tale of the famed standing wooden sculpture of the Buddha, still housed there. This image ranks as one of the most celebrated Buddhist statues in Japan, so popular and widely revered that roughly one hundred copies of the image remain, most created during the Kamakura period (1192–1333).[69]

The *Origin Tale* set of illustrated handscrolls claims that the Seiryōji image was in fact the very one that was carved during the Buddha's lifetime, modeled on the Buddha himself. The East Asian Buddhist tradition credits King Udāyana (sometimes "Rudrāyana"; Jpn. Udennō) as the devotee who so longed for the Buddha during his absence that the king ordered the creation of the first portrait sculpture of the Buddha as a replacement.[70] Indeed, the Seiryōji image, now understood by scholars as a precious example of tenth-century Chinese Buddhist sculpture in wood, has been much more thoroughly researched than the *Origin Tale* set of scrolls, which postdates it by over half a millennium.[71] Yet it is to such narratives as this scroll that we must turn to assess the reasons for the lasting importance of this image in late medieval Japan. The third through sixth fascicles of the *Origin Tale* depict the image's creation and its numinous powers. They relate the circumstances of its royally ordained carving, while the Buddha was away preaching to his mother in the Trāyastriṃśa heaven; the Buddha's return and recognition of the image as equivalent to himself; the transfer of the image from India to China; its transport to Kyoto by the cleric Chōnen (938–1016); and its eventual enshrinement at the Seiryōji, where it manifested wonders.

The *Origin Tale* scroll depicts the statue as a living being in its own right, not as a mere inanimate representation of one. Illustrations in its fascicles show the image moving to sit alongside the Buddha; carrying (and, in turn, being carried by) the Indian monk Kumārāyana on his journey to Kucha; communicating to Chōnen its wish to travel to Japan, through his dream; and moving to change places with its copy commissioned by Chōnen. Not content merely to retell episodes in which the image acts like a living being, the text of the *Origin Tale* scroll declares in no uncertain terms: "This auspicious sandalwood image (Jpn. *zuizō*) is unlike ordinary wooden images. It should be considered equivalent to the flesh-body of the Tathāgata."[72] Nor was this claim an invention of the text's anonymous author, for the Seiryōji image had functioned as a proxy for the Buddha's original "flesh-body" from the time of its creation. When its interior was opened for conservation in 1954, the image was found to include a range of contents, including internal organs made of silk, as well as a tooth attributed to the Buddha.[73] The animation of this image—through such enclosed objects and through the creation of such narratives as the *Origin Tale* scroll—exemplifies with particular clarity a much broader tendency in the attribution of life to Buddhist images. The reverence devoted to the Seiryōji image as a substitute Buddha, and the tale of its creation and authorization by the Buddha, are not innovations, but connect Japanese practice to its continental antecedents.

The *Origin Tale* begins with two introductory illustrated fascicles, representing the "prehistory" of the Seiryōji image—which is to say, the life story of its model, the Buddha Śākyamuni himself. Like the eighth-century *Illustrated Sutra*, the sixteenth-century *Tale* also draws upon a continental prototype for its iconography. As demonstrated by the art historian Tsuchiya Maki, the illustrations in the first two fascicles of the *Origin Tale* draw extensively upon the woodblock prints of the illustrated *Origins and Transmission of the Śākya Clan*.[74] Examination of the paintings included in these fascicles shows how the hold of continental models over medieval Japanese artists' depictions of the life of the Buddha had relaxed, if not released. Compared to the illustrations in the eighth-century editions of the *Illustrated Sutra*, the images in the *Origin Tale* scrolls engage in visibly more complex relationships to their predecessors. Only some of the designs for the *Origin Tale* illustrations copy outright from corresponding sections of the *Origins and Transmission*. Others either incorporate minor changes to its models, or draw instead from iconography already in circulation in Japan.[75] In designing illustrations for the *Origin Tale*, Kanō Motonobu treated the *Origin and Transmission* designs not as a body of authoritative models requiring faithful duplication, but as a storehouse of prototypes that he could borrow from, refuse, or reshape as needed.

The illustrations of the *Tale* imply that the woodblock print edition of the *Origins and Transmission* must have reached Japan by the early sixteenth century. Given the time of this reception, the lack of later influence in Japan by the *Origins and Transmission* becomes all the more striking. To date, only one other painting of the life of the Buddha produced in Japan has been definitely linked to the iconography of the *Origins and Transmission*.[76] Further, the Japanese reprinting of the *Origins and Transmission* excludes the images altogether.[77] The apparent lack of interest by Japanese artists in the iconography of the *Origins and Transmission* contrasts dramatically with its extensive impact on the continent; the book was reproduced not only in China, but also in Korea and Vietnam.[78] In the visual arts, the *Origins and Transmission* iconography influenced major programs of Ming-dynasty Chinese temple murals and late Chosŏn–dynasty Korean Buddhist painting alike.[79] In light of this disparity, it is impossible to take at face value Tsai Suey-Ling's sweeping claim for the *Origins and Transmission* as "most influential illustrated book on the life of the Buddha in East Asia,"[80] as long as "East Asia" is taken to include Japan. In early modern Japan, the *Origins and Transmission* text seems to have had only attenuated influence. There, the most influential illustrated text was the *Original Ground of Śākyamuni*, to be discussed in the following chapter.[81]

Apart from the selective reproduction and adaptation of iconography from the *Origins and Transmission*, the first two scrolls of the *Origin Tale* also differ from their Chinese predecessor in textual content. These scrolls dramatically rearrange and truncate the textual sources of the *Origins and Transmission*. Almost every chapter of the *Origins and Transmission* begins with the formulaic "Such-and-such a scripture says," invoking the authority of the scriptural text in question. Through such repeated reference to and rearrangement of canonical texts, the *Origins and Transmission* implicitly stakes a claim to its conformity with—and comprehensive control over—the body of canonical writings. By contrast, the abbreviated biography of the Buddha presented in the first two *Origin Tale* fascicles is written almost entirely in

Japanese grammar, quoting Chinese scriptural passages only sparingly. It presents just a rough summary of the corresponding sections of the *Origins and Transmission*, which are here explicitly rearranged according to the rubric of the Eight Phases. Interestingly, one scripture cited twice by name in these fascicles is none other than the *Scripture of Past and Present Cause and Effect*. Although this is the key source for the text in these two fascicles, the *Origin Tale* adapts it freely and also borrows from other texts. Kurobe Michiyoshi observed that this biography is "a transmutation, and a Japanization, of the *Scripture of Past and Present Cause and Effect*."[82] While it is not possible to define "Japanization" in a way that is not circular, the *Origin Tale*'s rearrangement of canonical materials nonetheless does herald later developments.

Thus, in the version of the *Origin Tale*, there is no pretense to a comprehensive command of the scriptural literature to explicate the many events of the life of the Buddha. Even the gesture of scriptural citation loses its pride of place: of the fourteen passages comprising the text of the first two fascicles, only two parrot the standard introductory formula of the *Origins and Transmission*. By transposing that formula to the end, they effectively reduce it to a footnote: "[The preceding] appears in such-and-such a scripture."[83] Just as the text uses the Eight Phases framework to structure the entire life narrative, so too does it explicitly adduce Zhiyi's scheme of the Four Teachings and the Five Periods to recount the specific order and significance of the Buddha's preaching career.

As the preceding consideration of sources and their reception in two handscroll types has shown, these Japanese illustrated narratives of the life of the Buddha continue to present him as an instructor. They either reproduce the text of his scriptural biography intact, or they fashion summary accounts, however abbreviated, that are ultimately traceable to such scriptural biographies. In these respects, the two different handscroll types display more continuity than discontinuity, although they were produced across a span of more than six hundred years. But the two handscroll types also differ considerably in their treatment of precedent and authority. The illustrators of the *Illustrated Sutra* endeavored to reproduce designs in a continental style and to align them rigidly with textual content of the scripture that they depicted. By contrast, Motonobu and the author of the text of the *Tale* still sought to preserve the overall orthodox structure of the Buddha's life, even as they selectively drew upon, abridged, and rearranged the visual and textual models provided by the *Origins and Transmission*.

Furthermore, the biographies of the *Tales* and the *Origins and Trans-*

mission present different conceptions of the Buddha's importance. In the episodes of *Origins and Transmission* that take place between the Buddha's awakening and his *parinirvāṇa*, the Buddha's primary task is to save a vast number of people through his instruction, sometimes requiring display of his superhuman powers, and typically incorporating moral exhortation. After the death of the Buddha, it is his teaching that survives to be transmitted to China to flourish there. This sequence of events is embodied by the succession of teachers—both Indian and Chinese—who appear after the Buddha's death and dominate the second half of the *Origins and Transmission*.[84] By contrast, in the account of the *Tales*, the Seiryōji image does not so much carry on the preaching career of the Buddha as render him altogether superfluous. Moral instruction is no longer a priority. This parting of the ways, as it were, exemplifies a general pattern across the *longue durée* of life narratives of the Buddha in Japan: accounts that depend upon scriptural authority are gradually displaced by retellings with a growing degree of self-confidence and self-sufficiency, a trend increasingly apparent from the turn of the sixteenth century onward. Put another way, by the end of the sixteenth century, cultural production surrounding the Buddha began to place less emphasis on his role as a teacher.

In addition to these two handscroll forms, a separate body of narrative paintings extant in Japan depicts various scenes in the life of the Buddha. Almost all these paintings depict only one scene—the Buddha's *parinirvāṇa*—and these exist in a vast profusion. A much smaller group, though, depicts multiple events in the life of Śākyamuni. Such images are often known as "paintings of the Eight Phases of the life of Śākyamuni" (*Shaka hassō zu*), though the selection of events, and even the actual number of events depicted, varies considerably.[85] Of the eleven such paintings (or sets of paintings) surveyed in Watanabe Satoshi's magisterial study of this type, all but two survive on silk (in polychrome) or paper (in ink).[86] Nine of the eleven paintings are easily portable; among these, just one complete group is extant: a set of eight hanging scrolls, dated to the mid-fourteenth century, owned by the temple Jikōji, in Hiroshima Prefecture.[87] Incomplete but noteworthy extant sets of hanging scrolls include a thirteenth-century work whose remaining scrolls are now split between the Kuonji, in Yamanashi Prefecture, and the Nezu Museum, in Tokyo; another fourteenth-century set, owned by the Jōrakuji, in Shiga Prefecture; a fifteenth-century set now in the collection of the Metropolitan Museum of Art, in New York; and a sixteenth-century ink painting, in the collection of the Mibudera in Kyoto.[88]

Two extant paintings on silk depict the life of the Buddha, each complete in a single panel. One of these is the oldest known painting of the Buddha's life to survive in Japan, dated to the late twelfth through early thirteenth centuries, and owned by the Daifukudenji, in Mie Prefecture.[89] The second of these single-panel paintings, now in a private collection, was likely produced in the interval between the Daifukudenji and the Jikōji paintings.[90] On the other hand, murals are nearly absent from Watanabe's list; this absence reflects the gradual supersession of static murals by portable painting in Japanese temple art.[91] Watanabe's survey uncovered only one extant set of murals, painted in the late thirteenth or early fourteenth centuries onto the inner walls of the "Many-Treasures" (Tahōto) pagoda at the Jōmyōji, in Wakayama Prefecture.

The existence of other murals portraying the life of the Buddha in premodern Japan is now known only via accounts in surviving texts. The most prominent of these remains the painting of the Eight Phases at the Hōjōji, a temple completed in 1022, first destroyed in a great fire of 1058 and not rebuilt after another fire in 1317. The painting appears in *A Tale of Flowering Fortunes* (*Eiga monogatari*, completed by 1107), the tale of the rise of the Fujiwara clan to its position of hegemony at the imperial court of the Heian era. In its account of the ceremonies marking the completion of the temple, the text offers the following picture of what the reigning emperor saw on his visit there:

> On the open doors the Emperor saw paintings of the Eight Phases, beginning with Śākyamuni's birth from Māyā's right side and the bath administered from the sky by the two dragons, Nanda and Upananda: pictures showing how the Buddha, as Prince Siddhartha, resolved to enter a life of religion while he was being carefully reared at Śuddhodana's Palace; how his father the King, deeply concerned, presented him with 500 daughters of neighboring Kings, none of whom he loved; how his father then decided to show him the gardens and groves in all directions, and sent him out with a retinue of officials; how gods from the Pure Abode appeared to the Prince as aged, ill, and dead men; how the Prince, at the age of nineteen, left home in the middle of the night on the Eighth of the Second Month in the year of the Senior Water Monkey to become a monk; how Candaka went disconsolately back, leading the horse from the royal stables; how everyone in the Palace—the King, the Prince's wives, and all the countless Palace ladies—shrieked and wept; how Śākyamuni subjugated demons, attained enlightenment, turned the wheel of the Dharma, and ascended to the Heaven of the Thirty-Three to act as a filial son to Māyā—all the events that culminated in the evening when the Buddha entered Nirvāṇa beside the double-trunked sal trees.[92]

The inclusion of a suspiciously precise date for the Great Departure according to the Chinese sexagenary cycle here ("year of the Senior Water Monkey") reflects another inheritance from the continental scholastic tradition's study of the Buddha, which by the end of the sixth century CE had already produced two rival calculations for the dates of events in the Buddha's life.[93] What is perhaps more interesting is the placement of the paintings: as the gateway to a hall enshrining a main image the cosmic Buddha Mahāvairocana in an esoteric configuration typical of the latter Heian period. This implies that the life of Śākyamuni was important less on its own terms than as one element within a visual program positioning him as a temporary manifestation of the cosmic Buddha.[94]

The works enumerated in Watanabe's list, all anonymous, lack documentation attesting to the circumstances of their creation; most are now removed from the sites and ritual contexts of their creation, and all too often, they survive only in fragmentary form. Inscriptions (cartouches) within some of these paintings originally named specific scenes or characters, but the text is often no longer legible. Some versions of the visual narrative, such as the Jikōji set, lack such labels altogether.[95] For these reasons, it is usually possible only to make informed guesses about the significance and intended use of this body of paintings.

Although evidence is scarce, elite ancient observers appear to have expected such depictions to tell the story of the life of the Buddha, and to reflect on authoritative texts. Accordingly, secondary scholarship about these images has repeatedly pointed to the likelihood of their use in "preaching with, or by means of, pictures" (*etoki*).[96] In Japanese historical sources, the use of temple murals as visual aids in explaining the Buddha's life is attested as early as 931. An entry for that year in the diary of an imperial prince recounts his visit to the now-defunct temple Jōganji: "We viewed the paintings on the pillars of the life of Śākyamuni (*hassō jōdō*), and the chief abbot (*zasu*) explained their meanings."[97] Educated observers also recorded their curiosity about the meanings of images of the life of the Buddha. An 1106 record of a pilgrimage to temple sites in Nara, written by a devoutly Buddhist student at the University Bureau (Daigakuryō), includes a short description of two pagodas at the Yakushiji. (Each of the four outer walls of these two pagodas originally depicted a scene from the life of the Buddha in sculpture, but now only scattered fragments from the Western Pagoda survive, having been buried when the pagoda burned down and having been excavated centuries later.[98]) Observing that the Buddha of the *parinirvāṇa* scene was extending his right arm, he noted, "Based upon the account of which sutra was this image created? This is most dubious."[99] As these instances suggest, narrative depictions of the life of the Buddha could be expected to embody fixed meanings and to derive from scriptural accounts.

Around the turn of the fourteenth century, however, increasingly conspicuous alterations—no longer attributable to any scriptural account of the life of the Buddha—began to accumulate in the visual repertoire. Watanabe's study emphasizes the incorporation of certain noncanonical narrative elements, found in the Jikōji and Jōrakuji sets of handing scrolls. Like some of its successors, the Jikōji version gives a nonstandard version of the Buddha's Four Encounters (*shimon shutsuyū*, lit. "excursions from the four gates"). It deletes the final encounter with a renunciant, transforming it instead into an encounter with a woman in childbirth—an alteration anticipated in the Dunhuang body of literature about the life of the Buddha, but unsupported by any scriptural account.[100] A related transformation occurs in the Jōrakuji scroll depiction of the prince's ascetic practice in the mountains. Here the prince is presented not merely in debate with the hermit sage, but also as serving him by delivering firewood and water to his hermitage.[101] (See fig. 1.) This narrative development—which proved hugely influential in the later medieval literary tradition—resulted not from any canonical biography of the Buddha, but instead from the "Devadatta" chapter of the *Lotus Sutra*, in which the Buddha speaks of his own past:

> For Dharma's sake, I abandoned realm and title, leaving the government to my heir. . . . At that time there was a seer who came and reported to the king, saying, "I have a great vehicle; its name is the *Scripture of the Lotus Blossom of the Fine Dharma*. If you can obey me, I will set it forth for you." When the king [the Buddha's former incarnation] heard the seer's words, he danced for joy, then straightaway followed the seer, tending to whatever he required: picking his fruit, drawing his water, gathering his firewood, preparing his food, even making a couch of his own body; feeling no impatience, whether in body or in mind. He rendered him service for a thousand years, bending all efforts to menial labor for Dharma's sake and seeing to it that he lacked nothing.[102]

This account unambiguously refers to a former life of the Buddha Śākyamuni—that is, the Buddha of the *Lotus Sutra*—but medieval Japanese storytellers were nonetheless unhesitant to import it into such depictions as the Jōrakuji image. (As the following chapter shows, the

FIGURE 1 From *The Eight Phases of the Life of Śākyamuni* (detail of Panel Four). *Shaka hassō zu* (fourteenth century). Held by the temple Jōrakuji, Shiga Prefecture.

loving depiction of the prince's suffering in his selfless service to the ascetic master went on to become a staple fixture of tales of the life of the Buddha in early modern Japan.)

The key factor here is not merely the *Lotus Sutra*, but the medieval intellectual milieu that valued it so highly—one centered upon Tendai Buddhism, which venerates the *Lotus* as the most complete teaching of the Buddha. By the late medieval period, Tendai teachings had begun to displace scriptural accounts as sources for depictions of the Buddha. Each of the extant seven scrolls of the Jōrakuji set incorporates a cartouche with a few lines of Chinese text related to the scene depicted in the painting. Virtually none of these draws directly on Chinese-language scriptures; instead, they draw on commentative literature, with a heavy bias toward the writings of Chinese Tiantai patriarchs important to the Japanese Tendai tradition: Zhiyi (538–597), Guanding (561–632), and Zhanran (711–782).[103] The aspiration to present an orthodox biography of the Buddha thus lives on in these paintings, but by the time of their creation, the sources considered to exemplify that orthodoxy had shifted away from scriptures themselves and toward Tendai commentative literature about them.

Taken together with the aforementioned handscroll editions, the preceding discussion may suggest the survival of a formidable quantity of narrative biographical artwork depicting the life of the Buddha from ancient and medieval Japan. By the standards of the medieval period, though, the list is not necessarily noteworthy. As noted unequivocally by the art historian Kevin Carr, "in comparison with the plethora of medieval images recounting the life of Prince Shōtoku, those depicting the biography of the historical Buddha are much fewer and less varied."[104] Nor is Prince Shōtoku the only indigenous Japanese Buddhist figure whose life story seems to have been more commonly painted than the historical Buddha's. In fact, the medieval period saw an efflorescence of narrative depictions of the biographies of indigenous figures, in quantities that far outstripped the number of depictions of the life of Śākyamuni. Among works extant from the late thirteenth through the late sixteenth centuries, for instance, there survive no fewer than *twenty* sets of handscrolls depicting the life of Kūkai.[105] Figures who themselves lived during the medieval period received similar treatment: from roughly the same span of time, there also survive at least one dozen sets of paintings—some as handscrolls, some as hanging scrolls—portraying the life of the cleric Shinran.[106]

Far from abating at the end of the medieval period, the production of such illustrated biographies in hanging scrolls vastly accelerated during the early modern years, aided by new printing technology and the distribution of such scrolls by denominational centers. Writing in 1999, one art historian observed that hanging scroll depictions of the lives of famous Japanese clerics were produced and extant in such vast numbers during the early modern period that an accurate count of them would demand state mobilization on the scale of a national census.[107] New hanging-scroll depictions of the life of the Buddha Śākyamuni continued to be produced during the early modern period, but they could not begin to match the sheer number of depictions of Japan's indigenous saints.

In addition to medieval paintings whose subjects span the major events the life of the Buddha, however those be defined, a further medieval subgenre of the *parinirvāṇa* image enumerates events from the sequence of the Buddha's life through a different organizing principle. Works in this subgenre are now known as "Eight Event–nirvana paintings" (*hassō Nehanzu*), a category more precisely broken into "nirvana paintings with the biography of the Buddha" (*Butsuden Nehanzu*) and "paintings of nirvana transformation scenes" (*Nehan hensōzu*). Hybrid works, both subcategories combine the standard *parinirvāṇa* image of the Buddha on his deathbed, enlarged and placed in the center, with smaller, peripheral paintings along some or all of the sides. These peripheral scenes portray either major scenes from throughout his life (nirvana biography painting), or events taking place immediately before and after his *parinirvāṇa* (nirvana transformation scenes).[108] (In very rare instances, both iconographies may be combined.[109])

The origin of these iconographies is as yet unclear. Both the biography and transformation paintings distantly recall the medieval vita paintings of the lives of Latin and Byzantine saints, which combine enlarged iconic portraits of the saints in question with smaller narrative panels of life events surrounding that portrait, running in strips on all or some sides.[110] The Japanese works are also reminiscent of a classic design in late Pāla-dynasty South Asian sculpture, which organized the key events of the life of the Buddha, each representing the stupa at which it took place, in a semicircle surrounding an enlarged representation of the Defeat of Māra.[111] On the continent, however, no extant prototype remains to suggest that the nirvana biography painting style originated outside Japan. Meanwhile, continental models for nirvana transformation paintings do survive, but only in Japan, and the attribution of some continental works remains a disputed topic.[112]

In the Japanese case, the creation of such hybrid images of the Buddha's *parinirvāṇa* was closely associated with a novel medieval liturgy focused on the final extinction of the Buddha. This was a work composed by Myōe in 1215: the *Nirvana Ceremonial* (*Nehan kōshiki*), itself a part of Myōe's longer *Ceremonial in Four Sessions* (*Shiza kōshiki*). Composed after Myōe had abandoned his second and final attempt to travel to India, the *Ceremonial in Four Sessions* encompasses four individual encomia. These praise the merits of (1) the Buddha's *parinirvāṇa*, (2) the sixteen great arhat followers of the Buddha, who remain in the world after his departure; (3) the *bodhi* tree and the other sites associated with the Buddha's life in India; and (4) the Buddha's bodily relics, or *śarīra* (Jpn. *shari*). Like other *kōshiki*—a category that Nils Gülberg translated into English as the "ceremonial" form—the *Nirvana Ceremonial* uses the vernacular language to expound Chinese-language scriptural sources. A great deal of it hews closely to scriptural precedents, and it draws most heavily upon (and explicitly names) the *Latter Portion of the Sutra of the Great Parinirvāṇa* (*Da banniepan jing houfen, T* 377), which is a textual addendum to the *Sutra of the Great Parinirvāṇa* (*Da banniepan jing*, *T* 375), the most influential account of the death of the Buddha in East Asia.[113]

However, the *Nirvana Ceremonial* is no mere vernacular gloss of scriptures in Chinese; it is also a recognized work of literary merit in its own right.[114] "Myōe's *Ceremonial in Four Sessions*," claims the authoritative encyclopedia for Japanese music, "is [a work at] the pinnacle of this [the Kamakura] period, for the excellence of its content, style, and melody."[115] Its final section, the dedication of karmic merit, includes particularly striking metaphors: "We will outfit ourselves with the great ship of the Vow, set it afloat on our tears of longing, raise the sail of orthodox faith, and propel it with the breath of our adoration."[116] Such vividness of expression surely helped the *Ceremonial* spread to a variety of Buddhist institutions, and to become a widely practiced liturgy for commemorating the death of the Buddha in Japanese Shingon temples.[117] As the core of the ritual program for the *Dharma Assembly of Permanence and Bliss* (*Jōraku-e*), the *Nirvana Ceremonial* had established a foothold in the massive Shingon complex atop Mount Kōya by the early fourteenth century, and is still regularly practiced there today.[118] Nor are these rituals any longer the exclusive preserve of Japan's Buddhist institutions: as recently as August 2014, the *Dharma Assembly of Permanence and Bliss* was performed at the National Bunraku Theatre in Osaka, and in February 2015, the entire *Ceremonial in Four Sessions* was performed, spanning two days, at the Spiral Building in Tokyo, in commemoration of the eight-hundredth anniversary of its first performance.[119]

This liturgy enjoys a close association with the aforementioned hybrid depictions of the Buddha's *parinirvāṇa*. In the late 1970s, art historians began to suggest that the *Ceremonial* had been stimulated by Myōe's exposure to Song- (960–1279) or Yuan-dynasty (1206–1368) depictions of the *parinirvāṇa* and the wonders attendant upon it.[120] Building on this notion, further scholarship argued that Myōe may have been inspired to choose specific scriptural passages for the ritual based on the scenes depicted in such nirvana transformation paintings as those now held by the Kōzanji in Hiroshima, the Saikyōji in Nagasaki, the Eifukuji in Ōsaka or the Jōtokuji in Kagawa.[121] More recent research argued that the nirvana transformation scene image jointly held by the Jishōin and the An'yōin in Okayama Prefecture was likely designed specifically to serve as a main image (*honzon*) for the *Nirvana Ceremonial*.[122] Other paintings in the same Eight Event–nirvana form—such as the Muromachi-era (1338–1573) work now held by Tsurugi Shrine in Mie Prefecture—seem not to have been explicitly produced in accordance with the *Nirvana Ceremonial*, but nonetheless were later incorporated into its practice: a copy of the ritual program was passed down along with the Tsurugi Shine painting.[123] Finally, the art historian Watanabe Satoshi speculated that the nirvana biography paintings resulted from the merging of standard *parinirvāṇa* images with biographical paintings that treated each scene equally, for use either in Myōe's ritual or in another *parinirvāṇa* rite employed in Tendai temples.[124]

The medieval performance of the *Ceremonial in Four Sessions* would, then, have fused scriptural accounts of the death of the Buddha with vernacular interpretation, poetry, song, and visual explanation. In one sense, this ritual typifies the didactic nature of presentations of the Buddha's life before the early modern period. In another sense, though, its didactic scope is limited. As the art historian Donohashi Akio noted: "The *Nirvana Ceremonial* is centered upon the events and wonders (*kiseki*) surrounding the *parinirvāṇa* of Śākyamuni; the biography of the Buddha itself is not preached" as a part of it.[125] While Myōe's text recounts individually moving moments—such as the Buddha's display of his golden skin and Mahākāśyapa's anguish at his late arrival—there is no comprehensive biography to be found in the *Ceremonial in Four Sessions*. The passage closest to a complete retelling of the life of the Buddha comes in at the end of the second section in the four-part program, the *Ceremonial of the Traces of the Tathāgata* (*Nyorai iseki kōshiki*). In this brief passage, Myōe's *gāthā*s enumerate the Eight Great Stupas:

The Stupa of the Site of His Birth, in the palace of King Śuddhodana.
The Stupa of the Attainment of the Way, beneath the Bodhi Tree.
The Stupa of the [Turning of the] Wheel of Dharma, in the grove at the Deer Park.
The Stupa of the Designation, at Jetavana.
The Stupa of the Bejeweled Staircase, by the city of Kānyakubja.
The Stupa of [the Preaching of the *Greater*] *Prajñāpāramitā* [*Sūtra*], at Rājagṛha.
The Stupa of Vimalakīrti, in the garden of Āmravana.
The Stupa of the *Parinirvāṇa*, between the Śala trees.[126]

Notably, this list does not conform to the standard set of the eight stupas which became important in the late Indian or Tibetan traditions, nor was it based on the list of Eight Phases that received the widest acceptance in Japan. Rather, this list recapitulates a list of *gāthās* from the *Great Vehicle Contemplation Scripture of the Mind Ground of* [*the Buddha's*] *Original Lives* (*Dasheng bensheng xindi guanjing*, *T* 159), a sutra translated into Chinese early in the ninth century, with slight changes to the names of the stupas.[127] (It also substantially tallies with the list of stupas from the *Sutra of the Titles of the Eight Great Numinous Stupas*.[128]) For all his desire to return to the roots of Buddhism and its practice in India, Myōe remained powerfully entrenched in his own cultural sphere.

The Biography of the Buddha as Homiletic Text

In a similarly didactic vein, tales of the life of the Buddha also figure in the records of sermons given in ancient and early medieval Japan. The text now known as the *Tōdaiji Notes for Sermons* (*Tōdaiji fujumon kō*; hereafter, *Notes*) was probably compiled in the first decades of the ninth century, and no earlier than the end of the eighth. This modular collection of fragments, recorded by an unknown monastic hand, includes a number of episodic stories and verbal formulae for use in rituals sponsored by patrons wishing to make merit for their deceased parents.

Extant only in a conspicuously rough copy, the single surviving manuscript of the *Notes* is shot through with pronounced abbreviation. Scrawled lines connect passages, suggesting that the text was not necessarily to be read in the order of its original recording. The formulaic nature of the text is evident again in the utter lack of names of contemporary individuals; in the inclusion of phrases roughly translatable as "Insert name of ritual patron here," "Insert title of ritual service here," and so on; and in the following note, presumably addressed to the preacher, concerning the use of the text as a whole: "[These] phrases should be used in accordance with the time and according to whether donors are rich or poor, monastics or laypersons, or male or female. Add or subtract language as appropriate."[129] Although written in classical Chinese, the text includes grammatical particles helping the reader to parse the syntax, marking the earliest datable appearance of the Japanese vernacular *katakana* script. This clue further indicates that the document functioned as written notes for an oral performance.

Within the *Notes*, a short sketch of the life of the Buddha appears in lines 156–67, wedged between a passage explaining why the Buddha is the "peerless one" (*mujōson*) and a passage glorifying the Buddha's compassion in ministering even to beggars lying in their own filth by the roadside. A translation of the first two lines of the brief passage alone suffices to suggest the telegraphic nature of the text, which must have been used primarily as an aid to memory:

> The causes and conditions [i.e., the origin tale or history] of Śākyamuni [Buddha]. Prabhāpāla *etc.* A white elephant *etc.* [Queen Māyā's] right side *etc.* Seven steps *etc.* [The king] ordered the great sage to prognosticate based on the signs *etc.* [The sage] wept *etc.* The highborn men of the world and their daughters assembled in this palace. Those of high talent in this world assembled. Reading a text, they asked the learned doctor but he did not understand. The prince gave instruction *etc.* Four gates *etc.* [The prince] saw the flowers in the garden *etc.* He left the fortress at dead of night *etc.* The four kings *etc.* King Śuddhodana was lost in agony for seven days *etc.* Six years *etc.* Bathed *etc* . . . .[130]

Strikingly, this highly abbreviated biography does not allude to the *parinirvāṇa* of the Buddha, which is mentioned only in a separate passage within the *Notes*, at the end of a short summary discussion of the three bodies of the Buddha. The exposition in this second passage is still more economical: "The Buddha's transformation body resides in its Pure Land, attaining the Way through eight phases and transforming sentient beings. Entry, infancy, childhood, asceticism, attainment, defeat, turning, annihilation, *etc.*"[131] Each term in the final list represents one of the Eight Phases (*hassō*) as conventionally defined in the Buddhism of East Asia: the bodhisattva's (1) entry into the womb of his mother, (2) infancy, (3) childhood, (4) ascetic practices, (5) attainment of the Way, (6) defeat of Māra, (7) first turning of the wheel of the dharma, and (8) *parinirvāṇa*.[132] Brief as it is, then, this passage therefore marks a very early occurrence in Japan of a kind of epitome of the full account of the life of the Buddha Śākyamuni.[133] In this text, we see instruction in the story of the Buddha's life embedded in a sermon calling on ritual patrons to trust in him to assist their relatives in the other world, and the main events of the Buddha's life used to illustrate a key doctrine in the Mahāyāna, that of the Buddha as a being with multiple bodies.

The retelling of narrative episodes from the life of the Buddha is also documentable for specific lectures in the late Heian period. Despite its title, the surviving portions of the *Notes Taken while Listening to One Hundred Sessions of Sermons* (Jpn. *Hyakuza hōdan kikigaki shō*, ca. 1110) cover only some twenty days' lectures from a royally sponsored series of dharma talks, which—again, despite its name—was reportedly planned for one hundred daily sessions but was later extended to a full three hundred days.[134] While the dates of the lectures and the titles of the monastic lecturers are known, the identity of the sponsoring imperial princess and the precise purpose for the lectures remain disputed.

On the seventh day of the third month of 1110, a monk of the Tendai denomination—known only by his monastic courtesy name Kōunbō and therefore of uncertain identity—lectured on the story of the Buddha's reunion with Rāhula after the Buddha's awakening. Kōunbō combined this account with a story hailing from a different textual tradition, concerning the Buddha's dispatch of Maudgalyāyana to bring Rāhula back to him as a renunciate. Reminded of her promise not to defy the dharma, a promise that she made to Śākyamuni during his existence as Sumedha, Yaśodharā ultimately accedes to the request. First, however, she excoriates him for his treatment of her:

> The Buddha must not call for this prince [Rāhula] as well. I am afraid that I feel only resentment toward him. Even when he left the palace and renounced the world, he never told me that he would. And even though he conducted [his austerities and practice] for twelve years, for some reason he never came home even once.[135]

Despite such occasional complaints, most of the sermons summarized in this collection end with exhortations to faith, but Kōunbō chooses to end this episode with the scriptural prediction of Rāhula's future Buddhahood. The implicit suggestion in this homily is clear: the sponsoring patron of the lecture series ought, like Rāhula, to have faith in the Buddha, which will contribute to her good rebirth in the next world. Because the lecture series was initially devoted to the *Lotus Sutra*, it would also be appropriate to see this account in the context of that more famous text.

The Life of the Buddha in the Training of Young Monastics

Like the homiletic materials, texts written for young monastics in ancient and medieval Japan also use the biography of the Buddha for purposes of teaching. Of the two texts treated in this section, the first is by far the better known. It is the *Illustrated Three Jewels* (*Sanbōe*, henceforth *Three Jewels*), a famous anthology originally prepared in 984 CE. The courtier and minor official Minamoto Tamenori (d. 1011) composed it for the imperial princess Sonshi (also read "Takako," 966–85), soon after she took the tonsure and shortly before her death. The text names and draws upon a range of canonical sources, often attested through the medium of Chinese encyclopedic compilations. Although any pictorial illustrations that might have originally been attached to the text have long been lost, it probably began its existence as an illustrated scroll, perhaps as a distant descendant of *The Illustrated Sutra of Past and Present Cause and Effect.*

The second instructional text, by contrast, is an obscure, anonymous work, titled simply *A Biography for the Instruction of Children.* Probably a product of the late fourteenth century, it is extant in just two manuscript editions, the earlier dating from 1402, the latter from 1421.[136] These record only the names of the copyists, and no author. While the *Three Jewels* has a long history of comment and reproduction, from the time of its composition to the present, the *Biography for the Instruction of Children* was rediscovered only late in the twentieth century.

In both of these texts, the story of the Buddha's life frames instruction in "doctrinal classification" (Jpn. *kyōsō hanjaku,* typically abbreviated to *kyōhan*). Given the weight of Tendai interpretations of Buddhism through much of Japan's classical and early medieval eras, it is only natural that these instructional texts—separated by roughly four hundred years—would both recapitulate the orthodox Tendai scheme. Conventionally attributed to the founder of Chinese Tiantai Buddhism, Zhiyi (538–597), the fully developed, polemical form of this classification actually owes more to the early Koryŏ-era monk Ch'egwan (d. 971?).[137] Zhiyi had, famously, tried to make sense of the bewildering variety of Buddhist scriptures coming to China in translation, each claiming to represent the word of the Buddha. Zhiyi classified the sutras that he knew into five periods of the Buddha's preaching, assigning to each a distinctive "flavor." It was Ch'egwan who interpreted these periods and flavors not as stages of accomplishment among the Buddha's listeners, but rather as a "device to rank sūtras based on their contents and ultimately to defend the superiority of the *Lotus Sūtra* and the [Chinese Tiantai] School."[138]

By far the older, longer, and more aristocratic of these two works, the *Three Jewels* also has a more complex history. Its intended reader, Sonshi, suffered ostracism at court, and appears to have expressed a strong interest in Buddhist practice. In 982, she underwent a private ordination, of the kind increasingly common for women in Japan after the ninth century, when court-sponsored ordinations of nuns ended. But in 984 she took the unusual step of receiving a further ordination from Ryōgen (912–985), who was at the time head of the Tendai monastic establishment based on Mount Hiei—the only known ordination of any nun by him.[139] This was also the year of the completion of the *Three Jewels,* further suggesting Sonshi's serious effort in Buddhist study. Meanwhile, the author of the compilation, Tamenori, had his own personal connection with Mount Hiei: he very likely participated in a mixed association of laymen and Tendai monks, whose members assembled twice yearly on Mount Hiei to pursue Buddhist practice, prominently including Pure Land devotion.[140] Given this background, the overwhelming dominance of Tendai doctrines in this text is only to be expected.

The *Illustrated Three Jewels'* discussion of "Buddha" in the eponymous first of its three volumes is remarkable, as it devotes hardly any space to recounting the life of Śākyamuni or of any buddha. This volume treats Śākyamuni in its preface, expounding on his distinctive bodily signs, his divine powers, and his transcendent body. Here, the narrative of his life as Siddhartha is allotted just one sentence: "He was born in the palace of a king and, while still in his youth, rejected the Five Cravings and left his father's house, and when he sat under the Tree of Enlightenment, he subdued the Four Forces of Evil and became a Buddha."[141] Following the preface, the body of the volume covers thirteen of Śākyamuni's previous lives, recounting a series of familiar birth stories. The "Buddha" volume, then, is less an account of the Buddha's awakening than a kind of shopping list of ingredients—here, perfections—indispensable to the making of a fully-fledged buddha.

The preface to the second volume (concerning dharma) treats the preaching career of the Buddha, beginning, "Among all the teachings of Śākyamuni—from the day he was enlightened to the night he entered Nirvāṇa—none are untrue."[142] The text then proceeds through each of the five stages as arranged by Ch'egwan, lingering on the preaching of the *Lotus Sutra* and omitting reference to the *Nirvana Sutra*. The narrative of the Buddha's life in this preface, then, represents just the barest scaffolding on which to hang the standard Tendai account of the doctrines that he preached. In a text that broadly emphasizes narrative over doctrinal discourse, this section is kept concise and to the point.

This scaffolding is further elaborated in the late medieval *Biography for the Instruction of Children*. Like the *Three Jewels*, the *Biography* also makes frequent reference, by name, to specific canonical sources, revealing a particular debt to the *Sutra of the Collection of Authentic Deeds of the Buddha*.[143] The Tendai text also follows its predecessors in adopting other conventions of existing biographical writing about the Buddha.[144] As in the description of the temple adornments in *A Tale of Flowering Fortunes*, it also adduces the years of the sexagenary cycle to fix events of his life in time. As did the Dunhuang *Sutra on the Achievement of the Way*, it recounts the trial by fire of Yaśodharā and Rāhula. Like *Notes Taken while Listening*, it tells of Yaśodharā's resistance to the

Buddha's demand to induct Rāhula into his sangha, and her eventual capitulation. The *Biography* also narrates Devadatta's failed attempts to assassinate the Buddha and take control of his sangha, continuing to the *parinirvāṇa* of the Buddha, the cremation and division of his relics, the compilation of the sutras, and the transmission of Buddhism to China, and thence to Japan.

The *Biography*—chronologically the last medieval work treated in this study as a didactic or canonical biography—does not merely point to the same canonical past as its predecessors. To be sure, like the *Three Jewels*, the *Biography* also uses the account of the life of a Buddha as a framework for discussing the Five Periods of the Buddha's preaching, with their attendant scriptures. Unlike the *Three Jewels*, however, the *Biography* exhibits a sustained preoccupation with doctrinal matters, devoting to their discussion some two-thirds of its total length, and including the *Nirvana Sutra* in its purview.[145] Unlike Sengyou and the style of critical reading inaugurated in his *Genealogy of the Śākya Clan*, this text simply notes and records discrepancies between conflicting scriptural accounts without trying to adjudicate among them.[146] True to its title, the implied purpose of the work is that of transmitting a basic body of knowledge; critical considerations can wait.

More remarkably, as Gotō Akio pointed out, the text breaks with its predecessors in at least two important senses. First, it is the first confirmable independently circulating textual biography of the Buddha composed in Japan.[147] Even if the narrative is a framework containing an exegesis of the Buddha's preaching, that scaffold is not itself embedded in a larger narrative structure. Second, the *Biography* sets a cosmically vast stage for the unfolding of its story, beginning not with the birth of Siddhartha or any birth stories of previous lives, but instead with the story of the "three innumerable aeons" (Skt. *tri-kalpāsaṃkhyeya*, Jpn. *san-asōgikō*) of existence; it places our Buddha Śākyamuni among his predecessors in the current aeon, the Kalpa of the Present.[148]

Sengyou's record aside, an interest in the cosmic lineage of buddhas is by no means novel within the Buddhist canons. For one early example, we may turn to the *Great Discourse on the Lineage of the Buddhas* (*Mahāpadāna-suttanta*), dating from a relatively early stratum of the Pāli canon. In this text, Śākyamuni recounts the history of the seven buddhas of the past, of which he is the last, demonstrating through a detailed retelling of the career of the buddha Vipaśyin, the first of the seven, that each has fulfilled precisely the same course of life events constitutive of buddhahood. In fact, early Indian accounts of the life of the Buddha seem more concerned with his place in a lineage of buddhas extending back to prehistory than with the particular events of his final lifetime. In the Japanese context, however, the *Biography* is the first of multiple texts to commence the biography of Śākyamuni not with his stay in Tuṣita heaven or tales of his previous births, but with the making of the cosmos and his buddha-lineage itself.

These two educational texts for young monastics survived through fame and through chance. The *Three Jewels* is now firmly enshrined in the pantheon of Japanese literary history, while the *Biography* slipped through to the present in just two manuscripts. Nonetheless, they suggest the role that the life of the Buddha could play in monastic education.

For roughly the first millennium of Japanese contact with tales of the life of the Buddha, his life story was relatively stable. Continental treatments of that life to reach Japan overwhelmingly sought to root their authority through the citation of recognized scriptural accounts. Japanese clerics learned and mastered that technique of citation, rehearsing it whenever they composed their own biographies. The persistent interest in asserting orthodoxy in these biographies is not unrelated to the monastic environments in which they were produced. As we will find in the next chapter, the biography began to change shape only when authors outside of those environments began to retell it.

TWO

The Buddha as Local Hero

Accounts of the life of the Buddha were not static in ancient and medieval Japan; as the previous chapter demonstrated, different authors and artists could—and did—draw upon different texts and episodes for a variety of purposes in their production of new accounts. Nonetheless, through the early sixteenth century, Japanese retellings of the life of the Buddha continued to depend heavily on continental precedents, particularly on literature considered canonical by Japanese clerics.

This chapter shows how tales of the Buddha's life changed when storytellers' concern for canonicity waned. By discussing popular Buddhist narratives produced from the late sixteenth century through the seventeenth century, it traces the opening of a rift within such Japanese tales. These texts—mostly from the first half of Japan's Edo or early modern period (1603–1868)—mark the point at which narratives about the Buddha begin to leave the conventions of their continental counterparts to go their own way. These narratives made the tale of the Buddha accessible to wider audiences in Japan through changes both to language and to plot. Altogether, they add up to a process of "vernacularization," in terms of both structure and content. The vernacular Buddha from them went on to dominate popular cultural production until the twentieth century. He had become a local hero.

In the sense used here, "vernacular narrative" does not only mean "narrative written in the Japanese language." As with early Chosŏn–dynasty accounts in Korea (late fourteenth century to late sixteenth century), early medieval Japanese canonical accounts of the Buddha's life (late twelfth century to late fourteenth century) initially survive the shift to inscription in the vulgar tongue. The earliest known Japanese vernacular sequence of stories from the life of the Buddha dates from the first half of the twelfth century, from the *Tales of Times Now Past*. Although written in Japanese, the *Tales* version of the Buddha's life is conservative in terms of plot.[1]

Rather, the structural vernacularization of the life of the Buddha accelerated when the tale entered into new narrative genres: first, the world of the so-called companion books (*otogizōshi*) circulating in the late medieval years; and second, the new genre of the puppet theater (known variously as *ayatsuri ningyō, ningyō jōruri*, or Bunraku), which began in earnest early in the seventeenth century.[2] Constraints imposed by these new generic forms altered the storytelling of the life of Śākyamuni, lessening the influence of older sources of authority. Further, with the shift in genre came a concomitant alteration in the producers and consumers of these tales. Until the late medieval period, high-ranking Buddhist clerics and their elite patrons were the chief producers and consumers of biographical texts. From the early seventeenth century onward, though, the biographies of the Buddha became commodities to be purchased and consumed by a wider literate audience. The Buddha and his life thus entered the custody of commercial authors, professional chanters, and writers in the puppet theater, and became subject to the vagaries of the publishing market.

Multiple forms of authority were attenuated in this process. First, the canon of scriptural and para-scriptural biographies composed in Chinese began to lose its sway over Japanese narratives. When commercial authors could not find sufficiently interesting material within the canon, they looked to sources outside the biographical corpus, or simply invented new ones. Like a space probe hurtling away from Earth and finding it increasingly difficult to lock onto a radio signal from home, these late stories of the Buddha unfold at a palpable distance from the gravity of the orthodox canon. Second, within the narratives in question, the figure of the Buddha begins to lose the authority that it previously embodied. These stories usually still narrate his awakening, but the retelling of that process, and the glorification of every facet of the Buddha's life, are no longer their central preoccupations. Other characters and other subplots appear, hijacking the narrative flow. Śākyamuni often cuts a poor figure; in fact, these tales seem to be as much concerned with his suffering as with his salvific power. The diminution of his status is particularly apparent in the scenes of his awakening, which ceases to result from his accumulation of karmic merit from time immemorial, and owes increasingly to the intervention of others.

To illustrate these developments, this chapter considers four representative texts or bodies of text, in roughly chronological order, from the late medieval period through the seventeenth centuries. While the set of texts here does not comprehensively chart the rewriting of the life of the Buddha in the early modern period, it does point to the important developments in the plot.

Declining Concern for the Canon

Shifts in narrative genre, in the custodians and audience of the narrative, and in the sources for biographical tales are well exemplified in two extended prose narratives that emerged in Japan's latter medieval period. The first, the *Program of the Eight Phases of the Life of the Tathāgata Śākyamuni* (*Shaka nyorai hassō shidai*), seems not to have circulated widely; only a few manuscript copies survive, one of them incomplete.[3] They survived in monastic contexts and appear not to have been disseminated any further. By contrast, the second group of sources, the *Original Ground of Śākyamuni*, developed into the single most popular life of the historical Buddha in Japan from the late sixteenth century through the first half of the seventeenth. Unlike the *Program*, the *Original Ground* literature, as I will call it, survives in a wide range of forms, including manuscripts, illustrated handscrolls, hand-illustrated books, books printed in early movable type, illustrated books printed from woodblocks, and even an adaptation for the nascent puppet theater.[4] They represent no unified corpus, but rather a group of closely related narratives. Some texts in this literature are known under variant titles, including *The Biography of the Fundamental Aspiration behind Śākyamuni's Emergence into the World* (*Shaka shusse honkai denki*), *A Vernacular Biography of Śākyamuni the Honored One* (*Tsūzoku Shakuson denki*) and simply *The Tale of Śākyamuni* (*Shaka monogatari*).[5]

Both the *Program* and the *Original Ground* literature comprise long and coherent prose narratives (not merely a succession of episodes strung together, as in the case of the sequence in *Tales of Times Now Past*). They were both written primarily in Japanese grammar, with occasional citations of text in Chinese. One other feature that they share is an apparent mismatch between their content and the genres by which we know them today. In medieval Japanese Buddhism, a *shi-*

dai, or "program," ordinarily signifies a ritual manual, which is to say, a "sequence" of events. But no ritual program is attested in conjunction with the *Program of the Eight Phases*. Similarly, the term *honji*, used for the "original ground" of the larger narrative corpus, typically refers to a distant Buddha or bodhisattva who appears in Japan as a "manifest trace" (*suijaku*), a Japanese deity who echoes or mirrors its foreign foundation—a kind of local representative or incarnation. This mode of relating Buddhist deities to indigenous ones in Japan has its roots in the Tendai doctrine of the Heian period. However, by the late Muromachi period, the term *honji* had also become the namesake for a genre of vernacular prose stories, *honjimono*, that "tell about the former lives of Buddhas, gods, and the origins of temples and shrines" and "show the strong influence of the *honji-suijaku* theory."[6] In the case of the *Original Ground of Śākyamuni*, though, this label does not quite fit. Nearly all the versions in the *Original Ground* corpus fail to end with the standard formula for denouement in a *honjimono*—in other words, a conclusion that relates how the foreign deity came to Japan. (Within the corpus, only the version for the puppet theater mentions the appearance of Śākyamuni in Japan, in the form of a deity enshrined on the eastern side of Mount Hiei.[7])

Broadly compared, the *Program* derives primarily from canonical biography, orientated to the Chinese canon and its various digests, while the *Original Ground* literature represents the start of a distinct vernacular tradition. Previous scholarship has adduced the *Original Ground* literature as pivotal in the indigenization of the story of the Buddha's life. Kurobe Michiyoshi wrote: "*The Original Ground of Śākyamuni* . . . is biographical literature about the Buddha representative of Japan's medieval period, [marking] a point of arrival for the biographies of the Buddha brought to Japan, which transformed over generations in the Japanese climate."[8] Hank Glassman concluded his discussion of the text with a corresponding observation: "The story of a young prince living in ancient India who set out to defeat rebirth in samsara, a story told over so many centuries in so many places, is here shaped to the narrative logic of the late medieval Japanese imagination and tuned to the local conventions of emotional response."[9]

To identify the *Program* as relatively canonical does not mean ignoring its innovations, which lie in harmonizing Tendai doctrinal concerns with the biography of the Buddha. Like the vast bulk of its predecessors, the *Program* is comprised of a pastiche of references to various sutras. It includes a standard, repeating formula for citation ("The scripture says . . ."), although it does not always name its particular sources.[10] At certain key points, it cites important passages in untranslated Chinese, suggesting that its intended audience had some degree of literacy in both languages. In its infrequent and haphazard style of citation, the *Program* forms a kind of bridge between the relatively conservative biographical literature of the ancient and early medieval periods in Japan, on one end, and the *Original Ground* literature, on the other, whose prose does not cite any scriptures by name.[11]

A few examples from the *Program* will suffice to show its relatively conservative character. Its accounts of the Buddha's birth and of his awakening rely heavily on conventional Chinese-language sources. The Buddha's birth takes place, as usual, while his mother Māyā is standing under an *aśoka* tree in the garden of Lumbinī:

> The Lady . . . cherished a tree known as the "tree of no sadness" [an *aśoka* tree]. In this tree are mixed purple and green, like the tail of a peacock; its stalk is red, like the light red of sandalwood; its scent is fragrant, like ox-head sandalwood. When, entranced by this fine tree, she reached up to break off a branch, the prince was born from her right side, as she felt nothing.[12]

The infant goes on to manifest the typical miracles and, as he generally does in East Asia, to declare that he is the only honored one in heaven and earth. The description of Māyā's death, slightly later, is similarly conventional:

> His mother, the consort, taken helplessly by the winds of impermanence, was reborn in the Trāyastriṃśa Heaven. This is because . . . a mother who gives birth to an avatar [Jpn. *gonja*] is fortunate and worth the utmost veneration. As a result, she abandons her karma in the lower realms, and inherits the karma in the upper ones. Thus, by virtue of the merit of giving birth to the prince, the Lady was reborn in the Trāyastriṃśa Heaven seven days later.[13]

The divine birth and its consequence for Māyā have canonical foundation but still are not wholly stereotyped. The "winds of impermanence" to which Hank Glassman called attention in the *Original Ground* narrative are already in evidence here.[14] Attested as early as the thirteenth century, the trope likening impermanence to a wind that scatters the flowers might not be original to medieval Japan, but its general currency there is beyond doubt.

Likewise, the *Program* narrates the awakening of the prince in a more or less standard way, with only slight adaptation. The scene has Siddhartha sitting under the *bodhi* tree. As is to be expected, Māra comes to contest the prince's right to claim the seat. After the weapons of Māra's army fail to harm or dislodge Prince Siddhartha, the *Program* supplies the prince with the following words of challenge:

> The Prince asked Māra, "On account of cultivating what good karmic roots of old, and dependent upon what merit, have you now become the demon king of the three realms, and do you now oppose me?" Māra was stupid and knew not of cause and effect; ignorant of the karma of his previous lives, he could not reply to the Prince. The Prince told Māra [in Chinese]: "In the past, you held a single Dharma-meeting of Non-obstruction, which is why you have now attained your destructive [power]; but in the infinite sea of saṃsāra, I [alone] have made various offerings for all sentient beings." [In Japanese,] these words mean: "You once held a Dharma-meeting of Non-obstruction, so you became the great demon king of the three realms. But I, in the very midst of the infinite sea of saṃsāra, made infinite vows for the sake of all sentient beings, cultivated the superior and boundless practices, and gave variously to all sentient beings. What is more, I gave with no regard for my life, and have now been reborn finally in order to become a Buddha. To compare your merit to mine, it would be like a mustard seed. To compare my merit to yours, it is like Mount Sumeru. You cannot use your merit to topple mine."[15]

The prince's testimony is here doubled by the operation of the quotation from scripture: As the character of the Buddha-to-be cites his own behavior in past lives, so too does the text of the *Program* itself cite an authoritative source in its "original" scriptural language (at least from the point of view of medieval Japanese). The text then consolidates that citation by interpreting—and extending—the Chinese source in the medieval Japanese vernacular. (That the Chinese scriptural citation here represents a slight adaptation of the received text does not compromise its gravitas.[16])

The *Program* goes on to recount in standard terms the attack of Māra and his horde, and their capitulation. But next, instead of recounting the prince's awakening, the text seeks to explain it in doctrinal terms. It points to the ultimate nonduality of awakening and delusion, even appealing by name to the authority of the founder of the Tiantai school, Zhiyi—positions typical of the Tendai monastic context in which this text was likely produced. This particular doctrinal overlay is new to the literature of the Buddha's life, but it merely supplements, and does not displace, what is already a fairly conventional retelling of the defeat of Māra. In this account, the understanding of the inner workings of the Buddha's awakening may be novel, but the propriety of the claim by the prince to awakening is never in doubt.

In the following episodes of the Buddha's preaching to his mother (who has been reborn as a deity) and father (who is still a king), the *Program* reconfirms the Buddha's supremacy. Positioned late in his preaching career, these familiar episodes draw on ancient biographical traditions that were already subject to a good deal of malleability. Although the Buddha's visit to the Trāyastriṃśa heaven features in accounts of his life from South Asia onward, there is no consensus, canonical or otherwise, as to what he taught his mother there. For instance, some scholastic traditions claim that only the Abhidharma was taught there, but Tibetan texts describe not only the preaching of the Abhidharma, but also the preaching of several different *dhāraṇī*s, or spells.[17] This tendency to flesh out the heavenly sermon with a *dhāraṇī* began in China: in a sutra probably originally composed in Chinese, the *Mahāmāyā Sūtra* (*T* 383, ca. 500 CE), the Buddha ascends to heaven and preaches a long *dhāraṇī* to his mother "as a token of gratitude" to her for giving birth to him. The unnamed *dhāraṇī* preached in this text focuses on the healing of disease, listing fever, malaria, insanity, nightmares, talking in one's sleep, childhood epilepsy, and so on.[18] It is fairly clearly this is not intended to assist in Māyā's salvation, which the Buddha has already enabled by this point in the text.[19]

In the world of the *Program*, the Buddha skips the usual visit to the Trāyastriṃśa heaven to preach to his mother, instead taking his leave of her when she descends to see him off at his funeral. He does, however, arrive at the deathbed of his father, King Śuddhodana, where he takes his father's hand and comforts his father by telling him that he, the king, has "cut off the *kleśa*s [delusions] of the three realms" and is therefore guaranteed awakening.[20] The Buddha attempts to lift his father's coffin in a final filial gesture, only to find that the cosmos will not permit an awakened being to do so: the earth shakes, and the Four Heavenly Kings descend to take the Buddha's place. This too is completely standard in terms of the canon.

In summary, the *Program of the Eight Phases of the Life of the Tathagata Śākyamuni* is, in one sense, the culmination of the Tendai-centered retellings of the life of the Buddha. Beginning with the Buddha's kingly lineage of wheel-turning kings and ending with the enshrinement of the Buddha's relics, this ranks as one of the few texts from ancient or medieval Japan to narrate a complete life of the Buddha in prose. Unlike the twelfth-century *Tales of Times Now Past*, the life story in the *Program* stands independent of any larger structure. Further, unlike the roughly contemporary *Biography for the Instruction of Children*, the *Program* employs Tendai doctrinal interpretations of the Buddha's life without subordinating the entire narrative to them. Yet, like its predecessors, this retelling resides squarely inside a long tradition of sifting, selecting, and recombining biographical narratives from various texts. Like its predecessors, it attributes canonical status to these and cites them by name, if not consistently or clearly. This text brooks no question about the status of the Buddha as the center of this life narrative, and as the ultimate source by which to reach salvation.

Breaking the Medieval Mold

By contrast, the *Original Ground* literature equivocates about the Buddha's exalted status. To be sure, some demotion of the historical Buddha is nothing new in the mature Buddhist tradition: Mahāyāna sutras in the mold of the *Lotus* emphasize that the *real* Buddha is transhistorical, and dismiss Śākyamuni as a mere shadow of his transcendent self. Chan literature includes colorful dismissals of Śākyamuni: "Followers of the Way, don't take the Buddha to be the ultimate. As I see it, he is just like a privy hole. Both bodhisattvahood and arhatship are cangues and chains that bind one. This is why Mañjuśrī tried to kill Gautama with his sword, and why Aṅgulimāla attempted to slay Śākyamuni with his dagger."[21] In these two representative examples, though, something else supersedes the figure of the historical Buddha, elevated to a position of greater authority.

The *Original Ground* literature of late medieval Japan does not, of course, declare Śākyamuni a privy hole, but in other ways it does compromise the authority of the Buddha. First, from the beginning of the story, the Buddha's body is treated like a normal physical object, not a mere emanation from a cosmic source. As the account of the *Program* reminds us, the canonical tradition often stresses the Buddha's painless entry into the world. It also typically observes that the mothers of Buddhas all inevitably die seven days after giving birth, and sometimes adds that their bodies are unable to bear the joy of producing a Buddha-to-be. However, the puppet-theater version of the *Original Ground* offers no such excuses: "The consort Māyā, desirous of a deutzia flower, raised her right hand. When she tried to break off the flower, her right side ruptured, and she fell to the ground, writhing."[22] What kills her is none other than this "rupture," through which the infant Buddha emerges.[23] The charge that the Buddha was ultimately unfilial by causing the death of his mother was apparently on the minds of apologists for Buddhism from its early days in China.[24] Strikingly, the biographical narrative here seems to accept it; such developments imply that the *Original Ground* literature is relatively unconcerned with apologetics.

Like his mother's body, the body of the Buddha in the *Original Ground* literature also displays an unusual fragility. To be sure, the body of Śākyamuni does suffer in more typical versions of his life story. The famous attacks inflicted on the Buddha by his evil cousin Devadatta were well known in Japan, but the canonical literature accounts for these with some care: Devadatta's ability to injure the Buddha's foot with a large boulder, for instance, may be explained away as a result not of Devadatta's overpowering strength, but of Śākyamuni's own residual bad karma from a previous life. Significantly, Devadatta's infractions typically plunge him into hell.[25] However, such qualifications explaining the Buddha's injuries disappear in the *Original Ground* literature. In the version of the story for the puppet theater, the Buddha is adorned with an *ūrṇā*, a tuft of white hair between his eyes. This hair is typically considered one of the emblematic physical signs of Buddhahood. In the puppet-theater version, though, the Buddha gives a different explanation for it: "The scar from the beatings from the hermit's staff when I was undergoing austerities on the mountain is this *ūrṇā* between my eyes."[26] Later Edo-period retellings push this idea further. Sometimes, in classic Zen style, they even locate the Buddha's awakening at the time precisely at the moment when his master, the hermit Ārāḍa Kālāma, is beating him savagely.

In general, the *Original Ground* literature transforms in the figure of Ārāḍa Kālāma, attributing to him a new centrality. Following continental precedent, earlier Japanese biographies of the Buddha usually either split him into two figures, enumerating Ārāḍa Kālāma (or the two) as master(s) whose limited teaching could not satisfy the young seeker Siddhartha; or they simply excluded him from the narrative altogether. In no prose narrative prior to the sixteenth century does Ārāḍa Kālāma ever guide the prince to awakening, but this is precisely what he and other "heretical" masters accomplish in the *Original Ground* literature and subsequent works. This shift amounts to a radical devaluation of the power of the Buddha, who in this literature ceases to attain awakening through his own cumulative efforts.

As indicated by Kurobe Michiyoshi, this new depiction of Siddhartha as training under Ārāḍa Kālāma likely derives from an effort to align the biography of the Buddha with the account of the *Lotus Sutra*. Previously we have seen the result of such alignment in the form of the Jōrakuji depiction of the prince's meeting with the ascetic master. The original context of the "Devadatta" chapter clearly distinguishes the *Lotus* story from the lifetime of Śākyamuni, but this distinction went unnoted by the authors of the *Original Ground* literature, who apparently delighted in the tale of backbreaking menial service in exchange for the *Lotus*.

Such creative appropriation from the *Lotus Sutra* appears elsewhere in the *Original Ground* literature. Borrowing and adaptation from this passage in the *Lotus Sutra* appear vividly in one printed (1643) version of the *Original Ground of Śākyamuni*. Here, after twelve years of the prince's grueling service to a hermit on Mount Daṇḍaloka, the hermit at last consents to transmit the Buddha-dharma to the prince. He grants the prince a robe of tiger skin and discloses that this is not the first time that he has made such a bestowal of the teachings. In the past, the hermit reveals, the prince was a great king who had practiced the Six Perfections and abandoned his kingdom, and who was searching for the dharma. As in the narrative present, then too the hermit was actually named Scripture of the Lotus Blossom of the Fine Dharma, and he demanded that the king pierce his body with four-inch nails five times a day for ninety days. When the king completed this ascetic practice, Scripture of the Lotus Blossom of the Fine Dharma granted the king the *Lotus*.[27]

Like the general framework of the prince's service to a hermit, this detail was drawn from an account of a former life of the Buddha: once, in the past, the Buddha was a king who renounced his kingdom; he subjected himself to ninety days of his body being pierced by nails in exchange for two verses of Buddhist teaching.[28] Returning to the narrative present of the *Original Ground*, the hermit again grants the *Lotus*, this time to Siddhartha. As the hermit notes in his encomium for the scripture, "That *Scripture of the Lotus Blossom of the Fine Dharma* is wondrous and wondrous again. All the Buddhas of the three ages achieve awakening through this scripture; and the Buddhas of the Ten Directions, too, attain Buddhahood through this scripture."[29] In no uncertain terms, the narrative here is animated by the claim of the *Lotus Sutra* to undergird the awakening of all buddhas.

Devotion to the *Lotus* is characteristic of the Tendai tradition, but it was also widespread throughout medieval Japanese society. Because this text does not demonstrate intellectual features distinct to medieval Tendai thought, it is not easy to link this interpolation specifically to the Tendai intellectual milieu of the late medieval period. As soon as the hermit makes this pronouncement, he reveals to the prince that he is actually an incarnation of the Buddha Vairocana and sends the prince off. In the Mahāyāna world of this text, two buddhas may work side by side in the same realm, but this revelation attenuates the interest in this story just the same. If some other buddha is already active in this world, then what is the significance of Siddhartha's struggle and awakening?

Perhaps the heavy emphasis on the bestowal of the *Lotus Sutra* is what makes the prince's subsequent meditation so colorless. The Buddha-to-be finds his way to the rock to which Vairocana directed him, aided by a divine boy "of fourteen or fifteen." The boy tells him that this is the spot on which all buddhas of the three realms attain awakening, and describes the rock in detail, saying that its roots penetrate five hundred *yojanas* down to the hells, and further to the discs of wind, water, and fire at the base of this world. "Thus," the boy goes on, "no matter how the heretics seek to topple this rock, it will not move."[30] Then the boy flies away to the west, revealing at the last minute that he is actually an incarnation of the Buddha Amitābha. (In other versions of the *Original Ground*, he reveals that he represents other figures.)

> Then, just as the boy had said, in order to prevent the prince from attaining Buddhahood, all of the heretics, along with Māra, king of the Sixth Desire Heaven and Devadatta, along with several tens of thousands of heretics [*sic*], came and attempted to smash that rock. But the Venerable Śākyamuni, previously forewarned, did not panic in the least, nor did the rock move, and the opposition of the heretics ended in vain. He became the Buddha Śākyamuni, Sole Honored-One in the Three Realms.[31]

Although the skeleton of the canonical plot survives here, the muscle of narrative elaboration has shriveled considerably, especially in comparison with the account of the *Program*. Gone is the Buddha's self-assured report about his voyage toward enlightenment over countless lifetimes, gone the testimony of the earth, gone the submission of Māra and his hordes, gone the Tendai doctrinal explanation for awakening. In the *Original Ground* literature, Śākyamuni's triumph lies not in the quality of his meditation, but rather in being in the right place and sitting still.

This Buddha, then, cuts a rather uninspiring figure, an impression still more prominent in the version of these same events in the *Original Ground* tale for the puppet theater. Having endured the beatings of Ārāḍa Kālāma "for the sake of his mother" and having received the tiger skin robe from him, the prince awakens in a passage straddling the fourth and fifth acts of the drama.

> The Buddha spread the grass the boy had given him, and meditated [upon it] for six years, without moving even a hair. In the sixth year, during the night of the fifteenth day of the tenth month, he saw Venus rise in the sky, and forthwith acquired the body of a Buddha. Since then, he has been venerated as the Teacher of the Three Realms. This is an indescribable boon to us. [End of act four.]

> [Beginning of act five.] The *śramaṇa* Gautama was awakened. Because he had meditated for so long, he could not move his legs even a little, and he was at his wit's end. At that point, the hermit Ārāḍa Kālāma arrived. He said, "Ah, *śramaṇa*, so you have attained awakening," and prostrated himself in reverence. "From now on, your name will be the Buddha Śākyamuni. Hurry and go down to Middle India, and save sentient beings! Since you can't move easily after your long meditation, take this *bodhi* wood [*sic*] as your cane. [See fig. 2.] Hurry and go down! I am the spirit of awakening in the *Sūtra of the Lotus of the Fine Blossom*, and I take my leave of you."[32]

In the puppet theater's account, the Buddha achieves his awakening seemingly with no opposition greater than his own tingling legs, which have fallen asleep after years and years of meditation. He apparently does not even *know* that he has become the Buddha Śākyamuni until Ārāḍa Kālāma tells him, and he cannot rise to walk again until his master fashions a cane for him from the *bodhi* tree. (See fig. 2.) This conspicuous devaluation of the events surrounding the Buddha's awakening is a late innovation, distinct to the 1661 "true text" associated with the puppet theater, but it appears elsewhere in the corpus of early modern tales. If this gesture was added as a gag, then presumably it was one that played off the stage as well as on it.

Not incidentally, the motif of a newly awakened Buddha—who nonetheless needs to be informed that he has in fact become the Buddha—survived through (or was newly recreated in) the twentieth-century manga of the Buddha's life by Tezuka Osamu, and its anime film adapation. In both of these versions, the god Brahmā appears to the newly awakened Śākyamuni to inform him of his achievement and charge him with his task of teaching. In the manga, he also zaps the Buddha's forehead with his staff, producing his characteristic *ūrṇā*, in another plot development reminiscent of the puppet-theater version of the *Original Ground*.[33] These innovations in the manga outraged one devout lay Buddhist, writing for a website based in Singapore, who decried these changes to the scene of the Buddha's awakening as "utter

FIGURE 2 From the *Original Ground of the Tathāgata Śākyamuni* (detail). *Shaka Nyorai go-honji* (Edo period). Photograph courtesy of Waseda University Library.

nonsense" and "an outrageous demotion of the Buddha's supreme spiritual status!" (emphasis in the original).[34] Another online contributor to the same website complained of the treatment of this scene in the anime version:

> What is also funny to the average Buddhist . . . was that there was no emphasis on the enlightenment during that one especially eventful night. Also not depicted was what he became enlightened to. Perhaps the most deviant (and demeaning) of all is that he needed someone to awaken him to the fact that he had awakened! The theatre laughed at this point, as many knew the story was totally off in this regard.[35]

Such self-assured expressions of indignation and contempt nicely corroborate film critic Yomota Inuhiko's more general observation about Tezuka's manga: "Some people in established [Buddhist] groups . . . who want to confirm only the greatness of the Sage of the Śākyas, might even hurl the book away in a rage."[36] These reactions also corroborate the present chapter's argument about the *Original Ground* literature as the point of departure for a literature of the Buddha's life free from institutional constraints.

Nor is it only the scene of the awakening whose transformation begins with the *Original Ground* literature. In another variation, the Buddha's supremacy in his preaching career to his parents also erodes; his messages to his mother, reborn in the Trāyastriṃśa heaven, are particularly unstable. In one edition, he lectures her on impermanence and thus liberates her. In a printed edition, he enables her to attain Buddhahood by preaching the aforementioned *Mahāmaya Sutra*. As with the varying accounts of the moment of awakening, in this case too it is the puppet-theater version that most deemphasizes the power of the Buddha himself: after ninety days of reunion, the Buddha announces that he must return to Middle India to meet his father. The deified Māyā breaks down in tears, to which he replies:

> If you make a copy of my appearance, and chant the Name of [the Buddha] Amitābha morning and evening, then you will certainly be born in the Pure Land. The great king [Śakra, king of the Trāyastriṃśa heaven, whose consort Māyā has become] thought of this approvingly, and summoned Viśvakarman, celebrated in Middle India, and explained to him the matter. "Very good, sir," he replied. In an instant, he copied the appearance of the Venerable Śākyamuni, after which time Śākyamuni took his leave and returned to Magadha. After that, the kingly couple and their people venerated the image of Śākyamuni morning and evening, and eventually were born in the Pure Land.[37]

This short passage packs a number of innovations decentering Buddha's presence in the narrative. In place of the *dhāraṇī* taught to his mother in the *Mahāmaya Sutra*, we here have an unexplained endorsement of the *nenbutsu* practice of calling upon a different figure, the Buddha Amitābha. The account of the creation of the first image of the Buddha has been moved: It is no longer inspired by the longing of the earthly king Udayana to see the Buddha even in his absence, but now serves only the gods. While the gods of the Trāyastriṃśa heaven do manage to escape from samsara, they escape into a Pure Land, presumably Amitābha's.

When the Buddha of the *Original Ground* visits his dying father, the king, he preaches another novel message. In a speech that probably draws upon Shinran's (1173–1262) citation of the *Sutra on the Ocean-Like Samādhi of the Visualization of the Buddha*, the Buddha tells his father that bad karma is like "a forest of *eraṇḍa* trees, forty *yojanas* square," so noxious that anyone who smells it dies. But imagine, continues the Buddha, that at the base of this tree sprouts a lone *gośīrṣa-candana* tree, whose "fragrance fills the air, finally transforming the forest and giving it everywhere its own fragrance."[38] So too, the Buddha continues, can a single, small *nenbutsu* transform even vast quantities of poor karma and lead to salvation.

The passage cited by Shinran from the *Sutra on the Ocean-Like Samādhi of the Visualization of the Buddha* clearly means "visualization of the Buddha" as a meditative practice, not the *nenbutsu* as it was typically understood in seventeenth-century Japan, as the verbal calling on the name of the Buddha Amitābha. But in Shinran's hands, this passage became a tool by which to affirm the orthodoxy of his interpretation of *nenbutsu*. In all likelihood inspired by Shinran's reframing, the manuscript, print, and puppet-theater versions of the *Original Ground* all mention the Buddha Amitābha explicitly in the Buddha's sermon to his dying father. This shift carries the tale here firmly into the territory of medieval Japanese religious practice.

The cumulative effect of the transformations to the Buddha's life story as occasioned by the *Original Ground* narratives suggests a substantial loss of prestige and power for the Buddha, and for the scriptural tradition that had previously told his story. Because the matter of authorship remains unclear for almost all the texts cited in this section, it is of course impossible to prove that control over the narrative had by this point slipped out of clerical circles and into the hands of lay authors. At the very least, though, it is clear that the mature permutations of the *Original Ground* literature require less specialized knowledge about Buddhist texts (and concomitantly less ability to navigate through classical Chinese) than do the *Program* or the *Biography of the Fundamental Aspiration behind Śākyamuni's Emergence into the World*. If the authorship is unclear, though, then it is still possible to make educated guesses about the audience.

A Vernacular Buddha for Page and Stage

The *Original Ground* literature supplied much of the material for the *Tale of Śākyamuni in Eight Phases* (*Shaka hassō monogatari*), whose earliest extant edition dates to 1666. As the single most influential Japanese biography of the Buddha from that time until the late nineteenth century, the *Tale* abridged or excised some existing biographical materials and rearranged or invented others.

The *Tale* reworked the account of the Buddha's birth as domestic drama, concocting an elaborate, sororicidal rivalry between his mother, Māyā, and his aunt Mahāprajāpatī (designated here, as in the *Original Ground* literature, as "Gautamī"). Additionally, the *Original Ground*'s reinvention of Ārāḍa Kālāma as the master who makes possible the Buddha's awakening is expanded in the *Tale*, which piles on further masters and inflicts harsher trials. And in its most startling innovation, the *Tale* completely does away with the standard version of the Buddha's awakening experience, replacing it with a *jātaka* tale originating in the Mahāyāna *Mahāparinirvāṇa Sūtra*. Finally, its treatment of the Buddha's preaching career evinces a striking lack of concern for content or coherence. In the *Tale*, the Buddha's preaching initially conforms to the Tendai model but also incorporates a classic Chan origin story, with no effort to reconcile the two.

Citation of scriptural biographies—so important for centuries of hagiography—reaches a new level of innovation here, as the *Tale* adduces even nonexistent sutras. The presentation of Buddhist doctrine in the *Tale* is frequently shaky, suggesting a lack of authorial command over Buddhist vocabulary. One cost incurred by the Buddha's vernacularization, then, was the consignment of the previous literature to the realm of the incomprehensible. At least as far as its popular interpreters were concerned, canon had become a foreign language.

Before investigating these developments in the text of the *Tale of Śākyamuni in Eight Phases*, it will first be useful to sketch out the long and wide scope of its influence over later tales of the Buddha's life. The *Tale* is, to all indications, more textually stable than the *Original Ground* literature, and was popular over a much longer span: by the end of the Edo period in 1868, this text had appeared in reprint in multiple urban centers in at least four years—1684, 1693, 1823, and 1827. The *Tale* motivated the production of a succession of commercially successful works spanning more than two centuries. A few decades after its first publication, the great dramatist of the puppet theater, Chikamatsu (1653–1724), extensively adapted it as his play *A Birth Assembly for the Tathāgata Śākyamuni* (*Shaka nyorai tanjō e*, possibly first performed in 1714).[39] The play premiered on the eighth day of the fourth month, doubtless in order to capitalize on the tradition of commemorating the birth of the prince on that day. As was not uncommon in the mid-Edo period, Chikamatsu's play reached audiences beyond the theater, circulating in print both as a chanter's text and, later, as a digest picture book (1749).[40] Despite the checkered career of the puppet theater itself, *A Birth Assembly* survived to grace the stage, in its entirety or in excerpts, at least as late as 1930.[41]

The mid-nineteenth century saw a new wave of commercial adaptations of the *Tale of Śākyamuni in Eight Phases*. Collectively, these mirrored some of the key innovations in genre and publishing technique of the late Edo years, accomplishing the re-vernacularization of the Buddha into the languages of the new creative genres. Around 1845, Mantei Ōga (1819–1890) began to publish installations of what would become the longest of these adaptations, a colossal reworking in the *gōkan* format (illustrated bound books, sometimes serialized): *Eight Phases of the Life of Śākyamuni, A Japanese Library* (*Shaka hassō Yamato bunko*), released with interruptions from 1845 to 1871. In its later phase, Mantei Ōga's work was illustrated in part by a maverick artist of the late Edo and early Meiji years, Kawanabe Kyōsai.[42] Despite amounting to fifty-eight chapters and becoming one of the longest works of fiction for the period, its narrative never even reached the *parinirvāṇa* of the Buddha.

In 1854, the Kabuki playwright Sakurada Shizuke III (1802–1877) adapted Ōga's text for the stage, under the title *The Flower-Viewing Hall, a Japanese Library* (*Hanamidō Yamato bunko*).[43] This too inspired the ephemera typically associated with Kabuki theater, including prints of the actors in famous scenes from the drama, which were published both before and after the Meiji Restoration. Performed in its entirety or in excerpts as late as 1910, Sakurada's adaptation was even restaged with a female cast in Kyoto in 1902.[44] Presumably, it was a scene from the drama by Sakurada Shizuke III that gave rise to a 1913 silent film version of the *Eight Phases* (now lost), which starred the itinerant Kabuki actor turned early star of the silver screen, Onoe "Googly-Eyed" Matsunosuke (1875–1926). Mantei Ōga's tale additionally inspired an illustrated erotic adaptation, issued in 1860 and still extant.[45]

The year of the premier of *The Flower-Viewing Hall, a Japanese Library*, 1854, also saw the release of the illustrated *True Record of Śākyamuni, Origin of the Eight Schools* (*Hasshū kigen Shaka jitsuroku*) by Umebori Kokuga II (a.k.a. Reitei Kokuga, Hagiwara Otohiko, etc.; 1826–1886).[46] The *True Record* narrated the Buddha's life, building on material in the *Tale* by creatively locating in the Buddha's biography the origins of practices characteristic of later Japanese Buddhism, including the geneses of cremation; *zazen*, or seated meditation; and Shūgendō mountain asceticism. Judging from the number of copies remaining, this was his most widely read work.[47] One reader of this text was the British scholar and diplomat Ernest Satow (1843–1929), who produced a detailed synopsis of it as the major source for the life of the Buddha in the 1884 edition of a guidebook to Japan, which he coauthored.[48] However greatly these stories may diverge from the "canonical" biographies of the Buddha, they all took their cues from the seventeenth-century *Tale of Śākyamuni in Eight Phases*.

Among the early modern Japanese biographies of the Buddha, only the *Tale* has been translated into English in anything more than a summary version. The British-born missionary John Laidlaw Atkinson (1842–1908)—among the first Protestant missionaries to work in Kobe—chose to render it into English as a means of *dissuading* impressionable readers from interest in Buddhism. In 1893, he published an English version of the *Tale* under the title *Prince Siddhartha* [*sic*]*: The Japanese Buddha*. In the book's final chapter, Atkinson conceded the Buddha may have been the "light of Asia," but insisted nonetheless that the Buddha was not an adequately bright one: "At its best . . . [the light of the Buddha] has been more like the light of the moon, clear, luminous, and cold, rather than like the sun, bright, glowing, and life-giving."[49] Atkinson made no effort to produce a literal or scholarly English version of the *Tale of Śākyamuni in Eight Phases*. He could not resist the urge to scatter footnotes denouncing the Buddha and his religion throughout the text, and he appended three scathingly critical chapters of his own to the main exposition.

Whatever the infelicities associated with the reworking of the Buddha's life in the *Tale*—and there are several, even to readers who do not share Atkinson's prejudices—they very evidently did not repel early modern Japanese readers, who seem to have consumed the story with gusto. Because the *Tale of Śākyamuni in Eight Phases* tells a story that is, in certain key respects, unfamiliar outside the early modern Japanese context, and because it so powerfully shaped later works (whether they derived from it or reacted to it), it will be useful to highlight some of its more powerful innovations in some detail.

First, this version of the life of the Buddha demonstrated a heightened interest in domestic drama at the palace. Like the theatrical version of the *Original Ground of Śākyamuni*, the *Tale of Śākyamuni in Eight Phases* also begins not with the Buddha's kingly or spiritual lineages, nor with tales of any of his own former lives, but rather with King Śuddhodana's reign and his taking of the sisters Māyā and Gautamī as his consorts. Unusually, though, the *Tale* deviates from the standard description of the sisters by making Māyā the younger sister.

In this version, Māyā dreams of a visitation by a tall golden-treasure stupa, from which emerges the Buddha atop a white elephant. He explains to her that he would like her to "lend him her womb" so that he may be born to save all beings.[50] When she protests that she is a filthy being, burdened by the "five obstacles and the three forms of subservience," the Buddha informs her of her former life, in which she was a princess unjustly exiled through the plotting of an evil stepmother.

But by writing out one thousand copies of the *Sutra of the Liberation Blood Bowl* and by reciting it ten thousand times, the princess earned rebirth in her current exalted status as consort to the king. Thus purified by her sutra copying, he continues, she is now suitable for his purpose. After lotus flowers have blossomed from her hands in response to his presence, the Buddha "parted her . . . breasts and, like the casting of a shadow, took up residence in her womb."[51]

The king and his courtiers rejoice at the news of Māyā's pregnancy, but Gautamī could hardly be more distraught at the threat to her position. She summons her lackey, General Ba, and threatens to kill herself so that she may haunt Māyā and the unborn prince as a vengeful ghost. The general persuades her instead to summon two mountain ascetics, versed in thaumaturgy, to come to curse Māyā. Gautamī accordingly feigns a rapprochement with Māyā, inviting her to visit so that the ascetics, hidden from view, may observe Māyā's face to complete the curse.

After Māyā departs, the ascetics build altars to "subdue" (*chōbuku*) her, installing an image of her and performing sacrifices to bring about her destruction. In the midst of the ritual, the image comes to life and turns to Gautamī, pleading in vain for mercy. Gautamī cuts off its plea, declaring that she no longer considers Māyā her sister. Gautamī has the ritual completed and gleefully instructs the general to pay the two ascetics. No sooner have they received the money, though, than they are paralyzed, are swallowed up by the earth, and plummet as far as the golden disc at the base of the world. (In the theatrical adaptation of the *Tale* from 1669, cosmic justice comes not from below, but from above: Red and white demons descend from the clouds, seize the ascetics, and rip them in two.)

The defeat of the ascetics does not end the conflict. (At this point, the theatrical adaptation inserts a scene depicting the defeat and routing of General Ba and his henchmen by forces loyal to the king, whom the general has sought to depose.) Māyā sinks into despair, even though the court physicians assure her that she is well and will have an easy birth before long. But she malingers for two more years, suffering from her ill health as well as the court gossip and the smoldering resentment of her sister. Finally, one night, she dreams of the fetal Buddha-to-be, who "parts her breasts and emerges from her body, radiating light, and immediately appears before her in the form of a shining boy with the thirty-two marks."[52] He preaches to her and consoles her. Among other things, he tells of Gautamī, whose jealousy at one point changed her into a giant snake that "blotted out the sun and the moon," and about the ritual she sponsored to obstruct his birth.[53] Although he could in fact choose to be born at any time, he continues, he is waiting so as not to deepen Gautamī's wrath and therefore worsen her karmic burden. Urging his mother to be patient, he takes her breasts in his hands, opens her bosom, and returns to her womb. Her womb then takes on the appearance of a transparent jewel into which she can see, confirming to her that the Buddha told the truth. She awakens and writes down the events of her dream so as not to forget them. (In the version for the puppet theater, Māyā sees into her womb *after* she awakens, in what may be a way of emphasizing the reality of the condition.)

Even after the prophetic dream, Māyā's anguish does not end. Though she insists that she really is pregnant, the court physicians find no precedent for such a prolonged pregnancy and determine that she must be ill. They prescribe a drug (in some later versions of the story, explicitly identified as an abortifacient), but she refuses to take it. The king summons one hundred soothsayers to pronounce judgment upon her condition. Ninety-nine of them conclude that she is ill. But one soothsayer—like the fortuneteller Asita of the more conventional biographies—breaks down in tears, heartbroken that he will die without a chance to encounter the Buddha to whom, he assures everyone, Māyā is about to give birth. The king is nonplussed. Here the theatrical version of the story goes to further pains to assure him: stars fall from the sky, including Venus, which sprouts a bud from which emerges a goddess, who informs the king and all present, in no uncertain terms, of the impending birth of a Tathāgata. By contrast, in the 1666 published version of the text, the king is left doubting, though Māyā receives a third visit and sermon from the Buddha in her dreams.

The finale to this domestic drama occupies the third book and more of the *Tale of Śākyamuni in Eight Phases*. Alone, it takes up practically the whole of the final act of its theatrical adaptation. In this section, Māyā has been pregnant for three years when she receives word that King Śuddhodana will hold a flower banquet at the Lumbinī Garden, during which she is to receive pride of place as mistress of the flowers. On seeing her radiant form, everyone is astonished, and Gautamī repents for having ever resented her gentle, elegant sister. Through the power of the Buddha, the narrative editorializes, her repentance cancels out countless eons of bad karma. The king allows everyone present to break off flower blossoms to adorn Māyā's crown. This, the text parenthetically remarks, is the origin for the later practice of offering flowers to the Buddha. The king next permits Māyā herself to break off flowers from the treasure tree, but as she approaches it, her labor pains start, and she realizes that the prediction of her dreams is now coming true. For the final time, the Buddha addresses her from within her womb; a golden light shines from the heavens; and the infant Buddha emerges from beneath her robes. He walks for seven steps, declares that he is the sole honored one in heaven and on earth, climbs upon her lap, and takes her breasts in each hand to suckle. But Māyā falls asleep, never to recover, and here the narrative leaves her. Her attendant Udāyin shows the king her writings, which vindicate her fully. The king orders her remains to be enshrined in a towering treasure stupa to be placed atop a mountain to the east of her former quarters, which Udāyin builds.

By contrast, the theatrical version does not shy from depicting both Māyā's last moments and her enshrinement in the stupa. Here, as Māyā is about to give birth, a *kalaviṅka* bird addresses her from the heavens, informing her that she is about to abandon this Sahā world and that she will be reborn in the Pure Land. The announcement provokes tears from Māyā, the king, and even Gautamī, who testifies to her repentance and asks to be reborn on the same lotus blossom as her sister. The golden stupa descends from the sky, and when Māyā presses her palms together in reverence toward it, the Buddha is born from within the robes of her right side. The four doors of the stupa open, and Buddhas emerge from it to praise her, while peacocks, phoenixes, and *kalaviṅka* birds sail through the sky, singing their benedictions. In this narrative, it is only at this point that the court ladies offer Māyā flowers, in order to establish karmic connections with the Buddhas, in what will become the occasion of "offering flowers on the eighth day of the fourth month."

In the theatrical version, the infant Buddha declares himself to be the sole honored one in heaven and in earth, walks his seven steps, and climbs upon his mother's lap, disappearing into the treasure stupa together with her. When Udāyin does obeisance to the stupa, the Buddha emerges from it to be scooped up by Udāyin. Accompanied by heavenly music, the Lady Māyā, having achieved the fruit of Buddhahood, ascends to heaven in what must have been a diverting display of the latest seventeenth-century special effects. It is only at this point, at the very end of the final act of the *Tale*, that the chanter's text touches on the remaining key events of the life of the Buddha, almost as an afterthought. Even counting both the Buddha's descent from the Tuṣita heaven and his birth, the theatrical version of the *Tale of Śākyamuni in Eight Phases* still touches on only five of the titular eight events.

In both its versions, then, the *Tale* exemplifies some of the tendencies dominant in commercially popular biographies of the Buddha through the end of the Edo period, and hence also exemplifies some of the legacies of the Edo period to the Buddha's biography. As in the *Original Ground* literature, the prince and the enlightened being that he becomes still putatively live in India, but they inhabit an ever more unmistakably vernacular Japanese setting. Even without recourse to illustrated versions of these tales—and all the popular narrative and theatrical versions of the life of the Buddha produced illustrated editions during the Edo period—the verbal descriptions suffice. Here, high-ranking ladies appear at court seated behind screens; a capping ceremony is held for the coming-of-age of the prince, in the courtly style; everyone writes with brushes; the king presents the prince with a palace divided into four sections, one for each of the four seasons of the Japanese climate; and on the return of the Buddha to the palace, his son, Rāhula, presents him not with an aphrodisiac sweet, but with the more dignified offering of the sleeve of his robe, which he had left behind as a keepsake.

The *Tale of Śākyamuni in Eight Phases* freely reinvents characters from the canonical lives of Śākyamuni. A number of these reinventions take place right at the court of King Śuddhodana. The king's senior consort Gautamī is hardly exemplary in this tale: she abandons herself to jealousy and attempts to kill her own sister. Even after she repents, she returns to her old ways, as an evil stepmother who bullies Yaśodharā throughout her pregnancy and beyond. Gautamī and Yaśodharā reconcile only in the eighth and final book of the *Tale*. The Buddha's allies diverge from precedent as well. Perhaps because of Gautamī's transformation into a flawed character, the *Tale* does not make her the first nun, an honor that it bestows instead upon Yaśodharā. On the other hand, perhaps it was because the authors of the *Tale* could draw on an established tradition of the trials and suffering of Yaśodharā that they found relatively little need to change her story for dramatic purposes. The minister Udāyin, whom some canonical texts represent as one of the messengers dispatched by King Śuddhodana to urge his renunciant son to return to the palace, reprises that role in this text. Perhaps taking a cue from that precedent, the authors of the *Tale* recast Udāyin a larger role, making him into the prototypical loyal retainer so important in Edo literature. During Māyā's trials, Udāyin and his unnamed wife stand as her only allies.

Outside the palace, other characters also adopt new roles. Unlike the narratives of the *Original Ground* literature, the Buddha of the *Tale* studies under multiple masters. One of the ascetics whose teaching the renunciant prince masters and discards in the canonical corpus, Udraka

Rāmaputra, here becomes his first childhood teacher. Although the king sends the young prince to board with Udraka for instruction in the secular arts, the young prince effortlessly exceeds at them all, even as he requests Udraka to teach him how to become awakened and repay his mother's beneficence. Udraka reports the will of the prince to the king, who has the prince brought home.

The next teacher reinvented in the *Tale* is Ārāḍa Kālāma, whom the *Tale* splits into two hermits, Ārāḍa and Kālāma, following the *Sutra of Past and Present Cause and Effect*. As in the *Original Ground* literature, here too the renunciant prince serves Ārāḍa, but this Ārāḍa is a more demanding master: he grants the prince the precepts and orders him to fetch water and firewood, but beats him each time for choosing living materials, thus breaking the precept against killing. (See fig. 3.) During the second beating, the prince "stops breathing, and becomes insentient," and Ārāḍa has to bring him back from the dead with his esoteric powers. This occasions a series of rebirths, not merely symbolic, after each of which the prince advances in his practice and receives a new name.

FIGURE 3 From the *Tale of the Eight Phases of the Life of Śākyamuni* (detail). *Shaka hassō monogatari* (rpt. of 1827). Photograph courtesy of Waseda University Library.

When the prince climbs still higher up the mountain, he meets Kālāma, who assigns him a more demanding schedule: he is to pass perpetually through three mountain sites, practicing one hundred days each of standing, sitting, and reclining meditation, with no eating or sleeping allowed. When in the course of his ascetic rigors the prince does start to nod off, divine boys come to chastise him as a heretic, binding him to a nearby tree so tightly that he cannot breathe. He endures soundlessly, keeping his vow of silence. The boys recognize his seriousness and release him. Ascending the mountain still further, Siddhartha meets his final master, the Brahmin Bira, who assigns him another punishing course of meditation. Like the other mountain ascetics, Bira also gives the prince a new name, deeming him "Ascetic of the Himalayas."

Because it is the name that the prince will bear at the time of his awakening, this choice is particularly pregnant. By identifying the renunciant prince this way, the *Tale of Śākyamuni in Eight Phases* sets the stage for a climax that departs both from awakening narratives of the Chinese Buddhist canon and from their reworking in the *Original Ground* literature. In the *Tale*, the Buddha awakens not by meditating on a rock under a tree, but rather by enacting what is usually a *jātaka* narrative of his former life as the "Boy of the Himalayas" (Jpn. Sessen dōji). With its locus classicus in the Mahāyāna *Mahāparinirvāṇa Sutra*, this *jātaka* tale proved especially popular in Japan.[54] In an era without buddhas, the story runs, the mountain ascetic Boy of the Himalayas surrendered himself to a man-eating *rākṣasa* demon in exchange for the latter half of a famous poetic summary of the dharma: "All conditioned phenomena are impermanent, subject by nature to birth and extinction. When birth and extinction have been extinguished, the bliss of quiet extinction is realized."[55] In this narrative of self-sacrifice, the Buddha-to-be is not in fact harmed. The demon spares the boy and reveals himself to be the god Śakra, who has tested the Buddha-to-be and found him worthy.

The repositioning of this *jātaka* tale as the immediate trigger for Śākyamuni's awakening sharply distinguishes the *Tale of Śākyamuni in Eight Phases* from any other biographical traditions about the Buddha. This *jātaka* had in fact already appeared in the variants of the *Original Ground* literature, which typically used it as a preface to the life of Śākyamuni proper. (The *Original Ground* chanter's text for the puppet theater excludes it.) Since other elements of the *Tale* version demonstrably derive inspiration from the *Original Ground* corpus, it is at least possible that the authors of the *Tale* simply transposed this *jātaka* tale from the story's preface to its climax. The temptation by Māra and his attack on the meditating prince—a scene at the heart of most narratives of his life—are entirely absent from the *Tale*.

With this displacement, the vernacularization of Śākyamuni in Japan entered a wholly new phase. Ancient and medieval presentations of the life of the Buddha assumed a wide variety of forms (sculpture, painting, poetry, pedagogical text, sermon, illustrated manuscript), and they selectively emphasized particular moments from the biography, but they generally maintained a core of key events in some received order. Likewise, as the medieval period continued, writers displayed a growing interest in bringing the biography of the Buddha into alignment with the broad Tendai hermeneutical project that dominated intellectual life at many of the great temples. This development—apparent in both the *Biography for the Instruction of Children* and the *Program*—certainly did subordinate the biography of the Buddha to a novel exegetical purpose, but it used that biography as scaffolding, without uprooting any of its foundational elements.

By contrast, the *Tale of Śākyamuni in Eight Phases* manifests little sense of any coherent doctrinal project from within the world of Buddhist textuality, whether exegetical or exhortative. Having said that, the medieval interest in reconciling the preaching career of the Buddha with the sequence attributed (however inaccurately) to Zhiyi is not wholly effaced here. The Buddha's forty-nine-year-long preaching career unfolds in the conventional five periods of the Tendai "division of the teachings."[56] But the very next chapter of book 8 of the *Tale*, for its part, tells a different kind of origin story, here set at the Jetavana Monastery, instead of its usual location, at the site of the Buddha's preaching on Vulture Peak. In this tale, framed as the beginning of the Buddha's preparations for his *parinirvāṇa*, he ascends an elevated seat, takes in his left hand a blue lotus flower, preaches a brief sermon, and then holds up the flower. While his other disciples do obeisance to him, Mahakaśyapa alone rises, puts away his cushion, and enters the abbot's quarters. The Buddha summons him, but he continues to stare off into space. Observing this, the Buddha declares that he is transmitting the "merit of the Mahāyāna" (Jpn. *Maka'en no kudoku*) to Mahākāśyapa, and then puts the flower directly in his hand. He deems Mahākāśyapa the "Tathāgata after my death," which the text of the *Tale* identifies with the first bestowal of any monastic rank.[57]

The juxtaposition of the Tendai tale with the Chan narrative demands explanation, but none is forthcoming. The tale of the flower and the transmission to Mahākāśyapa presumes the inferiority of the Buddha's "apparent" or "revealed" teachings. Without those teachings to disparage, there would be no grounds within the various Chan schools for the claim to a separate, superior, "private" transmission. The tale of the flower as a symbol of the private transmission of the Buddha's awakened wisdom to Mahākāśyapa first appeared in Chinese Buddhist literature no later than 1038. From the time of its creation onward, it manifested a polemical challenge to the "revealed" teachings in Chinese Tiantai.[58] From the eleventh century onward, as institutional rivalry between Chan and Tiantai monastic establishments heightened in China, the distinctiveness and verifiability of the Chan transmission to Mahākāśyapa remained in dispute, making this scene a battleground for competing Buddhist groups. Outside of specifically Chan contexts, continental biographies of the Buddha rarely include this scene, but when they do, they make precisely this claim for the superior value of the transmission of the dharma through the flower.

In the *Tale of Śākyamuni in Eight Phases*, though, what distinguishes the version of the flower narrative—and what signals the absence of any overarching doctrinal emphasis in this text—is precisely the lack of any such rhetoric about the superiority of mind-to-mind transmission. In fact, both the flower account and the Tendai-influenced catalog of the Buddha's preaching in the *Tale* lack their ordinary polemical valences. In this text, the Tendai-derived account of the Buddha's teaching in five periods makes no assertion of the superiority or finality of the *Lotus Sutra*. Nor does it echo Zhiyi's adoption of the metaphor of the "five flavors," which likens the stages of the Buddha's preaching to increasingly refined dairy products, ranked from raw milk to ghee: all of the same substance but adapted to the tastes of a range of palates. Likewise, although in the *Tale* the Buddha transmits the "merit of the Mahāyāna" to Mahākāśyapa in a scene clearly modeled on the "raising of the flower" narrative, it excludes the standard rhetoric of the entrustment of the eye of the dharma or of wordless transmission from mind to mind. More puzzling still, this document does not seem to engage in any kind of irenic project of harmonizing the two versions of the Buddha's teaching, either. It simply juxtaposes them with no evident effort to connect them, much less to reconcile their differences.

Such apparent lack of interest in canonical sources in the *Tale* has puzzled some scholars of Japanese literary history. Aoyama Tadakazu noted that it shows little facility in dealing with Buddhist technical terms, and little interest in "canonical" Buddhist doctrine. Commenting on such tinkering with the canon, and on the apparent inability of the authors of the *Tale* to understand and explain key Buddhist ideas (or their lack of interest in doing so), Aoyama diagnosed the *Tale* as "neither a novelistic 'translation' (Jpn. *hon'yaku*) of [canonical] biographies of the Buddha, nor a piece of literature for the propagation of Buddhism."[59] Likewise, noted Izumoji Osamu tartly, "The *Tale of Śākyamuni in Eight Phases* insouciantly adopts records without any sources (*tenkyo naki kiji o heizen to saiyō*), and evinces an attitude of 'anything goes, as long as it's interesting.' This is not material for helping us to understand 'Buddhism.'"[60] But such evaluations presume that early modern literature be either didactic or entertaining, and leave little middle ground.

Concepts of what properly counts as a "Buddhism" suitable for propagation or understanding, though, are persuasive only to the extent that it is possible to distinguish precisely that which is canonical from that which is vernacular, that which is authentically Buddhist from its vulgar, debased reflection. It is far from obvious that Japanese Buddhist institutions themselves rejected such "inauthentic" writings out of hand. In 2003, under the floorboards in a hall at the Bukkōji in Kyoto (the head temple of the Bukkōji subdenomination of True Pure Land Buddhism) were found some 3,500 woodblocks used in printing, dating from the latter seventeenth century to the Meiji era. Among them was a complete run of blocks used for a well-known vernacular collection of Buddhist stories of karmic retribution, *Tales of Cause and Effect* (*Inga monogatari*, first published in Osaka in 1661), attributed to Suzuki Shōsan (1579–1655). But the trove also included substantial portions of the woodblocks for the *Original Ground of Śākyamuni* and the *Tale of Śākyamuni in Eight Phases*.[61] Whether the temple itself engaged in the publication of these texts, or was merely storing woodblocks produced by commercial publishers, was not immediately clear.[62] A newspaper report quoted the scholar of early modern printing who inspected the woodblocks: "It's unexpected that they were found in a temple, but they might have been used in preaching to its patrons."[63] While some Buddhist clerical intellectuals issued objections against "popular" versions of the life of Śākyamuni, then, there remains the possibility that some Buddhist institutions saw fit to include those works in their output of publishing and preaching.

Commercial Theater after the *Tale of Śākyamuni in Eight Phases*

Narratives descended from the *Tale of Śākyamuni* went on to dominate commercial storytelling through the end of the nineteenth century. Chikamatsu's *Birth Assembly for the Tathāgata Śākyamuni* (1714) exemplifies these later developments. It follows the *Tale* in several major respects: it inherits some of the reinventions of figures of the life of Śākyamuni from the *Original Ground* literature and from the *Tale*; it assigns new identities and new plotlines to other established characters; it creates further new characters; and it extracts episodes from the Buddhist canon and integrates them into the life of the Buddha. The plot as a whole appeals to urban commoners, valorizing self-sacrifice and honesty, and elevating simple piety above riches. But there is little spare or restrained about Chikamatsu's stagecraft here. As in the theatrical versions of the *Original Ground* and the *Tale*, visual spectacle (particularly the vivid scenes of battle and mutilation) must have delighted the play's audience.

Chikamatsu's play maintains some of the more colorful innovations of its Japanese predecessors from the sixteenth and seventeenth centuries. Gautamī reprises her sororicidal role as rival to a pitiable Māyā; Udāyin and his wife, Kichijōnyo, assume their posts as consummately loyal retainers; and Ārāḍa Kālāma, reunited into a single body, again sets a punishing course of ascetic training for the prince on Mount Daṇḍaloka. However, existing characters also take on new roles in this drama. For instance, Devadatta and Gautamī actually begin this story as established partners in crime. Immediately after the birth of the young prince and the manifestation of his special status, Māyā dies on the spot. Gautamī swoops in with her minion, General Ba, to condemn the newborn for killing his mother. For, as she says, unlike other creatures,

> Humans and animals both have just one gate from which to emerge into the world. To fail to take that route and to be born rending apart his mother's side. . . . is first among the Five Heinous Crimes. Could we possibly elevate him to the rank of King of the Five Regions of India? I have made Devadatta my adopted son. That newborn might be my nephew, but he is a foe of my sister's. [*To General Ba*] Strangle him to death![64]

Fortunately for the newborn, Kichijōnyo and the court ladies are prepared: the flower poles that they carry actually conceal spears, and soon Udāyin rides to the rescue on horseback. He flaunts a straw figure of Māyā and a prayer petition by Devadatta and Gautamī—proof that Māyā's death is actually *their* doing—and the day is saved.

But the action scenes are not ended. After the prince grows up and leaves the palace in the middle of the night, the valiant Kichijōnyo fights one final battle. The morning after the prince's departure, she goes to the sleeping palace guards and angrily orders them to wake up to look for the prince, but the guards reveal themselves to be in the service of Gautamī, led by one Hakuryōton. They have come to abduct Yaśodharā to be Devadatta's bride. The loyal Kichijōnyo hoists Yaśodharā onto her back and battles her way to a garden wall. Kichijōnyo then lifts Yaśodharā onto the wall, enabling Yaśodharā to flee while Kichijōnyo stays behind to hold Hakuryōton at bay. They fight until each of them is mortally injured: "Hakuryōton, whose fortune had run out, thrust his shin onto the pile of purificatory sand. Kichijōnyo crawled over to the spot where he was writhing and climbed upon him. She stabbed him through unhampered, lifted up his chin, and with a cry cut off his head."[65]

Having escaped the palace, Yaśodharā spends most of the rest of the play searching for her husband. Her sole companion is the faithful Udāyin, who accompanies her to find Siddhartha, a task that echoes his canonical role. They at last discover him in the mountains, serving Ārāḍa Kālāma. From the next valley away, they watch as Ārāḍa Kālāma beats the renunciant prince almost to death, and cannot endure to see him suffer. They draw close and offer to do his chores in his place. Beaten and broken, he replies, weeping, that he does not mind the blows, as he has set his heart on saving all sentient beings; his tears, the narration reports, add to the water in his pails. When Ārāḍa Kālāma sees the water that the prince has fetched, he detects the reflection of Yaśodharā in it and sets again to punish Siddhartha, this time with sixty strokes of his staff.

Until this point, the interactions between Siddhartha and Ārāḍa Kālāma more or less resemble those of the *Original Ground* and *Tale* accounts. But in Chikamatsu's retelling, Yaśodharā's attachment to her husband is the catalyst to prompt his awakening. Even as he is suffering from the merciless beating of Ārāḍa Kālāma, Siddhartha enters a meditative state. When he arises, he overturns the water from his pails onto the earth, enters his master's cavern, and makes a mudra. He then recites verses from two points in the "Expedient Devices" chapter of the *Lotus Sutra*: "The dharmas from their very origin / Are themselves eternally characterized by the marks of quiet extinction," and directly thereafter, "Within the Buddha-lands of the ten directions / There is the Dharma of only One Vehicle. / There are not two, nor are there yet three." Finally, he shuts himself up in the cave, which is surmounted by a *bodhi* tree.[66]

Ārāḍa Kālāma prostrates himself before the cave, and in yet another homage to the *Lotus Sutra,* he reveals that he is in fact a manifestation of the ancient Buddha, Victorious through Great Penetrating Knowledge (Skt. Mahābhijñājñānābhibhū)—the "otherwise obscure" subject of the "Expedient Devices" chapter—before fading away.[67] As in both the various versions of the *Original Ground* and the *Tale,* Ārāḍa Kālāma turns out to be much more than a mere heretical master.

Unable to believe their eyes, Yaśodharā and Udāyin also prostrate themselves before the cave, and soon the door opens to reveal a fully awakened being. The narration tells us what they see: "The Buddha Śākyamuni has thirty-two] major marks and eighty minor ones. In the radiance from his *ūrṇā* are mountains and rivers, grasses and trees, beings in the six paths and born in the four ways. The faces of people shine white, so white (*Hito no omo shiro, shirojiro miyuru*)."[68] By placing the site of the Buddha's awakening within a cave, emphasizing his radiance, and using the distinctive phrase *omo shiro,* Chikamatsu's text unambiguously links the awakening of the Buddha with the ancient myth of Amaterasu, the solar deity who shut herself up in a cave and plunged the world into darkness. According to the *Record of Ancient Matters* (*Kojiki,* 712), "*Ara omoshiro ya*" were Amaterasu's first words on her return to the outside world. Chikamatsu's play thus superimposes Amaterasu's story onto the life narrative of the Buddha, even as it selectively retains elements of the biographies that precede it: the *bodhi* tree, Ārāḍa Kālāma's divine identity, and the connection between the awakening and the *Lotus* among them.

Chikamatsu's most original alterations to the tale of Śākyamuni derive from his original uses for characters outside the canonical biographies. One is the Buddha's disciple Cūḍapanthaka (Jpn. Shurihantoku, here abbreviated to Panthaka, or Hantoku), who is famous in Pāli Buddhist sources as a monk so dimwitted that he could not remember his own name, much less the Buddha's teachings. The Buddha gave him a broom with which to clean the floor, directing him to remember "calming" with one sweep and "insight" with the next. Chikamatsu's text reinvents Cūḍapanthaka as the foolish, long-lost son of Udāyin, who is carried off as a boy by an eagle at the end of the first act and rediscovered years later, living with new adoptive parents, in the third. In the third act, the adoptive parents—a hunter named Rintanshi and his wife, Rurisennyo—give shelter to Yaśodharā and Udāyin, who are trying to find Siddhartha while escaping from Devadatta and his minions.

Years before this scene takes place, Rintanshi had discovered the child about to be ripped apart by an eagle. At that time Rintanshi saved him, but he and Rurisennyo have since been frustrated by Cūḍapanthaka's inability to learn even one letter from the alphabet. (In a nod to the Indian setting, this alphabet is a Japanized version of the Arapacana Sanskrit syllabary.) Seeing Cūḍapanthaka as a reincarnation of their own dead child, they vowed to Brahmā and Śakra, promising to refrain from killing if only Cūḍapanthaka would recover. This vow has forced them to quit hunting and therefore plunged them into poverty. Accordingly, they secretly plan to turn in Yaśodharā for her bounty, and Rintanshi instructs Cūḍapanthaka to sweep the floor until Rintanshi gives a signal, when Cūḍapanthaka is to take the broom and beat Udāyin if he resists.

Before the plan can be set in motion, though, a lone dove barrels into the miserable hut and flaps around, unable to escape. Poor Cūḍapanthaka mistakes the resulting uproar for his signal, swings the broom, and fells the dove. At this point the plot is exposed, and Udāyin twists Rintanshi's arm until he agrees that, like a dove fleeing from hunters, a noble lady also deserves sanctuary. Udāyin and the adoptive parents reveal their identities, and everyone weeps. Thus Cūḍapanthaka reappears in this text as a fool with a broom, with which he unintentionally saves Yaśodharā.

The play is not done with the foolish son yet. A party of hunters storms in and demands the dove. They have been hunting on behalf of their master Devadatta, who has pledged a daily sacrifice to the Indian god Maheśvara (Jpn. Makeishura-ten) of one thousand beasts and one thousand birds—and that dove, they go on, was the thousandth one. Unable to use the dove that Cūḍapanthaka has killed, they demand an equivalent amount of human flesh from the man who killed it. Seemingly out of nowhere, they produce a balance scale.

Having hidden Yaśodharā away, Rintanshi tries to take the place of Cūḍapanthaka, but Udāyin will not permit his son to do anything as unfilial as forcing his adoptive father to cut into his own body. Hands shaking, Udāyin slices flesh from Cūḍapanthaka's thigh and weighs it on the balance scale against the dove's body, but the balance hardly moves. Hearing his parents wail, Cūḍapanthaka has a sudden epiphany. He rises and proclaims: "Cutting off piece by piece—what a bother! I'm going to put my whole body on the balancing pan, so take [what you need] and return the rest!"[69] He manages to lift his thigh onto the pan, but the scale still hardly moves.

To this point, Cūḍapanthaka has enacted a strikingly close parody of the celebrated ancient *jātaka* tale of King Śibi, who (at least, in the version of his story familiar in Japan) shelters a dove from a pursuing hawk and offers an equivalent amount of his own flesh in exchange. In the *jātaka* tale, no matter how much flesh is cut from the king's body, the balance does not shift. Finally, the king declares his willingness to offer his entire body in exchange for the life of the dove. It is only at this point that the hawk reveals that it is actually Śakra, king of the gods. The king—later to be reborn as Śākyamuni—has passed the test of his generosity.

By contrast, in Chikamatsu's version, there is no such divine sanction for self-sacrifice. Instead, Cūḍapanthaka kicks the balance into pieces, exposing it as rigged. The hunters flee the hut, and Cūḍapanthaka is cured of his stupidity, attaining awakening at last. Any of a range of canonical sources or Japanese compilations could have given Chikamatsu the raw material for these tales; for the basic account of Cūḍapanthaka, one likely source is *Sand and Pebbles* (*Shasekishū*, 1279–1283); for a popular retelling of the *jātaka* tale, the *Three Jewels*.[70]

The final act of the play expands on the role of Rurisennyo, inserting her into two additional episodes based on existing Buddhist tales. Gathering funds with which to support her son, who has now become a monk, Rurisennyo has entered service in the mansion of the wealthy Sudatta. At this point in the narrative, Sudatta still follows Devadatta's teaching. Sudatta has even built the Jetavana Monastery, intending to make an offering of it to Devadatta. When Sudatta discovers that the lowly maidservant Rurisennyo has been saving rice from her wages to give to the Buddha's sangha, he accuses her of theft and throws her out.

At just that time, the Buddha comes to Sudatta's home with his followers and asks him to hand over the rice that Rurisennyo has saved for alms. Sudatta refuses, only to discover to his astonishment that neither he nor his servants can budge the small sack. Still recalcitrant, Sudatta taunts the Buddha and his followers, saying that they may have the rice if they can take it without passing through his gate. At the Buddha's bidding, Cūḍapanthaka stretches out the arm holding his begging bowl until it extends all the way to the rice, whereupon the sack opens and the rice flows upward and into the bowl of its own accord. This display of superhuman powers prompts a tearful conversion for Sudatta, and affords the Buddha and his band an opportunity to preach about ideal religious practice. As the disciple Pūrṇa lectures Sudatta, "A human being who entrusts himself to and nourishes the Buddha is himself a god."[71] Similarly, in the words of the Buddha himself:

> This Cūḍapanthaka was so stupid and dull that he was practicing just one word and one *gāthā*, but the sincerity of his faith surpassed ten thousand fascicles of texts. . . . Devadatta has committed to heart eighty thousand treasuries of Dharma, and mastered every kind of learning in the trichiliocosm, but because he has gone over to the heretical paths and has no aspiration for awakening, it is all like steaming sand to make rice.[72]

It is not difficult to imagine why a scene like this might have appealed to an audience of commoners.

The following scene, the final in Chikamatsu's play, again spotlights Rurisennyo's humble circumstances and echoes this message. Sudatta, now converted to the Buddha's cause, orders ten thousand lanterns lit to illumine the Buddha's path to visit his mother in the Trāyastriṃśa heaven (a scene not itself represented in this play). Meanwhile, Rurisennyo has no money, and is driven to cut off and sell her hair to afford enough oil for just one lamp. When the time comes for the Buddha's send-off, a great wind blows through, extinguishing all the lamps donated by the rich Sudatta. Only Rurisennyo's humble lamp, fueled by her sincere faith, stays lit. The Buddha arrives and tells them that Sudatta's vanity has darkened his lamps, whereas the straightforward faith of Rurisennyo and her husband cannot be extinguished by any wind or water. The Buddha further predicts that Rurisennyo will attain Buddhahood in a future age, whereas Sudatta will fall into extreme poverty and become a "penniless hungry ghost." These two episodes featuring Rurisennyo come from sources within Buddhist literature, but not from *jātaka* tales or other stories of the Buddha's life.[73]

Chikamatsu's version takes a different stance toward the canon than its predecessor in the *Tale*. Unlike the anonymous authors of the *Tale*, Chikamatsu had considerable facility with Buddhist sources; his innovations result less from any evident difficulty in reading or understanding the previous narrative traditions than from a playful willingness to rearrange and parody them.[74] Although this chapter has discussed only a few examples from his play, they suffice to suggest the extraordinarily dense, multilayered pleasure of his writing. Chikamatsu inherited the earlier Edo-era narratives' interest in visual spectacle and melodrama, but onto that interest he also layered other, originally unrelated stories. Thus the Buddha's moment of awakening is, in some sense, also Amaterasu's illumination of the world. Cūḍapanthaka does not merely teach the moral of simple diligence as a path to awakening, but also repeats verbatim the heroic self-sacrifice by King Śibi, who was himself a previous life of the Buddha Śākyamuni. Audiences who could grasp these subtexts might well have savored their intertwining in the story. In the middle of the nineteenth century, Chikamatsu's inheritors would prove similarly unhesitant to rearrange and adapt material from other sources to fill out their own biographies of the Buddha.

By the middle of the seventeenth century, the new storytelling tradition inaugurated by the *Original Ground* literature apparently became the default version known to much of the Japanese public. In one sense, this is another case of the replacement of one text by another as discussed by Michael Emmerich in his study of the late "reception" of the *Tale of Genji*.[75] In the case of the Buddha's life story, the vernacular replacement eventually registered even in the writings of Buddhist clerics. Yamagata Genjō (1866–1903), a Shingon Buddhist cleric who had served as a military chaplain in the First Sino-Japanese War (1894–1895), wrote in 1897 of the need for his warrior-readers to emulate the spirit of Śākyamuni. He began his description of Śākyamuni's training thus: "Śākyamuni's study was polished by the sharp sword of Ārāḍa [Kālāma]; his courage was tempered by Ārāḍa's iron rod."[76] Nor was this a slip: as Yamagata's summary of the life of Śākyamuni proceeds, it is clear that he adopted the vernacular account of the Buddha's awakening, though it is unclear whether he did so as an expedient for communicating with readers unfamiliar with the canonical versions, or because he himself knew only this version. The more prominent Zen cleric Kawaguchi Ekai (whose unsuccessful effort to reform the objects of Buddhist worship was mentioned in the introduction to this study) was initially interested in Buddhism by his grandmother, who gave him one of the nineteenth-century vernacular biographies to read.[77]

Nor, again, did the arrival of competition in the form of European-style geographical or historical knowledge immediately displace established ways of telling the late-Edo version of the Buddha's life. At least as early as 1886, Tokyo raconteurs had begun to hold public displays of magic-lantern slides representing the very places in India where the Buddha had lived and died.[78] The positioning of the Buddha as a historical being who had inhabited a distant but real land, however, did not come to dominate popular consciousness in Japan for decades to come. Even as late as 1903, other enterprising artists working in the same mass medium were still peddling guides to magic-lantern presentations about the life of the Buddha—told, as before, not according to findings of the latest archaeological excavations in India, but according to the familiar vernacular sources.[79]

As succeeding chapters of this book demonstrate, some Japanese clerical biographers of the Buddha maintained efforts to reassert orthodox versions of his life through the end of the nineteenth century and into the twentieth. On the other hand, intellectuals with less deference to the needs of Buddhist institutions—laypersons and reformist clerics—tended to pass over the vernacular tradition in silence. For their part, though, secular writers of fiction in twentieth-century Japan did not forget the vernacular biographical tradition altogether. By the 1920s, even as the vernacular biographical tradition was falling out of favor with readers and theatrical audiences, secular authors began to tell the life story of the Buddha again. They employed new forms, added new characters, interwove new plot complications, created new characters, and displayed new purposes in their writing. Able to make reference to an ever-growing base of source texts, they modulated their relationship to the canonical Buddha ever more deliberately. In their hands, the local hero lives on.

THREE

The Buddha as Exemplar

Tales of the "vernacular Buddha," as considered in the previous chapter, formed just one kind of popular hagiography in Edo Japan. Commercial authors during that period also produced a profusion of vernacular stories of other religious heroes—mostly domestic saints from Japanese history. While these performances and publications won over commercial audiences, they could also raise the ire of Buddhist institutions, whose opposition even led to legal action. Objections to the vernacular Buddha, on the other hand, came not from institutions but from individual Buddhist clerics who were not in a position to speak for large denominations. These objections led to the form of biographies calculated to reassert some version of the canonical literature. The authors of the two such "reparative" biographies considered in this chapter each conceived of the Buddha as an exemplar, but they used very different strategies to document that exemplary status. The first response, written late in the seventeenth century by a scholar-cleric named Gentei (1621?–1705?), substantially recapitulated medieval ideas about the supermundane identity and role of the Buddha. It thus largely inherited received images of the historical Buddha.

The chapter then proceeds to another published response to the vernacular tales. This was the work of the scholar-nun Kōgetsu Sōgi (1756–1833), who hewed close to orthodox scriptures when she composed *Light of the Three Ages* (*Miyo no hikari*), which she wrote in elegant neoclassical Japanese prose. Kōgetsu's presentation of the life of the Buddha strongly reflected her tutelage under the monastic reformer Jiun Onkō (1718–1805). Her work inherited and originally developed his fresh commitment to rigorous inquiry into the scriptural canon, and repositioned the Buddha as a model of practice for Buddhist clerics and the laity in later days. In the 1880s, half a century after Kōgetsu's death, Buddhist institutions struggled to recover from a host of new pressures and attacks. A group of reformist clerics rediscovered Kōgetsu's work during this period, and enlisted it in their program of defending Buddhism by reviving the pure practice of the monastic precepts.

Reasserting an Orthodox Biography

Little about the rise of commercial publishing in early-seventeenth-century Japan—and the parallel growth of commercial stage performances—necessarily posed any intrinsic challenge to Buddhist institutions. Through most of that century, Buddhist texts actually maintained a major presence in the commercial book market.[1] Eventually, of course, titles with Buddhist themes ceded pride of place to a range of other commercial publications. Nonetheless, through the end of the Edo period, large and powerful temples (such as the Nishi Honganji, head of one major branch of True Pure Land Buddhism) could still maintain close ties with commercial publisher-booksellers. These commercial agents not only printed their patrons' religious texts, but also offered favorably biased representations of their patrons in their secular commercial publications, such as guidebooks.[2] In the sphere of Nichiren Buddhism, the Edo period saw a flourishing in the printing of popular biographies of Nichiren in vernacular language, which were produced by lay authors and published in commercial settings. In a closely related phenomenon of the latter half of the Edo period, Kabuki performances of the life of Nichiren took root in Nichiren temple fairs (*kaichō*), a development suggesting that those temples countenanced such retellings.[3]

On the other hand, commercial publishing and performance could also pose threats to Buddhist institutions. From the middle of the seventeenth century, the head temple of the other major branch of True Pure Land Buddhism, the Higashi Honganji, resorted to a series of protests and legal challenges against representations of its founder, Shinran, in commercial settings. It generally lodged objections against retellings of the life of Shinran in print, but it could also protest against the stage performances with which those print retellings were associated. Popular plays for the puppet theater (such as the *Record of Shinran* [*Shinran ki*, 1648] and their associated printed texts) proved problematic for the Higashi Honganji when they broke with the orthodox biographies of Shinran. True Pure Land institutions found it particularly challenging when those commercial versions presented Shinran as a wonderworker, contradicting the more sober official account of his life.[4] In other cases, even when commercially printed texts copied such biographies word for word, they nonetheless threatened the Higashi Honganji's monopoly over the distribution of its authorized account. As late as the early nineteenth century, the Higashi Honganji was still issuing protests against representations of Shinran, though now on the Kabuki stage. The protests and legal measures carried out across the Edo period did garner some temporary victories for the Higashi Honganji, but on the whole, commercial publishing proved too resilient to crumble under such pressure.[5]

Another strategy for counteracting the emergence of unpalatable new popular narrative tales of venerable figures lay in the creation of counternarratives. In the case of the Buddha Śākyamuni, this process began even within the *Original Ground* literature itself. A relatively late addition to the *Original Ground* corpus, the *Tale of Śākyamuni* (*Shaka monogatari*, dated to 1611), exemplifies an effort to capitalize on the success of the tale by reinserting into it selected episodes from the orthodox biographical literature. Credited to the otherwise obscure Jusen'in Nissen (n.d.), this version of the *Original Ground* tale incorporates a number of scenes not evident elsewhere in the corpus. It is the only member of the corpus to include the prince's impregnation of Yaśodharā with his finger before his departure from the palace, as well as the distribution of the relics of the Buddha after his cremation.[6] Again, in other versions of the *Original Ground* literature, the creation of the first Buddha sculpture is either elided altogether or attributed to the decision of Śakra, ruler of the Trāyastriṃśa heaven where the Buddha preaches to his mother.

By contrast, the *Tale of Śākyamuni* restores the version common in the Buddhist scriptural canon of East Asia, in which it is the earthly King Udāyana who commissions the creation of the sculpture.[7] The *Tale of Śākyamuni* seems to be the only version of the *Original Ground* literature to assign clear ages to the events in the Buddha's life, and it cites various scriptures by name, placing a special emphasis on the *Lotus Sutra*. Given this clear doctrinal orientation and the particular style of the clerical name of its author, the text was likely produced by a cleric of the Nichiren denomination, who attempted to rewrite the

Original Ground literature as a mode of spreading devotion to the *Lotus*.[8] Be that as it may, Nissen's version seems to have enjoyed little success: it survives as one manuscript among the many dozens of versions of the *Original Ground*.

Buddhist clerics of the Edo period could thus either embrace or reject vernacular versions of the lives of their founders. Buddhist institutions as institutions, though, seem not to have objected to the various vernacular versions of the life of the historical Buddha circulating from the early Edo period. While institutions appear to have kept silent, at least two individual Buddhist clerics were sufficiently moved by the vernacular retellings to compose and distribute responses to them. The prolific seventeenth-century True Pure Land clerical apologist Gentei wrote a number of defenses of texts important to the various Pure Land and True Pure Land denominations. Among this body of work focused on distinctly Japanese forms of Buddhism, we also find a defense of the orthodox accounts of the life of the Buddha: *Rousing the Record of the Life of Śākyamuni* (*Shaka ichidai ki kosui*, 1684).

Gentei's very decision to write this long, scholastically elaborate text suggests that he did not regard the popular narratives as merely harmless entertainment. In their place, this work strives to provide a comprehensive, easy-to-read life of the Buddha. It begins with the origins of the Śākya clan and works through a number of the Buddha's previous lives even before reaching his final incarnation. The eighth and final volume of the work takes place after the Buddha's cremation and the dispersal of his remains in stupas. It also narrates the passage of Buddhism from India to Japan, via the narrative of the reincarnation of the Chinese Buddhist master Huisi (515–577) as Japan's Prince Shōtoku.[9] Perhaps it was Gentei's aim for sheer comprehensiveness that led him, in classic Buddhist fashion, to devote so much of this work to lists: the four modes of birth; the ten types of demons whom Śākyamuni defeated under the *bodhi* tree; the twelve divisions of the Buddhist canon; the four modes of preaching by the Buddha; and so on. Such pedagogical detours are surely informative, but they do little to sustain the reader's interest in the narrative.

Gentei's work does not explicitly name the sources whose "errors" it was intended to correct, but it does adduce some arguments that might well belong to them. One section of *Rousing the Record* bears the title "Māyā's Life Ends Seven Days after Giving Birth to Siddhartha," with the explicit subtitle "A Statement of His Innocence of Any Evil Deed." Concerning the death of Māyā and her rebirth in heaven, Gentei writes: "[Some] ask if the Buddha didn't rupture her right side, for which reason she died seven days later, and he is guilty of the first Evil Deed [of five]." To counter this accusation, Gentei cites arguments made in several sutras: Māyā's lifespan was about to end regardless; a mother who saw her son renounce the world would die of heartbreak, in any case. He also cites the words of an unnamed Buddhist master who noted, in effect, that Māyā may have lost a finite, transient life, but in the end, the Buddha enabled her to attain eternal nirvana.[10] Gentei may well never have read the text for the puppet-theater version of the *Original Ground of Śākyamuni*, but it is at least possible that he was aware of its matter-of-fact assertion of Māyā's death from the Buddha's "rupture" of her side.

Following its medieval predecessors, Gentei's apologia also expresses little awareness of the uneven historical positions of its source texts. This conspicuous lack of interest in history appears vividly when Gentei must adjudicate among mutually conflicting accounts of events from the Buddha's life. In the seventh volume of his text, Gentei considers the date (month and day) of the *parinirvāṇa* of the Buddha. Gentei finds five contradictory dates in the relevant literature: the fifteenth day of the second month, the eighth day of the second month, the eighth day of the fourth month, the fifteenth day of the third month, and the eighth day of the ninth month.[11] Among these, he chooses the fifteenth day of the second month—because, he notes, the second month is when all things reproduce, when the spring rains fall, when the snows melt in mountain valleys, when the rivers swell and flow again. (The second month of the Chinese lunar-solar calendar is closer to March in the Gregorian calendar than to February.) He concludes: "When [the calendar] reaches this time, deluded sentient beings give rise to the conception of permanence. To shatter this conception, the Buddha preached that all dharmas have the aspects of impermanence, change, and dissolution."[12]

To be sure, Gentei's argument here makes perfectly good sense as a form of medieval Japanese exegesis, which presumes that every element of a sacred text conceals a secret meaning in consonance with profound doctrine. His case is reminiscent of the explanation of medieval Tendai reading strategies by Jacqueline Stone, as "a hermeneutics grounded in a particular insight or *a priori* position believed to carry greater authority than the literal or surface meaning of the text."[13] Gentei was neither a medieval figure nor a Tendai cleric, but in the mode of interpretation that he practiced here, the Buddha's intention to liberate sentient beings is treated as a priori truth. As an exemplar pointing the way to awakening, the Buddha could never have permitted such an important matter as his death to take place on an arbitrary date. At the same time, though, Gentei's apologia works here to cancel out or deny difference, or outright contradiction, as mere surface illusions.

Outside the Buddhist sphere, though, Gentei's intellectual contemporaries during the late seventeenth and early eighteenth centuries were becoming preoccupied with the question of the historical position of texts. Particularly in the world of Confucian studies, scholars grew increasingly concerned not just with the nature of orthodoxy, but with the very question of how to read texts composed in a different environment far from the present in geography, language, and cultural setting. They began to seek for moral guides within the contingency of history itself, in terms other than the abstract and transcendental.[14] As the following section shows, when these ideas were integrated into a Buddhist context through the work of Jiun Onkō, they would produce a very different reading of Śākyamuni's life and value.

Jiun Onkō's Career before Kōgetsu

The scholar-cleric Jiun Onkō (1718–1804) stands as one of the most influential Buddhist intellectuals of late Edo-era Japan. Several facets of his life project carried over into the work of his disciple Kōgetsu, so they merit attention here. In his youth in modern Osaka, Jiun was sent to train in Shingon Buddhist institutions, and his formal denominational affiliation remained with Shingon, though later he would pursue Zen training as well. Crucially, he also spent some years in Kyoto, where he enrolled at the private academy called the Hall for Studying Ancient Meanings (the Kogidō, in Kyoto). Founded by Itō Jinsai (1627–1705), and at the time of Jiun's enrollment directed by Jinsai's son and successor Itō Tōgai (1670–1736), this school taught the Confucian classics but rejected the interpretations of these classics then dominant all across East Asia, based on the works of the Song-dynasty philosopher Zhu Xi (1130–1200). In their place, the school instead promoted the rigorous philological interpretation of original texts in their original contexts. Jinsai's school rejected what we now call Song-dynasty "Neo-Confucianism," understanding it as not the fulfillment of the ancient Confucian teachings, but as an impediment to their understanding. Jiun absorbed these lessons as a youth and later sought to apply them to Buddhism.

There are, then, important parallels between the projects of Jinsai and other historically minded scholars of the Confucian tradition, on the one hand, and the new interest in the roots of Buddhist history by figures like Jiun, on the other. Nonetheless, Jiun was no mere philologist or theoretician of language, and he also displayed a keen interest in the problem of proper monastic practice throughout his career. From roughly the time that he took up the abbacy of the temple Chōeiji (in modern Higashi Osaka) in 1744, Jiun attempted to return to the original practice of Buddhism. He began his lifelong project of reproducing the monastic discipline practiced by the Buddha Śākyamuni, which he called the "*vinaya* of the True Dharma" (*Shōbōritsu*).

The project of revivifying this discipline took multiple forms. In his first years at the Chōeiji, Jiun took the unusual step of beginning to induct his trainees into the full *bhikṣu* precepts (Skt. *upasaṃpadā*, Jpn. *gusokukai*). These precepts, given to fully ordained monks in South Asian practice, had long since been superseded in Japanese Buddhism by later monastic codes produced in China. In particular, the *Net of Brahmā Sutra* (*Fanwang jing*)—probably composed in China during the fifth century—had dominated the practice of monastic discipline in Japan since its embrace by Saichō (767–822). Jiun sought to relativize the authority of such later developments, and to replace them with forms of practice that he attributed to the Buddha's day.

In 1749, he produced an additional monastic code for his trainees, the *Fundamental Institutions for the Sangha* (*Konpon sōsei*).[15] This code created a hierarchy of sources of guidance for correct practice. While allowing for some exceptions due to the climate and cultural practices of Japan, it ranked the Indian precepts above the *Net of Brahmā Sutra*. For instance, Jiun's trainees were to practice only the spirit and not the letter of "burning the body" (e.g., by burning off a finger as an offering to the Buddha). This form of asceticism is endorsed by the *Net of Brahmā Sutra* but forbidden by the earlier Indian precepts.[16] Again, in his *Fundamental Institutions*, Jiun stated clearly that monks of any Japanese denomination would be allowed to train at the Chōeiji, as long as they obeyed the precepts. In this way, Jiun began his efforts to overcome the internecine divisions among denominations and institutions that had become so prominent in Edo Buddhism. Here we find an early application of Jiun's ideal of returning to "the age of Śākyamuni."[17]

Later in his life, as Jiun peregrinated from place to place in western Japan, the same impulse propelled his intensive research into the Sanskrit language, as well as his efforts to reconstruct the correct form of monastic wear. Jiun continued these projects even after moving his base of operations to a retreat on Mount Ikoma, to the east of Osaka, which he named the Hermitage of the Twin Dragons (Sōryūan). A nun patron and follower of Jiun had donated the hermitage; in fact, nuns played a leading role among the many devotees, both lay and clerical, whom Jiun attracted.[18] As another sign of his devotion to the historical Buddha, Jiun chose for the main image for his hermitage a statue of the Buddha at his moment of awakening. This image is one of very few in Japanese Buddhist sculpture to show Śākyamuni making the "gesture of touching the earth" (*bhūmisparśa mudrā*). In it, the Buddha is seated on a lotus blossom supported by two dragons, which inspired Jiun's name for his hermitage.[19]

In 1771, Jiun left the hermitage, having accepted an invitation to move to Kyoto to take up the residence at the temple Amidadera (now defunct). There he remained until 1776, when he returned to the Osaka area. It was during this short but eventful period that Jiun made contact with the imperial court and became a mentor to the future nun Kōgetsu, who was at the time still named Nobuko and at service to the imperial court.

From Court Lady to Scholar-Nun

Nobuko was but a scant four years older than the master she served, Prince Sadamochi (1760–1772), the ill-fated younger son of Emperor Momozono (reigned 1747–1762). Sadamochi's elder brother, known to history as Emperor Go-Momozono (reigned 1771–1779), had an unhappy reign: still in his minority when his father died, he suffered from infirmity throughout his short life, and produced a daughter but no male heir. Sadamochi's untimely death in 1772 meant that Go-Momozono's demise would inevitably eventuate in a succession crisis.[20] The instability ensuing at court after 1772 might have encouraged Nobuko—then still a teenager—to seek an alternative to secular life. Nobuko's aunt Michiko (1718–1789) had served as wet nurse to Sadamochi. In 1773, when Michiko visited the Amidadera to hear Jiun preach, Nobuko probably was by her side. At the same time, Michiko and Nobuko also began their brief but significant acquaintance with one of Jiun's senior nun-disciples, Yōzan Gimon (a.k.a. Yōzan Gibun, 1739–1773), who passed away not long after.[21]

Nobuko and her aunt Michiko were reportedly so impressed with Jiun and Gimon that they persuaded the former consort of Emperor Momozono, Kyōraimon'in (courtesy name for Fujiwara Tomiko, 1743–1796), to receive the precepts herself, in lieu of their direct bestowal upon her son, Go-Momozono. Kyōraimon'in joined with Dowager

Consort Kaimeimon'in (1717–1789) to sponsor Jiun's delivery of lectures on the Ten Good Precepts, which he later published (*Jūzen hōgo*, whose first version was completed in 1775).[22] Also in 1774, Michiko accepted the monastic precepts, becoming the nun Erin. In 1775, the next year, Nobuko followed in her footsteps, becoming the nun Kōgetsu.

Some years after Go-Momozono's death in 1779, Kyōraimon'in accepted Jiun's counsel and moved to revive the Chōfukuji, one of two convents with this name located in what is now Ukyō Ward in metropolitan Kyoto. This, the smaller and less prominent temple called Chōfukuji, bears the "mountain name" Mitsujōzan and claims a founding in antiquity. By the medieval period, it had apparently become a Zen monastery, and by the mid-Edo period, the Katsuranomiya cadet branch of the imperial family patronized it.[23] Intending to dedicate merit for the repose of her deceased family (Prince Sadamochi and three former emperors: Go-Sakuramachi, Momozono, and Go-Momozono), Kyōraimon'in sponsored the refounding of this institution as a Shingon convent, dispatching the nuns Erin and Kōgetsu to reside there in 1782. They held ceremonies to mark the completion of the temple renovations two years later, in 1784. A leading scholar of Jiun, Kinami Takuichi, claimed that this represents the first instance of the conversion of an ancient monastery into a convent in Japanese Buddhism.[24] While this particular assertion may not be wholly accurate, the pattern of converting convents into monasteries is overwhelmingly more common across Japanese history. The late demarcation of the Chōfukuji from a monastery to a convent is extraordinarily unusual.

The material fittings of the restored Chōfukuji suggest a strong interest in the historical Buddha. Its main image (*honzon*) is a replica of the celebrated tenth-century sandalwood statue of the standing Śākyamuni, enshrined at the Seiryōji. The Chōfukuji also enshrines a stone carved with the footprints of the historical Buddha (*bussokuseki*).[25] Like the Seiryōji-style image of Śākyamuni, the footprint stone seems to have been given by the imperial court. Such stones with carvings of the Buddha's footprints appear in Japan from as early as the Nara period, but they began to spread widely only in the early nineteenth century. If the temple diary of the Chōfukuji is accurate in recording a date of 1786 for installation of the carved stone there, then the Chōfukuji could have been one pioneer in that trend.

These choices suggest a high degree of interest in and concern for the life of the historical Buddha—an emphasis wholly consonant with

Jiun's thought. These material elements of devotion are of smaller scale than, for instance, the roughly contemporary (ca. 1776–1800) stone diorama of events in the life of the Buddha, designed and installed at the temple Sekihōji by the artist Itō Jakuchū (1716–1800), located to the southeast of Kyoto.[26] Nonetheless, the Chōfukuji's version of the Seiryōji Buddha and its stone footprints imply a similar effort to materialize the historical Buddha, allowing his devotees to conduct their prayers and lives in his very presence. It was in this environment that Kōgetsu wrote her own biography of the historical Buddha.

Kōgetsu's Project within Jiun's Circle

Kōgetsu, now remembered as the "founding restorer" of the Chōfukuji, resided at the temple for the remainder of her life, where she devoted decades to the composition and dissemination of a biography of the Buddha in vernacular prose. While the text is Kōgetsu's work, she composed it with influence from other members of Jiun's circle. There is, first of all, the question of why Kōgetsu would ever have decided to write such a biography at all. Kōgetsu's preface to the text, dated to 1813, offers one clue. After a mention of the need to maintain the sangha, she remarks:

> The *śrāmaṇerikā* [female novice nun] Yōzan Gimon, who had deep a aspiration in that matter [of sustaining the sangha], read an intractable (*moteatsukau*) book from the present day, called *The Record of the Eight Phases of the Life of Śākyamuni* (*Shaka hassō ki*). She was heartbroken that people who read such books would think that they were true. She gave rise to the aspiration to write down the story (*en*) of the Eight Phases according to the exposition in the Tripiṭaka [the Buddhist canon], but her life was too short for this vow to be fulfilled, and now it must be fifty years in the past [since then].[27]

In this explanation, Kōgetsu's rationale for the creation of a new biography is deeply rooted in present conditions: the lack of awareness of the orthodox biography of the Buddha among the reading public. Kōgetsu next explains how she determined to carry on Gimon's mission:

> While I have had the aspiration to carry on her vow from my youth, I have passed my days in vain. But I revived that aspiration, wishing only that, even at the age of sixty, with deep karmic impediments and many illnesses, if any years should still be left to me, then that with the protection of the Three Treasures, I would fulfill the

vow of old. Heedless of my lack of literary talent and my poor writing, I have reverentially attempted to assemble the records of the origin of the Śākya clan, and of the Eight Phases and Attainment of the Way by the World-Honored One.[28]

Thus the work credits Gimon with its own immediate inspiration. Needless to say, it is not hard to imagine that Kōgetsu was at least as concerned as Gimon had been about the proliferation of the vernacular biographical narrative, instead of the orthodox one.

Later in *Light of the Three Ages*, Kōgetsu links Jiun more directly to her decision to write the piece. In remarks near the end of the fourteenth chapter, she explains the meanings of the three parts of the Tripiṭaka. After recording some sharply critical observations about the sad state of the sangha in the Japan of her day, Kōgetsu writes:

If I go on in this vein, then there will likely be many [readers] who say that this [just] sounds like an old nun complaining away, but my late [master], the Venerable One from the Twin Dragon Hermitage in Yamato [i.e., Jiun], longed for the world graced by the presence of the Buddha, and always spoke of how things were then, so I have longed only for the era of the True Dharma. Also because of the original vow by the *śrāmaṇerikā* Yōzan [Gimon], this wish was impossible for me to abandon, and I just continued writing, hoping that it might be an aid for people of aspiration in looking back on days of old.[29]

As this paragraph shows, Kōgetsu positioned her work within a broader circle of reform, devoted to a return to the world of the historical Buddha.

Which of the vernacular narratives originally troubled Gimon, and why? As we have seen, there is indeed an early *jōruri* puppet play titled *Record of the Eight Phases of the Life of Śākyamuni*, and it did circulate in published form no later than 1669. However, it is by no means clear that this was the specific text to which Gimon objected. Apart from the published version of the *jōruri*—which is not widely extant today—it seems at least equally likely that Gimon might have read at least some of the longer *kanazōshi* work on which it was based, the *Tale of the Eight Phases of the Life of Śākyamuni* (*Shaka hassō monogatari*). Unlike the *jōruri* version, the *kanazōshi* tale seems to have circulated quite widely, even to the end of the Edo period. A copy of it sits among more than a dozen titles about Śākyamuni found in the catalog of the Edo-period Ōnoya Sōhachi (Daisō) lending library of Nagoya, made when its contents were listed for auction in 1899.[30] Whichever specific account proved so upsetting to Gimon and perhaps to Kōgetsu, it is not difficult to guess which parts of the vernacular story might have been problematic. Mahāprajāpatī's abuse of her sister, Māyā, and later of her daughter-in-law, the prince's wife Yaśodharā, might have struck Gimon as particularly egregious. Gimon might also have taken umbrage at the account of the founding of the nuns' order in the *Tale of the Eight Phases*, which has little to do with the orthodox version.

While Gimon's precise contribution to *Light of the Three Ages* is a matter for speculation, Jiun's contribution does survive in rich documentation. A number of manuscript drafts for the book, kept at the Chōfukuji, were published in the 1920s as part of Jiun's complete *Works*. Some of these drafts were produced by Kōgetsu, and then checked and annotated by Jiun. Others are Kōgetsu's records of Jiun's preaching. Many of these cover specific elements of the biography of the Buddha, addressing such topics as the genealogy of the Śākya clan; the Buddha's kingly lineage; the archery competition between the young Prince Siddhartha and his cousin and rival, Devadatta; the early education of Prince Siddhartha (including a discussion of the Siddham alphabet, which he is said to have studied); the thirty-two major and eighty minor marks of the Buddha; the origins of the nuns' order; the renunciation of the world and ordination of the members of the Śākya clan; and the lives of such characters as Siddhartha's second consort Gopī, or King Bimbisāra. Even taken together, these drafts do not completely prefigure the whole text of *The Light of the Three Ages*, but they do form the core of a number of its sections.

These manuscript drafts—all coauthorships of one kind or another—offer multiple insights into Kōgetsu. First, they demonstrate the breadth of Kōgetsu's Buddhist learning. The drafts attributed to Kōgetsu translate (or sometimes cite) passages from the Chinese of a number of canonical texts, including the *Minor Section of the Monastic Code of the Root Group That Teaches That All Exists*, the *Dharmagupta Monastic Code*, the *Sutra of the Arising of the World* (*Qishi jing*, *T* 24), the closely related *Sutra of Cosmology* (*Da loutan jing*, *T* 23), and the *Sutra of the Collection of the Authentic Deeds of the Buddha*. Significantly, the focus of attention here lies squarely within the earliest layer of texts among those translated into Chinese from South Asian accounts of the life of the Buddha. While this approach may today seem self-evident and soundly historicist, it was novel in the Edo-period genre of published Japanese accounts of the life of the Buddha. Edo-era predecessors to Kōgetsu's work—such as the vernacular *Tale of the Eight Phases of the Life of Śākyamuni*, or even the apologetic account of the life of the Buddha by Gentei—had shown little awareness of the varying historical positions of their source texts, not distinguishing between different sources on the basis of the date or place of production. They had instead attempted to integrate the Buddha's life story, primarily to be found in the "Hīnayāna" parts of the Chinese Buddhist literature, with canonical texts more highly prized in Japan—with the *Lotus Sutra* as a conspicuous example. Kōgetsu opposed this tendency.

Second, the manuscript drafts attest to Kōgetsu's uncommon degree of facility in multiple styles of prose, both Chinese and Japanese. Some of these drafts represent Kōgetsu's original rendering of key passages from texts from the Chinese Buddhist canon into *kanbun kundokutai*, a style of rewriting or reading Chinese text using the grammar of classical Japanese. Others, written in a more colloquial style of Edo-era Japanese, represent Kōgetsu's notes from talks given by Jiun. To be sure, Kōgetsu was not the only woman of her period to evince deep engagement with Chinese-language sources, which were not part of the typical education for girls and young women. Born about a generation before Kōgetsu, the intellectual and author Arakida Reijo (1732–1806) produced copious original works in addition to Japanese-language adaptations of popular fiction from China.

Nevertheless, Kōgetsu's production differs from Reijo's in its circulation. Although some of Reijo's works did circulate in manuscript—to her apparent horror—there is no evidence that any saw publication during her lifetime. In any case, women who left evidence of advanced facility in reading Chinese, like Reijo and Kōgetsu, were undeniably exceptional in their day. Indeed, *any* kind of female authorship of prose narrative (with the exception of travelogues) was exceptional by the late Edo era.[31] To be sure, by the end of Kōgetsu's life, the rise of the popular *ninjōbon* genre of romance and sentiment, which addressed itself to women, does suggest a growth in female readership, but the authors of those texts remained male.

Content, Method, and Form in *Light of the Three Ages*

A complete examination of *Light of the Three Ages* lies beyond the scope of this chapter, but it is possible to catalog some distinctive notes it strikes. Needless to say, Kōgetsu rejected the new subplots that had accumulated in the Edo-era vernacular tradition of the biography of the Buddha, including the powerful motif of Mahāprajāpatī as a sororicidally jealous big sister. On the other hand, Kōgetsu's text also reincorporated certain elements of the Buddha's life story that had long since fallen out of favor in Japan by the early nineteenth century. Two chapters relating such episodes merit special attention, in part because they both abruptly reappeared in a later vernacular version of the biography from 1845, the *Illustrated Record of the Life of Śākyamuni* (*Shaka go-ichidaiki zue*), written by Kōkadō Isai (a.k.a. Yamada no Kakashi, 1788–1847) and illustrated by no less an artist than Katsushika Hokusai (1760–1849)—a semblance too great to chalk up to coincidence.[32] (See fig. 4 for Hokusai's treatment of the prince's sufferings.)

These chapters are "Concerning the Renunciation of the Aunt of the World-Honored One, Mahāprajāpatī" (chapter 12) and "Concerning the Karmic Reason for the Extinction of the Śākya Clan" (chapter 23). These two episodes are well attested in both South Asian sources and in their translations and adaptations within Chinese Buddhist literature, so they were naturally known in Japan as well. Notwithstanding their presence in Chinese scriptural texts, these episodes had not attracted much attention in Japan since the first half of the twelfth century, when they were treated in the *Tales of Times Now Past*.[33] Because Kōgetsu decided to include these topics after a lapse of nearly seven

FIGURE 4 From the *Illustrated Record of the Life of Śākyamuni* (detail). *Shaka go-ichidaiki zue* (1845). Photograph courtesy of Waseda University Library.

hundred years, we may presume that they bore some special meaning within her text. These two chapters were likely included in *Light of the Three Ages* because they each show the Buddha as an exemplary figure—and because they therefore offered a device with which Kōgetsu, like her mentor Jiun, could criticize the practice of Buddhism in the Japan of her day.

In the first of these two episodes, the Buddha's aunt and adoptive mother, Mahāprajāpatī, founds the order of nuns. This founding of the nuns' order itself was not unknown to the vernacular tradition: the chronicle of sisterly resentment, as elaborated in the *Tale of the Eight Phases of the Life of Śākyamuni*, had included its own account of the founding of the nuns' order. Here it made the Buddha's former consort Yaśodharā its founder, an innovation with no basis in the canon. Nor in this version does the Buddha have to be persuaded to allow the ordination of nuns; he simply remembers that Yaśodharā had vowed to become a nun in a previous life.[34] As if to rebut this variation, Kōgetsu instead retold the canonical tale of Mahāprajāpatī's repeated, urgent petition to the Buddha to accept her and five hundred other women of the Śākya clan (including Yaśodharā) as nuns. As in most canonical versions, here too the Buddha makes the usual protests, but he is finally persuaded, on cue, through the intervention of his disciple Ānanda. Kōgetsu cited multiple sutras by name to tell this story, and she referred to the Buddha's aunt not with the name common to the vernacular biographical tradition—Gautamī (Kyōdonmi)—but rather by the transcription or the translation of her name found in the many of older canonical materials: Makahajahatei or Daiaidō, "Great Lover of the Path."

Kōgetsu's innovation in this retelling comes from her distinctive framing for the story: she begins this chapter with a tale of Yaśodharā instead of Mahāprajāpatī herself. Picking up a different thread from canonical literature, Kōgetsu recounts how Yaśodharā attempted to seduce the Buddha when he first returned to the palace after his awakening, by giving him an aphrodisiac sweet. When the Buddha refused her, she fled to a tower and tried to kill herself by jumping from its height. She was saved, Kōgetsu continues, only through the power of the Buddha, and later went on to become a nun and attain the fruit of the arhat.

Women may have the potential to be awakened beings, Kōgetsu implies here, but in order to attain awakening, they must first cope with significant encumbrances. After telling the story of the founding of the nuns' order, she appends her own comments enlarging on this theme:

The writer [I, Kōgetsu] thinks this: Even though people of such great virtue [i.e., the founding nuns] were women, and even though they aided the World-Honored One in his transformation [of deluded beings], and left not a speck of injury upon the Buddhadharma, the World-Honored One was contemplating as far ahead as the Latter Days, and admonished them rather deeply. If we take a look at the nature of the women before our eyes in this era, then we find that they rarely appear to have true wisdom, that they are all heartless and arrogant, that they think themselves to be clever, and that even if they do happen to renounce the world, they forget the days of old . . . and break the vow made by Mahāprajāpatī.[35]

This passage is in keeping with Kōgetsu's insistence on the maintenance of the precepts, but it is also by no means optimistic about women's adherence to them. Although it would be impermissibly anachronistic to look for feminist sentiment in any eighteenth-century Japanese writer, it is also striking to find here that a highly literate and well-read nun has embedded the story of the acceptance of women into the monastic establishment within passages about the foolishness of women, both in the Buddha's day and in her own. Kōgetsu did not hold only women accountable for adhering to the precepts, but she gave women no quarter, either.

Adherence to the precepts would not be meaningful without a strong notion of karmic causality, in which skillful actions incur good results and vice versa. It was likely to emphasize this point that *Light of the Three Ages* includes a detailed exposition of the annihilation of the Śākya clan in its twenty-third chapter. In this well-known story, the Śākyas' humiliation of the young prince of the kingdom of Kosala, Virūḍhaka (Jpn. Ruri), sets in motion a series of events that lead to his eventual ascent to the throne, his invasion of the Śākya realm, and his slaughter of its people. Awakened and omniscient as the Buddha may be, he nevertheless tries more than once to deter Virūḍhaka and to protect his relatives, but all in vain. In the end, he realizes (and the reader learns) that the workings of karma are so ironclad, and so inevitable, that not even a buddha could stop them. Kōgetsu remains a careful scholar here, noting, for instance, discrepancies in the numbers of Śākya clan members as given by multiple sources.

Of course, what goes around comes around, and after the extermination of his clan, the Buddha predicts that Virūḍhaka's recompense for the slaughter of the Śākyas will come as death by fire within seven days. Virūḍhaka learns of this prediction and, desperate to escape the fire, builds a palace in the middle of a lake, moves his court there, and waits. Day after day, nothing happens. On the seventh day, when everyone is preparing to go home, one of his court ladies is getting dressed to celebrate the imminent departure. She leaves her jewelry on top of her pillow (presumably one made of wood). Although the day has been cloudy, the sun suddenly comes out and the jewelry focuses its rays, which start a fire on the pillow. The fire instantly spreads from the pillow to the structure as a whole. All of the court manages to escape, except for the king and his wicked advisor. Some "strange creature, not even a human" comes and bars the door, trapping them inside until they burn to death.[36] (In Hokusai's illustration of this episode, revenge comes not through cosmic principle or its anonymous servants, but in the hands of an angry god of thunder, who smites Virūḍhaka and all his followers with his thunderbolt.[37])

At the end of the chapter, Kōgetsu appended her own extended commentary to this story. She began with a general argument about the necessity of being on one's guard against producing bad karma, but then moved into a more specific discussion of the state of Buddhist practice in Japan. Here she turned her critical gaze upon the "single-practice" Buddhist denominations, still dominant in her day:

> Saint Hōnen, Saint Nichiren, and others appeared in a world in disorder, long after the *saṅgha*-treasure had hidden itself away. They lamented that the sentient beings of those times would all fall into the Evil Ways, and they tried by any means possible to capture the hearts of sentient beings who would be ill at ease because of the turmoil of the times, even were they urged with all eloquence either to uphold the precepts, or to still their thinking and practice meditation. They recommended that people simply have faith without doubt, and singlemindedly recite the name of the Buddha, or the title of a sūtra, and then they would save sentient beings when they had been born into a Buddha-land, having made karmic connections to escape from the three worlds. This is a most blessed expedient, but it is not a precedent to cite in a felicitous time [such as ours], when the storm has passed. . . . I would like anyone with faith, whether monastic or lay, to look back to the era graced by the World-Honored One; to restrain body, speech, and mind, according to the Buddha's precepts; and then, in addition, to chant the name of a Buddha or the title of a sūtra, or to practice seated meditation or esoteric ritual.[38]

Indeed, the "single-practice" movements of Hōnen, Shinran, and Nichiren, born during times of sociopolitical disorder, all stressed not only that observance of a key single practice surpassed upholding any of the moral precepts, but also, more sweepingly, that the exigencies of the particular degenerate era at hand had foreclosed the possibility of meaningful precept practice. They all had some theory of time according to which the era had already entered its terminal phase, the End of the Dharma (Jpn. *mappō*), or its Latter Days (Jpn. *sue no yo*, a phrase that Kōgetsu herself used often), though they disagreed vigorously about which specific practice best suited the new time. While she did not belabor this point, Kōgetsu seemed to endorse their overall premise of choosing a practice that suits the era. However, she neatly turned the tables on the founders of these "single-practice" movements by declaring that her own era—which Anglophone historians still call the Pax Tokugawa—was no longer a world of disorder, but a period propitious for the reestablishment of the sangha. Now that meaningful practice of the precepts is again possible, Kōgetsu claimed, the practices distinctive to the various Buddhist lineages should cede pride of place to observance of the precepts.

Even after the conclusion of this chapter, Kōgetsu was still not quite finished with the story of the decimation of the Śākya clan. At the end of the seventh chapter of *Light of the Three Ages*, after narrating the distribution of the Buddha's relics and their enshrinement in stupas, she noted a troubling detail: one of her sources mentions that, among the kings who came to demand the relics of the Buddha, there was "the king of Kapilavastu, a relative of the Tathāgata" when he was still a prince. Although her source does not mention the fate of the kingdom, she noted that its capital had already been destroyed at this stage. To her credit, Kōgetsu made no effort to argue away this inconsistency. "There are many variations in the account of the *parinirvāṇa*," she noted, "but I have relied upon the *Ekottarāgama*, and for the rest the *Mahāparinirvāṇa Sūtra* and its addendum, taking from and mixing in the *Genealogy of Śākyamuni* (*Shijia pu*), and making note of their imperfections."[39] In the hierarchy implied here, Kōgetsu expressed a clear preference for an early Indian compilation over a later Mahāyāna sutra and a Chinese collection of texts—a hierarchy that echoes Jiun's own.

One final distinctive point about Kōgetsu's work lies in its use of style and form. That Kōgetsu had facility in multiple writing styles is evident from her drafts, written either in *kanbun kundokutai* or a colloquial style. For *Light of the Three Ages*, though, she chose a style reminiscent of so-called "neoclassic prose" or "imitative ancient prose" (*gikobun*). This style emulates the prose of such Heian-era masters of prose as Murasaki Shikibu or Sei Shōnagon. Because its models lie in works by premodern Japan's canonical female writers, it may appear at first that it is only natural or even inevitable for Kōgetsu—who, like her predecessors, also served at the imperial court—to have selected it. But there is little "natural" or "inevitable" about Kōgetsu's choice of this style. Kōgetsu's prose certainly does leave an elegant impression, but it does not begin to replicate the full range of auxiliary verbs used by Heian authors, instead resorting to a small range of classical compound auxiliaries that circulated as frozen units, and whose components' individual semantics had been lost. Kōgetsu's prose also reflects (probably inadvertently) the influence of postclassical changes to Japanese grammar. For instance, it sometimes substitutes the attributive form (*rentaikei*) when the final form (*shūshikei*) is technically the correct conjugation. Such linguistic features reveal that Kōgetsu was composing in a style not wholly native to her.

More important than the grammatical specificities of the prose, though, may be the sociolinguistic environment in which *gikobun* functioned after the eighteenth century. This Edo-era neoclassical prose style did indeed draw on works by women, but its developers and practitioners were men. And not just any men: the style was particularly favored by followers of the Kokugaku, or "National Learning" movement, who employed it as part of a larger historicist project of uncovering a distinctly Japanese tradition from the past. For National Learning scholars like Motoori Norinaga, to write in *gikobun* would therefore not merely have been a marker of elegance and familiarity with the classical tradition. Instead, it would have represented the self-conscious removal of historical accretions to expose the latent ancient truth beneath. This is, in fact, precisely what *Light of the Three Ages* attempts to do for the history of Japanese narratives of the life of the Buddha.

The work resonates with other themes in National Learning. Kōgetsu mentions Japan only infrequently, but always with words of praise. In the fourteenth chapter, after discussing the contents of the Tripiṭaka, Kōgetsu noted: "The *vinaya* have been transmitted to Japan and even in this era, we keep the Three Treasures. I believe that this is all proof (*shirushi*) that this country is a land of the gods, superior to other nations."[40] This remark may not be quite as chauvinistic as it sounds, since Kōgetsu goes on to specify that it is owing to the intervention of the Kasuga deity that Japan's precept lineage survived eras of disorder; that is, were it not for the custodianship of the gods, the people of Japan alone could not have carried on the precept tradition. But on the whole, Kōgetsu's comment here is still in line with the nativist insistence on the distinctiveness and special position of Japan.

Light of the Three Ages also evinces departures from the *gikobun* style. It is densely packed with Buddhist technical terms and proper nouns with South Asian antecedents. These are here uniformly rendered in

Chinese script. Perhaps more surprising is Kōgetsu's use of quotations of verse from canonical texts and (much less frequently) Chinese commentaries, including Sengyou's. Even in its 1830s printing, Kōgetsu's work punctuates these quotations to make them more readable, but it does not rewrite them for the reader in *kanbun kundokutai* style. This is quite different from the sort of exercise in which Motoori Norinaga engaged when he rewrote *kanbun kundokutai* from the *Record of Ancient Matters* in order to "restore" the "original" ancient Japanese language obscured by its Sinicized script. By contrast, Kōgetsu's deliberate reproduction of these passages—mostly *gāthās* purporting to represent the thought or speech of narrative characters—suggests her effort to retrieve and cite the voices of the past in as authentic a form as possible.

Light of the Three Ages in Early Meiji Japan

The publication of Kōgetsu's work near her own time came about, we are told in comments by her disciple Gikan (n.d.), because visitors who had heard of her composition urged her to publish it. Gikan's testimony reports that Kōgetsu set about revising the manuscript, but was able to finish revising only the first two volumes.[41] Kōgetsu's own preface is dated 1813 (tenth year of Bunka), but an additional preface, contributed by a monk at the temple Sangūji, also to the west of Kyoto, is dated 1830 (the thirteenth year of the Bunsei era), suggesting that Kōgetsu's work was first published no earlier than 1830, and possibly after her death in 1833.[42] There is little evidence of the immediate reception of her work, except for the aforementioned strong possibility that Kōkadō Isai adopted elements from it for the *Illustrated Record of the Life of Śākyamuni*.

In 1882, the third-generation abbess of the Chōfukuji after its restoration under Kōgetsu, Hiramatsu Shunsei (n.d.), had *Light of the Three Ages* reprinted from the original blocks, which had survived at the temple. This may well have been the edition that was known to Fukuda Gyōkai (1806–1888), a leading figure in the Pure Land movement and in the early Meiji Buddhist world more broadly. Gyōkai regarded Jiun with the highest admiration, and he worked to disseminate Jiun's Ten Good Precepts. It was at one of Gyōkai's lectures that his disciple, the fellow Pure Land priest Hiroyasu Shinzui (1848–1922), first learned of *Light of the Three Ages*. In 1885, Hiroyasu collaborated with a number of other clerics to republish the book in a new, illustrated edition. According to the preface that Hiroyasu wrote later that year, they funded the printing of one thousand copies by selling subscriptions in advance. (Some fifteen years later, Hiroyasu would depart for the Korean peninsula, where he served briefly as the head of the Pure Land Buddhist mission to Korea, taking up his post in 1901 and returning to Japan the following year.[43])

The various endorsements that Hiroyasu secured for the new edition of the book, finally published in 1888, succinctly communicate what the male Buddhist intellectuals of his day found valuable in it. Gyōkai probably spoke for more than one reader with his effusive praise for the style: "The style of this book certainly calls to mind the literary pursuits of a certain court lady, written on the paper of the *Great Prajñāpāramitā Sutra* when she was in seclusion at the Ishiyamadera."[44] He is referring here, of course, to the popular medieval legend according to which Murasaki Shikibu began to compose the *Tale of Genji* while staying at the celebrated temple, using sutra paper for a decidedly non-Buddhist purpose. Other contributors of endorsements wrote approvingly of her work's careful attention to the canon, and noted their hopes that Kōgetsu's work would help "correct" the various popular biographies of the Buddha that were still circulating in the early Meiji years. One wrote:

> As for early works written about the life of the Buddha, there are the *Tale of the Eight Phases* and the *Record of His Life*, and many apart from those, but none of these are correct. They treat the olden days of his Causal Stage [i.e., his bodhisattva career] as though . . . they were matters of the present, or else they mix in fiction, and are the doings of "wise guys" (*sakashirabito*) who only seek profit [from selling them]. Thus, there are many people who are confused, and even the religion (*kyōhō*) is injured in no small part.[45]

In the estimation of such early Meiji Buddhist intellectuals, Kōgetsu's work was, therefore, considered not only elegant in style, but also an antidote to the vernacular "fictions."

Like Kōgetsu herself and the clerical backers of the 1880s reissue of her work, authors of other original accounts produced around this period also attempted to counter the vernacular tradition of tales of the Buddha's life. In 1882, the Sōtō Zen cleric Tokumitsu Shōryū (n.d.) published a *True Biography of the Venerable Śākyamuni* (*Shakuson shinjitsu denki*), whose narrative chronology begins with the formation of our universe and ends with the compilation of the Buddhist scriptures after the *parinirvāṇa* of the Buddha. In the prefatory material, Tokumitsu described his frustration with the persistent influence of the illustrations of the Edo-period material, particularly the *Japanese Library*, even in texts that are otherwise orthodox. Material in his book, Tokumitsu assured his readers, would derive only from reliable sources.[46] As had been the case for Kōgetsu, though, Tokumitsu's effort to restrict the narrative to canonical sources did not preclude the expression of his own interests. For instance, he included the story of the Buddha's willingness to wash with his own hands the body of a monk who had suffered from a long illness, and whose smell and filth repelled the other monks.[47] Although attested in multiple canonical sources, this tale hardly appears in other biographies produced in Japan after the *Tōdaiji Notes for Sermons*.

In 1902, another Sōtō Zen cleric, Itō Shundō (d. 1939), published the similarly titled (but much longer) *True Biography of Śākyamuni* (*Shaka jitsu denki*). In his preface, Itō positioned this book as a long-overdue response to questions he received during his missionary work in Hokkaidō in the early 1890s, presumably directed toward the ethnic Japanese newly sent to "settle" the island. "The existing biographies of Śākyamuni in our country have many unbelievable stories, and there are even some with [outright] errors, especially the narrative 'playful compositions' (*gesaku*). Please show us a good, reliable book."[48] The complaint about "playful compositions"—a retroactively applied, Meiji-era term of derision for popular literature of the later Edo period—receives further elaboration in one of the conventions that Itō set out before the main body of his work:

> Item. There are many books in the world that record the Eight Phases in the life of Śākyamuni, but few people look over the biographies of the Buddha which he preached himself and which were compiled by eminent monks in India and China. Instead, many read books written by the authors of "playful compositions" in Japan, such as the *Record of the Life of Śākyamuni*, the *True Record of Śākyamuni [Origin of the Eight Schools]*, or the *Japanese Library of the Eight Phases of the Life of Śākyamuni*. Among the works above, the *Record of the Life* and the *Japanese Library* do not explain events in the correct way, but they instead record groundless fictional tales, on account of which people err in their belief and interpretation.[49]

The production by clerics of narratives to "correct" the "distortions" of popular commercial literature suggests that late-Edo presentations of the life of the Buddha remained a concern among Buddhist intellectuals at least through the early decades of the Meiji period. Nonetheless, these biographies are essentially inward looking, directed to a readership already disposed to accept the validity of Buddhist scriptural accounts, and searching for a biography that adduced its authority from those accounts.

As the following chapters will show, however, by the time Itō's book was finally published, a different set of intellectuals had already begun to explore the life of the Buddha. While they dismissed the Japanese vernacular accounts, they did not unquestioningly accept the Buddhist scriptural canon as the ultimate authority, either. These scholars would also understand the Buddha as an exemplar, but not in his traditional sense.

FOUR

The Buddha as Fraud

A thinker who has never been ranked among the biographers of the Buddha is, in fact, the most important one. Today generally remembered as a Shintō fanatic and a notorious cultural chauvinist, the early-nineteenth-century scholar of National Learning, Hirata Atsutane (1776–1843), also engaged in a long and serious study of Buddhism. Among the most virulent intellectual opponents of Buddhism in premodern Japan, Atsutane undertook that research with the express purpose of discrediting Buddhism, and he achieved some success. In the final decades of the Edo period, his followers' polemics helped to galvanize anti-Buddhist sentiment, contributing to the severe persecution of Buddhism in the early 1870s. In the course of that research, however, Atsutane became the first intellectual in Japan to treat and to critique the life of the Buddha on the basis of the texts in which it appeared. Working in both negative and positive critical modes, Atsutane sought to strip away layers of fabrication and historical accretion, to uncover Śākyamuni as he had really lived and preached, and to retell his story within the context of the India that he inhabited. Other Japanese intellectuals had attacked the Buddha before, of course, but not in this mode. To destroy the Buddha, Atsutane inadvertently became his first critical biographer.

As this chapter shows, scholars writing in English have recognized Atsutane's historical importance but largely dismissed his textual scholarship, instead stressing the emphasis that he placed on folklore studies in his later years. Even in his intellectual maturity, though, Atsutane continued his investigations into the Buddhist classics, with a particular focus on early texts often neglected in Japan. He critically inherited Taoist and Confucianist criticisms of the authenticity of the Buddhist canon. Within his influential *A Mocking Discourse upon Emerging from Meditation* (*Shutsujō shōgo*), completed in 1811 but first printed only in 1849), Atsutane built on methods inherited from Tominaga Nakamoto (1715–1746). Atsutane developed Nakamoto's understanding of the body of texts describing the life of Śākyamuni as retroactive constructions whose contradictions betrayed the disparate circumstances of their assembly. Using this text-critical method, Atsutane went on in the *Mocking Discourse* to demythologize the Buddha, reducing him to a trickster and a fraud, although recognizing him as a powerful wonder-worker. Later, as part of his monumental but incomplete *Compendium of Indian Records* (*Indo zōshi*, 1826), Atsutane revisited the story of the life of the Buddha. This time, he changed emphasis: Rather than foreground the criticism of the life stories of the Buddha, Atsutane now highlighted the story itself, largely shorn of the details he found unpalatable or objectionable. Incomplete and overshadowed by the *Mocking Discourse*, the *Compendium* suggests the level of critical work on the biography of the Buddha that would be possible using Chinese materials alone.

The *Compendium* seems to have circulated only among Atsutane's disciples, but the *Mocking Discourse* circulated widely, if illicitly, to appreciative readers of many kinds. A number of leading Buddhist clerical intellectuals of the late Edo period read it and condemned it, but they could not parry it. This chapter takes up one representative attempt at the refutation of Atsutane—the *Whisk for Swatting Away a Fly* (*Tsuiyō barae*) of 1867—to suggest just how difficult it could be for Buddhist clerics to grasp the nature of Atsutane's argument. To be sure, many of Atsutane's claims would not prove defensible after his own era. However, in his unwavering insistence on the historically contingent and retroactively constructed character of the biographical literature, and in his naturalistic account of Śākyamuni as a human being (albeit a "bizarre" one), Atsutane proposed problems demanding serious attention in the years after the Restoration.

Approaches to Atsutane

Hirata Atsutane polarizes his readers. Anglophone critics typically offer a reluctant admission of his historical importance, combined with a lingering distrust of his character and his standards as a scholar. Monographs about Atsutane produced in the present century have returned Atsutane to his rightful place as a key intellectual of the late Edo period, but typically by setting aside his work as a scholar of the written word; instead, they explore the adroit politicking that won him a place in the institutional world of late-Edo-era National Learning, or they frame Atsutane's work as a species of proto-ethnography. The focus in this scholarship on Atsutane as a Shintō thinker (and secondarily, as a plagiarist of European ideas) has obscured his relevance as a scholar of Buddhist texts, including his work as a biographer of the Buddha.

Since the late nineteenth century, writers of English have typically acknowledged Atsutane's historical importance, even as they cast aspersions on his standing as an intellectual and as a person. Basil Hall Chamberlain (1850–1935), the eminent early British gentleman-scholar of all "Things Japanese," noted as much in his oft-reissued book of the same title (1890): "Unfortunately Hirata was very bigoted as well as very learned. Consequently the reader must always be on his guard . . . for Hirata never scrupled to garble a sacred text, if he could thereby support his own views as to what the sacred writers *ought* to mean."[1] An Anglophone pioneer of religious studies in Japan, Anesaki Masaharu (1873–1949), deemed Atsutane "a man of great ability but a bigot of doubtful character."[2] Such evaluations typified the suspicion of Atsutane expressed in English from the period before 1945.

The wholesale appropriation of Atsutane by ultranationalists in Japan during the Fifteen-Year War (1931–1945) did not ameliorate this perspective. In 1954, Donald Keene did the Anglophone world a service in returning scholarly attention to Atsutane and his interest in Europe, even as he issued this caution: "Hirata's conclusions are usually foregone and not very original."[3] As recently as 2011, a writer could characterize Atsutane as "probably the most important and also the most radical ideologist of Restoration Shinto," but cast aspersions upon his consistency: "This fanatical propagandist of 'pure Shinto' also, quite astonishingly, picked up aspects of Christian thinking and modified these for his concept of Shinto."[4] As these representative evaluations suggest, the key foci of interest in Atsutane have lain in his Shintō theology (which may be recognized as original, but is typically discounted as xenophobic) and his incorporation into it of ideas from early modern Christianity.

On the other hand, recent English-language monographs no longer simply condemn him as a bigot, but neither do they demonstrate much appreciation for Atsutane's interpretation of written texts. Mark McNally's *Proving the Way: Conflict and Practice in the History of Japa-*

nese Nativism (2005) surveyed the extraordinary schemes to which Atsutane resorted to secure his institutional place in the lineage of his self-proclaimed predecessor in National Learning, Motoori Norinaga (1730–1801)—despite the fact that Atsutane never even met Norinaga in person, much less directly received instruction from him. McNally's work asserts that the mature Atsutane was, nonetheless, less interested in the "textualism and philology" of Norinaga than in "eschatological matters."[5] This study further contends that Atsutane was able to distinguish himself from the text-bound successors of Motoori only by leaving texts behind. As this study stresses, Atsutane refocused his scholarly interest upon the unwritten testimony of the folk as the first experts in Japan, particularly their accounts of the "supernatural."[6]

In a similar vein, Wilburn Hansen's study, *When Tengu Talk: Hirata Atsutane's Ethnography of the Other World* (2008), examined one representative writing about the "supernatural" by Atsutane: *Strange Tidings from the Realm of Immortals* (*Senkyō ibun*, composed in 1822). Hansen characterized Atsutane as a kind of proto-ethnologist who recorded, edited, and disseminated testimony from a boy who claimed to have been abducted to the invisible world of the mysterious "mountain men." Like McNally's work, Hansen's study also notes Atsutane's "mistrust of history" and "privileging of oral modes of communication over written modes."[7]

Scholarship in this mode has performed a valuable service in restoring Atsutane to his historical and institutional contexts, and in taking his claims seriously. It has properly recognized that the mature Atsutane's espousal of a distinctive theology of national superiority, however odious, does not necessarily taint everything he ever wrote. Nonetheless, Anglophone scholars have yet to grapple with the text-critical work conducted by the mature Atsutane. Far from ignoring textual sources in his mature phase (i.e., after 1811), Atsutane actually conducted copious surveys of textual evidence in Chinese from a wide range of sources—not merely European scientific writings or Catholic tracts in Chinese translation, as has already been noted, but also the voluminous texts of Taoism and Buddhism, among others.[8] In fact, it was only after completing the paradigmatically anti-philological study *Strange Tidings from the Realm of Immortals* in 1822 that Atsutane either completed or set aside work on such writings, including his *Record of the Legend of the Yellow Emperor* (*Kōtei denki*, 1824), *Compendium of Indian Sources* (*Indo zōshi*, 1826), and *Legends from Chinese Antiquity* (*Sekiken taikoden*, 1827).

Most English-language scholarship has overlooked these sources in its pursuit of Atsutane's Shintō theology.[9] Of the limited scholarship to take up Atsutane's interest in Indian texts, one article analyzes the *Compendium of Indian Sources* to show Atsutane's interests in Vedic accounts of creation and in the geography of India.[10] Other discussions of Atsutane's writings on Buddhism have considered their anti-Buddhist polemics and their complex relationship with elements of medieval Japanese Shintō theology. An article by a scholar of medieval Japanese religion, Iyanaga Nobumi, identifies Atsutane as the Japanese writer whose "works on Buddhism were the most significant, both in quantity and quality, of any composed by a non-Buddhist author before Meiji."[11]

In Japanese, a richer assortment of scholarship treats Atsutane's work on Buddhism.[12] As might be expected, Japanese Buddhist scholar-clerics have often seen little of worth in Atsutane's work. In 1955, for instance, the True Pure Land Buddhist historian Kashiwahara Yūsen (1916–2002) wrote that, in Atsutane's work, "Buddhism, Confucianism, Christianity, Dutch Studies, and so forth: Everything was used opportunistically in the construction of his academic theories." Kashiwahara was particularly horrified at Atsutane's willingness to incorporate goblins and magic into his theory, about which he wrote, "It goes without saying that criticism of Buddhism from such positions can have nothing scientific or objective about it."[13] Other scholarship coming from outside Buddhist studies still exhibits a reluctance to put Atsutane's work in dialogue with any but its most immediate predecessors, or to consider it alongside the responses issued near its own time. Most pressingly for our purposes, scholarship about Atsutane by Japanese Buddhist researchers tends to locate Atsutane as an anti-Buddhist activist, or more rarely as a scholar of Buddhist texts. Here too, previous work has largely disregarded Atsutane's role as a biographer of the Buddha.

Precedents from China for Atsutane's Textual Critique

Atsutane inherited centuries of accumulated critiques of Buddhism, particularly from China. One such legacy was the claim that the Chinese Buddhist canon was itself derivative or forged. In China, particularly after the fall of the Han dynasty (220), Taoist and Buddhist polemicists accused one another of plagiarism, with each side claiming that its opponent had stolen and rewritten its own sacred texts. With the late Tang period came a growing interest in Confucian exclusivism; with the rise of Neo-Confucianism during the Song period came a new battery of arguments against Buddhism, recapitulating the accusation of plagiarism. Nonetheless, even the founding figures of Song Neo-Confucianism neglected to investigate the contents of Buddhist translations into Chinese in any detail. In Japan, Neo-Confucian exclusivism manifested as an independent intellectual force at the start of the seventeenth century. Its advocates dutifully repeated the standard denunciation of Buddhist scriptures as inauthentic forgeries, but again, without engaging in serious textual investigation. For his part, Atsutane granted a measure of credence to this argument, but he also charged that his predecessors had neglected the careful study of Buddhist texts.

Indian Buddhist sutras already record a considerable quantity of criticisms of the Buddha by rival teachers.[14] Buddhist institutions in India and points further east faced rivals as different from one another as the Indian Advaita Vedānta thinker Śaṅkara (ca. 800 CE) and the Neo-Confucian scholar of the late Koryŏ and early Chosŏn dynasties in Korea, Chŏng Tojŏn (1342–1398). As different forms of "Buddhism" arose, so too did the challenges to it multiply, indicting its philosophical incoherence, metaphysical errors, or undermining of social cohesion. While some opponents of Buddhism criticized its systems of epistemology, they showed strikingly little interest in the question of how Buddhist intellectuals could correctly know their own tradition. Those critics seem typically to have been content to adduce the teachings of Buddhism—however they understood those—and then to refute them. Problems of textual mediation failed to draw much attention.

This pattern held in early China, whose nascent Taoist movement both drew upon Buddhism and engaged in rivalry with it for patronage. In these disputes, textualist criticism, such as it was, largely spoke to a contestation over origins. From at least 166 CE, elite Chinese Taoist clergy and their lay sympathizers began to proclaim the story of the "conversion of the barbarians" (Ch. *huahu*). According to this story, all of Buddhism ultimately derives from the instruction of the high Taoist sage Laozi (sixth century BCE). Various versions of the story claim that Laozi entered India to teach the Buddha, dispatched a follower to become the Buddha, or even manifested himself as the Buddha, all to subdue the wild and uncivilized inhabitants of that foreign land. Such tales may have begun as a way of reconciling Taoist and Buddhist teachings. Regardless, by the beginning of the fourth century CE, Taoist writers began to use them to proclaim the superiority and authenticity of Taoism. In their later and more aggressive forms, such arguments voiced assumptions of the superiority of what, for lack of a better term, we must simply call "Chinese civilization."

As competition for patronage intensified, debates between elite Taoist and Buddhist sympathizers took place at various rulers' courts, reaching the greatest intensity from the fifth through the seventh centuries. For a typical example, we may look to the treatise *Laughing at the Tao* (*Xiaodao lun*), presented to the emperor of the state of Northern Zhou in 570 CE. In it, the layman and court official Zhen Luan invoked such plagiarism as one argument in his arsenal against Taoism. Zhen first cited stanzas from a Taoist scripture that nearly duplicated verses from the Chinese translation of the *Lotus Sutra*, but merely substituted "Tao" for "Buddha." He then accused Taoists of rationalizing this duplication by claiming that the Buddhist *Lotus Sutra* had, in fact, derived from their Taoist scriptures. Zhen retorts that while Chinese ("eastern people") may be fooled by this kind of rank deception, the *Lotus* has proper precedents in "the western regions," and therefore it is the *Taoist* version that is fraudulent. He pressed his point home: "There is not a single reference to the Buddha in the *Way and Its Power* (*Daode jing*). Nor do the eight collections of Buddhist texts ever talk about the Tao. All other Taoist texts were made up later, stolen from Buddhist sūtras."[15] Even at the height of such debates, neither Buddhist nor Taoist participants expressed deep interest in exploring the textual history of Buddhism in its own right. With the institutional destabilization of Buddhism brought on by the persecution of Emperor Wuzong (reigned 841–847), which peaked in 845, such court debates between Buddhists and Taoists largely ended.[16]

Confucian scholars inherited the banner of anti-Buddhist critique by the latter phase of the Tang dynasty, but even their leading lights expressed relatively little interest in Buddhist texts per se. Han Yu (768–824)—perhaps the most important reviver of Confucianism and critic of Buddhism during the Tang dynasty—wrote a short treatise, "Essentials of the Moral Way" ("Yuandao," ca. 805). This has been characterized as "among the most important texts in the history of Chinese thought."[17] In it, Han Yu indicted the foreignness, and therefore inferiority, of the Buddha; condemned the economic consequences of the flourishing of Buddhist temples; and vilified the social consequences of Buddhist practice. Han referred to particular Taoist passages (if only to condemn them) and to a variety of Confucian documents (to support his case), but he mentioned not a single Buddhist text by name. Later intellectuals furthered Han's revalorization of Confucianism, reworking it into the movement known to the Anglophone world as Neo-Confucianism. They also inherited this attitude of dismissal. Cheng Yi (1033–1107), a Neo-Confucian philosopher of the early Song dynasty, actually cautioned against the study of Buddhism, even for purposes of refuting it: "If one tries to investigate all its theories, it is probably an impossible task. Before one has done that, he will already have been transformed into a Buddhist."[18] Such admonitions could not have encouraged even the bitterest enemies of Buddhism to learn enough about its texts to criticize them from within.

Sustained historicist criticism of Buddhist texts therefore did not flourish in the Neo-Confucian context. A case in point is Zhu Xi (1130–1200), the scholastic giant of the latter Song dynasty. Zhu Xi's assault on Buddhism relied on grounds similar to Han's, but it also incorporated a critique of Buddhist texts as well. Given the prominence of the Chan (Zen) movement in the China of Zhu Xi's day, it is wholly natural that he concerned himself principally with repelling, and co-opting, Chan thought and practice. On the other hand, Zhu Xi's attitude to the corpus of Buddhist texts claiming origins outside of China was dismissive in the extreme:

> Of the books of the Buddhists, at first there was only the *Sutra in Forty-Two Sections*, its language extremely rustic and coarse. Later, with the passage of time, [other sutras] were all assembled through the efforts of Chinese literati together. As in the period of the Jin and Song Dynasties [265–479], people set themselves up as lecturers, asking, "Who is Śākyamuni?" "Who is Ānanda?" "Who is Mahākāśyapa?" They posed difficult questions to one another, recording these in books, to deceive and oppose one another. These mostly plagiarized the thought of the *Laozi* and the *Liezi*, altering and expanding it in order to embellish their teachings.[19]

Another passage by Zhu Xi reiterates this notion more succinctly: "Of the Buddhist books, only the *Sutra in Forty-Two Sections* is ancient. The rest were made through the embellishments of Chinese scholars."[20] Of course, Zhu Xi's evaluation here followed the precedent of Chinese dynastic histories, which claimed this sutra as the first Buddhist text to reach China after a dispatch of imperial emissaries in the middle of the first century CE.

The classification of the *Sutra in Forty-Two Sections* as the sole authentically foreign work within the corpus of sūtras in Chinese represents a particular irony. Like the more famous *Dhammapada*, this short text assembles excerpts from a range of other sutras, none of which it prefaces with a typically Buddhist formula, such as "Thus have I heard";

instead, it consistently employs the formula "The Buddha said," implicitly casting the Buddha as a kind of Confucian sage. No parallel compilations of the same texts exist in other canonical Buddhist languages. In the evaluation of its translator, Robert Sharf, it "bears certain unmistakable Chinese stylistic features," including "passages that are most certainly interpolations by a Chinese editor."[21] To contemporary text-critical scholars, then, the Indian provenance and antiquity of the *Sutra in Forty-Two Sections* are anything but self-evident. Reflecting on this misstep by Zhu Xi, one historian of Neo-Confucianism observed: "It would . . . appear that [Zhu Xi] did not know very much about earlier Buddhist history or doctrinal developments."[22] Another sought to account for Zhu Xi's understanding of Buddhist scriptures by placing him in context: "But it is not really surprising, because he merely reflected the general situation of his time. Few Neo-Confucians cared to read Buddhist books. Certainly [Zhu Xi] read many more than his contemporaries. . . ."[23] In other words, Zhu Xi certainly may have been largely uninterested in the Buddhist scriptural canon—at least, aside from Chan works—but even that relatively low level of engagement was unusually robust for a Neo-Confucian scholar of his day.

Neo-Confucian texts and ideas arrived in Japan alongside the other elements of Song dynasty elite culture, which found their first home in the system of the Five Mountain (Gozan) Zen monasteries of Kyoto and Kamakura, which started to be conceived of as a unit by the fourteenth century. By the start of the Edo period, some monks from the elite Zen monasteries had begun to reject the long-dominant notions of Confucian-Buddhist unity and to defect from their positions. One such malcontent was Fujiwara Seika (1561–1619), a Zen monk who as a youth entered the major Kyoto temple Shōkokuji, in which he ultimately ascended to the high position of master of the meditation hall ("Chief Seat," Jpn. *shuso*). After extensive study of Neo-Confucian texts and a failed attempt to cross over to China, he ultimately chose to laicize and marry, probably no later than 1598.[24]

Seika's younger pupil Hayashi Razan (1583–1657), disenchanted with his own studies at the Kyoto Zen temple Kenninji, left and laicized without accepting full ordination around the same time. As experts in the new Confucian learning, these men rapidly captured the attention of the warlord who founded the Edo military government, Tokugawa Ieyasu (1543–1616). Seika delivered Ieyasu lectures even before leaving his temple, and in 1600, he debated before Ieyasu against two Zen monks hailing from it, including its abbot Saishō Shōtai (1548–1608).[25] For his part, Razan profited from the lasting support from the house of

Tokugawa, which from 1607 employed him as clerk and advisor, and later patronized his family Confucian academy.

Razan maintained an aggressively anti-Buddhist ideological stance, for which he drew extensively upon Zhu Xi, as well as Zhu Xi's contemporaries and successors. He also adopted Zhu Xi's criticism of the Chinese Buddhist texts as forgeries crafted on the basis of indigenous texts in China. Razan's articulation of these ideas appears in the *Dialogue between a Confucianist and a Buddhist* (*Ju-butsu mondō*).[26] The *Dialogue* became the first of a succession of exchanges and recriminations between representatives of the Buddhist and Neo-Confucian traditions in Edo-era Japan.[27] Throughout the *Dialogue*, Razan makes repeated reference to the charge of the forgery of Buddhist texts. That appropriation, he says, accounts for the instances in which Buddhist texts resemble those in the other traditions. His opponent Teitoku replies by distinguishing between form and content: just because Buddhist ideas may have been rearticulated in a Chinese-style form does not necessarily change their core. For Japanese people to wear clothing based on Chinese models, for instance, does not make them plagiarizers of Chinese garb. And to disprove the accusation of forgery by translators, Teitoku reminds Razan of the large scale and high level of expertise of the translation enterprise in China, as well as its imperial sponsorship; there could have been no need to forge texts. Finally, Teitoku attempts to turn Zhu Xi's disparaging words about the *Sutra in Forty-Two Sections* against him. In recognizing this text as an authentic production of the Buddha, Teitoku contends, Zhu Xi inadvertently acknowledged the historical reality of the Buddha. As a real being in history, the Buddha naturally could have created those scriptures.[28]

Heir to over a millennium of debates such as these, Hirata Atsutane selected useful elements from the broader Neo-Confucian critique of Buddhism. Of Razan, for instance, he wrote: "Master Dōshun [i.e., Razan] is the person who first revealed—after a fashion—that the Buddha-dharma has concealed the facts of our [land's] antiquity, and that its monks commit wickedness."[29] Of course, Atsutane was no partisan of Confucian rationalism, and he criticized Confucian thinkers as excessively petty and unwilling to explore the deep mysteries of the realm of the gods.[30] However, he did make some limited use of Confucian authors as allies against Buddhism. In his *Mocking Discourse upon Emerging from Meditation*, Atsutane cited with approval Zhu Xi's statement that the arrival of Buddhism had brought confusion of values and a lack of distinction between right and wrong.[31] He also praised the attacks upon Buddhism by Chinese Confucian scholars, including

Han Yu, whose "Memorial on the Bone of Buddha" and "Essentials of the Moral Way" he specifically named.[32] In virtually the same breath, though, he condemned Chinese Confucian scholars for failing to admit that their own ancient texts included ideas parallel to the Buddhist notions of karmic retribution and reincarnation, which he found in the *Zuo Commentary on the Spring and Autumn Annals* (*Zuozhuan*) and the *Classic of Changes* (*Yijing*).[33] "Those people known as Confucians," he writes, "are, as I always say, narrow-minded; if you tell them the fact that the Confucian texts that they read have words just the same as the teachings of the Buddha, then they become greatly angered."[34]

Likewise, Atsutane accepted only part of Zhu Xi's accusation of Buddhist plagiarism. Atsutane's verdict on this case comes in the twenty-third volume of his *Compendium of Indian Records*, which comments on the account of the rise of the Mahāyāna as it is given in a popular medieval Japanese primer of instruction in the fundamentals the various denominations of Japanese Buddhism.[35] Here Atsutane cites the words of his predecessor in textual criticism, Hattori Ten'yū, commenting upon the criticism of Zhu Xi by one Lin Xiyi:

> Lin Xiyi said, "Zhu Xi said that the accounts of the Buddhists [lit., "the Śākya clan"] derive from [the Taoist works] the *Zhuangzi* and the *Liezi*. I am afraid that this is not so. . . . The Buddha emerged in the West. How could he have plagiarized [from them] here? [Zhu Xi's] excessive faulting [of the Buddha] is not equitable." But the main intent of Zhu Xi's attack, and Xiyi's defense, are both biased and not equitable. I [Hattori] say that nothing prevents the accounts of the Buddhists from deriving from the *Zhuangzi* and the *Liezi*. This is because, as they say, sometimes the pupil outstrips the master. (And although the Buddha certainly did emerge in the West, how can we know that in translation, the sutra reciter, the scribe, or the emendator did not augment and embellish the texts using the *Zhuangzi* and the *Liezi*?) Thus, setting aside other sutras for the moment, I believe that such texts as the *Vimalakīrti nirdeśa sūtra* have many passages comparable to the *Zhuangzi* and the *Liezi*.[36]

This particular example is notable, since the *Vimalakīrti nirdeśa sūtra* was enthusiastically accepted during the earliest phase of Buddhist texts' entry into China, a period in which the interpretation of Buddhist texts through Taoist notions held sway.

In general, however, Atsutane was not content to accept the reduction of Buddhist texts to bastardizations of the Chinese classics. Notably, he judged the controversial *Sutra in Forty-Two Sections* to be a compilation of excerpts from other Buddhist sutras, created in China at the very earliest stages of its transmission there, when the complete body of scriptures could not yet be translated.[37] To be sure, like Zhu Xi, Atsutane certainly did believe the vast bulk of the Buddhist sacred literature to be later creations, retroactively attributed to the Buddha. But unlike Zhu Xi, Atsutane did not merely dismiss the Buddhist texts as pale reflections of materials already circulating in China. Rather, he sought to demonstrate the grounds for that position through an investigation of the corpus of Buddhist writings itself. Near the start of his *Mocking Discourse upon Emerging from Meditation,* he argued:

From times of old, the people of Yamato [Japan] have . . . discussed and attacked the Buddha-dharma, but none of them has examined the Buddhist books well. . . . In general, if in debate one speaks only of one's own side's claims, then [one's opponent] will not advance to grant them. This is as the Chinaman (*Karabito*) named Su Ziyou said: "When one skilled in speaking with others uses the words of that person to speak to him, then the debaters of the world will obey. . . ." This truly hits the mark. Thus, in order to expound the various Ways, I use Confucian books for talking about the Confucian Way, and Buddhist books for the Buddhist Way.[38]

Atsutane elaborated elsewhere, urging his audience to use care even when examining the commentative tradition within Buddhism. They ought to avoid commentaries if at all possible: "Someone who really wants to ferret out the true shape of the Buddhist sutras . . . should read only the texts themselves" (*honbun bakari de yomu ga yoi koto de gozaru*), resorting to commentaries only to look up unfamiliar names and terms.[39] For, as in a passage of Tenyū's which Atsutane incorporates into his *Compendium of Indian Records*: "Originally all the intentions of the sutras were simple, and nothing was hard to understand. But later commentators made unnecessary and forced explanations, and since they wished to make the sutras terribly profound, that which was clear grew dark, and that which was simple grew abstruse."[40] Failure to register the importance of textual criticism, Atsutane charges in the *Mocking Discourse,* has misled the opponents of Buddhism to focus upon the wrong target: the Buddha himself, rather than the process of textual accretion that actually gave rise to the existence of the Buddhist canon.

As I have said, all the Buddhist scriptures, without exception, were attributed to Śākyamuni and forged by later Buddhist followers, but most people today, such as the Confucians, firmly believe that they all really emerged from the mouth of Śākyamuni, and that Ānanda wrote them down. Thus they direct their scorn against Śākyamuni. Everyone who attacks the Way of the Buddha in these times is so. Even if, like me, they understand that the Buddhist scriptures were all words fabricated by later followers of the Buddha, and that nine-tenths of them are not [even] words spoken by the Buddha, and even if they argue about the matters that must be argued—still, among the people who set up these ideas and attack the Buddhadharma, there might just be one person out of one hundred who can understand this idea and speak it. The other ninety-nine will all [merely] denounce Śākyamuni.[41]

In other words, held Atsutane, previous critics of Buddhism had generally overlooked the mediated nature of the knowledge of Buddhist teachings. They had fixed onto the presumed originator of the teachings (Śākyamuni) without studying textual evidence to distinguish a history internal to the body of Buddhist teachings themselves, or inquiring into how these teachings relate to one another. This is precisely the tactic employed by Atsutane himself.

Critical Method in Atsutane's *Mocking Discourse*

In writing the *Mocking Discourse*, Atsutane consciously drew inspiration for its title—as well as considerable methodology and content—from Tominaga Nakamoto (whose name is also read as "Tominaga Chūki," 1715–1746). A merchant-class scholar who wrote a brilliant historicist critique of the formation of the Buddhist canon, Nakamoto left his most important surviving work under the title *Emerging from Meditation and Then Speaking* (*Shutsujō kōgo*, also read *Shutsujō gogo*, 1745), which was published shortly before his early death.[42] Through critical philological inquiry, Nakamoto showed in this treatise that the various texts in the canon did not all represent the words of the Buddha, but had been created by different parties, at different historical moments, to different ends. The growth of the Buddhist canon, he contended, resulted largely from one-upmanship among various competing Buddhist parties, each seeking to subsume and outdo its predecessor. From the twentieth century onward, Nakamoto's writing earned him positive comparisons to the likes of Voltaire and Lessing, and he was regarded as a herald of "scientific scholarship."[43]

Within *Mocking Discourse*, Atsutane explained that he had learned about Nakamoto from a reference in the work of Motoori Norinaga, whom Atsutane regarded as his master, and he described how he embarked on a furious search through the bookstores of Edo and Osaka in order to acquire a copy of Nakamoto's work for himself. There is also no doubt that Atsutane adopted many specific cases and arguments from Nakamoto's work for his own text, though he did not emulate Nakamoto's pose of neutrality. For their part, scholars writing in English have generally not connected the two works in a positive way, instead dismissing Atsutane's scholarship as unapologetically derivative. One study characterized the *Mocking Discourse* as "finally, a mere vilification" of Buddhism, written by a man "beside himself with anger."[44]

But the *Mocking Discourse,* for all its sneering polemic and overheated rhetoric, is no collection of empty invective. Its argumentation guides readers through a novel effort to locate the Buddha within his Indian intellectual and religious environment, shuttling among teachings attributed to the Buddha, the background Indian traditions that they supersede or from which they appropriate, and Atsutane's own, admittedly idiosyncratic, cosmological assumptions. Atsutane's work makes no pretense of disinterested, clinical evaluation, so we may take it for granted that Atsutane's research to confirm his cosmological and theological ideas—"verified" by evidence from the texts in Chinese—is less the product of his investigations than their catalyst. Likewise, there is no doubt that Atsutane preselected the canonical passages that best suit his own purposes; he was no exegete obliged to follow any given Buddhist denominational system, working with a given set of scriptural materials.

Despite these limitations, the *Mocking Discourse* ambitiously attempts to sketch the whole sweep of Buddhist history in Atsutane's eyes, starting from the wretched Indian homeland of its birth and proceeding finally to the lamentable ascendency of the corrupt Buddhist clergy in his own day, and their hateful monopoly over the practice of funerals. The basic operation of the *Mocking Discourse* is comparison, involving Atsutane's juxtaposition of one Buddhist text against another, or (again, following Nakamoto) Atsutane's comparison between the material in a Buddhist text and his "common sense." In simple prose strongly influenced by the oral vernacular of the late Edo raconteur, the *Mocking Discourse* begins with a description of India, drawn largely from the writings of Xuanzang (602–64). It moves on to discuss the entirety of the Buddha's life at length, before surveying the creation and contents of the Buddhist canon and proceeding to the movement of Buddhism from India through China and to Japan. It ends with a long denunciation of Buddhism in its Japanese form. To this completed book Atsutane added an appendix—which often circulated independently of the main body—with additional condemnations of two large and powerful movements within early modern Japanese Buddhism: the True Pure Land and Nichiren denominations.

Broadly construed, Atsutane's narrative of the Buddha's life begins with the arising of the world and ends with the compilation of the canon, thus spanning most of the first two of the three volumes of the *Mocking Discourse*. As promised in the introduction, the *Mocking Discourse* does cite Buddhist texts in support of Atsutane's critique of the canonical biographies of the Buddha, invoking texts (such as the Āgamas) that had long suffered neglect in Japan. Like his predecessor Jiun Onkō, Atsutane had limited access to Indic languages; while he sometimes offers glosses or etymologies for Sanskrit words, he seems not to have used any sources in Indic languages himself. Nor did Atsutane limit his attention to texts linked to the mainstream Buddhist traditions.

The *Sutra on the Ocean-Like Samādhi of the Visualization of the Buddha*, for instance, includes esoteric elements out of place in mainstream Buddhism, and the sutra's purported author, Nāgārjuna, was a critic of certain elements in mainstream Buddhism as well. Atsutane read these texts through a rather highly developed interpretive hermeneutic and did not cite them all for the same purpose. The unusual citation of the esoteric *Visualization of the Buddha*, for instance, is solely for the purpose of ridiculing its narrative. Nāgārjuna's commentary is valuable to Atsutane because it represents for him the rationale for the use of magical displays in Buddhism.

It is difficult to overstate the importance of this shift in the object of critique, which assumes no internally coherent message and looks instead to the question of medium. Unlike his predecessors, Atsutane did not begin by assuming Buddhism to be a coherent entity, laid out by the Buddha and subject to various later doctrinal and philosophical elaborations. Rather, following Nakamoto, Atsutane found that discarding the presumption of coherence, like picking out a thread holding together a worn sweater, could trigger the unraveling of the entire system. And true to his promise, in the *Mocking Discourse*, he largely refrained from direct citation of proof texts outside the Buddhist canon while citing, by title, an impressive array of texts from the Chinese canon. To name a few: Atsutane identified the *Dīrghāgama* as the source for his discussion of the Buddhist tale of the origin of the world; the *Sutra of Past and Present Cause and Effect* and the *Buddhacarita* as sources for the month and date of the birth of the Buddha; the **Upāyakauśalyanāmamahȳānasūtra* as a source for rationalizations explaining the death of Māyā and the justification of the marriage of Śākyamuni; the *Sutra on the Ocean-Like Samādhi of the Visualization of the Buddha* for some absurd consequences of that justification; the *Sutra of the Five Dreams of the Buddha as Bodhisattva*, the **Dvādaśa-varṣa-viharaṇa-sūtra*, and the

Sutra on the Past Activities of the Buddha in support of his contention that Śākyamuni had three wives and three children; Nāgārjuna's *Treatise on the Great Perfection of Wisdom*, concerning the performance of miracles by bodhisattvas; and the *Sutra on the Favorable Circumstances for the Awakening of the Prince* as a source for a catalog of the Buddha's miraculous powers.

We cannot, of course, take this list of titles at face value. Like his predecessor Nakamoto—from whose work he cribbed or otherwise adapted a number of passages—Atsutane also made copious use of encyclopedic compendia of scriptural excerpts produced in China, such as the *Pearl Grove of the Dharma Garden* (*Fayuan zhulin*, *T* 2122, compiled in 668). But as had been the case with Nakamoto, to decry Atsutane's scholarship for its mistaken citations—on the assumption that his argument would not stand had he cited all his sources to our exacting standards—is really to miss the creative thrust of his argument. As the discussion of Nakamoto in *Of Heretics and Martyrs* put it, "Comments of this sort merely served to illustrate [the] argument all the more."[45]

By following Nakamoto's use of the comparativist method, Atsutane distantly anticipated some aspects of the modern Buddhist studies born in Europe, a discipline long preoccupied with uncovering older texts, and long suspicious of the demonstrably late emergence of the texts of the Mahāyāna. For his part, Atsutane explicitly endorsed Hattori Tenyū's disdain for the Mahāyāna scriptures and Tenyū's comparatively higher evaluation of the Hīnayāna. Indeed, the critique of Buddhism that Atsutane inherited from Nakamoto and Tenyū has typically been encapsulated in Japanese secondary scholarship as the "argument that the Mahāyāna was not spoken by the Buddha" (Jpn. *Daijō hi-bussetsu ron*).

This formulation is not incorrect, but Atsutane notably insisted that even the so-called Hīnayāna sutras were produced long after the *parinirvāṇa* of the Buddha—a position still widely accepted by scholars of Buddhism today. Adducing the *Treatise on the Great Perfection of Wisdom* Ch. *Dazhi dulun*; Skt. **Mahā-prajñāpāramitā-śāstra* and the preface to the *Great Exegesis* (Ch. *Apidamo dapiposha lun*; Skt. *Abhidharmamahāribhāṣā*), Atsutane contended that the canon of the Mūlasarvastivādins was produced some four hundred years after the death of the Buddha, at an assembly of monks sponsored by the king of Gandhāra.[46] Atstuane thus self-consciously broke with the pious tradition according to which the disciple Ānanda, having heard all the Buddha's teachings, recited them back at the monastic assembly at which the Tripiṭaka was first assembled—a scene placed at the end of a number of biographical accounts for the Buddha. How, Atsutane asked, could Ānanda possibly have heard all of the Buddha's teachings if he was born only on the night of the Buddha's awakening? Atsutane rejected the various efforts to account for the twenty years of preaching that he missed: that Ānanda had heard from other people; that the Buddha had repeated them for him; that gods had repeated them to him; that the Buddha had emerged from his coffin to recite to him; that he had heard them in meditation, and so on.

Merely demonstrating scriptural contradiction rooted in conflicting historical situations (such as the conflict between adherents of different schools of Buddhist practice, with devotion to different textual traditions), and thus refuting the claims made by Buddhist texts, did not suffice for Atsutane. At the end of his discussion of Śākyamuni's Four Encounters, he wrote,

> All of the Buddhist sutras were written down, their lies intact, in the generations long after Śākyamuni died; therefore, they [basically] have no truth, but within them are interspersed some true facts. Those facts are unmoving, when the reader thinks well of the context and chews over it. The lies of the writings can be recognized when the reader picks out these unmoving facts and considers them to be standards [for evaluating the text]. The best way to read all of the Buddhist sutras is to put one's mind to using one or two facts to reflect upon the fabricated accounts, and to use the fabricated accounts to learn the facts. Unless one does so, one will be misled.[47]

Thus, even as he employed a basically comparativist method, Atsutane did not limit his interest solely to the inconsistencies among various Buddhist texts. Rather, he presumed that a core of "unmoving" truth undergirds even some of the "lies" of the Buddhist canon. Here Atsutane suggested that patient scrutiny of the Buddhist texts, then, would have something to offer even the nativist opponents of Buddhism.

What Atsutane regarded as "true," or even plausible, though, hardly agrees with post-Enlightenment sensibilities about "truth." Although Atsutane ultimately rejected the tradition by which the Buddha was born from his mother's right side, he did not summarily dismiss the possibility of that mode of birth. "Narrow-minded Confucianists and the like might complain about this [account of the birth] and cast doubt on it without even inquiring into its reason, but seen from a tolerant mind that embraces the Ancient Learning, this [mode of birth] is not impossible."[48] Elsewhere in the text, Atsutane decried the role played by superhuman powers (Jpn. *jinzū*, Skt. *abhijñā*) in the commentative and scriptural accounts of the life of the Buddha. After citing a long passage on the topic from the *Treatise on the Great Perfection of Wisdom,* Atsutane reframed it in an unbecoming mode: "One should reflect well on this. It's no different from the technique for illusion in a great feat of [stage] magic."[49] And after recounting the claim of the Buddha's ability to teleport his body, to split into a thousand or a million bodies, to pass through earth and stone, to tread on water or the empty space, and so forth, Atsutane noted acidly:

> This thing called "superhuman powers" seems, as the *Treatise on the Great Perfection of Wisdom* says, to be something that develops when one mortifies the body in meditation and trains well. Here is my attempt to explain why it develops: In the deep mountains and dark valleys, where people do not venture, there are many creatures, such as the evil spirits of the land and water, or the *tengu* hobgoblins. Thus, it appears that, as the Buddha was training [in the peaks and valleys], he wound up consorting closely with these things, and finally came to control them.[50]

But even this accomplishment, Atsutane continued, was no real feat; celebrated clerics from Japanese history had done more or less the same thing from antiquity onward, befriending tigers, and making servants of demons, or foxes, or the spirits of the dead. Throughout the *Mocking Discourse,* Atsutane doggedly insisted that Śākyamuni was no enlightened sage, but merely an "ordinary person" or a "worldling" (Jpn. *bonjin, bonbu;* Skt. *pṛthagjana*). We might characterize Atsutane's attitude as a tenacious form of philosophical naturalism, but only on the condition of recognizing that his perspective on "the natural" presupposed the real existence of spirits, hobgoblins, and magical displays.[51]

However such powers could be obtained, Atsutane did not tire of reminding his audiences of their vulgarity. As we have already seen from the summary of the *Sutra of Past and Present Cause and Effect,* some scriptures claim that after the Buddha's awakening, his former ascetic companions rose to greet him, in spite of their own best efforts to shun him. They asked to become his disciples, and when the Buddha approved and told them to follow him, their hair and beards instantly fell off of their own accord, and robes instantly appeared on their bodies. Commenting on this use of the Buddha's powers, Atsutane likened the ascetics' transformation to a stage technique popular in the *kabuki* theater of his own day: "Why, this is just like the feeling that one has when watching a quick change on stage by [the actor] Onoe Shōroku [1744–1815]! What a trick!"[52] Atsutane thus demoted the Buddha's superhuman powers to the stunts of a mere stage entertainer.

Atsutane's *Mocking Discourse*: Demythologizing the Buddha

As the previous examples show, when the *Mocking Discourse* tackles the story of the life of the Buddha, it does so in a caustically ungenerous mode, attempting throughout to expose the "truth" underlying the events of the life of Śākyamuni. Like Kōgetsu's roughly contemporaneous project, Atsutane's biography of the Buddha starts with the creation of the universe, as related in the *Dīrghāgama*. This famous story tells of the first sentient beings, whose unhampered greed plunged them into a protracted fall from grace. As they transgressed again and again, their heavenly bodies lost their radiance and their ability to fly, and their bodies began to suffer from the new burdens of gender distinction, property, and caste stratification. Atsutane's version of this story takes a skeptical slant. Discussing these beings' original consumption not of human food but of "joy," Atsutane challenged its plausibility: "How could they have eaten joy? It's the same as the eating of dreams by that beast called a *baku*," a mythical monster known from Chinese sources, and a fixture of early modern Japanese folklore.

In the end, the *Dīrghāgama* account concludes, these first beings declined so precipitously, and their struggles over property intensified so furiously, that they had to elect the first kings to keep the peace. Following the *Dīrghāgama* account, Atsutane traced the descent of these kings, through the rise of the Śākya clan from the progeny of King Ikṣvāku, down to the life of the Buddha's own father, King Śuddhodana. Perhaps to suggest that the conventional tale of Māyā's divine pregnancy was beneath contempt, Atsutane here skipped it to launch directly into a discussion of the birth of the prince. While allowing for the possibility that the Buddha really was born from his mother's side, Atsutane instead decided to dismiss the unusual events found in the accounts of the Buddha's birth as later textual accretions. These include the traditions of his miraculous speech at birth and the worship of him by the image of Brahmā to which he was presented. Of the death of Lady Māyā seven days after the birth, Atsutane wrote: "It is a lie to say that he was born from her side, but in any case, she died from an extraordinarily difficult delivery."[53] As we have already seen, this is a possibility presented in the puppet theater and denied in previous apologetic accounts of the life of the Buddha. For Atsutane, though, this tale is a means by which to reconcile the story of the strange mode of birth with the rapid decline and death of his mother.

Atsutane likewise dismissed the accounts of the young Siddhārtha's prodigal intelligence and the scriptural accounts of the transformation of the god from the Heaven of the Pure Abode into the four men—aged, sick, dead, and renunciant—whom the prince encountered on his trips outside his father's palace. How, asked Atsutane in a matter-of-fact way, could a young prince have mastered all the academic disciplines of his day, besting all his teachers, and yet not know about the phenomena of sickness, old age, and death? Why should the gods have even needed to raise in him the aspiration to awakening? Hadn't the bodhisattva intended from the time he was reborn in the Tuṣita heaven to become a Buddha? Hadn't he instructed the gods while in his mother's womb, and announced his intention immediately after his birth? Such scornful observations recur in Atsutane's *Mocking Discourse* whenever the gods intervene in the life of the prince. For instance, Atsutane flatly dismissed the tradition according to which a god instructed a cowherd girl to feed the Buddha-to-be when he had starved himself to the brink of death. "If the gods had been tagging along with him so closely," he wrote, "then they would never have made Siddhārtha do all those foolish things."[54] Such elaborations are all later inventions, Atsutane claimed, to conceal the truth: the Buddha was, from start to finish, merely a worldling who never attained awakening.

Atsutane's insistence on the this-worldly character of Śākyamuni extended, of course, to his family life. Railing against the "twisted minds of later followers of the Buddha, which commit evil partiality," Atsutane held that a range of sutras proved that the Buddha *actually* had *three* consorts and *three* children.[55] Further, Atsutane dismissed irenic claims that some of these variant names refer to the same wife. According to his calculations, the third child, Sunákṣatra, must have been conceived after the departure of the prince from the palace, proving, at least to Atsutane's satisfaction, that after the Great Departure, the prince must have later returned to the palace to impregnate his third wife. So much, then, for his renunciation.

There is, of course, the problem of why a bodhisattva would ever marry and have sexual congress in the first place. Taking a cue from Nakamoto, Atsutane heaped scorn on ways in which canonical literature explains away the apparent presence of sexual desire in a bodhisattva—including the claim, for instance, that the prince-bodhisattva had no sexual desire of his own, but rather took consorts in order to prove to the world that he was no eunuch but had a working penis. Evidently drawn by the discussion of this topic in the *Sutra on the Ocean-Like Samādhi of the Visualization of the Buddha*—which he probably derived from the Chinese scriptural synopses in the *Pearl Grove of the Dharma*

Garden—Atsutane offered an unusually long quotation of its Chinese text in his *Mocking Discourse*. As this quotation begins, one of the female attendants of the bodhisattva-prince Siddhārtha complains that, despite having served him for eighteen years, she has never even seen his penis, much less observed him having intercourse. All the female attendants then start to crow that the prince is not, in fact, a man at all. As the sutra claims, one afternoon, while taking a nap, the prince let his robe slip open to reveal his genitals.

At that time, the prince made a white lotus flower appear from his penis. Two or three flowers, red and white, clustered above and below it. Having seen them, the ladies again said: "Thus this divine man has the mark of the lotus. How can his mind have defilement?" When they had said that, they sobbed and could not speak. At that time, within the flower there suddenly appeared a penis in the shape of a boy. The ladies saw that and spoke further to one another: "Now the prince will manifest a wonder." The penis that had suddenly appeared [now grew into] a shape like an adult man. When the women saw this, they could not contain their joy at his manifestation of this mark. Then the mother of Rāhula [i.e., Yaśodharā] saw his penis, flowers clustered on it like a heavenly cotton tree, on top of each numberless great bodhisattvas holding white flowers, surrounding that penis, appearing and disappearing.[56]

Atsutane's evaluation of this tale is curt and dismissive: "The priests who came after [the Buddha] . . . were surely trying to cover for Śākyamuni, but this is what is known as 'pulling so hard for someone that you pull him down' (*hiiki no hikidaoshi*)." In other words, here Atsutane argued that contradiction between the Buddha's bodhisattva nature and his life as a householder had the paradoxical effect of making that story even more improbable; as Atsutane caustically observed earlier in this discussion, "These are all lies of the sort that we popularly call 'hiding your head but not your ass.'"[57] As metaphorical ostriches, we might say, the biographical accounts in the Buddhist canon are fooling only themselves. In his survey of the biographical literature, Atsutane cited few passages with such a distinctly Mahāyāna (or even Vajrayāna) character, but this text is clearly not one from which he hopes to extract any truth; rather, its citation exposes the absurd results of retroactive efforts to "cover for Śākyamuni." It is, in short, the true face of any biography that does not treat the Buddha as just another human being.

Atsutane made an equally scathing evaluation of Siddhārtha's practice, holding that the prince punished himself trying to escape from samsara, only ultimately to realize that the cycle of birth, death, and rebirth is not the sort of thing from which anyone could ever escape. For his part, Atsutane assumed that the creator deity Musubi no Ōkami divinely ordained birth, old age, disease, and death; therefore, he wrote, "No matter how much one runs around, rushing to discard these things and to brush them away, these four . . . will not be shaken off."[58] Traditionally, of course, the prince adduces a different motive for ending his grueling asceticism and taking nourishment: "If I were to take this worn-out body and then achieve the Way, then those heretics would surely say, 'His starving himself is the cause of his nirvana!' I should accept food, and only then attain the Way." After citing this passage in its Chinese version, Atsutane offered his own vernacular gloss, beginning with a disclaimer about the evident weightiness of its concerns: "In order not to be overawed by this sort of thing, those who read the Buddhist scriptures should think through their context well, and take the meaning without becoming entangled in the rhetoric." The reference to "nirvana" here, for instance, should, he says, be read for its real meaning: death. In his vernacular gloss of this passage, Atsutane re-represents the Buddha's plan after his acceptance of food thus: "He thought, 'After first eating and gaining some strength, I should abandon my asceticism, and announce myself as having attained the Way of liberation from samsara." At such deception, Atsutane, perhaps predictably, expressed outrage: "Could there ever be such a Buddha? How hateful. He had only to admit that when he didn't eat, he grew uncontrollably hungry, and that he could not find liberation from samsara."[59] Atsutane had equal disregard for the traditions of the Buddha's struggle against and victory over Māra: "And even apart from these, there are abundant falsehoods, all spoken to give Śākyamuni weight. There is not one worth taking up."[60]

Atsutane illustrates the preaching of the "Buddha" (to whom he continues to refer as merely "Shaka," the abbreviation for "Śākyamuni") as dominated by the Buddha's theft and reworking of Brahmanical doctrines, on the one hand, and by the Buddha's relentless bullying of his disciples and family, on the other. The Buddha's posturing as an awakened being, preaching of the Four Truths for Noble People and the Twelvefold Chain of Dependent Origination, display of superhuman powers, and teaching of impermanence were all techniques with which to "subdue" (*kuppuku*) the five ascetics who formerly were his colleagues. His teachings about reincarnation, the heavens and the hells, and the rewards and punishments for human activities were similarly intended to frighten his audience into believing him. Taking advantage of the belief in Brahmanism among the people, the Buddha used his magic to make it seem that the Brahmanical gods paid him reverence. What is worse, the Buddha had no choice but to crib his major doctrines—of "heaven and hell, karmic retribution, and regulation of the mind"—from his rivals. Citing Nāgārjuna's *Treatise on the Great Perfection of Wisdom,* Atsutane pointed out that, of course, "people with sense" attacked the Buddha, accusing him as follows: "The Buddha's wisdom does not emerge from his person; he merely uses his magic to confuse the world."[61] As Atsutane wrote, the Buddha replied by denouncing everyone who came before him as "heretics."[62] The displays put on by the Buddha to convert Uruvilvā Kāśyapa and his disciples—such as his extinguishing their sacred fire, his manifestation of Brahmā, or his trick of dividing his own body into countless numbers of copies—were actually nothing more than fox magic.

Atsutane gleefully denounced the Buddha's treatment of the members of his own clan. When the Buddha returned to Kapilavastu, Atsutane observed, he not only made his father, King Śuddhodana, worship his feet, in a most unfilial manner; he also cruelly demanded that all his relatives become his disciples. Atsutane finds particular pathos in the case of the Buddha's half-brother, Nanda. The Buddha tricked Nanda into accepting a begging bowl and hence compelled him to become a monk. When Nanda refused to ordain and tried to go home, Atsutane insisted, he was bullied until he gave in: "The Buddha used his majestic powers to compel Nanda to renounce home, shutting him up in a silent chamber." And again, Atsutane quoted from a different text: "The Buddha forthwith commanded the barber to shave Nanda's hair, but Nanda would not consent, and shouted at the barber, 'Must you shave the head of everyone in Kapilavastu?'"[63] Even after Nanda lost his hair and entered the sangha, he still tried to go home, and hid from the Buddha in the shade of a tree. Unwilling to let Nanda go, the Buddha used his powers to rip the tree up by its roots. Only when the Buddha took Nanda to heaven and to hell did he succeed in cajoling and frightening Nanda into complete submission. Atsutane similarly related the tale of Rāhula's ordination: his mother, Yaśodharā, was unwilling to part with him, and could not be persuaded by Maudgalyayana or Mahāprajāpatī. Atsutane put in her mouth a litany of complaints: Why did the prince marry me, only to abandon his home? It is proper to leave an heir for the world, but now the prince has gone, and he wants even Rāhula to become a monk, too, which will cut off the royal line.

What kind of justice is that? Atsutane had the king repeat her lamentation: "The scriptures even say: 'King Śuddhodana lamented to the Buddha: "At this rate, my country will be extinguished forever!"'"[64]

It should come as no surprise that Atsutane had no patience for the received accounts of the Buddha's *parinirvāṇa*. For him, the Buddha's death was by no means deliberate, nor was it a mere display of dying, as an expedient means; rather, the Buddha simply died of eating spoiled food, suffering from food poisoning all along. Atsutane took particular umbrage at the scriptural accounts that have the Buddha maintain that the donor Cunda actually earned merit by offering the final mushroom dish—as much merit as that obtained by the cowherd girl who offered milk gruel at the end of the asceticism by the prince. This Atsutane dismissed as preposterous: "There could be no merit in feeding someone poison and killing him."[65] To Atsutane, the Buddha's issuing of such outrageous pronouncements signaled only that he was a "poor loser," unwilling to admit when he has been beaten. It may be less the Buddha's falsities than his affectations that offend Atsutane.

Dispensing entirely with the traditional stories of the final moments of the Buddha, Atsutane focused instead on the traditions surrounding the fate of his body after his death. According to the scriptural tradition in the *Sutra on the Ocean-Like Samādhi of the Visualization of the Buddha*, when the Buddha was on the verge of death, he issued forth a golden radiance, but only some people—those with faith—could see it; those who doubted the Buddha beheld merely "a thin, ashen Brahmin." Atsutane accepted the story but inverted the values it carries. The Buddha's golden form was visible only, Atsutane speculated, to *deluded* mourners, or perhaps, he conceded, the radiance appeared erratically because the Buddha had aged and his superhuman powers had faded accordingly. Other episodes within the narrative of the death of the Buddha similarly inflamed Atsutane's ire. The claim that the Buddha provisionally manifested his death as an expedient display for his disciples was, Atsutane wrote, just another case of "pulling so hard for someone that you pull him down." Why, asked Atsutane, should the Buddha's disciple Mahākāśyapa have been late to the Buddha's extinction in the first place? When the Buddha entered *parinirvāṇa*, hadn't he emitted light and sound that could be observed in all the heavens and all the hells? Wouldn't Mahākāśyapa have seen these signs? And why didn't Mahākāśyapa fly back at once, using his superhuman powers, rather than walk? While Atsutane cast doubt on these parts of the death account, he cited without any apparent skepticism a "bizarre thing" done to the Buddha's body by Ānanda, according to Nāgārjuna's

Treatise on the Great Perfection of Wisdom: Ānanda displayed the Buddha's penis to the women in attendance on him, to cause them to despise their female forms and aspire to rebirth as men.[66] Gleefully, Atsutane gloated, this strange behavior later became one cause for Ānanda's disciplining by Mahākāśyapa, which was rescinded only when Ānanda belatedly achieved the status of an arhat.

The Life Story of the Buddha as Residue

In part because it circulated widely in both manuscript editions and moveable type editions, Atsutane's *Mocking Discourse upon Emerging from Meditation* stood as his most influential public statement about Buddhism—particularly its extremely popular and widely reproduced appendix, "Concerning Two Buddhist Denominations, Enemies of the Gods." By contrast, Atsutane's much longer *Compendium of Indian Records* did not see print until well into the twentieth century, and its manuscript editions in circulation late in the Edo period often included only two volumes, encompassing the "Chapter on the Legends of the Land of India" ("Indo denzū bon"). These seem to be the only volumes to be released in fair copy during Atsutane's lifetime. Further, unlike certain other works that Atsutane left unfinished at his death, the *Compendium* was not completed by his disciples. On the face of it, then, the *Compendium* might appear to be a mere footnote to the *Mocking Discourse.*

In a way, the *Compendium* actually *is* a footnote—one long, extended footnote to the earlier *Mocking Discourse*. Seeing that much of its material overlaps with the material covered in the *Mocking Discourse*, scholars have hypothesized that it represents an effort to record documentary evidence in support of the case that Atsutane makes in the *Mocking Discourse*. But the differences between the two texts are jarring. While Atsutane's *Mocking Discourse* intersperses citations from scriptures among a diatribe in the vernacular, his *Compendium* embeds his own commentary within an immense volume of citations, principally from Buddhist sources. In the *Mocking Discourse*, Atsutane made fewer direct quotations from Chinese-language texts, and he typically glosses these in vernacular Japanese. On the contrary, the vernacular passages in the *Compendium* represent Atsutane's commentary on the Chinese-language passages at hand, offering at best an explanation of some of the proper nouns or technical terms in the Chinese, in whose support Atsutane sometimes cited the dictionary he used. There is, again, the difference in length between the two works: in its twentieth-century print addition, and including its appendix, the *Mocking Discourse* weighs in at some 227 pages. By contrast, the *Compendium* sprawls across some 571 pages—including its section of unfinished *Drafts*—itself a misleading figure, since so much of its commentative text is parenthetical, meaning that it is printed in a smaller point size than that used for the *Mocking Discourse*.

Thus, although these two works overlap considerably in their treatment of material, these differences in form and volume imply a stark difference in Atsutane's purpose for writing each. In the *Compendium*, a highly technical work of scholarship, Atsutane's goal is no longer simply to disabuse his audience of its ignorance regarding the truth about the deviousness and falsity of Buddhism. As multiple commentators have observed, the *Compendium* instead represents Atsutane's positive effort to extract truth from the tissue of lies of which, he charges, the Buddhist canon is mostly comprised. This difference is apparent in the attitude expressed by the text toward the sources it invokes. The citations of the *Mocking Discourse* are often followed by words of outright dismissal, whereas the citations of the *Compendium* tend to feed into explanations of the rationale for their selection.

Although the *Compendium* is incomplete, its projected structure would likely have loosely paralleled that of the *Mocking Discourse*, beginning with Indian accounts of the creation of the world and ending with the transmission of Buddhism from India, through China, to Japan. Multiple catalogs of Atsutane's writing differ on the number of volumes projected for the *Compendium*, one claiming thirty, the other twenty-five. Even if we accept the smaller estimate (as is conventional today), only eleven of those volumes are extant in a nearly final form, including the two in circulation during the Edo period. Available today are volumes 1 through 8, and then 20 through 23. Apart from those eleven volumes, the body of surviving *Compendium* material also includes *Drafts for a Compendium of Indian Records* (*Indō zōshi kō*), surviving in four long volumes. Later scholarship has postulated that the material in these would probably have belonged among the missing volumes, numbers 9 through 20. It is in the volumes of the *Drafts* that we find Atsutane's account of the life of the Buddha, told principally through quotations from canonical Chinese texts. However, in their existing form, the books are not all in any obvious order, and the quality and quantity of Atsutane's notes and annotation vary considerably.

The sections within the volumes of the *Drafts* that treat the life of

Śākyamuni are arranged as follows, including the chapter themes and numbers as Atsutane's manuscript records them:

VOLUME 1.

The destruction and arising of the world. Chapter 3.

The fundamental account of the arising of the world. Chapter 4.

The worldly lineage of the Buddha. Chapter 5.

The birth and rearing of the Buddha[-to-be]. Chapter 6.

The education and marriage [of the prince]. Chapter 7.

VOLUME 2.

The raising of the aspiration to awakening and the renunciation [of the prince]. Chapter 8.

The pursuit of the Way and the practice after the abandonment of asceticism [of the prince]. Chapter 9.

Chapter concerning the [creation of] images of the Buddha. [Unnumbered chapter.]

The three great calamities [at the end of the world cycle]. [Unnumbered chapter.]

The ancestry of the Gautama clan. [Unnumbered chapter.]

The sermon at the Deer Park. [Unnumbered chapter.]

VOLUME 3.

The *Sutra of the Great Foundation*. [Unnumbered chapter. Excerpts from the first volume of the *Dīrghāgama*, concerning the previous career of the first Buddha Vipaśyin (Pāli, Vipassī). Corresponds to parts of the *Mahāpadāna Sutta* (*The Sublime Story*) of the Pāli *Dīgha Nikāya*. Ends with Atsutane's note to himself: "Text above transcribes the account of the Buddha Vipaśyin. Almost useless as it is. To be considered carefully."]

[Untitled and unnumbered excerpts from the second through fourth volumes of the *Dīrghāgama*, concerning the final preaching of the Buddha, the events of his *parinirvāṇa*, and the division and enshrinement of his relics. Corresponds to parts of the *Mahāparinibbāna Suttanta* (*The Book of the Great Decease*) of the Pāli *Dīgha Nikāya*.]

As the preceding outline suggests, the volumes of the *Drafts* generally decline in degree of completion from the first through the last; each volume includes blank spaces, which Atsutane apparently intended to fill once he had access to the appropriate reference sources.

Within the *Compendium* proper, the more complete chapters also cite a wide number of sources. Investigating the texts invoked within the first three-volume chapter of the *Compendium*, "The Customs of the Land of India" ("Indo kokuzoku bon"), Kanno Hiroshi found that it adduced the following sources by title: forty-one Chinese-language sutras (Jpn. *kyō*), discounting overlap; three Chinese-language works of the monastic discipline, or *vinaya* (Jpn. *ritsu*); seventeen Chinese-language commentaries, or *śāstras* (Jpn. *ron*), originally composed outside of China; and a whopping forty-seven works composed in China.[67] From Kanno's list, it is clear that Atsutane wrote this section while relying extensively upon the *Dīrghāgama*, the *Ekottara Āgama*, the *Abhidharma-kośa* (attributed to Vasubandhu), the *Treatise on the Great Perfection of Wisdom* (attributed to Nāgārjuna), the *Treatise in One Hundred Verses* (attributed to Āryadeva) and its commentary, the *Collection of Terms and Definitions Used in Translation* (*Fanyi mingyi ji*, *T* 2131, compiled in 1143), and the records of journeys to India by the Chinese monks Xuanzang and Yijing (635–713).

As is the case with the *Compendium* as a whole, we cannot speak with assurance about the projected final form of the *Drafts*, but it is possible to make some educated guesses. The first volume of the *Drafts* is relatively polished, compared with the third and fourth volumes, but even it is evidently not yet in fair copy. Nonetheless, it follows the same basic pattern as the completed portions of the *Compendium of Indian Records*: (1) citation of a passage from one or more Buddhist sources in Chinese (typically, but not always, from sutras), followed by (2) citation of parallel or related passages from other sources, and/or (3) Atsutane's notes concerning the source(s) in question. To take one extended example: Atsutane's discussion of the birth and rearing of the Buddha-to-be suggests in capsule form how the *Drafts* differ from the *Mocking Discourse*. As with almost all sections in this work, it begins with quotations from Chinese-language Buddhist scriptures—here, citation from multiple texts:

> At that time, King Śuddhodana forthwith equipped his fourfold army, and escorted by one hundred million Śākyas, he entered the garden. Arriving at the place of the Lady [Māyā], he saw the wondrous signs on the body of the prince, and danced for joy. He joined his palms and made obeisance to the gods of heaven, and he advanced to hold the prince. Placing the prince in a jeweled palanquin, he took the prince into the palace. At that time, King Śuddhodana and the Śākya clan did not yet know of the Three Treasures. They took the prince to pray at a shrine to the gods, and then they returned to the residence of his consort. A full seven days after the birth of the prince, the life of his mother ended. Then his aunt Mahāprajāpatī suckled and cared for the prince, just like a mother. The Brahmins and soothsayers all proclaimed, "Hurrah!" Thus the prince was named Siddhārtha.[68]

Atsutane followed this quotation in Chinese immediately with a long annotation in Japanese, beginning with a summary of the sources he used: "This passage is based on the *Sutra of Past and Present Cause and Effect,* though I have also checked it against the *Avadāna of the Auspicious* [*Deeds*] *of the Prince* and other scriptures." This claim is not inaccurate, though as had been the case for his *Mocking Discourse,* Atsutane again relied for his paraphrases on the compendium of scriptural excerpts, the *Pearl Grove of the Dharma Garden,* of which he made liberal use.

Next, Atsutane offered notes concerning individual items in the passage that he cited. Atsutane's annotations in the *Drafts* and in the relatively polished *Compendium of Indian Records* are themselves composed in large part of citation or paraphrase from scriptural texts, interspersed with Atsutane's own words. These he often put in *warigaki* interlinear notes in smaller script, which in the following translation are rendered with parentheses.

> Well, I have already explained the fourfold army. (See my first chapter.) The reference to "one hundred million Śākyas" is too much. (All the Buddhist books give such exaggerated numbers that they have the contrary effect of losing touch with reality and often cause people to doubt even the facts. In China, too, there is the habit of exaggeration, but compared to India, they rarely lose touch with reality.) As for joining the palms, this is a basic kind of courtesy in India, and the reference to praying to the various gods is also the ancient custom of that land. The shrine mentioned in the phrase "King Śuddhodana and the Śākya clan did not yet know of the Three Treasures and went to pray at a shrine" is a shrine to Brahmā. This is another ancient custom of that land.[69]

As in the *Mocking Discourse,* but in a much more pronounced way, Atsutane here was in no small part interested in establishing the nature of the "ancient customs" of India—at least, to the extent possible using sources available to him within the literature of Chinese Buddhism. Again, as in the *Mocking Discourse,* Atsutane sometimes offered critical comments concerning the passage that he has reconstructed: witness his contemptuous dismissal of the Indians and their love of exaggeration.

More commonly, though, Atsutane offered critical remarks not about the "plausible" reconstruction, but about what he had chosen to exclude. One of the terms that Atsutane consistently excluded throughout his writings about the Buddha is the most common of the

Buddha's standard honorifics in East Asia, "The World-Honored One" (Jpn. Shakuson). For this, Atsutane substitutes the sneering phrase "the Buddha-ancestor" (Busso):

There is also the passage: "Then the image of Brahmā stood up from its seat and did obeisance to the feet of the prince, saying to the king, 'This prince is honored among gods and men, and the gods throughout space all do him honor; how could you come here and make him reverence me?'" This is the usual fabrication. (The *Sutra of the Display of the Deeds of the Buddha* even says, "The prince arrived at the shrine and spoke *gathas*, saying . . ." And: "The images of the gods manifested their original forms and did reverence to the feet of the bodhisattva. Then before him, they spoke *gathas*, saying. . . .") Next, there is the reference to the life of the mother of the "Buddha-ancestor" ending seven days after his birth; this is because it was a terribly difficult labor. A variant account in the *Sutra of the Authentic Deeds of the Buddha* even says, "The Sarvāstivādins say, 'His mother saw how wondrous was her newborn, and at once her life ended.'" (In order not to blame the Buddha for the death of the Lady Māyā, the sutras and commentaries say: "In the beginning the Buddha was in the Tuṣita heaven. When he contemplated the time, place, and rank [of candidate mothers], he observed the date on which the Lady Māyā was to die. Since the woman was fated to die on a certain day, [he reasoned,] if she gave birth to the Buddha, then through that merit, she would inevitably be born in the Trāyastriṃśa heaven, so he entered her womb; this is the meritorious expedient means of the bodhisattva." Such passages were all the sales pitches of later generations of apologists, built up to disguise the fault of the Buddha [in causing the death of his mother].) "Mahāprajāpatī" is the woman named above as "Great Lover of the Path." As she is the younger sister of Māyā, she is really the aunt of the Buddha, and the mother of Nanda. (See below for details concerning this mother and child.) Among the various wonders that the sutras narrate at the time of the birth of the Buddha are such as these: In eight lands, each king had a son; throughout the land, eighty thousand rich men each had a child, all sons. The various Śākyas, too, gave birth to five hundred sons on the same day, and even the animals each bore offspring, all male. Five thousand serving-women gave birth to five thousand strong men, and so on. Even among the fabricated accounts, these are the stupidest, most delusional explanations. (But it would seem that this is only how outsiders [to Buddhism] see it, while insiders run here and there declaring that these [miracles] are the finest thing ever.)[70]

As in the *Mocking Discourse*, here too Atsutane poured vitriol upon the Buddhist scriptures, and he again argued that the real reason for Māyā's early death was not her preordained rebirth in the heavens on a certain day, but the extraordinarily difficult labor she endured. What distinguishes this passage from its parallel in the *Mocking Discourse* is the position of these comments. For Atsutane was here not merely criticizing everything he cited from the Buddhist scriptures, as in his earlier work; instead, he was specifically noting and discussing those passages that he *decided not to cite* in his reconstruction.[71] In other words, Atsutane was here explaining why he had excluded certain elements from the narrative. By implication, then, the major quotation with which this section began ("At that time, King Śuddhodana forthwith equipped his fourfold army . . .") represents what remains when the outrageous falsities are detected and extracted. With Atsutane's vitriol now contained in the notes, that which remains—the root surviving the critical storm after it had blown away the leaves and branches, as it were—was nothing less than Atsutane's biography of the Buddha.

That biography exists only in fragments, but enough survives that it is possible to sketch elements from it. Atsutane apparently planned to treat the life of the Buddha comprehensively, as his citation and commentary for *Drafts for a Compendium of Indian Records* range from the tales of the cyclical development and devolution of the universe, through the Buddha's *parinirvāṇa*, cremation, and enshrinement. In his discussion of Buddhist cosmological origins, Atsutane was at pains to uncover the "truth" about Brahmā, whom Atsutane firmly held to be a disguised version of the Japanese deity Musubi-no-kami. Excoriating the Buddha for defaming Brahmā and the other Indian deities as unable to create the world, Atsutane set about attacking the denial of an omnipotent creator god as he found it in the *Dīrghāgama* and the *Twelve Gate Treatise*. Here Atsutane rehearsed and rejected the arguments in the *Treatise* for the impossibility of an omnipotent god who is self-created, who permits evil, who does not enjoy universal reverence, who made some fortunate and some not, who would monopolize a position to which all beings ought to have access through karmic merit, and so on. Atsutane could not resist fulminating against Nāgārjuna's arrogance, which Atsutane attributed to Nāgārjuna's legendary success in stealing into a kingly harem and having his way with the women there.[72] Elevating the fertility deity Musubi-no-kami to the level of cosmic creator, Atsutane was likewise hostile to the traditional Buddhist explanation for agriculture and sex as signs of decline, caused by greed and lust.

Turning to what we know as the ancient Indian caste system, Atsutane challenged the not-uncommon Buddhist downgrading of the Brahman priests below the *kṣatriya* warrior clans (of which the Buddha himself was a member). Even Xuanzang, Atsutane contends, may have been intoxicated with the Buddha, but he still correctly recorded the preeminence of the priests when he visited India. Far from the Brahmans being the pompous bullies of ancient India, Atsutane averred, it is in fact *the Buddha* who is the culprit for arrogance. The social disorder resulting from the Buddha's hostility to the caste system has, Atsutane continued, even reached the Divine Land of Japan, where a man who identifies his origins in an untouchable *caṇḍālā* family may—as Atsutane observed of Nichiren (1222–1282)—earn aristocratic treatment just by becoming a member of the "Buddha's clan." The institution of the *śramaṇa* ascetics was stolen from Brahmanical practice; the Buddhists ruined it by adding the practice of begging for food, another degraded custom brought by Buddhism to Japan.

As such examples suggest, Atsutane's *Compendium of Indian Records* acted like a photographic negative, plunging the figure of the Buddha into shade and highlighting that which the Buddhist traditions portray as already overcome. Even in this reversal, however, the biography of the Buddha himself is plainly apparent. However, this was not the work by which Atsutane's study of the Buddha came to be known widely within Japan.

The Dissemination of Atsutane's Thought

Even after Atsutane's death in exile in 1843, his *Mocking Discourse* initially circulated only among the registered disciples of his academy in Edo, the Ibukinoya. Like the vast bulk of Atsutane's works, it initially circulated in manuscript form; it was deliberately kept out of print and commercial circulation through the officially sanctioned booksellers' associations in Kyoto, Osaka, and Edo. After Atsutane's death, the Ibukinoya did put some of his works into print, but for sale only to the initiated and the trusted.

Even in the final decades of the Edo period, self-publishing and the circulation of text in manuscript were hardly unusual practices. The Edo period is today celebrated for the development of a thriving print culture and extensive trade in printed books, but books continued to circulate in large volumes in both manuscript and self-printed versions. According to the estimates of one historian of the Japanese book, Hashiguchi Kōnosuke, as many as one-third of the books circulating across the Edo period were self-printed, and commercially printed books made up no more than thirty or forty percent of the total quantity of texts in circulation, with the remainder in manuscript.[73]

Certainly, avoiding the scrutiny inevitably triggered by commercial publishing in the later Edo period—and particularly, avoiding the censure of the authorities for any criticism of Confucian or Buddhist institutions, both of which enjoyed the patronage of the shogunate—motivated Atsutane and his successors to shun the public commercial-publishing route. Accordingly, those relatively few works that Atsutane did have printed in his life relied heavily on subscriptions and donations by his disciples.[74] Despite this level of care, Atsutane still eventually faced official reprisal for his thinking. In 1840, publication of his works was proscribed, and in 1841, he was exiled from Edo to his birthplace in Akita, where he died within a few years. The precise nature of Atsutane's offense remains unclear; one of his twentieth-century biographers suggested that Atsutane's call for the return to ancient standards in the calendar and weights and measures threatened the shogunate's monopoly on setting such standards. Such challenges to the shogunate's cosmological authority over the measurement of space and time would likely have been viewed seriously in the 1830s and early 1840s, a time of famine and social volatility, on the one hand, and efforts at policy reform (the Tempō Reforms), on the other.[75] Even after Atsutane was exiled, the Ibukinoya, led now by Atsutane's adoptive son Kanetane (1799–1880), continued to operate in Edo, though it was forced to exert considerable discretion in the circulation of Atsutane's works. Only late in 1849 did the shogunate finally lift the ban on the publication of Atsutane's works.

By that point, however, the leadership of the Ibukinoya could no longer fully limit the circulation of Atsutane's works, for its rank-and-file members had begun to take matters into their own hands. A key disciple of the academy in this connection was Sakura Azumao (1811–1860). A Shingon cleric from modern Ibaraki Prefecture, Azumao had grown disenchanted with Buddhism and joined the Ibukinoya shortly after Atsutane left for exile. He is reputed to have publically burned his rosary and clerical robes in his temple garden before fleeing naked to a friend's home. There, the story continues, he allowed his hair to grow out before visiting a Shintō shrine, where he fasted and prayed for a week to purify himself.[76] Historical fact or not, the manifestation of such extremism seems perfectly attuned to Atsutane's temperament. In or around 1848, Azumao settled in Osaka, where he took a position as a low-ranking Shintō priest at the Ikasuri Shrine (popularly known as "Zama Shrine"). There he began to issue and sell his own privately printed editions of various National Learning texts, which are today known as "Zama editions" (*Zama-ban*). Azumao issued the *Mocking Dis-*

course in the summer of 1849, in defiance of the shogunal ban on the printing of Atsutane's works and the Ibukinoya's sensitivity toward this particular text.

To produce the Zama editions, Azumao used wooden moveable type, a technology by then already known in Japan for centuries but used only rarely. Setting the thousands of Chinese characters in moveable type was in fact more laborious than carving whole pages of text into wooden blocks, which could then be reused; moveable type hampered the use of illustrations and the addition of phonetic glosses next to characters, two key selling points in the late-Edo-era book market; and moveable type could produce only about one hundred copies with each setting. Accordingly, private printing with moveable type was not unusual when printers wanted to distribute works narrowly, within a particular school or movement and away from the scrutiny of commercial publishers. Because of the relatively small print runs of books produced with moveable type, shogunal authorities tended to turn a blind eye to them, reasoning that their influence would be limited.[77] Further, because the moveable type could be assembled and then taken apart, the printing process left no evidence in the form of carved blocks. Even when the printing was technically private, commercial publishers were often engaged in these projects, if discreetly.

Sakura Azumao's publishing project did not remain covert for long. By the third month of the following year, 1850, the Ibukinoya had discovered the production of these pirate editions, issued a protest, and ordered the moveable type used in their printing shipped to Edo.[78] Presumably, authorities at the Ibukinoya intended to make a demonstration to the shogunate of their good faith. Facing criticism from other parties as well, Sakura Azumao was forced to abandon his printing operations and leave Osaka in 1851.[79] In Kyoto in 1860, he gave shelter to a comrade active in the growing movement to overthrow the shogunate; for this crime, the authorities arrested him and imprisoned him in Edo. There he reportedly starved himself to death, refusing to eat the food of the shogunate. Meanwhile, sensitive to the inflammatory nature of the *Mocking Discourse*, the authorities at the Ibukinoya refrained from issuing their own printed edition of the text until 1870.[80]

By then, the text had already spread throughout the archipelago. At least ten distinct printings by Sakura Azumao of the *Mocking Discourse* survive, with the later editions produced rather shoddily.[81] Each text produced in these printings includes a standard disclaimer, stating that it was produced in a print run of one hundred copies. Even if we take that claim at face value, that still means that over one thousand copies could have resulted. As late as the early twenty-first century, those copies continued to circulate widely as easily available, barely antiquarian books.[82] Nor did urban readers enjoy any monopoly over the *Mocking Discourse*. A copy in the possession of a well-to-do farmer in the Ina Valley (modern Nagano Prefecture), who was a devout member of the Ibukinoya, was "one of the most popular books" in his library, "lent out ten times between 1858 and 1872."[83] Exemplified by cases like this one, the spread of Atsutane's ideas even to far-flung regions of the archipelago would be an important stimulus to the anti-Buddhist persecutions following on the heels of the Meiji Restoration in 1868.

Buddhist Responses to Atsutane's Criticisms

Perhaps surprisingly, not all Buddhist clerical readers of Atsutane's work criticized it. Late in 1840, the Sōtō Zen monks Saian Urin (d. 1845), the fifty-seventh abbot of the temple Eiheiji, and Kakugan Jitsumyō (1793–1857)—clerics on friendly terms with Atsutane—jointly contributed a brief preface in Chinese to Atsutane's *Compendium of Indian Records*. They wrote:

> Even among monks, few study the repository of the *sūtras* deeply and thoroughly. But here, the Layman Taigaku ["Great Ravine," i.e., "Ocean"] has read through the repository several times, seeking for the origin of the various schools, and illuminating the root of Zen in its single transmission. He has at last compiled his *Compendium of Indian Records* in twenty-five volumes, which lights the pure lamp of the sun and the moon, and dispels the darkness of delusions, past and present. He is truly an *udumbara* blossom in this Latter Age. He must have wished the partisans of the various schools to return to Bodhidharma's path of the "direct pointing" [at awakening]. How could it not have been through the power of a distant, great vow that he accomplished this? Could any of our compatriots not rejoice at this? He ranks with Layman Vimalakīrti of India, or Layman [Su] Dongpo of China. We bestow upon him the title of "Layman," by which we offer our congratulations. From now on, he will ever more tirelessly, for the benefit of future generations, spread the "path outside the teachings."[84]
>
> **A felicitous day in the eleventh month of Tenpō 11 [1840],**
> **Year of the Senior Metal Rat**
> **Elder Urin of the temple Eiheiji**
> **Kakugan of the temple Chintokuji (cipher)**[85]

Urin and Kakugan were possibly unaware that some decades prior to the date of this preface, Atsutane had already issued a critique of Zen, written primarily with materials from Japan: *An Explanation of the Way of Awakening* (*Godōben*, a multipart text that seems to have begun to take shape around 1811).

Atsutane once famously declared that he really, really hated three things: caterpillars, the Buddha, and death.[86] Given such comparisons, the preface contributed by Urin and Kakugan would seem to demand some explanation. Some scholars have, of course, attempted to reconcile these clerics' praise for Atsutane with his evident anti-Buddhist sentiment. Writing in 1916, an otherwise unknown contributor to a Buddhist denominational newsletter, by the name of Shigeki Denhachirō (n.d.), opined that Atsutane had, albeit unintentionally, actually become a scholar of Buddhism, "infused" (*kunsen*) with the teachings of the Buddha through his study of them.[87] Further, considering the admiration expressed in the preface for Atsutane's labors, Shigeki wrote: "It is only right and proper that [the preface] praised the *Compendium*. Buddhists regard what is correct as correct, without any self-interest. This lack of self-interest, i.e., 'selflessness,' is what ennobles the study of Buddhism."[88] In this interpretation, then, Hirata and the writers of the preface mutually profited from their work: "Hirata-*sensei's* deep study of the repository of sutras was to his own benefit, not the repository's; the Zen masters' words of praise were to their own benefit, not Hirata's."[89]

Other evaluations of Atsutane's position toward Buddhism have also represented him similarly—if not as a crypto-Buddhist himself, then as a concerned scholar who took to heart the rectification of Japan's Buddhist institutions. This approach is evident in a study published on the one-hundred-twentieth anniversary of Atsutane's death in 1963, by the scholar of Shintō Nishida Nagao (1909–1981). Although Nishida acknowledged that Atsutane had indeed produced a collection of anti-Buddhist books, he contended that these had actually been produced to the end of instituting "a great reform of Buddhism."[90] After all, he pointed out, Atsutane *had* produced the equally caustic *Summary of Vulgar Shintō*—not with the aim of eradicating Shintō itself, but in order to attack what he dismissed as its corrupt and inauthentic forms. Atsutane's apparently anti-Buddhist works, Nishida argued, could not be dismissed merely as such: "On reconsidering them and reading them carefully, I have to say that they are not anti-Buddhist books. They are both anti-Buddhist and not."[91] By the same token, "Atsutane was an opponent of Buddhism, and he also was not. Rather, I believe, he is a figure who should be thanked by the Buddhist community as a benefactor."[92] In support of this point of view, Nishida cited Kakugan's words from the preface.

Nishida's formulation may appear a rank attempt to have it both ways with Atsutane, but it is not uncorroborated by other evidence. Whether truly in the interest of the "reform" of Buddhism or not, Atsutane remained on friendly terms with other Buddhist clerics as well. In addition to Kakugan, with whom he directly associated, he was also acquainted with Fumon Entsū (1754–1834), a cleric who tried to demonstrate the compatibility of traditional Buddhist cosmology with new astronomical data coming to Japan from Europe, as Entsū regarded the established Buddhist world scheme as the ultimate truth. Atsutane also associated with the Shingon cleric Gyōchi (1778–1841), a pioneering historical phonologist and the leading scholar in the Japanese study of Sanskrit (written in the Siddham script) of his generation: Atsutane's diary records a Siddham study gathering with Gyōchi and others in 1817, and it also reveals that Gyōchi continued to participate in other gatherings at Atsutane's at least as late as 1825.[93] It is almost certainly no coincidence that this period coincides with Atsutane's intensive work on the *Compendium of Indian Records*. Nor, if we are to believe Atsutane's testimony, was his relationship with Gyōchi merely instrumental. In his *Japanese Writing in the Divine Script* (*Shinji hifumi den*, 1819)—a work in which Atsutane attempted to uncover an indigenous Japanese script used until the advent of Chinese characters—Atsutane praised Gyōchi as "my monkish friend, expert in the study of Siddham."[94]

Whatever Atsutane personally intended for Buddhism, his books nonetheless supplied arguments used by his followers to "reform" Buddhism through its curtailment or destruction. This threat to Buddhist institutions was clearly foreseen by the following generation of clerical intellectual readers of the work. In the final decades of the Edo period, popular fictional and theatrical accounts of the life of the Buddha continued to draw mass audiences, but the institutional and intellectual security of Buddhism in Japan had begun to unravel. In the domains of Satsuma and Hitoyoshi in far southern Kyūshū, the True Pure Land and Nichiren denominations had been banned since the start of the Edo period. From 1830 through the mid-1840s, the domain of Mito undertook an intense campaign of confiscating temple properties and the forced laicization of Buddhist clergy; this was one reason that the shogunate ultimately forced the domainal lord Tokugawa Nariaki (1800–1860) to retire and cede his position to his son in 1844.[95] By this period, criticisms of Buddhist institutions as an economic drain on the realm had gained considerable currency, particularly the works *Frank Words on Current Issues* (*Sōbō kigen*, composed in 1789) by Nakai Chikuzan (1730–1804) and Shōji Kōki's (1793–1858) *Secret Record of Dialogues about the Economy* (*Keizai mondō hiroku*, printed with moveable type in 1841).[96] Atsutane's *Mocking Discourse upon Emerging from Meditation* was thus only one of a number of anti-Buddhist treatises in circulation by the late Edo period, but it certainly ranks among the most influential.

Naturally, Atsutane's incendiary works—critical not only of Buddhists but also of Confucianists and even rival movements within Shintō—drew no small share of criticism from a range of positions. Outside the world of Buddhist clerics, inventive critics of Atsutane could dream up ingenious ways to make their point. One particularly original rebuttal, part of a collection dating from 1831, actually emerged within the National Studies community itself. It imagined no less authoritative a figure than Prince Shōtoku himself swooping down from the heavens to chastise a terrified Atsutane. The author of this rebuttal, whose precise identity remains unclear, has the apotheosized prince berate Atsutane with accusations of shoddy scholarship, plagiarism, and ungrounded interpretation of ancient texts. Although the author uses examples drawn from Buddhist texts to discuss textual criticism in a general sense, this short work does not specifically mention Atsutane's own criticisms of Buddhism.[97]

By the last decades of the Edo period, though, elite Japanese Buddhist intellectuals—including the most influential thinkers of various schools—were registering astonishment and distress over Atsutane's attacks. Based in Kyoto, the True Pure Land scholar-cleric Higuchi Ryūon (a.k.a. Kōzan-in, 1800–1885) was one of them. He had steadily ascended through the academic ranks at the Higashi Honganji's seminary (the Takakura Academy, predecessor to today's Ōtani University), finally attaining its highest non-administrative position, "lecturer" (*kōshi*), in 1865.[98] Around that time, Ryūon delivered talks and issued writings alerting his colleagues to the dangers posed to the True Pure Land institution by the various new critics of Buddhism. These works evince particular distress at Atsutane's *Mocking Discourse upon Emerging from Meditation*. In his *Words of Lamentation to Prevent Slander* [*of the Dharma*], *or A General Discussion of the Opponents of Buddhism* (*Gyobō gaitan, ichimyō hai-Butsu sōron*, 1863), Ryūon pronounced Atsutane as one of the two "worst slanderers of recent times."[99]

By the time he delivered his *General Discussion of the Opponents of Buddhism*, Ryūon already knew of a great number of Atsutane's writings, including the *Mocking Discourse* and its appendix, as well as *Compendium of Indian Records*, though Ryūon noted its incomplete state.[100] Ryūon seems to have found the content of Atsutane's polemic largely derivative: "That man Atsutane's abuse of the Buddhas and bodhisattvas is wholly inherited from Motoori [Norinaga]. Originally it was that Motoori who always called Śākyamuni the Great Liar and the Buddhadharma words of empty fabrication."[101] Ryūon also voiced the possibility of more nefarious sources for Atsutane's ideas: "I personally see the appearance one after another of [Atsutane and other] opponents of Buddhism as entirely the work of Māra and his minions. As for the Shintō that Atsutane discusses, there are many places in which it agrees with Christianity."[102] To Ryūon, then, Atsutane may have been not just an unusually virulent critic of Buddhism, but rather, an agent of cosmic forces ranged against the dharma.

Ryūon's alarm over the possible return of Christianity to Japan was no empty paranoia. By 1863, the shogunate was no longer able to block the influx of Christianity into Japan, in the form of European and North American traders, missionaries, and residents of treaty ports. To suggest that Atsutane was a crypto-Christian would, for Ryūon, have been tantamount to declaring Atsutane an agent of the ultimate adversary of the Buddha, Māra the Destroyer. Atsutane's demythologizing treatment of the Buddha as a mere human comparable to the figures in such heresies as Christianity proved offensive to Ryūon, who condemned Atsutane for "utterly disbelieving in the virtues that make the Buddha a Buddha," and for "considering the Buddha to be the same as Jesus or Mohammed."[103]

These views further found institutional support. Ryūon was soon named the titular director of the Institute for the Defense of the Dharma (Gohōjō), a scholarly center for apologetics established by the Ōtani subdenomination.[104] During its short lifespan (1868–1871), the Institute's curriculum included the study of both National Learning and Christian texts; Nanjō Bun'yū (1849–1927), who was later to found Sanskrit studies in Japan, would rank among its graduates.

Atsutane therefore attracted severe criticism, but Ryūon seems to have found little novel in his thinking per se. "However, what is surprising," Ryūon wrote in 1865,

> is that the [book of] abuse and invective, written by this Hirata [Atsutane], has become greatly popular; they say that these days, people who hate the Buddhadharma—even warriors and doctors, and the like—all seek it out and read it with pleasure. We truly live in a lamentable age. From days of old, there have been

many books in circulation to oppose Buddhism, but never one like this work of Atsutane.[105]

For Ryūon, what had changed in the realm of anti-Buddhist argument was not its content but its currency: no longer limited to the fringes of society, diatribes against Buddhism were finding traction with the ruling warrior class and well-educated doctors. Ryūon displayed acute awareness of the necessity of securing patronage and protection, and he noted that Atsutane had deliberately avoided all mention of the devotion shown by many generations of emperors toward Buddhism.[106] As Ryūon also noted, scholars of other persuasions agreed with Atsutane that the embrace of Buddhism had been harmful to Japan; accordingly, Ryūon countered, to attack Buddhism was to attack the belief held by emperors and lords, and hence to attack emperors and lords.[107] Efforts to legitimize Buddhism on the basis of appeals to its relationship with the imperial institution were, in fact, a staple of Buddhist apologetics as early as the Edo period.[108]

Ryūon's contemporary, the scholar-cleric Udana-in Nichiki (1800–1859), displayed an equally dismayed but more measured engagement with Atsutane's thought. Now remembered as the great synthesizer of early modern Nichiren doctrine and a pivotal educator and reformer in his own right, Nichiki embraced a number of controversial positions, bequeathing an intellectual agenda to later generations of thinkers in the Nichiren denomination. Considering the growth of anti-Buddhist sentiment in his times, Nichiki likewise sensed that the era had changed: "The Final Age of the Dharma began with attachment to appearance and the slander of the Truth; the present era is a time of attachment to Confucianism and the destruction of Buddhism."[109] Although Nichiki also demonstrated awareness of the unpublished *Compendium of Indian Records*, he displayed particular concern for Atsutane's *Mocking Discourse*, which he found "twice as good as that *Emerging from Meditation* [by Tominaga Nakamoto], and extreme in its superb views and blazing argument."[110] (Nichiki seems to have known of the *Mocking Discourse* only through a manuscript version; in 1850, he could still write that Atsutane's book "has not yet been printed."[111]) Though certainly not an admirer of Atsutane, Nichiki actually considered Atsutane's writing "good medicine," or a wake-up call to Nichiren clerics, rousing them to study well enough to defend themselves against it.[112] At the same time, Nichiki was sufficiently attuned to the dangers presented by Atsutane's argument about the authorship of the Buddhist sutras to contend that even if those sutras were not the words of

Śākyamuni himself, they could nonetheless represent supreme truth. His reluctance to set aside key canonical texts stands in contrast with his intellectual flexibility in certain other areas. Nichiki proved willing to discard other long-cherished Buddhist concepts when he found that they could not be substantiated—dismissing, for instance, the cosmology of the six paths of rebirth.[113]

While Ryūon and Nichiki both sounded the alarm about the *Mocking Discourse*, neither seems to have written extensively about the contents of its main body.[114] Because its appendix specifically targets the Buddhist schools to which each belonged, their interest in the appendix alone may have been inevitable. A number of rebuttals appeared to counter that appendix, but the best-known attempt at a comprehensive rebuttal to Atsutane's work from a Buddhist author—therefore, including a rebuttal to Atsutane's version of the life of the Buddha—was published only in the autumn of 1867, on the very eve of the Meiji Restoration. Written by Ryōgetsu (n.d.)—the otherwise obscure abbot of the Sōkenji, a Sōtō Zen temple in the modern Kyoto suburb of Kameoka—and titled *A Whisk for Swatting Away a Fly* (*Tsuiyō barae*), this appears to be the only refutation to enter print before 1868. Like Sakura Azumao, Ryōgetsu also published his polemical work using wooden movable type, likely to circumvent official scrutiny.[115]

Prefaces to this work by Ryōgetsu and his disciple Zetsugaku (n.d.) explain the circumstances of the compilation of the *Whisk*. Zetsugaku described having visited a bookshop in Kyoto, where he found the *Mocking Discourse* featured prominently. When questioned, the bookseller described it to Zetsugaku as a book that "refutes the Buddhist classics" by "an administrator (*shamu*) at the Ikasuri Shrine in southern Osaka," a clear mistake for Azumao's employer at the shrine, who contributed a preface to his edition. (Azumao himself seems to have occupied a relatively low position at the shrine: although Atsutane referred to himself by name in the body of the text, Ryōgetsu and Zetsugaku did not name him in their writing.) Zetsugaku brought back a copy to present to his master Ryōgetsu, who unexpectedly greeted the book with an expression of joy. "This," Zetsugaku quoted Ryōgetsu as saying, "is no impartial argument by a man of knowledge, but rather, a work of jealousy and self-righteous prejudice. It merely redounds on him, exposing his own side's flaws to the public."[116] Keen to help his rival air his dirty linen in public, the preface explains, Ryōgetsu composed a rebuttal, and Zetsugaku persuaded him to print it.

Ryōgetsu's foreword and other prefatory material suggest, however indirectly, that the Buddhist giant actually had much to fear from its

Lilliputian adversaries. When anything rots, Ryōgetsu explained, insects naturally spring forth from it; in a rotten era far removed from the life of the sage Śākyamuni, it is only natural that Buddhist leaders grow corrupt, giving rise to slanderers of the dharma with their heretical tracts. Among these, Ryōgetsu charged, the *Mocking Discourse upon Emerging from Meditation* is particularly odious, like a horsefly emerging from a dung heap to buzz around, disturbing one's sleep and dirtying one's food. Thus, Ryōgetsu told his readers, he composed *A Whisk for Swatting Away a Fly* to vanquish the buzzing annoyance. "These days, there are many who attack Confucianism and slander Buddhism. If we leave them alone, then, I fear, we will have no small worry over their harm and filth. This is the sole reason for which I raise the whisk."[117] Here, the choice of a whisk as metaphor is something more than mere rhetorical flourish: fly whisks, originally a practical implement for dislodging small creatures from the path without harming them, became in Chan and Zen Buddhism symbols of monastic authority and legitimacy, employed in actual teaching and featured in portraits.

The main body of the *Whisk*, which includes the discussion of the life of Śākyamuni, comprises a series of point-by-point rebuttals to specific passages from the *Mocking Discourse*. To this main body of the *Whisk*, Ryōgetsu appended a section of endnotes, citing other sources. He further added a short appendix in which he attempted to list every reigning or retired emperor to assume Buddhist guise—and in some cases, to take full monastic orders—across Japanese history. (The list enumerates a total of thirty-seven emperors and alludes to one hundred thirty princes of the blood who did the same.) Whether or not Ryōgetsu actually took direct inspiration from Ryūon, the two clearly concurred about the value of centuries of imperial endorsements in establishing the legitimacy of Buddhism in Japan.

In the main body of the *Whisk*, Ryōgetsu quoted Atsutane's words (sometimes in abbreviation) under the heading "The fly says . . . ," alternating with his rebuttals, under the heading "I swat it away, saying . . ." His text is long but repetitive. One of its fundamental premises, repeated ad nauseam, poses little difficulty of understanding: by neglecting the overarching intent behind the words of the Buddha, Ryōgetsu insisted, Atsutane preoccupied himself with superficial trivialities of no concern for the core message of Buddhism. Ryōgetsu maintained that, ignorant of the true teachings of Buddhism and of the functioning of instructive expedients provided by the Buddha, and unschooled in any Buddhist practice, the fly of the title merely misattributes the evil and duplicity in his own heart to Buddhism. Ryōgetsu thus paraphrased the

Platform Sutra of the Sixth Patriarch: "When a wicked man preaches it, even the True Dharma will be wicked; when a good man preaches it, even a wicked teaching will be true."[118] Or, as he addressed Atsutane more directly elsewhere: "You must not recklessly measure the mind of the Sage [i.e., the Buddha] with your own mind."[119]

Given this basic posture of condemnation of Atsutane, it may have simply been inevitable that Ryōgetsu's work would display little patience for Atsutane's methodology. For one, Ryōgetsu rejected out of hand Atsutane's claim to address the Buddhist tradition on the basis of a critical inquiry into its own texts. To Ryōgetsu, Atsutane was only deluding himself into believing that he had uncovered the core truths of the Buddhist texts:

> The fly says: When I argue about the various Ways, I use Confucian books to discuss the Confucian Way, and Buddhist books to discuss the Buddhist Way. In any matter, when someone knows the root and discusses it, then one's opponent will be unable to say anything [in rebuttal]. And once one has a grasp of the root, then one can understand all the leaves and branches. And based on this, once one is able to pull out the whole root, then often the leaves will be comprehensible of their own accord, without speaking or asking about them.
>
> I swat it away, saying: Because you have no eye with which to read the Buddhist books, you recklessly discuss the leaves and branches, vainly ignorant of the root. How laughable! What is questionable about your words is this: When someone grabs grass for thatch and pulls with all one's might, it is possible to pull out any amount of grass. But when one grabs weakly and pulls gingerly, then the root does not come out; instead, the one pulling gets hurt. You have no strength to grab hold of the root of the Buddha's intention, and are just gingerly tugging on the leaves and branches at the ends. I hope that you don't wind up cutting your hands and feet.[120]

Likewise, Ryōgetsu refused to countenance another core element of Atsutane's methodology: his conviction that, among the materials within Buddhist scriptures, genuine accounts may be meaningfully distinguished from fabrications through critical examination of text and context.

> The fly says: The way to read the words of the Buddha is to use one or two facts to consider [which words are] fabricated accounts. And one should keep in mind the method of using the fabricated accounts to learn the facts as one reads. Unless one does so, one will be misled.
>
> I swat it away, saying: Narrow-minded scholars of National Learning might speak recklessly and loudly, doubting [Buddhism] without even investigating why,

but seen from the broad mind of the study of Buddhism, they are pitiable. You do not know how to read the words of the Buddha, and even when you see facts, you make them into lies. It is like this: The sun and moon are always bright, but when they are covered by clouds and fog, their light is temporarily not apparent, but that does not mean that their light has gone away. If the clouds of your doubt were to part, then the light would appear of its own accord. When the minds of sentient beings are clear, the shadow of wisdom manifests within them. The mind of the Buddha is like the sun and moon, shining on all without partiality.[121]

Such repudiation of Atsutane's methodology sets the tone for Ryōgetsu's concrete refutations of the critical readings of the biography of Śākyamuni from Atsutane's *Mocking Discourse*. In a number of these refutations, Ryōgetsu displayed little concern with the niceties of Atsutane's argument. Countering Atsutane's insistence that no bodhisattva should have three wives and three children, Ryōgetsu pointed out that the Buddha was married only when he was, after all, still a prince of the world, before becoming the World-Honored One. As for the contradictions among various scriptural accounts of the prince's marital pairings and offspring, Ryōgetsu held that the Buddha teaches according to the capacity and needs of his audience, so there is no need to condemn the canon for inconsistency. Further, he adduced historical precedent in Japan for unusual modes of engendering pregnancy, which to him seemed not unlike the prince's pointing his finger at Yaśodharā's belly. Similar factors, he continued, may account for the contradictory numerical figures given for the Buddha's age at his renunciation and for the length of time he spent practicing austerities.

Against Atsutane's claim that the Buddhist sutras are all retroactive inventions whose content overwhelmingly fails to reflect the actual teachings of Śākyamuni, Ryōgetsu eschewed direct engagement with his argument, instead retorting that Atsutane had identified no suspects for this act of forged composition: "You do not say who, in which land, forged the sutras; instead, you are just aimlessly firing your cannon at dark clouds, as usual."[122] In a similar fashion, Ryōgetsu repudiated Atsutane's accusation that Chinese Buddhists continually inflated the antiquity of the Buddha in order to present him as increasingly storied and venerable. Here too, Ryōgetsu declined to engage with the specifics of Atsutane's argument, which were all borrowed from Tominaga Nakamoto. Instead, he declared flatly that, if there actually had been any later falsification, then it would have moved the Buddha's age in the *other* direction, toward the present, because of later Buddhists' wish to live even one year closer to the era of Śākyamuni.[123]

The problem of the Buddha's use and final loss of superhuman powers—a topic prominent in Atsutane's portrayal of the Buddha—reappears in Ryōgetsu's rebuttal. In this regard, Ryōgetsu relied heavily upon the classic claim, common to a number of Buddhist traditions, that mind itself manufactures all experience. Thus, he charged, when Atsutane compares the Buddha's powers to mere magic tricks, he both misunderstands the compassionate intention underlying the Buddha's use of his powers, and also neglects the broader Buddhist claim about the basic unreality of all experience: "The empty sky, the vast ocean, and the great mountain are all phenomena produced by one's own mind."[124] The Buddha's ability to divide his body into countless duplicates—a display of powers described in many sutras—is no different from these everyday objects of perception: "You must recognize that even a multitude of apparitional bodies is wholly a phenomenon produced by your own single mind."[125] Against Atsutane's damning invocation of Nāgārjuna's endorsement of the bodhisattva's reliance upon superhuman powers to convert sentient beings, Ryōgetsu countered that everyone has those powers, so they are nothing special. After all, as the classic Chan teaching has it, the activities of daily life are themselves wondrous superhuman powers. Even the apparent fading of the Buddha's golden radiance at the end of his life—a phenomenon which Atsutane blamed upon the weakening of the Buddha's magic powers—for Ryōgetsu also lay in the eye of the beholder, because "it is not the Buddha's fault whether you see or not."[126]

Again, to counter Atsutane's indictment of the Buddha's use of magic, Ryōgetsu also rejected Atsutane's invocation of the words of the Buddha—"I am now old in age, my body tired, my life nearing its end"—as an indication that the Buddha's magical powers had terminally weakened at the end of his life. On the basis of this passage, Atsutane had held that the inclusion among the eighty minor marks of the Buddha of "a countenance always youthful and never aging" must, therefore, represent a later accretion to the scriptural canon. In opposition to this interpretation, Ryōgetsu replied with a standard, if condescending, invocation of the Buddha's expedient means:

> I swat it away, saying . . . You must know that the Buddha is not a liar because of different explanations in two sūtras. There's originally no need to wait for this account. As you yourself acknowledge, the *Sutra on the Descent into Laṅka* says, "In forty-nine years, I have never preached a word." What a dimwitted man you are not to notice, though these tongs for the fire have burned you already! Well, I will have to give you some solicitous instruction, so listen! The account of the *Chūagonkyō* shows

> unmoving dullards like you that the matter of birth-and-death is great and that impermanence is swift; to drive you out [from samsara], it whips you in a spirit of kindness. And for those who are startled by a single whipping, [other sutras] show, with reference to their ability, that the Buddha's true adamantine body has the virtue of being "always youthful and never aging," and sometimes explain that the Buddha is always preaching on Vulture Peak.[127]

Ryōgetsu's riposte to Atsutane could be read as an admirable display of consistency, on the one hand, or as an attempt to drown out Atsutane's arguments through sheer relentless censoriousness. Either way, Ryōgetsu's writing plots and executes the retreat from whatever specifics Atsutane raises, shifting the point of contention away from the messy particularities of his case and transposing the controversy into the register of the eternal and essentially unchanging Mind. A readership already deferential to discourse in this register would presumably have welcomed Ryōgetsu's ideas. But for readers not already committed to such notions, Ryōgetsu's rebuttal could have offered little satisfaction or persuasiveness.

As this chapter has shown, Atsutane deserves to be recognized as a key biographer of the Buddha, even if his methodology was borrowed largely from Nakamoto, and his fundamental premises flawed. Just as such figures as Ryūon, Nichiki, and Ryōgetsu were attempting to come to terms with Atsutane, though, his basic reduction of the Buddha to a historical figure was already reaching Japanese readers from a different source, which they were equally powerless to ignore: European missionaries and their Japanese converts to Christianity.

FIVE

The Buddha as Character

From the 1860s to the 1910s, Japanese intellectuals' understanding of the historical Buddha underwent a stunning transformation. This ultimately produced a distinctly Japanese version of a human Buddha who could nonetheless be revered for his "great character." Although developed primarily by lay intellectuals and artists, the notion of the Buddha as a distinctly *human* exemplar would, by the end of this period, gain traction even in Buddhist clerical circles. The very reframing of the Buddha as a human being—which provoked widespread alarm in Buddhist circles in the middle of the nineteenth century—thus became his passport to relevance in the following one.

As this chapter shows, Japanese Buddhist intellectuals began the period embattled on multiple fronts. One such threat lay in the influx of nineteenth-century Euro-American Christianity. Almost as an afterthought, Christian missionaries brought threatening new arguments about the historicity of the Buddha, which undercut claims to his universality and omniscience. Traditional Buddhist doctrinal scholarship proved unequal to the task of refuting these arguments—or even properly understanding them—and the first efforts during the 1880s to recast Buddhism to fit the mold of European philosophy fared little better. By the 1890s, some Japanese Buddhist intellectuals had begun to experiment with the discipline of empirical history, as developed in nineteenth-century Germany. They initially attempted to retain a privileged place for the Buddha by adopting history without historicism (the elevation of historical contingency and individual characteristics over universal principles). Dependent on faith in the Buddha's transhistorical uniqueness, this effort at a solution would not have satisfied researchers not yet committed to Buddhism.

By the start of the 1890s, a handful of scholarly accounts from Europe and America of the life of the Buddha had become available in Japanese translation. In these sources, Japanese intellectuals discovered the possibility that the Buddha's life story was not mere falsehood, but had the qualities of literature. Meanwhile, through the middle of the 1890s, efforts to reconcile the traditional life story with the historical method foundered. Two projects—both initiated by intellectual lay leaders in the middle of the decade—delineated routes to reconciling historical study of the Buddha with the aspiration of transcendence. The art historian, critic, and educator Okakura Kakuzō looked to the life of the Buddha as an artistic theme for promotion in "Japanese-style painting," or Nihonga. Painters in this new style followed Okakura's lead, both in depicting the theme and in looking to Indian materials in order to ground it in "history." Their paintings consciously broke with existing traditions—ultimately inherited from the Asian continent—in depicting the life of the Buddha, largely eschewing the display of his superhuman powers. Built from South Asian materials and newly sensitive to the human dimensions of their narratives, these paintings nonetheless afforded the life of the Buddha a place in the transcendent realm of the fine arts.

Meanwhile, Okakura's former classmate at Tokyo University, the philosopher Inoue Tetsujirō, laid the foundations for a textual rapprochement between transcendence and historical research. A leading professor at his own alma mater and an influential ideologue in the service of the state, Inoue also explored Buddhism in his lectures and writings. From the mid-1890s, Inoue started to publish his speculations about the racial origins of the Buddha's line. In 1902, Inoue published a rigorously demythologized biography of the historical Buddha that proved highly influential for generations. Inoue's historicized Buddha, while rooted in empirical evidence, nonetheless partook of the universal, because Inoue understood him as a "great man" whose life unfolded on the pattern of other "great men" in history. Inoue was also a pioneer in introducing European conceptions of personal value, translating the German *Persönlichkeit* or *Person* into Japanese as *jinkaku*, the "rank" or "grade" of a person. Originating in post-Kantian German idealism, this term took on multiple meanings, including "character" and "personality." At the same time, the Buddha was also recognized as a historical figure, or *jinbutsu*.

By the end of the Meiji period, two prominent disciples of Inoue Tetsujirō had also produced new narratives of the life of the Buddha. Takayama Chogyū, a professional critic with a deep interest in the relationship between genius and society—and a devotee of Nietzsche and Nichiren, among other "great men"—published a starkly demythologized account of the life of the Buddha for young readers in 1899. Even with most of his mythic trappings gone, though, the historicized Buddha could still participate in a truly global pantheon: Chogyū's book was merely the first of a series of biographies from "world history." Each of its successors treated a figure in an implicitly comparable position: Confucius, Jesus, Bismarck, Hannibal, Mohammed, the founder of the Han dynasty, Nelson, and so forth. Meanwhile, Chogyū's classmate and close friend, Anesaki Masaharu, approached the life of the Buddha through a different comparative project. As the first Japanese scholar to research the Buddha's life through sources written both in Chinese and in the languages of South Asia, Anesaki postulated a process by which his *jinkaku* had become a *shinkaku*, or "divinity." But this was no aberration or fabrication: As European critics and scholars or religion had suggested, character—whether human or divine—resulted purely from natural, historical processes. Because the superhuman and divinized incarnations of the Buddha resulted from historical processes, they merited a proper place in Buddhism, and in the articulation of its moral vision.

Christian Critics Historicize the Buddha and His Teaching

In its final years, the Tokugawa shogunate was no longer able to police its borders. Euro-American missionaries from multiple confessions and denominations began to stream into Japan. They were restricted to residence in the treaty ports, but their Christian tracts could travel where they could not; the fall of the shogunate and the establishment of the Meiji government in 1868 did nothing to stop that inflow. The period spanning the 1860s to the 1890s saw the emergence of Christianity, particularly Protestantism, in Japanese public life. In these years, Japanese Buddhist leaders widely understood and condemned Christianity not just as a heretical teaching (*jakyō*), but also as a profound threat to themselves and to the welfare of the nation as a whole. They responded to missionaries and to Japanese converts with threats, harassment, protests, and impassioned refutations, in public speaking and in print.[1] Buddhist intellectuals applied themselves to repudiating published Christian critiques of Buddhism with particular zeal.

However zealously they argued, though, they struggled unsuccessfully to respond to Christian attacks on Buddhist cosmology, elemental theory, ritual practice, meditation, and other topics. Among the Christian accusations toward Buddhism, historical criticism of the Buddha and challenges to the provenance of his teachings proved particularly difficult to counter. Representatives of a new and menacing power, Christian critics nonetheless posed questions that Buddhist apologists could not avoid: When and where did the Buddha live, and as what sort of being? What did he teach, and what is the value of his connection to those teachings? How is it possible to reconcile the various conflicting sources describing his life and teaching?

Publications by two unrelated Protestant intellectuals—the Englishman Joseph Edkins (1823–1905) and the Japanese Takahashi Gorō (1856–1935)—posed these questions about Buddhism with new authority and new urgency. Composed for different audiences, in different languages, and under different polities, these influential critiques naturally differed in a number of points. However, they shared a common confidence in their exposition of the historically limited role of the Buddha, whom they recognized as a real individual and a philosopher of no little importance. They also concurred in pointing to the historical gap dividing the historical Buddha from the complete body of teachings attributed to him, even if they disagreed about the significance of that gap. And neither of these Christian polemics acknowledged those teachings as having lasting value.

Judging from the level of alarm and acrimony that it inspired in Japan, the anti-Buddhist Christian tract most influential in the earliest Meiji years was Edkins's *Correction of the Errors of the Buddhists* (Ch. *Shijiao zhengmiu*). Edkins, a British missionary dispatched to China by the London Missionary Society, first printed this text in Shanghai in 1857; he then reprinted it in Hong Kong in 1861, in an expanded edition. Through the Chinese book trade, it reached Japan via Nagasaki no later than 1865. Within Japan, the tract was widely republished, particularly by Buddhist apologists for the express purpose of its refutation. Editions punctuated to help Japanese readers navigate the Chinese prose appeared as early as 1867. Edkins nowhere indicates awareness of a specifically Japanese readership in this text, but his work became more important among Japanese readers than among the Chinese intellectuals to whom he originally directed it.

Although the bulk of the expanded *Correction of the Errors* excoriates Buddhist cosmology, ritual, and the like, Edkins devoted one of its twenty chapters to the Buddha Śākyamuni. On the basis of Christian doctrine, he argued that Śākyamuni, as a mere man, cannot save anyone from sin, but he also employed historical reasoning in his description of Śākyamuni. First came the problem of dating. Edkins dismissed the Chinese chronology for the date of the Buddha's birth as absurdly early, noting that Buddhists of different lands espouse conflicting dates: "Some might say that this disagreement in the date is no great matter, but I reply that if even the dating is unfixed, then there is even less evidence for the other [matters concerning him]."[2] In his discussion, historicity and verifiability thus emerge as criteria in which the Buddhist tradition is found sadly lacking.

Toward Buddhism as Edkins observed it in China in his own time, he manifested only contempt, but Edkins treated the historical Buddha less harshly: "On considering the Tathāgata's pity and intention to lead others to reform their evil ways and to return to the correct path, we see that they were all his good intentions. Among the wise men and the philosophers of the lands of the world, the Buddha was not of the lowest grade."[3] Elsewhere in the treatise, Edkins warned his readers not to ascribe any universal meaning to Śākyamuni: "The Buddha was merely a sage for one country, a great man for one generation."[4] There is no question that, for Edkins, the Buddha could not rank with Christ. On the other hand, Edkins did not deny the historical reality of the Buddha, though he did deny the reality of bodhisattvas revered in China.

While the historical Buddha received a conciliatory treatment, Edkins had harsher words for his relationship to the Buddhist scriptures: "The thousands of volumes of Buddhist scriptures are all said to have been spoken by Śākyamuni. To translate them from Sanskrit to Chinese required hundreds and thousands of years and the labor of hundreds of people. This is by no means a quantity that one person could preach at one time."[5] Unlike the Buddhist scriptures, Edkins held, Confucian and Christian texts came with trustworthy accounts of their provenance. Edkins further dismissed the contents of the Buddhist scriptures themselves: "If we were to debate the validity of the arguments of the followers of Śākyamuni, they would certainly cite their scriptures as evidence. They are unaware that the scriptures were all written by Indians, and that those Indians are, compared to people of other lands, full of lies and absurdities, and much without substance."[6] In this mode from European Orientalism—not so far from Hirata Atsutane's nativist vision of India—Edkins described the inhabitants of India as pathologically prone to lies and exaggeration.

Notwithstanding that dismissal, Edkins also allowed for relative levels of spuriousness even within the canon. He held up the "Hīnayāna" teachings as simple in comparison to the elaborate fantasies of the Mahāyāna. "In the Hīnayāna," he wrote, "the Tathāgata, in an era of evil, [merely] tried to transform people away from wickedness and to return them to the correct path. There was nothing especially lofty in his preaching."[7] Like many of his Victorian peers, Edkins envisioned the Buddha as a simple teacher whose instructions later degenerated into superstition, maintaining this conviction even decades after the publication of *Correction of the Errors*. In *Chinese Buddhism: A Volume of Sketches, Historical, Descriptive, and Critical* (1880), Edkins used the findings of European Buddhology to decry the "corruption" of Buddhist clerics in sixth-century China, who were accused of using magic:

> The use of charms, and the claim to magical powers, do not appear to have belonged to the system as it was left by Shakyamuni [*sic*]. His teaching, as [Eugène] Burnouf has shown, was occupied simply with morals and his peculiar philosophy. After a few centuries, however, among the additions made by the Northern Buddhists to popularise the religion, and give greater power to the priests, were many narratives full of marvels and impossibilities, falsely attributed to primitive Buddhism. These works are called the *Ta-ch'eng* [*Dacheng*] or "Great Development" [i.e., Mahāyāna] Sutras.[8]

Of course, Edkins was not correct to suggest that the texts of the Mahāyāna had a monopoly on "marvels and impossibilities." Nevertheless, such passages sufficed to move one reviewer of Edkins's book to take a more sympathetic stance toward the "Hīnayāna": "The more we learn about Buddhism as divested of all its supernatural and legendary trappings, the more are we struck by the depth and width of the genius which conceived it as a system."[9] Whether Edkins and his reviewer were unaware of the "supernatural and legendary trappings" evident even in the "Hīnayāna" scriptures, or whether they knew them but simply dismissed them, is perhaps beside the point. To condemn Buddhism in China as degenerate, it was necessary to posit a pure or prelapsarian form of Buddhism in history. Needless to say, Edkins's biases as a Protestant missionary are unconcealed here: the exuberance of ritual and miracle could, for him, never outrank personal piety.

The reduction of the Buddha to mere human thinker, and the assertion of an unbridgeable chasm separating him from the teachings attributed to him, returned in one of the first anti-Buddhist tracts published by a Japanese Christian convert: the *New Treatise on Buddhism* (*Butsudō shinron*) of 1880. Its author, Takahashi Gorō (1856–1935), spent the following years embroiled in debate with his Buddhist critics.[10] Although largely forgotten today, Takahashi was a major contributor to the world of early Protestant Japan.[11] He not only participated in committees translating the Bible for both Protestant and Catholic groups, but also translated voluminously and broadly from European and American literature. His astounding output included Japanese renderings of Johann Goethe's *Faust* (1904), the *Essays* of Francis Bacon (1908), Ralph Waldo Emerson's *The Conduct of Life* (1910) and *Society and Solitude* (1912), the *Meditations* of Marcus Aurelius (1912), the *Discourses* of Epictetus (1912), Plutarch's *Lives* (1915), and Thomas Carlyle's *Sartor Resartus* (1918). Takahashi also wrote prolifically in his own right. He was also a public figure: in 1893, he stood as the most prominent representative of Christianity in the so-called "debate between religion and education," pitting him against Inoue Tetsujirō.

Takahashi published his work decades after Edkins's book first appeared, and he wrote in Japanese, for a specifically Japanese audience. Nonetheless, like Edkins, Takahashi also couched his critique of Buddhism largely in philosophical and doctrinal terms, rather than in a historical mode. Thus, he objected chiefly to the flaws in the Buddha's teaching, indicting Buddhist notions of cosmology, physics, and causality. A Buddha whose declarations conflict so inescapably with modern science, Takahashi claimed, certainly could not have attained what Buddhist texts claim for him: "omniscient knowledge" (Jpn. *issai shuchi*, Skt. *sarvākārajñatā*). "Seen this way, it is clear that Śākyamuni was merely a wise philosopher. If Buddhists come so far in this argument, then they should surrender and admit this fact as it is."[12] Unlike Edkins, Takahashi identified a specific historical philosopher for comparison with the Buddha. "One thousand six-hundred-fifty years prior to the present day," he began, "there was in the land of Egypt a philosopher called Plotinus (said to be a disciple of Ammonius Saccas)."[13] After sketching out Plotinus's philosophy, Takahashi contended:

If we compare these arguments of Plotinus with those of Śākyamuni, then we find that, in regarding this world as unreal and in the desire to be absorbed into reality,

Plotinus also commits the error of contradicting himself. However, when it comes to explaining the occurrence of all phenomena, the arguments of Plotinus seem to be far superior. . . . If people say that Śākyamuni ought to be respected for arguments of the kind that he made, then there are others who deserve respect even more: none other than Plotinus and his like.[14]

Takahashi's text adduces no source for his knowledge of late antique philosophy in the Mediterranean world; it may well have derived from his years of study and collaboration with one of the earliest missionaries to arrive in Japan from the United States, Samuel Robbins Brown (1810–1880). However dubious his understanding of Plotinus, Takahashi used the comparison not only to discount the uniqueness and primacy of the Buddha, but also to argue that Buddhism was no better equipped to survive in the long run than had the school of Plotinus. Just as the original teachings of Plotinus had, he held, been corrupted by an admixture of magic and superstition, so too would Buddhist practice sabotage itself:

If we turn our attention to those who proselytized the path of Plotinus, then it seems that the Buddhists will end up as they did. [The followers of Plotinus] also made it their business to employ magic and spread myth. Thus, they wholly lost the point of their Way, which extinguished itself of its own accord. This, too, is an inevitable principle.[15]

Here the portrayal of the Buddha as a philosopher is hardly a concession, as in the case of Edkins's tract, but a mode of attack. True to his conviction that the "magic and superstition" may be dissociated from the traditional biographies of the Buddha, Takahashi excluded them from his brief sketch of the Buddha's lineage and life.

Also like Edkins, Takahashi pointed out that the Buddhist scriptures had been recorded long after the death of the Buddha, though he cited both Nakamoto and Atsutane by name on this point. Unlike Edkins, though, Takahashi refused to privilege the "Hīnayāna" texts, exemplified by the Āgamas, as originary Buddhism. Strikingly, he argued that although the Mahāyāna texts in fact long postdated the life of the Buddha in their formation, they nonetheless reflected his "intention":

In Śākyamuni was truly born the bud of Buddhism. The spontaneous blossoming of that bud into its Pratyekabuddhayāna and Mahāyāna forms was an inevitable principle. And if people doubt the Mahāyāna, then they must doubt the so-called Hīnayāna as well. That is because even the so-called Hīnayāna did not result from the hand of the Buddha. This being the case, in the end, the Buddha's Way will die out. Thus, I regard the Buddhism transmitted in the world today as springing in its roots from the mind of Śākyamuni, and I take the three vehicles, Hīnayāna, Prayetkabuddhayāna, and Mahāyāna, together as Buddhism. However, I am not saying that *the so-called "preaching of the Buddha" all sprang from the mouth of Śākyamuni.*[16]

To be sure, Takahashi's primary interest here lay in disallowing any form of Buddhism as authentically deriving from the historical Buddha himself. By that logic, all forms of Buddhism must be the same, because all are equally spurious. Nonetheless, Takahashi's formulation in this pamphlet, in which he admits the Mahāyāna texts as the proper descendants of their early Buddhist forerunners, foreshadows later developments among Buddhist intellectuals themselves. In the first years of the twentieth century, some Japanese Buddhist intellectuals would begin to accept that the Mahāyāna teachings may not have derived from the preaching of the Buddha, but they would argue nonetheless that those texts represented a development continuous with his original teachings. If only to secure a uniform condemnation of all Buddhist texts, Takahashi inadvertently suggested a way to tie late Buddhist texts to the intention of the historical Buddha.

The Defeat of Traditional Scholarship

Rebuttals by Japanese Buddhists followed the circulation of the tracts by Edkins and Takahashi. In their tone and mode of argument, they closely resembled the 1867 refutation of Atsutane by Ryōgetsu. Even Buddhist clerics and their lay sympathizers would eventually realize the failure of this mode, although only after the elapse of some decades.

Circulating amid the tumult surrounding the Meiji Restoration and the anti-Buddhist persecution of the early 1870s, *Correction of the Errors* attracted intense scrutiny: by 1872, at least nine refutations had been produced to counter it. Along with Atsutane's "Concerning Two Buddhist Denominations, Enemies of the Gods" and other texts, the *Correction of the Errors* was studied at the Ōtani denomination's short-lived Institute for the Defense of the Dharma, whose acting head, Senshōin Kūkaku (1807–1871), gave lectures upon it. Leading lights in other Buddhist denominations responded to the critique in writing. The most influential and widely circulated responses came from Ugai Tetsujō (1814–1891; surname also read "Ukai"), a Pure Land cleric who in 1874 rose to serve as the chief abbot of a powerful head temple in his denomination, the Chion'in in Kyoto, and who in 1885 assumed the title of denominational chief officer (*kanchō*).

Tetsujō published two refutations of the *Correction of the Errors*, first in a printed version of 1868—*An Initial Refutation of "Correction of the Errors of Buddhism"* (*Shakkyō shōmyū shoha*)—and then in an expanded version, printed in 1873 as *An Initial Refutation and a Re-Refutation of "Correction of the Errors of Buddhism"* (*Shakkyō shōmyū shoha narabi ni saiha*). Presenting the text of each chapter from the *Correction of the Errors* with a rebuttal, Tetsujō's works themselves attracted commentary and critique by other clerical intellectuals. On the other hand, the 1880 text by Takahashi invited refutations both in the Buddhist periodical press and in a book, *A Compass in a Sea of Mist* (*Bukai nanshin*) by the Sōtō Zen cleric Nōnin Hakugan (d. 1882). He published this tract at the end of his life, in 1881.

The publications by Tetsujō and Hakugan epitomize the failure of traditional Japanese doctrinal studies to counter the new historical arguments wielded by Edkins and Takahashi. Like the work of their contemporary and fellow apologist Ryōgetsu, the refutations by Tetsujō and Hakugan showed little recognition of the novelty of their opponents' arguments.[17] Given the sources for the arguments employed in Buddhist apologetics of the 1860s through 1880s, that gap in consciousness is not entirely surprising. As early as 1861, Tetsujō had already assembled and published *A Personal Record of Refutations of Heresy* (*Hekija kanken roku*), a collection of Japanese and Chinese refutations of Christianity. He separately reprinted a number of Chinese refutations of Christianity from the late Ming dynasty, originally written to counter the Jesuits in China. Tetsujō's arguments against Edkins naturally accomplish little not already done in the Ming-dynasty works.

In his rebuttal, Tetsujō cited Buddhist literature to counter Edkins, who had accused that very literature of unreliability. Tetsujō seemed unaware of the circularity of his approach to proving the validity of Buddhist literature by citing Buddhist literature itself. And if Tetsujō offered little novel argumentation, he saw little novel argumentation in his adversary. In fact, he accused Edkins of stealing arguments against Buddhism from Song-dynasty Neo-Confucians and their distant predecessors. To counter Edkins's argument for the late creation of the Mahāyāna scriptures, for instance, Tetsujō held that even the many heretics in India, "who try on every occasion to attack the Buddhadharma and to prevail over it," had never been able to show that the *Flower Garland Sutra* is a forgery. Against Edkins's accusation that

Nāgārjuna did not retrieve the *Flower Garland Sutra* from the palace of the Dragon King but wrote it himself, Tetsujō shot back that Edkins himself was copying a fifth-century Chinese criticism of the Buddhist scriptures as poor imitations of Taoist materials.[18]

More surprising, Edkins's demotion of the historical Buddha to the status of mere philosopher found no direct acknowledgement—much less refutation—in the writings by Tetsujō. Nor did Tetsujō's own critics necessarily notice that claim, either. Tetsujō's rival in the Pure Land denomination, Fukuda Gyōkai, wrote an evaluation of Tetsujō's rebuttal, but in it, he demonstrated little urgency around the account of the life of the Buddha. Gyōkai suggested explaining the biography of the Buddha on the basis a traditional Chinese compilation, Zhipan's thirteenth-century *Chronicle of Buddhas and Patriarchs,* because of its ease of comprehension. With reference to Edkins's discussion of the conflict among the multiple dates for the life of the Buddha, Gyōkai noted that even in great nations, chronicles conflict with one another. Gentlemen, he concluded, do not occupy themselves with such trifling concerns.[19] In other words, Gyōkai seems not to have grasped the difficulty that Edkins's argument implied for the circular use of Buddhist texts themselves as evidence for the truth of Buddhism.

Even commentators who did note Edkins's contention that the Buddha was just a man could not cope with it in historical terms. The anonymous author of the manuscript *"Correction of the Errors of the Buddhists" Spits at Heaven* (*Shakkyō shōmyū tenda,* early Meiji period) refused Edkins's declaration of the Buddha's humanity outright: the Buddha's true form is transcendent, wrote this author, but "because he pitied sentient beings lost in delusion, he manifested his emanated traces and displayed the Eight Phases of his life."[20]

Likewise, Hakugan's response to Takahashi displays no more concern for the nature of historical reasoning than had Tetsujō's. Similar to Tetsujō, Hakugan detected little new in his opponent's case. He too traced historical sources for Takahashi's ideas, in which he reached as far back as Zhu Xi's condemnation of Buddhist scriptures as spurious—"Of the Buddhist books, only the *Sutra in Forty-Two Sections* is ancient," while "the rest were made through the embellishments of Chinese scholars"—to accuse Nakamoto of developing that idea into his *Emerging from Meditation,* which in turn "infected" Atsutane.[21] To Hakugan, then, Takahashi stood as just one more inheritor of this centuries-long lineage of delusion. Hakugan, therefore, rejected outright the suggestion that the Āgama literature provided the basis from which the rest of the Buddhist canon developed, accusing Takahashi of "slurping up the leftover dribble" of his predecessors.[22] By the same token, Hakugan found Takahashi's biographical sketch of the Buddha so derivative and objectionable that he blanched even at refuting it.

> [This biographical sketch] also imitates the fabricated biographies of Tominaga and Atsutane, but it does not relate how the Buddha observed the five matters in the Tuṣita heaven, how he manifested the five signs of decay and the five miracles [after his birth] and was born in our world. It does not relate how he defeated Māra, turned the wheel of the dharma, or entered *parinirvāṇa*. The Eight Phases all resemble [those of] an ordinary unawakened person. . . . It is merely the fabricated explanation of the Buddha's birth, renunciation, and attainment of the Way, so it is not worth refuting.[23]

Further rebuffing Takahashi's simile of the blossoming of the flower of the Mahāyāna out of the "intention" of the Buddha, Hakugan instead contended that such blossoming is actually to be found elsewhere: *during* the life of the Buddha, or in the preaching assemblies for the various sutras, or in the words of each individual sutra. And finally, Hakugan would have no truck with Takahashi's comparison between the Buddha and Plotinus. "Based on the arguments in this chapter" of Takahashi's book, Hakugan wrote dismissively, "[the writing of Plotinus] is merely a shady imitation of the Buddhist scriptures."[24] He identified the *Sutra of the Heroic March* (Ch. *Shoulengyanlang jing*, *T* 945, Skt. **Śūraṃgamasūtra*) as a likely source of such counterfeit fabrication for the ideas that Takahashi attributed to Plotinus, and elsewhere as well. After subjecting the philosophy of Plotinus to a good thrashing for some pages, Hakugan charged: "If you still do not believe me, then I ask you: Does Plotinus have thirty-two major marks and eighty minor ones? Is there still a canon of scriptures from his lifetime to the number of six or seven thousand? If so, then present them. If not, then know that my defense is no falsehood."[25]

To note that the apologetic publications of Tetsujō and Hakugan failed to persuade Christian readers in Japan would be no small understatement. Hakugan's *Compass* met in turn its counter-refutation by Takahashi, *A New Interpretation of Buddhism* (*Bukkyō shinkai*), published in 1883, after Hakugan's death. It included an appendix titled "On the Absurdity of *A Compass in a Sea of Mist*" ("*Bukai nanshin* benmō"). In response to Hakugan's objection to the radical truncation of the biography of the Buddha in the *New Treatise on Buddhism*, Takahashi extracted a number of "strange events" from the former and final lives of the Buddha, only to dispense with them as nonsensical in their own right, or contradictory to the accounts of other Buddhist scriptures.[26] Responding to Hakugan's elaborate, point-by-point disproofs of the philosophy of Plotinus, Takahashi noted simply:

> From page sixty-nine to page seventy-four [of *A Compass in a Sea of Mist*], Hakugan refutes the arguments of Plotinus in chapter eleven of the *New Treatise on Buddhism*, taking them to be an imitation of Buddhism. But Plotinus expanded upon the arguments of the Greek philosopher Plato, so from the very beginning, his origins differed from Buddhism. Hakugan does not know of these matters, so there is no point in telling him.[27]

For a span after Hakugan's death, Buddhist intellectuals continued to criticize Christianity using established apologetic traditions, but their Christian critics were increasingly not alone in observing the shortcomings of such methods. Within decades, even leading Buddhist intellectuals began to question the utility of apologetics in the traditional vein. In 1903, the True Pure Land scholar-cleric Murakami Senshō (1851–1929)—then suffering a temporary period of exile from his subdenomination, brought on in part by his public pronouncement that the Mahāyāna teachings had not been spoken by the historical Buddha—had no choice but to condemn Tetsujō's approach:

> None of us scholars of Buddhism (*Bukkyōka*) feels drawn to Mr. Edkins, and needless to say, we have sympathy for Kiyū Dōjin ["A Man of the Way Whose Fears Are Groundless," the pen name under which Tetsujō published his refutations]. However, when we engage in research, private feelings ought not to intrude; using one's personal [beliefs] in the realm of debate is not the behavior of a gentleman. Thus, if I set aside my private thoughts, and view this case from the fair perspective of a third party, then it must be said that [Tetsujō's] refutation utterly misses the mark.[28]

As this quotation suggests, the self-conscious modernizers of Buddhist scholarship in Meiji Japan would build their new academic programs on the smoldering ruins of traditional doctrinal scholarship. The intellectual legacy left by Tetsujō and Hakugan, then, lies primarily in their exposure of the failure of established Buddhist intellectual practices to come to terms with arguments posed by their opponents, including arguments based in the study of history. Takahashi Gorō himself later turned away the Protestant Christianity that he had championed in his youth, and inclined toward the spiritualism also imported from Europe. His last years exemplify a particular irony: from 1924 until 1934, just before his death, Takahashi was employed to teach English literature at Komazawa University, founded in 1882 to promote the education of young monks of Sōtō Zen—the same movement from which Nōnin Hakugan hailed.[29]

Within a few years of Hakugan's death, though, Buddhist apologists had actively begun to enlist European learning in their stand against Christianity. In anti-Christian Buddhist polemics, the most important of the early modernizers was Inoue Enryō (1858–1919), born into a True Pure Land temple family and ordained in his youth. His education funded by the Higashi Honganji—headquarters of the Ōtani subdenomination of True Pure Land Buddhism—Enryō graduated from the Philosophy Department of Tokyo Imperial University in 1885, after which he laicized.

However, the termination of his affiliation did not spell an end to his interest in reforming Buddhism and combating the spread of Christianity. In the years following his graduation, Enryō used his training in European philosophy to mount a blistering attack on Christianity in *The Golden Needle of Truth* (*Shinri kinshin*, 1886–1887). Having indicted Christianity as irrational, he next set out an ambitious, ultimately unfinished, work to "prove" the logical coherence of the various Buddhist schools: *Theory of the Revitalization of Buddhism* (*Bukkyō katsuron*, 1887–1890). The *Prolegomenon* (*Joron*) to this long, serialized text, published independently in 1887, received an enthusiastic welcome from intellectuals, both clerical and otherwise. This text held that Buddhism—corrupt and weak as its institutions might be—had an intellectual legacy that could nonetheless be understood in philosophical terms; properly understood, Enryō maintained, this philosophical facet of Buddhism was compatible with European philosophy. Enryō now argued not only that Buddhism could hold its own against Christianity in religious terms, but also that it deserved the prestige that European philosophy enjoyed among Japanese intellectuals of the day.

Despite its vast scope, Enryō's work still refused deep engagement with history. From the start, Enryō took pains to distinguish the "philosophical" significance of Buddhism, which he believed defensible, from its concrete state in the Japan of his day, and even from its origins:

> By "Buddhism," I mean the Buddhism that has been transmitted to Japan; by the founder of its teaching, I mean Śākyamuni. Therefore, although some Christians are garrulous in their claims that the original texts of Buddhism are no longer in India, that the teaching of the Mahāyāna was not expounded by the Buddha, that Śākyamuni did not really exist, and so on, they do not concern me in the least.

> While we lack details of Śākyamuni's biography and the sources of his teachings are unclear, I am not the sort of ignorant man to believe a teaching because of a biography. I trust [in Buddhism] simply because what has been transmitted to Japan is consistent with philosophical reason, and what I reject is simply what is not consistent with philosophical reason.[30]

Enryō's work thus endeavored to enunciate universal principles by excluding historical contingency. True to his declaration in this preface, Enryō did not directly treat the life of the Buddha in his *Prolegomenon*. This does not, however, mean that Enryō could set aside the life of the Buddha altogether. In the *Prolegomenon*'s treatment of Buddhism as philosophy, Enryō revisited the doctrines taught by Śākyamuni as well as the order in which they were taught. For this discussion, he accepted the standard Tendai "division of the teachings" into five parts: the first comprised of the *Flower Garland Sutra* and the last, of the *Lotus* and *Mahāparinirvāṇa* sutras. Further, he devoted a separate chapter to the "Original Intention of Śākyamuni," in which he attempted to defend the Buddha's use of "expedient teachings" in philosophical terms. Even in this highly schematic and universalizing text, then, the teachings of the Buddha remain unavoidably mediated by time.

As did Tetsujō and Hakugan in their apologias for Buddhism, Enryō produced an intellectual defense of Buddhist ideas, while purposely distancing his argument from the person of the historical Buddha. Unlike Tetsujō and Hakugan—men whose religious study completed long before the Meiji Restoration—Enryō was the product of two kinds of elite education: he was conversant both in traditional Chinese and Buddhist learning, and in the latest ideas from Europe. After his laicization in 1885, he was at liberty to defend Buddhism in a selective mode, freely abandoning what he found strategically indefensible so as to hold on to what he could defend.

Nonetheless, in another sense, Enryō simply substituted one master discourse—the body of post-Kantian philosophy as he had imbibed it—for the now-discredited master discourse of traditional East Asian doctrinal studies. This new master discourse could win over parties unmoved by appeals to Buddhist doctrine. In 1887, Enryō and some of his friends founded the "Hall of Philosophy" (Tetsgakukan), a private academy that ultimately developed into today's Tōyō University. Takahashi Gorō attended the opening ceremony and published a critique of Enryō's plans in *The Cosmos* (*Rikugō zasshi*), the leading Japanese Christian journal of the day. Philosophy, Takahashi wrote, "is deemed the 'study of all other studies,' and is revered as the king of the disciplines."[31] Unlike all the other disciplines, he claimed, philosophy alone is not content with explaining individual experiences, but seeks out their ultimate causes. While this article objected to the curriculum at the Hall as a watered-down popularization of philosophy, Takahashi's language about the subject closely echoed that of Enryō in his opening address: philosophy is "a discipline which seeks out the principles of all things and fixes their general rules."[32]

The reluctance of such early Meiji Buddhist apologists to reply in kind to Christian invocation of history was no mere expression of parochialism—or, in Atsutane's language, of being a "poor loser." After all, allowance for historical contingency, for the endless panoply of modes for communicating the ineffable essence of awakening, had by their time been part of the Mahāyāna tradition for well over a millennium and a half, but it had derived its value from participation in a transcendent reality. The claim to find the truth of the Buddha's teaching in its history must have struck intellectuals of a traditional bent as a topsy-turvy distortion of the locus of truth. That truth, they knew, suffered no contingency. In response to Takahashi's prediction that Buddhism would die out as had the school of Plotinus, Hakugan retorted acerbically: "Buddhism in its intrinsic nature has no division between this realm and that; so how could it be only Plotinus who is extinguished? Even if the entire trichiliocosm were to be destroyed, there would still be no formation or destruction in this, our Buddha-dharma, which can never change in past or present."[33] For Hakugan and many centuries of Japanese Buddhist exegetes before him, the timeless nature of the dharma was part of its very definition. That nature was, thus, not subject to debate.

History without Historicism

Intellectual historians of modern Japan conventionally adduce a break in elite discourses around 1887, or Meiji 20. Scholars of the history of political thought, tracking the waning of the Movement for Freedom and Popular Rights, have pointed to the decline of natural law theory and the ascent of a new interest in the "preservation of the national essence," as one new formulation of the time put it.[34] One key forerunner of this shift was Katō Hiroyuki (1836–1916), the first president of Tokyo University, who in 1881 repudiated his previous arguments for natural law and moved decisively toward statism. The meaning of the apparent shift that Katō helped induce remains a topic of debate—

even before 1881, Katō was already using natural law theory to argue for the role of a government elite—but a broader methodological reorientation clearly began in the late 1880s. As the intellectual historian Yamamuro Shin'ichi observed, Katō's turn against the philosophy of natural law helped shift the metaphorical basis of mainstream legal argumentation from the natural sciences to the biological sciences—particularly, if not intentionally, to evolutionary theory, then known in Japan primarily through the social Darwinist writings of Herbert Spencer.[35] The dominant tropes in elite politics and law shifted accordingly: away from nineteenth-century physics, with its immutable, universal laws, and toward nineteenth-century conceptions of evolution in biological systems, which unfolds in a process of never-ending, individual contingency. Different metaphors suggested different methodologies: if nineteenth-century physics posited deduction from invariable, universal principles, then the new science of evolution called for close observation of specific individuals, and careful induction. In humanistic inquiry, evolutionary method resonated with historicism, which in its most radical forms threatens to expose every human endeavor as contingent and limited.[36]

The open-endedness of Darwinist theory, and its inherent potential to rationalize the subjection of Japan in a global hierarchy of exploitation and violence, ultimately drove statist intellectuals to look to other intellectual tools.[37] The new public discourse around national distinctiveness, though, exerted lasting effects. Expressed in such influential new periodicals as *The Japanese* (*Nihonjin*, founded in 1888) and *Japan* (*Nihon*, founded in 1889), it opened up space for serious discussion of Japan's historical heritage and cultural particularities without judging them inferior to their counterparts in Europe. In this context, even intellectuals with no particular loyalty to Buddhist causes could take up the historical study of Buddhism in Japan. Before he cofounded *The Japanese*, the philosopher and historian Miyake Setsurei (1860–1945)—then a recent graduate of the Department of Philosophy at Tokyo University—published a short and misleadingly titled *History of Japanese Buddhism* (*Nihon Bukkyō shi*, 1886). As the first and only installment of a projected multivolume history, this book never even reached the arrival of Buddhism to Japan in its narration.[38] Nonetheless, it sufficed to demonstrate Miyake's interest in showing that developments in Japanese religious history responded to evolutionary pressures.

Buddhist intellectuals, typically writing for apologetic purposes, also gravitated to the historical method, even if they did not embrace the relativism characteristic of so much early-nineteenth-century European historicism. Conventionally, scholars date the widespread acceptance of European-style historical scholarship by Japanese Buddhist intellectuals to the founding of the journal *Grove of Buddhist History* (*Bukkyō shirin*, 1894–1897). The leader in this publication project was Murakami Senshō, who lectured on "Indian Philosophy" at Tokyo University from 1890 until 1923.[39] Here, "Indian philosophy" stood for "Buddhist studies," which Murakami taught using Chinese materials, and focused principally on the Buddhism of East Asia. The turn to "history" as a methodology for the study of Buddhism, then, did not immediately entail the use of a new body of sources in Meiji Japan. Nonetheless, through the publication of this journal, Murakami led the turn from philosophical to historical scholarship concerning Buddhism.[40]

The inaugural issue of the *Grove* appeared on April 8, 1894, explicitly timed to coincide with the traditionally accepted month and day for the birth of Prince Siddhartha. It included the first installment of a four-part discussion by Murakami of the dating of the Buddha's life—both the years of his birth and death and the month and day of those events—for which he almost exclusively used sources in Chinese, relying heavily on Xuanzang's record.[41] In this series, Murakami argued for an extremely early dating for the life of the Buddha (1028 BCE to 949 BCE), and affirmed the observance of the traditional months and days for those events: the eighth day of the fourth month for the birth, and the fifteenth day of the second month for the death.[42] Concern for the dating of the life of the Buddha reappeared in later pieces written for the journal by Murakami, and articles treating South Asian topics appear scattered throughout the three years of the *Grove*: the geography of ancient India, the rulers and Buddhist patrons Aśoka and Kanishka, and the Buddhist assimilation of the Hindu deity Gaṇeśa.[43] Nonetheless, the great bulk of the articles in the journal treated China and Japan. Indeed, the biography that Murakami first explored in the *Grove* was not that of the Indian prince Śākyamuni, but rather that of the Japanese prince Shōtoku. Murakami's promotion of history as a method for academic Buddhist studies thus did not necessarily lead to new sources, or to new conclusions.

The Arrival of European Buddhology

Even before the release of the *Grove*, new accounts of the life of the Buddha were becoming available in Japan. The introduction to Japan of Euro-American scholarship about the Buddha—much of which employed a historical method—stimulated increasing interest, though still apologetic for the most part. The key mode for this introduction lay in the translation and publication of foreign texts. This section introduces a selection of early translations of such scholarship from the late 1870s through the 1880s, showing how Japanese translators' facility with such texts increased dramatically.

The assimilation of European scholarship about Śākyamuni in particular did not feature as a major goal for the first clerical students sent there. Conventional scholarship dates the introduction of the techniques of European Buddhist studies to Japan to 1884. In that year, the True Pure Land scholar-cleric Nanjō Bun'yū (1849–1927) returned to Japan, having completed his studies at Oxford under a pioneering scholar of "Oriental" religions, Freidrich Max Müller (1823–1900).[44] Nanjō went on to contribute mightily to the study of Buddhist scriptures through their Sanskrit editions, but he focused squarely on Mahāyāna texts valued in Japan, and he expressed little interest in the details of the biography of the Buddha. His later brief stay in South Asia in 1885 seems not to have changed that attitude, but rather to have deterred him from his plan to continue the study Sanskrit there. His later account of that trip indicates his sadness at witnessing the Hindu control over Bodhgayā and the dilapidation at the Deer Park. It also represents the German principal of the Benares Sanskrit College, George Thibaut (1848–1914), as personally discouraging Nanjō from the "useless" endeavor of study in such an "unhealthy land" as India.[45] When the occasion later came for Nanjō to speak about Śākyamuni, then, he had little to say. In a commemorative talk for the Buddha's birthday in 1896, Nanjō devoted most of his discussion not to the Buddha himself but to the fable of Barlaam and Josaphat, a widely circulated piece of Christian hagiography based in part upon the Buddha's life story. Presumably, Nanjō saw little new to observe about the biography proper, a topic that he found "not the slightest bit novel," and which, as he told his fellow intellectuals, had been "habitually on our lips since we were children."[46]

Likewise, experiences by Japanese clerical intellectuals of South Asia —which, like Nanjō's journey to Europe, began in the 1870s—took quite some time to register in Japanese narratives of the life or significance of the Buddha. A relatively high rate of casualties among those clerics must be counted among the key causes for the delay. Several of these men arrived in India and managed to engage in study or survey work, only to die shortly afterward. The True Pure Land cleric Fujii Senshō (1859–1903) was called away from his assigned fieldwork in Britain to join the first Ōtani Expedition in 1902, but his health declined during his stay in India, and he died from dysentery in Marseilles, on his way back to London, in June 1903. Another True Pure Land cleric, Shimizu Mokuji (1873–1903), son of Shimaji Mokurai and himself another member of the first Ōtani Expedition, stayed on in India to enroll in the Sanskrit College, only to die in Bombay of cholera in August 1903. The Shingon cleric Hori Shitoku (1876–1903) traveled to India, where he began to learn Sanskrit, and was touring historical sites in the company of the architect and historian Itō Chūta (1864–1954) when he contracted tetanus from an injury that he sustained in a horse carriage accident, and died in Lahore in November 1903.[47] Before leaving Japan, Fujii had produced the first part of an incomplete history of Buddhism that did treat the life of the Buddha, but like Shimizu and Hori, he died before his experiences in South Asia could manifest in his thinking about the historical Buddha.

Even prolonged stay in South and Southeast Asia could have but a glancing impact on the study of the Buddha's life story. The Tendai cleric Ōmiya Kōnin (a.k.a. Ōmiya Kōjun, 1872–1949) voyaged to South Asia on his own in 1895, and traveled and resided in the region for most of the period until his final return to Japan in 1906. (He too contributed to the Ōtani Expedition.) His years of study of Sanskrit in Calcutta included Indic versions of both Aśvaghoṣa's *Acts of the Buddha* and the *Exhaustive Narrative of the Play* [*of the Buddha*].[48] When, after his final return to Japan, Ōmiya lectured on issues in the biography of Śākyamuni in 1909, he nonetheless made relatively little use of these Sanskrit texts. Among the fifteen different sources that he adduced for the month and date of the birth of the prince, Ōmiya included just one Sanskrit source (the *Acts of the Buddha)*, while almost all the rest derived from Chinese Buddhist literature.[49] Among the thirteen different versions of the words first spoken by the newborn prince, none cited by Ōmiya came from a source in any Indic language (though here he did correct a mis-citation by Fujii).[50] In fact, all of the passages of scripture that Ōmiya cited in his lecture derived from the Chinese canonical versions. Doctrinally, too, Ōmiya's approach to the biography was relatively conservative, centering as it did upon the question of which scriptural account was most accurate. Ōmiya did make some concessions—for instance, allowing that the demons whom Siddhartha defeats immediately before his awakening, such as the daughters of Māra, are "personified expressions of an aspect of his mental state, or of the *kleśas*."[51] However, Ōmiya justified this reductive or psychologizing explanation through a rather standard appeal to Nāgārjuna's *Treatise on the Great Perfection of Wisdom*: "There is no lair of demons outside of one's clouded mind; outside of the deluded operation of one thought, there is no other Māra."[52]

The new European scholarship about the life of the Buddha thus first reached Japan through routes other than its clerical explorers abroad. European Buddhology came to Japanese shelves as part of the vast tidal wave of new information to flood Japan from the 1860s onward. As in other fields deemed critical to the nation—railways, mining, industrial development, and the like—the Meiji government directly managed much of the early translation of European knowledge. Working from 1873 to 1888 under the auspices of the Ministry of Education (Monbushō, created in 1871), a team of translators and proofreaders produced a Japanese edition of a popular British encyclopedia, *Chambers's Information for the People*.[53] Initiating and coordinating the translation was the legal scholar and heir to a lineage of experts in Dutch studies, Mitsukuri Rinshō (1846–1897), who had studied English in his youth and previously served as a translator. How Mitsukuri acquired a copy of *Information for the People*, and how he determined it worthy of translation, remain unclear.[54] It was, at any rate, one of the first encyclopedias produced anywhere for a mass readership on an industrial scale. It provided concise accounts of global knowledge whose mastery Japanese elites demanded: "Chemistry Applied to the Arts," "Civil Engineering," "Preparation of Food—Cooking," "Constitution and Resources of the British Empire," "Commerce—Money—Bank," and "Household Hints" ranked among the section headings.[55] Mitsukuri parceled out these and other individual sections among some ninety-six different translators, and he also translated a number of sections himself.

Encyclopedic in scope, *Information for the People* naturally treated religion, and it did not limit its coverage to Christianity. The headings in its third edition describe Asian systems as "Pagan and Mohammedan Religions," but its fourth edition—the one that was used by the Ministry translators—drops that designation for the more neutral "Mohammedanism—Hinduism—Buddhism."[56] The translation of this section, first published in 1877, fell to a disciple of Mitsukuri, the economist Ōshima Sadamasu (1845–1914). Ōshima appears to have been selected not for his knowledge of Buddhism but for his skill in English, and his translation of the subsection about Buddhism is not without infelicities. These are particularly noticeable in its treatment of Buddhist terms and names, for many of which Ōshima supplied either only *kana* transliterations, or literal translations, instead of using the standard

Japanese Buddhist vocabulary. Thus, Japanese readers might have been puzzled to find that the Buddha had been born in *Karirahasutsu* to King *Shudodana*, that his first sermon taught the "four great items," and that his doctrine presupposed the "movement of souls."[57]

Still, Ōshima's translation of the subsection did convey basic achievements of scholarship concerning the Buddha and Buddhism in Europe. Following the English original, Ōshima's translation began by pointing out that despite the venerable age and vast spread of Buddhism, Europeans had only just begun its systematic study with the acquisition of Sanskrit texts in Nepal by Brian Hodgson (1801–1894). "In 1844," Ōshima's translation continued, a "Mr. *Yūzen Borunaufu* published a book titled *An Overview of Buddhist History*. Truly, this was, at last, the origin of reliable theories about Buddhism in the West."[58] This "Yūzen Borunaufu" is, of course, Eugène Burnouf (1801–1852), the pioneering French scholar of Buddhism, and the *Overview of Buddhist History* is his *Introduction à l'histoire du Buddhisme indien*. Burnouf's achievements are illustrated in this capsule summary by Donald S. Lopez Jr.: "Eugène Burnouf was the first European to read a large corpus of Indian Buddhist texts in Sanskrit, and it is from these sources that he paint[ed] his portrait of the Buddha, a human Buddha."[59] Indeed, as Ōshima's translation went on to inform the Japanese reader, European scholarly consensus of the day held that the Buddha had been a historically real human being, and that he actually lived in India.

Although they lacked the resources of the Meiji state, clerical intellectuals within Japan were not slow to begin their own efforts to translate the findings of European and American scholarship into Japanese. In 1872, the young heir to the Ōtani subdenomination of True Pure Land Buddhism, Ōtani Kōei (1852–1923; a.k.a. Gennyo), used his connections with the new Meiji government to arrange for a tour of observation in Europe, against the wishes of the subdenomination's current head—his father—and other leaders. His small entourage, which had to leave in secret, included Ishikawa Shuntai (1842–1931), a scholar-cleric who arranged the travel plans.

Having studied at the Institute for the Defense of the Dharma before its closure, Ishikawa had ascended to high rank in the Ōtani administration, where he promoted its organizational reform. After returning from Europe in 1873, Ishikawa masterminded the creation of an Office of Translation (Hon'yaku kyoku) for the subdenomination. Just five short years later, in 1878, Ishikawa fell foul of a scandal whose details remain unclear. His resultant, if temporary, fall from grace robbed the Office of its patron, and it closed abruptly.

Over this short span of five years, the translators of the Office must have worked feverishly, because their labor left a great mass of unpublished translations from European languages. They included histories of Mormonism, outlines of Protestant and Catholic doctrine, and the first Japanese version of the *Life of Jesus* (*Vie de Jésus*, 1863). Written by a French scholar of the "Orient," Ernest Renan (1823–1892), this book had shocked European Christians by describing Jesus as a historical figure but not as a divine being. Needless to say, its translation into Japanese was motivated less by abstract intellectual considerations than by its potential utility in debates over Christianity. During its brief lifetime, the Office managed to print translations only of part of the *Sanskrit-English Dictionary* (1872) by the British Sanskritist Monier Monier-Williams (1819–1899), and of the chapter treating Buddhism from the first volume of *Ten Great Religions*, which had been released in 1871 by the New England Unitarian minister James Freeman Clarke (1810–1888). This chapter, which included Clarke's concise biography of the Buddha, was translated by a member of the Office staff, and published with interlinear commentaries written by Ishikawa himself, as *Evaluation of a Discussion of Buddhism* (*Bukkyō ronpyō*), in 1876.

Unlike Joseph Edkins, James Clarke was no obvious adversary against Buddhism—a point not lost on his Japanese readers. Shinohara Junmei (1836–1906), Ishikawa's colleague, contributed a preface to Ishikawa's *Evaluation*, including these words: "The work by this writer about Buddhism, the American Mr. James Clarke, is what is called 'equipped with both eyes'; it is not akin to [Joseph Edkins'] *Correction of the Errors of Buddhism*."[60] Universalist aspirations aside, though, Clarke's *Ten Great Religions* nonetheless represented an unmistakable apology for Christianity. As noted by Tomoko Masuzawa, Clarke's survey of world religions in fact represented them as "at best preparatory phenomena . . . whose transcendent aspirations [had] been from the beginning . . . doomed to fail."[61] And as Shinohara himself explicitly indicated in the preface, the translation by True Pure Land Buddhists of Clarke's work was not carried out in a spirit of reconciliation, but was instead prompted by the mutual failure of Christian and Buddhist disputants to understand one another's religious systems. In the previous era of the "closed country" (*sakoku*), Shinohara wrote, Buddhists and Christians had repeatedly battled one another in writing: "However, the followers of our religion (*kyōmon*) always said that Christians, ignorant of Buddhism, made delusory attacks, and that their arguments couldn't touch even its skin, much less its marrow."[62] Nonetheless, the arguments wielded by the Buddhist side had been equally ineffective: "Previously, Mr. Ishikawa had a book refuting Christianity. Its sincerity in refuting the heresy and manifesting orthodoxy moved us, but it was a shame that it was inadequate to refute the essence of Christianity altogether."[63] A more accurate understanding of Christianity would, Shinohara implied, enable Japanese Buddhists to defeat it decisively.

At the Office, then, *Ten Great Religions* was studied in order to explicate Christian understandings of Buddhism. Its translators' success in this endeavor was at best partial, though, owing mostly to the spotty quality of the translation, whose errors inspired Ishikawa to refute arguments never actually made in the English original. For example, Clarke's English original text, in its universalizing mode, positively noted points of resemblance between Buddhism and Catholicism. It quoted one "Mr. Medhurst," whose writing "mentions the image of a virgin, called the 'queen of heaven,' having an infant in her arms, and holding a cross. Confession of sins is regularly practiced."[64] In Japanese translation, this passage became something like: "A Mr. *Medarufu* deems a heavenly maiden as the 'main image' (*honzon*) of this religion. Images are painted of this goddess holding an infant, with a cross in her hand. Before this god, he said, there is confession (*zange*) of sins."[65]

Such "domesticating" translation into familiar Japanese Buddhist vocabulary—here, the use of *honzon* and *zange*—did not necessarily aid Ishikawa's understanding, and seems instead to have backfired. The previous description is credited to Walter Henry Medhurst (1796–1857), missionary in Shanghai from 1842 to 1856. It likely refers to an image of the bodhisattva Guanyin (Skt. Avalokiteśvara, Jpn. Kannon) in her guise of the bestower of children. The iconography of Kannon holding a child had been familiar in Japan since the Edo period, and continued to appear in Meiji art.[66] Ishikawa thus ought to have recognized it easily. However, the garbled translation of this passage instead prompted Ishikawa to retort: "These gods (*kami*) are probably the gods (*shoten*) of Lamaism (*Ramakyō*), which I cannot record in detail here. To speak of them as the main images in Buddhism is an outrageous fabrication."[67] Similarly, against the reference to "crosses" in Buddhism, Ishikawa asserted that this must be a mistake for the Buddhist swastika. He proceeded to assert that the Christian cross actually had derived from the Buddhist swastika, citing authorities as respectable as Renan and Burnouf in his challenge to Clarke.

Similar problems in translation hampered Ishikawa's reading of Clarke's summary of the life of Śākyamuni. Clarke's original text described the renunciation of the young prince in a fairly conventional mode: "So . . . he left the palace one night, and exchanged the position of a prince for that of a mendicant. 'I will never return to the palace,' said he, 'till I have attained to the sight of the divine law, and so become Buddha.'"[68] Perhaps challenged by the use of quoted speech in the English, the Office translator rendered this passage as follows: "Having made up his mind, he vowed, 'I will never return home again unless I achieve my aspiration.' Under the cloak of night, he left the palace, renamed himself 'Buddha,' and became a mendicant monk."[69] In reply to this translation, Ishikawa wrote indignantly: "'Buddha' is a term for the highest degree of awakening. It is not a name by which the World-Honored One names himself; how much less could he have used this name at the time of his renunciation. The error here is extreme."[70] Indeed, in no orthodox biography does the prince take "Buddha" as his title on leaving the palace, and to his credit, Clarke had made no such claim.[71] As these scattered examples show, the translations produced by the Office during its brief lifespan are an index of both the demand for foreign knowledge, and the immense challenge of assimilating it.

Even after the closure of the Office, translators continued to produce and disseminate Japanese versions of European scholarship about Buddhism and the Buddha. In 1887, there appeared a translation into Japanese of excerpts from a perennial bestseller by Thomas William (T. W.) Rhys Davids (1843–1922), *Buddhism: Being a Sketch of the Life and Teachings of Gautama, the Buddha* (first published in 1877, though the 1882 edition was used here). Along with his wife and collaborator, Caroline Augusta Foley Rhys Davids (1857–1942), T. W. Davids pioneered Anglophone scholarship concerning Buddhism through its texts in the Pāli language. After starting to study Pāli in British Ceylon, where he served as a colonial official (1866–1874), T. W. Davids returned to Britain, where he founded the Pāli Text Society in 1881. As a successor to Burnouf, Davids disseminated the rationalist image of a distinctly human Buddha within Europe and beyond its borders.

Under the new title *Flowers of Wisdom* (*Bodai no hana*), the Japanese translation of this, Davids's most important early work, was accompanied by a preface from a leading clerical promoter of precept practice, the Shingon cleric Shaku Unshō (1827–1909). Despite Unshō's endorsement for the translation as a whole, his preface nonetheless expresses reservations about the value of European scholarship concerning Buddhism: "Why is it that, for the most part, Westerners' glimpses of Buddhist principle give one the impression of being the views [of a frog] in a well? It comes from their ignorance of karmic causality and samsara."[72] Unshō's skepticism aside, there is no question that this translation, by one Kuwahara Keiichi (n.d.), demonstrated a rapid growth in Japanese facility with European Buddhist scholarship. Names and terms that had discomfited Ōshima a decade ago, in 1877—"Kapilavastu," "Śuddhodana," "Four Noble Truths"—appeared in Kuwahara's translation with notes referring readers to their familiar Japanese equivalents. Davids's text makes copious reference— often in Sanskrit—to texts and figures unknown in Japan, but Kuwahara seems to have been better prepared to cope with these challenges than were his predecessors; for instance, he successfully matched the Sanskrit title *Lalitavistara* with its two Chinese translations.[73]

Such improvements in the quality of translations from European languages would have aided Japanese readers' engagement with the major ideas of Davids. Davids stressed the "historical displacement between the life of the Buddha and the texts of Buddhism"—particularly the question of "how a charismatic human being, a great humanist philosopher who had risen up against the ritual, priestcraft, and institutional religion of his time, had over time been deified by his followers."[74] That emphasis on the gap between the historical Buddha and later accounts of his life is evident even in the table of contents in *Buddhism*: chapters 2 and 3, included in the Japanese translation of 1887, comprise "The Life of Gautama"; chapter 4, not included in this early Japanese translation, is a separate study of "The Legend of the Buddha." Even without the text of this latter chapter, Japanese readers of the 1887 translation could still have found Davids's idea in the first chapter of the text:

> There was certainly an historical basis for the Buddhist legend; and if it be asked whether it is at all possible to separate the true from the false, I would reply, that the difficulty, though great, is apt to be exaggerated. The retailers of these legends are not cunning forgers, but simple-minded men, with whose modes of thought we can put ourselves more or less *en rapport*; we are getting to know what kinds of things to expect from their hero-worship and religious reverence, and delight in the physically marvelous.[75]

Needless to say, Davids's point here rests on a distinctly Orientalist faith in the endless credulity of primitive peoples. But patronizing and belittling as it is, this argument could nonetheless have suggested novel possibilities for intellectuals in the Japan of 1887.

As we have already seen, in anti-Buddhist polemics across East Asia, critics of Buddhism had long denounced its scriptures as forgeries—in other words, as deliberate deceptions. Even in his sketch of the development of Buddhist literature, Tominaga Nakamoto portrayed the act of attributing late texts to the Buddha as a deliberate one. By contrast, Davids suggested that such attribution lacked not only malice, but perhaps conscious intention as well: it simply resulted from the innate dispositions of "simple-minded men" and could be understood on that basis. Their dispositions, Davids went on, were not so alien from "ours" as to be utterly incomprehensible. Japanese Buddhist intellectuals themselves would begin to grapple with this suggestion before long.

The translation of this passage from *Flowers of Wisdom* presages another development in Japanese discussions of the life story of the Buddha in its particular rendering of the English term "legend" into Japanese. Published decades later, in 1911, the first complete translation of Davids's *Buddhism* rendered "legend" here as *koden*: "ancient tradition," or "ancient account."[76] In the earlier, partial translation of 1887, though, Kuwahara had interpreted "legend" not as a cumulative cultural inheritance from ancient times, but as a fictive story (*shōsetsu*). Today, *shōsetsu* is the standard translation for the literary form of the "novel" and its European counterparts (Fr. *roman*, Ger. *Roman*, etc.). Until the 1880s, though, it referred mostly to vernacular fiction imported from China (*xiaoshuo*) and its Japanese derivatives, a usage that changed only gradually and fitfully.[77] Kuwahara's 1887 translation, which clearly counterposes *shōsetsu* against "history," inherits this notion of fictiveness.

To label accounts of the life of the Buddha "fictive" might seem no less disparaging than Atsutane's condemnation of them as "fabricated accounts," and some Japanese Buddhist intellectuals understood the treatment of the life of the Buddha as a "legend" in precisely this way. In 1894, the True Pure Land scholar-cleric Fujishima Ryōon (1852–1918), who had previously studied in France, published "The Legendary Śākyamuni" ("Shōsetsuteki Shakuson"). Here he mounted an attack on a claim made by the French scholar Émile Senart (1847–1928): Senart held that the Buddha may have been a real historical figure, but nonetheless denied that the life stories of the Buddha have any historical basis; they simply reflect the solar mythology of ancient India. Citing European critics of Senart, Fujishima maintained that the "legendary" reading of such religious figures as the Buddha or Jesus was merely a passing fad.[78] His conviction was unfounded: Even by Fujishima's time, Japanese intellectuals who did not dismiss the Buddha's biography in toto were still increasingly identifying "legend" within it.

Unlike Fujishima, not all Japanese Buddhist intellectuals objected to indications of literary qualities in Buddhist texts. From the 1890s, some of them actively began to advocate literary readings of those texts, on the basis of European scholarly discourses. One leading advocate of a literary mode of interpretation was Sakaino Kōyō (1871–1933), who devoted his life to the reform of Buddhism through scholarship and publication. Sakaino graduated from Enryō's Hall of Philosophy and had contacts with the influential Unitarian movement then active within Japanese Christianity. At the age of twenty-three, Sakaino assisted Murakami in the founding of the academic *Grove of Buddhist History*. In the November 1894 issue of the journal, Sakaino published "Historical Buddhism" (*Rekishiteki Bukkyō*), an essay that censured conservative Buddhist clerics, entreating them to defend Buddhism with history, not "forced interpretations" (*kenkyō fukai*). In this piece, Sakaino estimated that Western scholarship about Buddhism still lagged far behind Japan's, but he also warned that a refusal to employ historical methods in scholarship would ultimately cede the field to the Europeans and Americans.[79]

Even as he continued to contribute to the *Grove* over the following years, Sakaino seems to have grown aware of the danger of reductionism lurking in the thorough embrace of history as a master discipline. In articles contributed to a separate, reformist Buddhist journal in 1896, Sakaino issued a new call for the recognition of "Poetical Buddhism" ("Shiteki Bukkyō"). Identifying three "qualities" (*genshitsu*) within Buddhism, Sakaino now contended that the apparent "delusions" (*mōsō*) of Buddhist texts need not be read, with naive credulity, for what he called their "religious" qualities. Nor, he went on, need they be dismissed as "superstition" in favor of the texts' "philosophical" qualities. Rather, when read as the texts' "poetical" qualities, these "delusory" elements might be understood to express "ideals." While foolish common people might have confused or conflated these three qualities in Buddhist texts, Sakaino continued, eminent monks of past times would not have made such errors, instead appreciating poetry for what it is. Again criticizing the Buddhist clergy of his own day, Sakaino held that both traditionalists and philosophers "are together guilty of not understanding poetical Buddhism. If they held that ideals are delusory, then both *Faust* and *Paradise Lost* would be only delusion."[80]

As this allusion to European literary classics suggests, Sakaino borrowed from foreign precedents in making this argument. One of Sakaino's supporters in the liberal Japanese Christian press succinctly noted that Sakaino's notion of "poetical Buddhism" was an application of the interpretation of the Bible as "poetical expression" (here using the English words), a hermeneutic introduced to Japan by the liberal German missionary Otto Schmiedel (1858–1924; active in Japan, 1887–1892).[81] As part of his lifelong project of promoting "free inquiry" (*jiyū tōkyū*) into Buddhism, Sakaino continued to refine his ideas about different modes of interpretation, finally applying them to scriptural representations of Śākyamuni in the mid-1900s.

Such early, fragmentary efforts to assimilate European and American scholarship about the life of the Buddha did not, by themselves, engender any decisive shifts in Japanese scholarship about Buddhism. To begin with, none of these works remained a standard reference source in its own right; instead, they all quickly became historical artifacts from a transitional period. By the turn of the twentieth century, Japanese publishing houses were no longer just translating European encyclopedias, like *Chambers' Information for the People*, but had rather begun to produce their own encyclopedias in the European style. Later translators did not revisit Clarke's *Ten Great Religions* to produce a complete Japanese version, and the 1887 partial translation of Davids' *Buddhism* was superseded by the full—and more readable—retranslation of 1911.

Through the late 1880s, then, the European study of the Buddha seems to have exerted little influence in Japanese Buddhist circles more broadly, even in the isolated cases in which Japanese Buddhists made specific attempts to introduce the Buddha to an Anglophone readership. From 1888 to 1889, a group of students at the Honganji subdenominational academy published a short-lived English-language newsletter, *The Bijou of Asia*. Its fourth (and nearly final) issue, published in March 1889, carried the first installment of a "Life of Buddha." Uncredited but possibly composed by the editor of the newsletter, one Matsuyama Matsutarō (n.d.), the article offers a highly telegraphic summary of the life of the Buddha, translated from a reference work published in Japan in 1887.[82] The translation into English made few concessions to its readers beyond transcribing names and terms into their Sanskrit equivalents and translating dates into their Gregorian equivalents. What Japanese Buddhist outreach offered even to Anglophone readers at this point was simply the standard version of the Buddha's life as it was still circulating within Japan; even when addressing the Anglophone world, Japanese Buddhist presentations of that life did not yet reflect substantive engagement with European scholarship about the Buddha.

On the Limits of Historical Study

By the middle of the 1890s, then, cutting-edge Buddhist intellectuals had begun to reformulate their own broad textual and doctrinal inheritance by using modes derived from latter nineteenth-century European philosophical and historical practice. The world of Euro-American Christianity had begun to appear to some reform-minded young Buddhist intellectuals not merely as a monolithic threat, but also as a repository of intellectual developments that could be applied to the understanding of Buddhist texts—particularly developments from the more liberal versions of Christian theology, which exerted a disproportionate impact in Japan. Nonetheless, as the short-lived Buddhist reformer Furukawa Rōsen (1871–1899) declared in the title of a celebrated short essay of 1894, "We Have Entered an Age of Uncertainty" ("Kaigi jidai ni ireri").[83] As Furukawa warned, the historical study of Buddhist literature would, when fully assimilated, trigger consequences as distressing as they were inevitable:

> If Buddhists today were versed in the history of Buddhism, could observe the traces of its doctrinal development, and could use a clear eye for reading the sutras to make a critical evaluation of the sutras and commentaries, then they would naturally be lofty in knowledge, and thus would give rise to even a little dismay. While many students of Buddhism today are merely absorbed in the explication of words in one part of the Tripiṭaka, they must steel themselves for the great shock that will surely arrive.[84]

Even as he intimated a looming spiritual crisis, Furukawa encouraged the adoption of modern scholarly methods. Only by first passing through the "age of uncertainty," he held, could Japanese Buddhists enter the more developed "age of critique" yet to come. In the period of the 1890s, when Furukawa outlined the consequences of the application of historical study to Buddhist text and practice, more than one attempt to narrate a historically defensible life of the Buddha foundered in uncertainty. Although the authors of these works each inhabited a different position in relation to establishment Buddhism, they uniformly proved unequal to the "great shock" of the advent of historical scholarship.

Saji Jitsunen (1856–1920), a onetime True Pure Land cleric of the Ōtani subdenomination who had defected to Unitarianism in 1892, exemplified these problems when he serialized a biography of the Buddha in the Unitarian newsletter *Religion* (*Shūkyō*), from 1893 to 1894.[85] In its first installment, Saji set out his reason for writing the biography and the basic difficulty in doing so. As one effort at inclusiveness and as a high-minded display of tolerance, the Japanese Unitarian mission had begun to observe the birthdays of each of the "Four Great World Sages" (*Sekai shidai seijin*), beginning with the Buddha.[86] At the celebration for the Buddha's birthday on April 8 of that year, Saji wrote, he had given a talk, which he had then been asked to publish.

But what, he asked in the piece that he wrote, ought he to publish? Of course, Saji allowed, he could very well cobble together a biography of the Buddha by picking and choosing from all the available sources. In fact, while Saji may have given up on Buddhist institutions, his outline of biographical sources available to him suggests that he retained more than a passing familiarity with Buddhist learning. Beginning with the standard Chinese scriptures and derivative compilations, he continued through the Edo vernacular tradition—not neglecting Kōgetsu's *Light of the Three Ages*—before listing publications of his own time, including translations of such foreign works as T. W. Rhys Davids's *Buddhism*.[87]

Thus Saji's difficulty lay in evaluating the sources that he tracked down. As he wrote, the sources that already were accessible did not merely clarify Śākyamuni's achievements, but "also include wonders and absurdities, so that rather than an excess of such materials, it would be better to have a lack of them."[88] Anticipating Sakaino's chronologically later argument about the different "qualities" of materials commingled in Buddhist texts, Saji declared that he would like to "divide clearly the historical Siddhartha from the ideal, great Buddha Śākyamuni," but had found the task impossible. "Materials for the biography of Śākyamuni may be found without searching, and come without summoning," he went on, but among the sheer bulk, he could not find "building blocks already 'cut to size,' or anything of good quality and sturdy."[89] In the end, Saji could only critique the existing biographical tradition even as he retold it, interspersing passages derived from scriptural texts with his own commentaries, as Atsutane had done most of a century before him.

If Saji's case exemplifies the difficulties of retelling the life of the Buddha for an apostate—albeit one committed to irenicism—then it proved still more difficult for a devout layperson to reconcile the Buddha's life with historical and rationalist leanings. One work to exemplify this challenge came from the hand of a lay Buddhist educator, lecturer, and writer named Katō Totsudō (1870–1949). During his life, he taught in True Pure Land and Sōtō educational institutions, wrote prodigiously for the trans-denominational Buddhist press, and published over sixty books, many of which treated Buddhist themes—but he never became a Buddhist cleric. Katō's life thus illustrates the possibilities newly opened to intellectual Buddhist laymen in Japan at the last decade of the nineteenth century: he had no affiliation with any specific denomination of Buddhism, yet he made his living solely through teaching and publication, largely on Buddhist themes. Katō's success in this endeavor demonstrates that the ranks of spokesmen for Buddhism in modern Japan had, by his day, expanded to accommodate such intellectual laymen in prominent public positions.

In 1891, the twenty-one-year-old Katō self-published the first of his dozens of books, a pamphlet titled *The Great Sage Śākyamuni* (*Daishō Shaka*). Katō introduced his work with a quotation from the first sentence of *The Christ of History: An Argument Grounded in the Facts of His Life on Earth* (first published in 1855): "A change in the form of the argument for the proper deity of Jesus Christ seems to be demanded in our day."[90] *The Christ of History*, by the British minister John Young (1805–1881), sought to counter the corrosive effects on Christian faith of historical scholarship. Young argued that Christ's divinity could be defended on the basis of his historical humanity. Later editions of the book even included an appendix specifically dedicated to refuting the arguments of Renan's *Life of Jesus*. Though largely forgotten now, *The Christ of History* sold well in its own day: by 1906—slightly more than half a century from its first appearance—it had already passed through eight editions, and it had been translated into German (1858), Japanese (1889), and Arabic (1890).

Following Young's lead in presenting an argument for faith by using exclusively historical evidence, Katō asserted in his book's preface that "in our day of the development of the intellectual sciences," there was no longer anything for a critic to gain from "absurd and groundless biographies."[91] Like Saji, then, Katō attempted not so much to tell an innovative account as to edit or justify the existing ones through commentary, though he derived his version of the Buddha's life story from multiple sources. Even this less ambitious task, though, proved unexpectedly thorny. Katō noted the difficulties that he experienced in determining precisely what counted as "absurdity" and "groundlessness." In relating the episode of the birth of the prince, Katō omitted the specification of his birth from his mother's side, even as he retained other miracles from the traditional accounts: the newborn infant's seven steps; his declaration of his preeminence; and the appearance of lotus flowers at his feet and deities in the air. Katō defended this selection in his commentary to the chapter:

> As indicated in the preface, in editing this book, I have worked to eliminate [narrative] facts akin to superstition. However, for some of the acts of Śākyamuni—who possessed infinite power and infinite knowledge—it has been difficult for me all at once to distinguish what is a fabrication and what is not. Such accounts as the wonders of the birth, as discussed in this chapter, are just like the angels who sang of glory when Christ was about to be born before they returned to heaven, and their prophecy that people would be at peace. While these wonders are over one thousand years and countless tens of thousands of miles apart, they agree with one another. Could we reject these all as absurdities? I wonder if the real absurdity is always to regard such matters as absurd. For now, I will record them, and await [the judgment] of learned [readers].[92]

Struggling to integrate trans-historical elements into a biography grounded in a nineteenth-century empiricist notion of history, Katō vacillated before this and related passages. Writing about the tradition that the prince had, before leaving the palace, impregnated Yaśodharā by pointing his finger at her belly, Katō again found himself at a loss. Was it a fiction? An expression of his superhuman powers? Or simply a matter of such antiquity as to be unknowable?[93]

Of course, Katō was not so hesitant in the treatment of every supernatural event in the narrative; he more decisively eliminated the conventional role of the deity of the Pure Abode in inspiring the prince's renunciation, and he couched the description of Māra's attack in psychological terms, as "evil thoughts and delusions" that "came and went in Śākyamuni's breast."[94] Still, it is significant that Katō conspicuously avoided the wholesale elimination of the biographical wonders. Like Sakaino, he seems to have been wary of the relativizing implications of a thoroughgoing historicism.

Katō's *Great Sage Śākyamuni* many not have reconciled the biography of the Buddha to the demands of history, but it did augur a new development in the overall framing of that biography. Katō began the body of his account by locating Śākyamuni not in the Buddhist cosmos, nor in the historical setting of ancient India, but among a universal pantheon of global "heroes" (*eiyū*): the Japanese warlord Toyotomi Hideyoshi (1536/7–1598), the French general Napoleon Bonaparte (1769–1821), the Scottish inventor James Watt (1736–1819), the Italian explorer Christopher Columbus (1451–1506), and a litany of others. In the world of heroes, he continued, each occupies a distinct field: politics, entrepreneurship, literature, religion (here he specifically named Confucius and Christ), and so forth. Katō returned to this theme in the final chapters of his book, arguing that the Buddha had in fact outdone his rivals—as a political leader who changed Indian society; as a poet who composed thousands of scriptures (in this work, Katō did not question their provenance); as an author of prose who transformed countless people; and as an "entrepreneur" (*jitsugyō no yū*) whose influence spread around the world, presumably like a banker's money or an inventor's creations.[95] Katō may not have first devised this comparison between the Buddha and other idols of late nineteenth-century Europe, but he gave it a rousing articulation. As this chapter will later show, the inclusion of the Buddha among a global pantheon of "great men"—including those from the fields of religion and philosophy—would become a key to his newfound popularity in Japan from the turn of the century.

As the examples of Saji and Katō suggest, even writers who maintained no allegiances to the Japanese Buddhist establishment—a clerical apostate to Unitarianism and an up-and-coming young Buddhist layman—could struggle to fashion a historically defensible life of the Buddha in the 1890s. We might therefore expect an intellectual at the heart of a Buddhist denomination to have found the problem still more intractable. However unexpectedly, though, this was not the case for the discussion of the Buddha's life in the first volume of *A Short History of Buddhism* (*Bukkyō shōshi*, 1894), by the True Pure Land cleric Fujii Senshō, whose early death cut short a promising career as a scholar of Buddhism.

Among Buddhist clerics in late nineteenth-century Japan, Fujii stood out as a man of firsts: to begin with, he was the first ordained cleric of the Honganji subdenomination to graduate from the Tokyo Imperial University Department of Philosophy, in 1891. Unlike Inoue Enryō, who had hailed from the Ōtani subdenomination, Fujii remained a cleric after graduating and took up a teaching position at the Honganji academy (Bungakuryō), predecessor to today's Ryukoku University.[96] He took the role of groom in the first Buddhist-style wedding in Japan (held in Tokyo, at a hall inside the complex of the temple Tsukiji Honganji, in 1892).[97] He further ranked among the first modern Buddhist clerics to inspire a character in a work of fiction by a contemporary author: in 1904—the year after Fujii's death—the novelist Shimazaki Tōson (1872–1943) published a short story, "The Shade of the Palm Leaves" ("Yashi no hakage"), whose unnamed protagonist overlaps with the historical Fujii.[98]

Fujii was dispatched by his denomination to London to study the religious situation in Britain in 1900. Before he could finish that task, he was summoned to India in 1902 to join the survey team for the first of the continental expeditions sponsored by Ōtani Kōzui (1876–1948), heir to the leadership of the Honganji subdenomination. From October 1902 to May 1903, Fujii labored to study Buddhism in India, visiting sites directly associated with the life of the Buddha—such as Bodhgayā and Rājagṛha—as well as a number of other sites, including the Buddhist cave temples at Ajantā and the Indian Museum in Calcutta. (Anesaki Masaharu, who stopped in India and stayed for roughly half a year on his way back to Japan from Europe, took lodgings with Fujii and accompanied him on his expeditions.) His overexertion damaged his already fragile intestinal health, and he died—likely of dysentery—on his way back to London, at the French port of Marseilles. (Shimazaki Tōson granted his fictional protagonist a more romantic death, lying in a sickroom in Colombo, Ceylon, tended by a fellow Japanese cleric who was also studying abroad.)

Composed before his overseas travels began, Fujii's *Short History of Buddhism* also marks an original achievement in scholarship about the Buddha. Like other notable attempts to compose grand Buddhist histories during the Meiji years, it was never completed. Nonetheless, its two published volumes distinguished a key moment in modern Buddhist intellectual history, revealing how Japanese Buddhist clerics began to adjust their historical self-understanding to the new standards employed in secular academic histories. This achievement is not a little surprising, considering that Fujii wrote and published his *Short History* even as he served as an instructor in the Honganji subdenominational academy.[99] On first glance, it is difficult to reconcile the devotion to doctrinal orthodoxy that would have been expected of Fujii as an educator with sentences such as these, with which he opened the preface in his first volume:

> What is History? Accounts of the development of human knowledge and the advance of civilization: These we call "history." Thus, the facts that make up history must rely upon definite sources. Fantasies of the sort in legends (*shōsetsu*) or in tales of wizards must never be intermixed with it.[100]

In fact, Fujii's substantial preface to his biography of the Buddha explicitly declares his historical methodology: historical writing must describe social facts in relationships of cause and effect.[101] Socially static societies—for Fujii, presumably including Japan before the Meiji period—do not have history proper, but inhabit an "age of ancient stories and tales of wonder."[102] History must be written impartially, so that even biographies of the Buddha "must always be read with a critical faith achieved through understanding (*hihyōteki geshin*)."[103] Indeed, a historical account of the Buddha must be readable by outsiders as well as insiders: "Śākyamuni must not be made the 'private property' of Buddhists."[104] Such positions must embody the legacy of Fujii's European-style education at the Imperial University. However, at the end of his preface, Fujii gestured obliquely to the limitations imposed on his scholarship by his institutional affiliation: "Heedless of the sort of passive restraint given me by my situation, I am recklessly attempting to do something that scholars will condemn. Hearing of this, who would not laugh at my foolishness, and pity my lack of thought?"[105]

Indeed, Fujii did lose his teaching position in 1897, though the cause lay in internecine battles at the academy and not in his scholarship. Even incomplete, his *Short History* stands as a pioneering synthesis of European scholarship about Buddhism with sources from the Chinese-language tradition. Fujii carried out his long discussion of the Buddha's life in dialogue with the works of European scholars, most of whose writings Fujii could not yet have read in Japanese translation. His first volume cites the findings of—among others—T. W. Rhys Davids; Monier Monier-Williams; the British Sanskritist Charlotte Manning (1803–1871); the French Catholic missionary to Burma, Paul Ambroise Bigandet (1813–1894); the German Sanskritist Hermann Oldenberg (1854–1920); and the British missionary to Ceylon, Robert Spence Hardy (1803–1868). With his facility in reading the Chinese Buddhist scriptures, Fujii was able to compare and contrast the findings of these scholars, whose evidence came from South and Southeast Asia, with the scriptural tradition as known in Japan. Through such comparative work, Fujii tried to determine, for example, the precise genealogy for the prince, and the ages at which he accomplished various deeds of his life.

Despite these historical investigations, Fujii also posited another level of meaning to the story of the Buddha's life. For example, he began his seventh chapter, concerning the Buddha's renunciation of the world, with a statement distinguishing the "inner truth" (*naijitsu*) from the "external appearance" (*gesō*) in his life story.[106] For the Buddha, the events of his life are mere "expedients" (here Fujii used not the technical Chinese term *hōben*, but the more colloquial Japanese *shimono*); for human knowledge, though, the "inner truth" of these events is inaccessible. "If you try to expound them anyway," Fujii continued,

> then they become either tales of the strange, or talk to no end. These tales of the strange, and talk to no end, do not transmit the Śākyamuni who was held in awe as the Teacher of Gods and Men, or revered as the World-Honored One. Therefore, I must limit my brush to narrating the manifestation of his external appearance. However, although I stop at his external appearance, depicting the sixteen-foot body and the monastic robes of Śākyamuni, his inner truth and his external appearance do not exist apart from one another, so when I adduce the external form, the inner truth will become manifest on its own. Whether or not that inner truth is recognized is not to be known from the description, but depends solely on the capacity of the person, able to read and able to see. In other words, in order for me to be able to enshrine Śākyamuni into history, I cannot but content myself with this.[107]

While the "sixteen-foot body" (*jōroku*) credited to the Buddha may itself seem to represent a "tale of the strange," it is in fact the conventional measurement attributed to Śākyamuni in his historical lifetime. Juxtaposing that body, amenable to description, against an unknowable "inner truth," Fujii's text thus wavers here, as elsewhere, in its reliance upon the discipline of history. This passage certainly points out the limits of history, but not as a gesture of methodological humility or skepticism; rather, it indicates the existence of a separate reality to which historical research affords no access. Like Murakami Senshō, Fujii appears to have felt the need to supplement the conclusions that could be derived from historical rationalism alone.

The review of the *Short History* by Anesaki Masaharu, published in 1897, noted the tension between the book's overarching historical framework and its ventures—or, perhaps, slippages—into the realm of the transhistorical. On the whole, Anesaki's generally laudatory review praises the book's methodological foundation: "There is no question that this book should be seen as a history, not as a book of religion."[108] In the final lines of his review article, though, Anesaki chastised Fujii's inability (or unwillingness) to apply the historical method consistently:

> I greatly regret that the author occasionally appears to let his prose run beyond historical writing. When he does that, the author does not strive to manifest the spirit of Śākyamuni as a great man in history (*rekishi jō no ijin*), but rather eulogizes him as though he were made of the concepts added by later generations. . . . The author's confusion between the historical Śākyamuni, and Śākyamuni seen in a po-

etical manner [more literally, "as reflected in poetic vision"], may have no little influence over the value of the *Short History of Buddhism* as a work of history.[109]

These comments aside, Anesaki held Fujii in great respect. He contributed a glowing encomium to the posthumous publication of Fujii's writings, praising Fujii's selfless work with Buddhist sculpture and epigraphy in the museum at Calcutta during the summer of 1902. In the eulogy, Anesaki lamented:

> The study of the characteristics of Buddhist sculpture, a field strongly related to the changes in Mahāyāna Buddhism, has died along with [Fujii]; not only have his achievements not appeared, but not even many people have understood the pains which he took. I regret to the utmost the possibility that they should be buried and forgotten.[110]

By the time that he had composed these words, though, Anesaki had set out a very different solution to the problem of finding value in the life of the Buddha, while describing him in historical terms.

Over a few short decades, Japanese Buddhist intellectuals' responses to European and American writing about the life of the historical Buddha had traveled a great distance. Traditionalist efforts to counter Christian attacks on the established understanding of the Buddha—carried out in print from the late 1860s through the early 1880s—inadvertently exposed the unsuitability of conventional apologetics to comprehend Christian descriptions of the Buddha, much less to refute them. By the latter 1880s, leading apologists for Japanese Buddhism had begun to appropriate the tools of European philosophy, both to attack Christianity and to reformulate Buddhist doctrines to participate in the prestige then accorded to European thought. Over the same period, European scholarship about the life of the historical Buddha began to filter into print in Japan, generally through translations undertaken for the defense and development of the nation and of Buddhist institutions. The 1890s saw the rise of inquiry into Buddhism through its history, a field whose standards in Japan drew heavily upon the late-nineteenth-century European discipline. The empiricist character of that discipline, however, itself proved hazardous to intellectuals' efforts to consolidate and defend a Buddhism rooted in "fact." In the study of the life of the historical Buddha, empiricism threatened to dissolve traditionalist narratives without leaving any compelling reason to revere him, or even to find him particularly important. As it turned out, it would be secular scholars, affiliated with the secular academy, who pointed a way out of this dilemma. Before exploring their solution, though, it will be useful to consider how the turn to "history" in the search for the historical Buddha registered a different medium: not the printed word, but the painted image.

Painting the Life of the Historical Buddha in Late Meiji Japan

As we have seen, starting in the 1890s, Japanese intellectuals self-consciously began to rewrite the life story of the Buddha. But intellectuals wielding the written word were not the only producers of culture to experiment with historically informed representations of that life story. During the same decade, scenes from the life of the Buddha began to occupy an important role in contemporary painting in the "Japanese style," or Nihonga. The attempt to incorporate historical materials into biographical painting was first inspired by a book published in the United States, and later culminated in a series of journeys by Japanese artists to South Asia.

In 1895, the art educator and cultural broker Okakura Kakuzō (a.k.a. Tenshin, 1863–1913) issued a call for a painting competition to represent scenes from the life of the Buddha in a new form. A number of young artists heeded the call, and their production ranked among the foundational works in the repertoire of modern Nihonga. But their efforts to innovate were dogged by critics' accusations of inauthenticity in their pieces. Beginning in 1901, Okakura and his disciples made multiple sojourns in India, one consequence of which was a new body of works to depict the life of the Buddha. These efforts to incorporate a "historically authentic" visual language for depicting the Buddha paralleled the textual effort to refound accounts of the Buddha in historically defensible ways.

Christian publications and translations of Euro-American academic writings were not the only windows through which Japanese readers could glimpse new, foreign accounts of the life of the Buddha. During the latter Meiji years, more creative efforts to retell his life story also became available in Japanese. Poetic renditions of the tale were translated into Japanese throughout this period: the first two books of the epic poem *The Light of Asia* (1879), a phenomenally popular work by the British author Edwin Arnold (1832–1904), were translated and published in Japanese in 1890.[111] A full translation was published in 1911.[112] The German-American A. Christina Albers' (1866–1948) *Buddha: A Poem* (n.d.) also entered Japanese, as *The Tale of Śākyamuni* (*Shakuson monogatari*), in 1909.

The most influential creative retelling of the life of the Buddha to enter Meiji Japan, however, was undoubtedly *The Gospel of Buddha According to Old Records* (1895; c1894), a book by the German-American philosopher and publisher Paul Carus (1852–1919). Sympathetic to Buddhism and desirous of a true, scientific religion that would unite all world faiths, the liberal Carus issued books from his publishing firm, Open Court. He also produced two journals: the *Open Court* (1887–1936) and the *Monist* (1890–1919). In Japan, the Rinzai Zen cleric Shaku Sōen (1859–1919) and his pupil Suzuki Daisetsu (a.k.a. D. T. Suzuki, 1870–1966) orchestrated the rapid translation and publication of the *Gospel* in 1895. As previously demonstrated by Judith Snodgrass, their actions signaled not so much an appreciation of Carus's recasting of the Buddha in the idiom of the New Testament as an effort to appropriate the prestige and authority embodied by its author, a bona fide German philosopher who had earned his doctorate from Tübingen in 1876.[113]

Buddhist intellectuals in Japan were not the only parties who attempted to draw on the prestige of Carus' work. Another leading cultural producer of the time to take interest in it was Okakura Kakuzō, who by 1895 had already labored on behalf of the Tokyo School of Fine Arts (Tōkyō Bijutsu Gakkō) for over half a decade. By this point in his life, he was already well traveled: he had already been abroad to Central and Western Europe (1886–1887), participated in an ambitious survey of temple and shrine cultural properties in western Japan (1888), and spent over four and a half months traveling in Qing China (1893).

Okakura took part in a broad refashioning of Japanese aesthetics both to develop traditional forms and to appeal to a new base of global (Euro-American) connoisseurs and consumers. He had already begun to market Japan to the newly rising economic powers of his day by masterminding the construction of the Phoenix Pavilion (Hōōden), which represented Japan at the 1893 World's Columbian Exhibition, held in Chicago. Now, in 1895, Okakura decided to sponsor an open painting competition, taking Carus's *The Gospel of Buddha* as its subject matter. In October of that year, the journal *Painting Digest* (*Kaiga sōshi*) published Okakura's "Notice of a Call for a Prize for Buddhist Painting." Its "Plans and Rules" included the following conditions.

1. About ten paintings will constitute one set. The subject matter must be the biography of the Buddha, as contained in *The Gospel of Buddha*, written by Dr. [Paul] Carus and translated by the layman Suzuki Daisetsu. However, the type of painting may be in ink, or crayon, or pencil, or pen.

2. In order to make the works easily reproducible as normal photographs or by photolithograph, color may not be used.
3. The breadth of the painting will be that of an ordinary book, that is, around five inches in width and seven and a half in height. It is acceptable for works to be larger than this, as long as they may be reduced in size.

. . .

5. The purpose of this project is not only to encourage interest in Buddhism; we also intend to widen its scope, and to give a new stimulus to Buddhist art (*Bukkyōteki bijutsu*). In general, previous Buddhist images (*butsuzō*) have all copied the single posture of the Buddha in meditation (*zenjō*). There are as yet none that artistically (*bijtusuteki ni*) conduct observation (*kansatsu*) of the many events of the life of the Buddha. This is a great shortcoming for Buddhist art. In Christianity, there are exceedingly many celebrated paintings that show the life of Jesus, by such artists as [Julius] Schnorr, [Gustave] Doré, [Heinrich] Hofmann, or others—not to mention such masters as Rafael [i.e., Raffaello Santi], [Peter Paul] Rubens, or Rembrandt [Harmenszoon van Rijn]. This project is an effort to direct the interest of the public toward this shortcoming; given the degree of progress in Japan at the present, making up for this shortcoming should be an easy task.
6. The judges will be: the Venerable Shaku Sōen, abbot of the Enkakuji in Kamakura; Louis Prang, the American publisher of art in the city of Boston in America; and Dr. Paul Carus, writer for the Monist and the Open Court in the city of Chicago in America. . . . .[114]

As these excerpts from his call for entries suggest, Okakura's call for paintings of the life of the historical Buddha represented anything but an unreflective turn to hoary tradition. As this study previously suggested, narratively charged scenes from the life of the Buddha had, with few exceptions, been at best marginal subjects for Buddhist painting and sculpture since the start of the Edo period. Of course, Okakura's lament concerning the absence of paintings "that conduct artistic observation of the many events of the life of the Buddha" is disingenuous at best. Okakura had himself acquired one fascicle of an extant roll of the *Illustrated Sutra of Past and Present Cause and Effect* for the collection of the Tokyo Art School before its opening in 1889. Further, Okakura's name appears as cosigner to a letter of appraisal, dated to June 1892, for a latter Kamakura-period single-panel painting of the life of the Buddha, now in a private collection.[115] There is, then, ample reason to believe that Okakura was actually acquainted with the legacy of the life of the Buddha in premodern Japanese art.

Okakura's rhetorical turn in the "Notice of a Call for a Prize for Buddhist Painting" does suggest, however, that he saw little of value in the established visual tradition, which had been adapted from paintings of the Buddha's life from China and Korea. Commissioned by and designed for Buddhist clerics and temple settings, polychrome and therefore expensive to reproduce, the inherited visual tradition could not answer Okakura's call for a new visual vocabulary, which could be appreciated by the reading public and inexpensively reproduced in the medium of print. Rather than attempt to revivify the medieval Japanese iconography of the life of the Buddha, Okakura suggested models exclusively from the world of European art. Although not well known today, the nineteenth-century artists whom he named in the competition notice—the German Julius Schnorr (1794–1872), the Frenchman Gustave Doré (1832–1883), and the German Heinrich Hofmann (1824–1911)—produced a phenomenally popular body of religious illustration. These included Schnorr's *Illustrated Bible* of 1860, illustrated with some 240 woodcut-engraved scenes from both testaments of the Bible; Gustave Doré's French *Holy Bible* of 1865 and its English-language adaptation of 1867, each with over 230 illustrations; and Heinrich Hofmann's large body of monumental oil paintings of the life of Jesus. To the tastes of the early twenty-first century, these illustrations may now seem excessively sentimental or melodramatic. Nonetheless, their ability to condense complicated narratives into easily comprehensible, emotionally moving scenes might well have impressed Okakura. Whatever aesthetic judgment Okakura passed upon these works, he could not have ignored their resounding commercial success. To replicate that success with the figure of the Buddha in Japan, though, would demand not just new media and techniques, but also new iconographies and representations.

Okakura's prediction that artists would find his assignment "an easy task" did not come to pass. Precisely how the competition ended, and even whether the panel of judges ever actually reviewed the works, remain unclear. Until 2004, no later edition of *The Gospel of Buddha*, either in English or Japanese, used paintings from Japan for its illustrations.[116] Nonetheless, works presumably produced in answer to Okakura's solicitation reached the Japanese public in the following year, 1896. They ranked among the paintings in the Nihonga mode—nearly 150 in total—accepted for the first competitive exhibition held by the Japan Painting Association (Nihon Kaiga Kyōkai), which was held in Tokyo that autumn. Over a dozen of the 150 paintings on display at the exhibit treated Buddhist figures or themes; among those, at least four treated events in the life of Śākyamuni: the *Birth of the Buddha* (*But-*

tan) by Kosaka Shōdō (1870–1899); *The Austerities of Śākyamuni* (*Shaka kugyō*) by Ōta Shiichi (n.d.); *Siddhartha Addresses an Angel* (*Shitta go tenshi zu*), by Terasaki Kōgyō (1866–1919); and another *Birth of the Buddha* (*Buttan zu*), by Shimomura Kanzan (1873–1930). The works by Kōgyō and Kanzan, pioneers in the Nihonga style and followers of Okakura, each won prizes. Both were chosen for reproduction in the November 20, 1896, issue of the enormously popular general-interest magazine the *Sun* (*Taiyō*), through which they would have reached readers throughout Japan's growing empire.

Other works also appear to have resulted from Okakura's competition. Another disciple of Okakura, the Nihonga artist Yamada Keichū (1868–1934), produced an entire a set of paintings of the life of the Buddha. The *Sun* reproduced seven of these in its September 1897 issue, under the title *Half of the Life of Śākyamuni* (*Shaka no hansei*). In the following year, 1898, Open Court published eight of Keichū's paintings from this series in a slim but lavishly produced volume with color plates, *Scenes from the Life of Buddha*.[117] Suggestive of Okakura's promotion of a new visual language for depicting the life of the Buddha, all the works in these two sets avoid scenes common in the existing visual tradition. Instead, these works by Keichū depicted relatively unfamiliar scenes, all from the life of the Buddha after his awakening: the god Brahmā's entreaty to the newly awakened Buddha to teach; the Buddha's conversion of his former ascetic companions, who became his first five disciples; the Buddha's acceptance of his sixth disciple, Yaśas; his conversion of King Bimbisāra; his meeting with his wife, Yaśodharā, after his return to Kapilavastu; and so on. These and other extant scenes overwhelmingly depict the Buddha, or his disciples, spreading the dharma. In them, Keichū eschewed the standard depiction of the Buddha instructing vast assemblies of beings, focusing instead on small groups of figures.

Although Keichū's depictions were not used for *The Gospel of Buddha*, Carus nonetheless promoted them to the extent of his ability. From September 18 to October 1, 1899, at Carus's behest, the Art Institute of Chicago held a display of thirty-three of Keichū's paintings.[118] For an exhibition catalog, Carus published a sixteen-page pamphlet, adorned with a photograph of Keichū and reproducing one of the paintings (the conversion of King Bimbisāra), with explanations for all thirty-three. The explanations are, in keeping with the tone of *The Gospel of Buddha*, heavily colored by comparisons to the life of Jesus, but more surprising are the subjects that Keichū decided to illustrate: such topics unfamiliar to the Japanese visual tradition as "Brahmā Worshiping the Buddha

Child," "Questioned by the Sages," and "The Betrothal."[119] In a final irony, these paintings, produced in response for a call for mass circulation, were ultimately packed away in a trunk and left in the attic of the Hegeler Carus Mansion in LaSalle, Illinois. Their existence forgotten, they languished for roughly a century, to be rediscovered only in 2001. At that point, six of the group of thirty-three were not recovered.[120]

Presumably inspired by the competition and Keichū's success in it, a range of Nihonga artists went on to produce pieces based on scenes from the life of the Buddha. Such pieces continued to appear in further yearly exhibitions held by the Japan Painting Association; from the inauguration of the government-sponsored Ministry of Education Fine Arts Exhibitions (Monbushō Bijutsu Tenrankai, abbreviated as Bunten), they became a staple in that prestigious venue as well. Okakura had secured a place for the Buddha within the newly introduced genre of "historical painting" (*rekishiga*). Its misleading name aside, this genre—like its progenitor in continental Europe—was as concerned with themes which we might call "religious" or "mythological" as well as with "historical" events. According to an analysis by the art historian Yamanashi Toshio, even as history was becoming an empirical discipline in Meiji Japan, "a dual structure of history and legend—which is to say, of the rational and the irrational—was always left intact."[121] As will become clear, though, the role of historical "truth" within "historical painting" was itself a matter for debate in late Meiji Japan.

The "historical paintings" of scenes from the life of the Buddha from the mid-1890s through the early 1910s reveal an ongoing search for new foundations upon which to build modern depictions. The aforementioned works by Kōgyō and Kanzan take different approaches to the problem. Kōgyō presumably drew inspiration for *Siddhartha Addresses an Angel* from Carus's depiction of the last of the Four Encounters of the prince: a "vision" of a "celestial messenger," who "vanished" after he finished instructing the prince in his destiny to become a Buddha.[122] (See fig. 5.) In turn, Carus seems to have drawn upon Aśvaghoṣa's account of a man "wearing a mendicant's garb, unseen by any of the other men," who is actually "a deity who in that form had seen other Buddhas and had come down to arouse the attention of the prince."[123] Notably, Aśvaghoṣa's deity makes no prophecy of the prince's future Buddhahood; the grandiloquence of the prophecy in the *Gospel* version is more reminiscent of the angel who appears to Mary to inform her that she will give birth to a savior. The eponymous angel of Kōgyō's painting seems to spring from the vision narrated by

FIGURE 5 Terasaki Kōgyō, *Siddhārtha Addresses an Angel. Shitta go tenshi zu* (1895). Photograph courtesy of Tokyo University of the Arts.

Aśvaghoṣa, via Carus, but he may also be kin to the diaphanous messenger in Gustave Doré's engraving of the Annunciation. (See fig. 6.)

For his part, Kanzan looked for models distant not in space but in time. In *The Birth of the Buddha,* Kanzan's "figures strongly suggest study of eighth-century Buddhist style" at the temple Hōryūji in

FIGURE 6 Gustave Doré, *The Annunciation* (1865).

Nara.[124] Treating a different moment from the life of the Buddha, Kanzan's later work *Cremation* (*Jai*, 1898) appears to cite the eighth-century sculptures of the Four Heavenly Kings (Shitennō) from the Kaidan'in at the temple Tōdaiji.[125]

These early experiments in reenvisioning the life of the Buddha met with critical reactions, ranging from grudging praise to outright hostility.[126] Reviewing *Siddhartha Addresses an Angel* for the newspaper *Yomiuri shinbun*, the art critic Seki Nyorai (1866–1938) contested the very premise of Kōgyō's painting:

Did he title the work *Siddhartha Addresses an Angel* to make viewers interpret the figure as an angel? . . . However, this "angel" is something we often hear of in Christianity, but not in Buddhism. And even if we did hear of angels in Buddhism, according to which scripture has the artist documented (*kōshō*) that the prince speaks to an angel when he is about to leave the palace?[127]

Nor did Seki's accusations of a lack of historical and doctrinal foundation end there. Why had Kōgyō depicted the god who abets the departure of the prince as a mendicant? If the figure were supposed to represent a mendicant, then why did he lack the ordinary straight staff of a Buddhist monk, and hold instead a wooden staff with a crook? In what source had Kōgyō documented the crown atop the head of the prince? The crown differs from previous depictions, Seki continued, "but we cannot imagine that [Kōgyō] has made a thorough archaeological investigation." Even the decorative pattern on the pillar in the painting, which "seemed as though it were faintly based on ancient Indian precedent," was found lacking.[128] Seki's complaint of a lack of fidelity would return in criticisms of other new versions of Nihonga paintings of the life of the Buddha.

Kanzan, too, faced no little criticism. Reviewers uniformly noted that his *Birth of the Buddha* (fig. 7) broke with established iconographic

FIGURE 7 Shimomura Kanzan, *Birth of the Buddha. Buttan zu* (1895). Photograph courtesy of Tokyo University of the Arts.

precedents for the depiction of this scene, but they did not all approve of his handling of the break. The reporter for one newspaper, for example, observed that "previous Buddhist paintings in our country have often followed Chinese painting," but that Kanzan's work, by contrast, "took into account the dress and customs of India, in accordance with the recent development of archaeology." Nonetheless, the reviewer still found the work "slightly lacking in elegance."[129] Writing for the *Sun*, Seki Nyorai had still more severe words for *Birth*. In his laundry list of flaws in the piece, Seki expressed strong reservations about the presentation of the figures: "In their visages, all the characters differ from previous Buddhist painting, but they can't be regarded as definitely Indian, either." Overall, Seki found the piece to be "lacking in vitality," and accused Kanzan of confusing that lack of vitality with elegance.[130]

Some professional appraisals of Kanzan's *Cremation* were still more severe. The author, philosopher, and critic Takayama Chogyū, quoted in the magazine of the Japan Art Institute, observed: "In the future, even religious matters will be interpreted historically. India will be regarded as a country in history, and Śākyamuni as a historical person; depicting historical facts will enable us to discover a hitherto nonexistent new territory."[131] By this logic, he continued, the reimagining of *Cremation* had to be excluded, since it lacked documentation. This Chogyū sought in the canonical Buddhist scriptures. Another, anonymous critic published a caustic attack on the piece in a different art journal. To this reviewer, the work "reeked of India"—a phrase meant as anything but a compliment. Despite noting the debt to Nara sculpture, the reviewer was unimpressed by the handling of other figures in the painting; he observed that the short figure crying on the left seemed to be not a child, but "a person soaked in brine," who had withered and shrunk as a result. The reviewer found the main subject of the painting equally unsatisfactory: "Hey," the reviewer taunted, "even Śākyamuni is a human in his emanation body. Just because he was burned on a pyre of aloeswood doesn't mean that he'd give off golden smoke." Ending on a sarcastic note, the reviewer sneered that it was a shame that Kanzan had not been born in the Nara period, when such a "monstrous painting" would have moved superstitious folk to tears.[132] Yet another reviewer, writing for *Painting Digest*, wondered what purpose this massive work could possibly fill; it would not be suitable for temple commemorations of the death of the Buddha, nor would it be the sort of painting to adorn "a normal house."[133] (See fig. 8.)

Much of the skepticism and hostility toward these paintings stemmed from doubt about the authenticity of their depictions. Critics

FIGURE 8 Shimomura Kanzan, *Cremation. Jai* (1898). Photograph courtesy of Yokohama Museum of Art.

of the latter 1890s correctly noted that these works broke with established iconographies and discarded traditional ritual utility, but they also charged those works with disregard for the genuine Indian past, whether it was to be understood through scriptural precedent or archaeological investigation.

From the early 1900s, practitioners of Nihonga responded to such criticisms by actively incorporating South Asian materials into their works. Unexpectedly, the opportunity to do so came from Okakura's difficulties. In 1898, frustrated with the increasing influence of European methods at the Tokyo School of Fine Arts, Okakura resigned from it to found his own rival private institution, the Japan Art Institute (Nihon Bijutsuin). Faced with problems in the operation of the Institute, Okakura opted to travel abroad to South Asia in 1901, where he spent most of a year, returning to Japan in October 1902. Okakura spent some of that time traveling to Buddhist sites in the company of the True Pure Land scholar-cleric Oda Tokunō (1860–1911), but his association with the Tagore (Thākura) family in Calcutta proved to be the most important encounter of his stay. They took him in, and he stayed at the mansion of Satyendranath Tagore (1842–1923) and may have had some association with his brother, Rabindranath (1861–1941), who would eventually win the Nobel Prize for Literature.

Okakura's own visit to India did not itself immediately result in new representations of the Buddha, but it did pave the way for the production of such images by later Nihonga artists who followed his lead. In

FIGURE 9 Yokoyama Taikan, *Śākyamuni Encounters His Father. Shaka chichi ni au* (1903; orig. now lost). Photograph courtesy of Yokoyama Taikan Memorial Hall.

the late Meiji period, these included two of Okakura's leading disciples, Yokoyama Taikan (1868–1948) and Hishida Shunsō (1874–1911), hosted by Satyendranath Tagore from February to July 1903; and Katsuta Shōkin (1879–1963), who in September 1905 set off to serve in Satyendranath's home as Nihonga tutor, and who also taught Nihonga at the Government School of Art in Calcutta before his return to Japan in July 1907. (Of course, not all the individuals whom Okakura introduced to India flourished; Hori Shitoku, who did not return, originally journeyed to India along with Okakura, at Okakura's behest, though Hori declined Okakura's suggestion to accompany him back to Japan.)

Taikan, Shunsō, and Shōkin each produced work based on the life of the Buddha, whether during his stay in India or after his return to Japan. Upon returning to Japan in 1903, Taikan painted *Śākyamuni and the Demon Women* (*Shaka to majo*) and *Śākyamuni Encounters His Father* (*Shaka chichi ni au*), and Shunsō painted *The Offering of the Milk Gruel* (*Nyūbi kuyō*). (See fig. 9.) In 1906, while still in India, Shōkin produced a work on the same theme as Shunsō's, titling it *The Buddha and Sujātā* (*Budda to Sujātā*). After his return to Japan in 1907, he completed a number of other biographical works: *Śākyamuni Departing from the Fortress* (*Shaka shutsujō*, 1907); *The Conquest of Māra* (*Gōma*) in two versions (1907); *Prince Siddhartha beneath the Jambu Tree* (*Enbuju ge no Shitta taishi*, 1908); and *The Evil Elephant Takes Refuge in the Buddha* (*Akuzō no ki-Butsu*, 1912).

Like their predecessors in the works of Yamada Keichū, the works produced by these three artists either treat parts of the Buddha's life story not commonly depicted in Japan or depict familiar scenes in unfamiliar ways. The presentation of gruel to the prince at the end of his ascetic phase, though known in Japan through Buddhist texts, appeared only rarely in the Japanese visual canon after the *Illustrated Sutra of Cause and Effect* (the incomplete set of paintings of the life of the Buddha at the Hōkiin, datable to the mid-fifteenth century, constitute one exception). Nor had the scenes of the Buddha's reunion with his father, or of the elephant sent to kill the Buddha by Devadatta, ever featured prominently in Japanese Buddhist painting. Even in cases in which there was an established iconography, it seems not to have hindered these artists: in their depictions of the prince's triumph over the forces of Māra, both Taikan and Shōkin dispensed with the traditional depiction of demons who attack the Buddha-to-be. Instead, Taikan painted only the voluptuous daughters of Māra in their attempt to seduce the prince—neglecting their famous transformation into wizened hags through the Buddha's meditative power, as depicted in the medieval versions preserved at the Daifukudenji, Jikōji, or other temples. Shōkin also defied the standard iconography, essaying a simple depiction of the triumph of the prince as he meditated alone under a tree. (See fig. 10.)

As demonstrated by the art historians Satō Shino and Narihara Yuki, such works by these three artists draw powerfully on their experiences and observations in India. For instance, Taikan was among the first Japanese ever to visit the ancient Buddhist cave temples at Ajantā.

FIGURE 10 Katsuta Shōkin, study for *The Conquest of Māra. Gōma* (1907; completed final work now lost). Photograph courtesy of Fukushima Prefectural Museum of Art.

His paintings cited a number of motifs from them, freely adopting and reworking bodily postures, animal forms, and ornamentation.[134] In depicting the Buddha's receipt of an offering of food from Sujātā, both Shunsō and Shōkin labored to humanize him, in part by placing him in a real-world environment—hence the quotation of Indian flora in their scenery.[135] Shōkin also traveled to Ajantā to study the murals there; when he depicted the Buddha's departure from the palace, he too made use of the Ajantā murals, quoting them in the facial features of the prince, the design for the prince's headdress, and the ornamentation on the pillar of the fortress of Kapilavastu.[136] (See fig. 11.)

Such deliberate use of citation appears to have afforded these paintings a cachet lacked by their predecessors. To be sure, critics expressed mixed overall opinions about these pieces as well, but they tended to grade them highly for their authenticity. Newspaper reviewers commended Taikan for his treatment of the human figures in *Śākyamuni Encounters His Father,* writing that viewing the painting was "like view-

FIGURE 11 Katsuta Shōkin, *Śākyamuni Departing from the Fortress. Shaka shutsujō* (1907). Photograph courtesy of Fukushima Prefectural Museum of Art.

ing a scene from ancient India," and noting that "the figures seem to have been sketched from life, based on Indians." One of the judges concurred in an opinion cited in an art journal. The painting had its flaws, he conceded, but "the artist traveled to India and has been able to present for the first time a Śākyamuni in an Indian style."[137] Another critic, writing for an art publication, noted that in Shōkin's depiction of the Buddha's conquest of Māra, the "physiognomy [of Śākyamuni] is assembled in a way not seen elsewhere, perhaps as a result of the artist's research in the actual land of India."[138] But such a standard cut both ways. In 1908, Shōkin's *Prince Siddhartha beneath the Jambu Tree* earned the scorn of art critics, in part for their low evaluation of the authenticity of the prince's appearance: "The figure is a European and doesn't seem to be an Indian."[139] Shōkin seems to have taken such criticisms to heart. Within a few years, he had wholly abandoned Indian themes, and even the human form has little place in his mature work.

Needless to say, not all Nihonga artists spent time abroad in India, and even those who did travel to India were not necessarily betaken with Buddhist art. Nonetheless, through the 1930s, a surprising number of Nihonga painters did venture to India—sometimes for extended stays—and did incorporate their experiences and observations into paintings of scenes from the life of the Buddha. Their ranks included Arai Kanpō (1878–1945), whose long interest in Indian Buddhist art engendered the production of a number of scenes from the life of the Buddha; Kiriya Senrin (1877–1932), whose 1915 handscroll illustrations were reused in postwar children's literature concerning the life of the Buddha; and Nousu Kōsetsu (1885–1973), who not only sojourned in India from 1917 to 1919, but who was later commissioned to paint murals of the Buddha's life at the temple established by the Maha Bodhi Society in Sarnath.

The Buddha as a Great Man

Even as visual artists experimented with the integration of historical motifs into the narrative of the life of the Buddha, elite Japanese scholars unaffiliated with Buddhist institutions also began to recast his life and achievements in the idiom of historical writing.

Inoue Tetsujirō, Takayama Chogyū, and Anesaki Masaharu—three key intellectuals in this process—all graduated from the Department of Philosophy at Tokyo Imperial University (until the establishment of Kyōto Imperial University in 1897, the only university formally accredited by the government), and each later taught at his alma mater, at least briefly. Although distinct and even idiosyncratic thinkers, they enjoyed intimate personal and professional relationships: Inoue taught Anesaki and Takayama, who were classmates and inseparable friends throughout their years at the Imperial University (1893–1896) and beyond; at Inoue's behest, Anesaki married his niece, Inoue Masu (1898); all three contributed extensively to the *Sun*, Japan's first general-interest magazine; and in response to Takayama's untimely death at the age of thirty-two (1902), Anesaki inaugurated a commemorative society in his honor (1903), spearheaded the posthumous publication of his *Complete Works* (1904–1906), and erected his portrait bust at his gravesite (1929).

Such deep and enduring relationships surely contributed to the common historical perspective in which each of these scholars represented the Buddha. Despite their differences, each of these intellectuals treated the Buddha as a human being whose life could be explained in the terms laid down by the naturalistic historical writing then current in fin de siècle Europe. By attuning their writing closely to contemporary European scholarly standards, they eluded the obstacles confronted by the likes of Katō Totsudō, Saji Jitsunen, and even Fujii Senshō, whose roughly contemporary works all tried to reconcile the demands of the new scholarship with traditional scriptural and institutional authorities.

Inoue, Takayama, and Anesaki thus grounded their scholarship not on the cosmic status of the Buddha, nor on his major and minor marks, nor on his superhuman powers. Rather, they located the basis for his authority in what they believed to be a more universal foundation: the cult of the "great man," often rendered in Japanese from the late nineteenth century onward as *ijin*. Their repositioning of the Buddha spanned the final decade of the nineteenth century and continued through the first of the twentieth, coinciding with a burgeoning of interest among Japanese intellectuals in such exponents of heroism and genius as the Scotsman Thomas Carlyle (1795–1881) and the German Friedrich Nietzsche (1844–1900).[140] To treat the Buddha as one of these heroes (*eiyū*) or as one of these geniuses (*tensai*) was no effort to limit him to a particular sphere; it was his passport to global or universal significance. "For, as I take it," declaimed Carlyle at the start of the lecture series published in 1842 as *On Heroes, Hero-Worship, and the Heroic in History*, "Universal History, the history of what man has accomplished in this world, is at bottom the History of the Great Men who have worked there."[141] Whether overtly articulated or not, such conceptions of the historical undergirded the study of the Buddha by this group.

As a member of the first class to graduate from Tokyo (Imperial) University (1880), as the first Japanese scholar to rise to the status of full professor in its Philosophy Department (1890), and as a dominating presence in the world of Japanese academic philosophy until his retirement (1923), Inoue Tetsujirō stands out as a representative Japanese thinker of his day. Inoue maintained close ties with the government establishment: after the promulgation of the Imperial Rescript on Education (1890), he was chosen to pen the single officially endorsed commentary (1891). He was also linked to more broadly conservative social forces, including institutional Buddhism, particularly after publically announcing that individual faith in Christianity was incompatible with loyalty to the Japanese nation. In articulating this position, he inaugurated a prolonged debate over the "Collision between Religion and Education," so named for Inoue's famous treatise ("Kyōiku to shūkyō no shōtotsu") of 1893. Scholarship to treat Inoue in English has generally focused on these events, which highlight his roles as reactionary and ideologue.

This emphasis makes it worthwhile to revisit Inoue's work across the span of the 1890s, particularly a long series of talks that he delivered between 1890 and 1897: *Lectures on Comparative Religion and Eastern Philosophy* (*Hikaku shūkyō oyobi Tōyō tetsugaku kōgi*).[142] Most of these lectures went unpublished at the time of their delivery, but the sections concerning the Buddha Śākyamuni did find their way into print, first in a series of articles published between 1894 and 1897. In 1902—well after the conclusion of his lecture series, and at the suggestion of his student Takakusu Junjirō—Inoue published his lectures about Śākyamuni as *A Biography of Śākyamuni* (*Shakamuni den*). This popular book had by 1909 undergone eighteen impressions, and it continued to be updated and reprinted as late as 1926.

Inoue's reputation as a scholar has long suffered from accusations of eclecticism or derivativeness, and in general, his body of material about the Buddha contains little to deflect that charge. These works give selective priority to the writings of European scholarly authorities on India and Buddhism, with which Inoue must have grown familiar during his seven years abroad in Germany. Further, Inoue's studies rely overwhelmingly on translations into European languages for access to Buddhist texts from South Asia, and they cite original sources only in classical Chinese, not in Pāli or Sanskrit. Inoue inherited his methodology from European practice as well: in a published lecture titled "Concerning Research into Buddhism," Inoue recommended to aspiring scholars (particularly those among the Buddhist clergy themselves) that they adopt a "historical-critical eye," and he stressed the value of the comparative study of different religions with Buddhism.[143]

Following a line of research leading back to Eugène Burnouf, Inoue contended that the Buddha was a universal figure, born in India but not of it.[144] In lectures published in the late 1890s, Inoue lauded the Buddha's "doctrine of equality" as "universal" (*ippanteki*), and he held that "the Buddha's doctrines parted ways with the character of his nation to become universal."[145] Inoue ended a list of the qualities distinguishing Buddhism from Brahmanism in a similar vein: "Brahmanism is a religion particular to the Brahman tribe (*shuzoku*), which is to say, to the Aryans; [however,] the Buddha did not establish a religion for a single people (*minzoku*), but preached the dharma for the [entire] world. This is the distinction between the particular and the universal (*fuhenteki*)."[146] Although still unusual in the context of 1890s Japan, Inoue's placement of the Buddha within world history closely followed the precedent of recent European scholarship.

To Inoue, it was not only the Buddha's teaching that was not properly Aryan, but also the Buddha himself. Dispute among Europeans over the proper racial identification of the Buddha had already accumulated a long history by Inoue's day: from the eighteenth through the early nineteenth centuries, the leading European hypothesis concerning the origin of the Buddha placed him in Africa—more precisely, in the Egyptian priestly class.[147] Inoue did not repeat this hypothesis, but he did make a strenuous—and strained—case against the identification of the Buddha as Aryan. To be sure, competing ideas about the ancestry of the Buddha continued to influence scholarly discourse in Inoue's day. Nonetheless, the identification of the Buddha with the Aryan heritage of South Asia was finding growing intellectual acceptance by the late nineteenth century, even as the term of art "Aryan" slipped from a linguistic designation to become a racial category, ongoing protests from its progenitor Max Müller aside.[148]

Troubled at the prospect that the Buddha's racial classification as Aryan might irrevocably align him with European civilization, Inoue contended instead that the Buddha's tribe, the Śākyas, was actually a subgroup of the Scythians described in ancient Greek histories. These he linked to the Sai (Śāka) tribe and the Yuezhi described in ancient Chinese records—meaning, he claimed, that the Buddha's people would be members not of the Aryan race, but of the "Turanian."[149] Conveniently, Inoue continued, the mixed race that had emerged on the Japanese archipelago in ancient times incorporated a large admixture of Turanian stock. "If this is really the case," Inoue concluded, "then we should not consider Śākyamuni to be the same as the Euro-Americans, but should instead say that he shares the same ancestry with us."[150] It is not difficult to imagine the appeal that such identification would have held for Inoue, who with his attack on Christianity was at that point leading the intellectual wing of Japan's nationalist vanguard. His article describing these points, "To What Race Does the Buddha Belong?" ("Shaka wa ikanaru shuzoku naru ka"), was published in the *Sun*'s October 1895 issue, with a short summary in English following that December.[151]

Inoue's argument in this piece met with a harsh riposte from one of the founders of historical Sinology in the modern Japanese academy, Naka Michiyo (1851–1908). Naka's article first appeared in the elite *Historical Review* (*Shigaku zasshi*) and was only later reprinted in the *Sun*.[152] Identifying Inoue's arguments as borrowings from "Western Indologists," Naka went on to enumerate their flaws: the Greek usage of "Scythian" was too vague, and in any event, the Sai and the Yuezhi peoples were distinct from each other; the purported dates of the Scythian migration and the dates of the Buddha's life were irreconcilable; and Inoue's effort to link the Sai people with the Śākya tribe ultimately relied only on a coincidence of similar names.[153] The description of the Śākyas' skill in archery, which Inoue had submitted as corroborating evidence for his identification of their clan with the Scythians, was, Naka wrote, merely a standard trope appearing throughout such Indian epics as the *Mahābhārata* and the *Rāmāyana*, and therefore "nothing limited to the Śākya tribe."[154] More damning still, Naka also observed that Inoue had mistranslated the name "Himalaya" with "Mount Qilian," the name of a range of mountains in faraway China.

Confronted with this critique, Inoue poured out his bile in a long article, "Concerning the Ancestry of Śākyamuni (A Reply to Mr. Naka Michiyo)."[155] In it, Inoue alternately excoriated Naka for not citing from Buddhist texts, chided him for asking unanswerable questions, and accused him of sheer mean-mindedness, deploring that "if he does enjoy such things as attacking others for their faults and humiliating them, then he truly has the mind of a petty man."[156] In addition to reiterating all his own major points, Inoue also defended his mistranslation of "Himalaya," and even insisted that the great Indian classics had been composed under the influence of Buddhism. While the force of these arguments exposed Inoue's wounded pride to the reading public, it also suggested the key role that Inoue envisioned for Buddhism in his greater intellectual project—nothing less than the articulation of a historical and intellectual vision of "Eastern Civilization" (*Tōyō bunmei*) that would stand on par with the "West." For the "East," Inoue wrote at the beginning of his rebuttal to Naka, Buddhism played a cultural role comparable to that of Christianity in the "West," which made scholarship on Buddhism a critical part of any project of self-articulation for scholars of the "East." "If we were to ignore the influence (*kanka*) of Buddhism, then we would be unable to enter deeply into the realm of the spirit and discern where the essence of Eastern Civilization is located."[157] Inoue found his exchange of articles with Naka sufficiently important to merit their complete republication in a separate pamphlet, *On the Race of the Buddha* (*Shaka shuzoku ron*, 1897).

If Inoue's body of articles from the 1890s tried to offer the Japanese a common ancestry with the Buddha, then Inoue's monograph *Biography of Śākyamuni* (*Shakamuni den*, 1902) signaled a still more ambitious attempt: to fix the Buddha firmly within a universal history of great men. The theme is evident even in his preface to the book, which explains for readers the book's superiority to its predecessors in the Buddhist scriptures. Through an "excess of devotion of later generations of Buddhists (*Bukkyō shinja*) to the character (*jinkaku*) of their founder," those later followers have "confused" his biography "with many tales of wonder and marvels," so that the biographies of the Buddha available in Inoue's day were "just absurd and groundless fiction (*shōsetsu*)."[158] By contrast, he announced, his work would draw upon both Eastern and Western sources to "make a faithful introduction of the true face of this universal great man (*sekaiteki ijin*), who has been buried among absurd and groundless tales."[159] Inoue's term for "universal" more literally signifies the "global," and manifesting Buddhism as a truly global religion was one of Inoue's starting points.

Far from finding the Buddha's relevance primarily within his Indian context, Inoue now echoed many of his European predecessors—starting with Burnouf—by pointing out that the Buddha belonged as much to other lands as to his birthplace. (Whereas his earlier 1895 article had specified the Buddha's position in Indian history, the corresponding chapter here, in the 1902 *Biography*, refers only to the Buddha's position in history generally, without specifying any particular place.) "The influence of a universal great man like Śākyamuni," wrote Inoue, "overcame the borders of India and spread both East and West. . . . Thus, the Indians alone must not monopolize him, for he is one of the sages common (*kōkyō*) to all of us human beings."[160] Indeed, Inoue's introduction to the book stresses the universal reach of Buddhism: it cites Rhys Davids's contention that there are more Buddhists than believers of any other faith in the world; and it draws upon Renan, Müller, and Schopenhauer, among others, to suggest the possibility of Buddhist influence in the formation of Christianity.

Inoue manifested a sanguine attitude about the future prospects for the dissemination of Buddhism as well. He gave his book this epigram from the German philosopher Arthur Schopenhauer (1788–1860):

> In India our religions will never at any time take root; the ancient wisdom of the human race will not be supplanted by the events in Galilee. On the contrary, Indian wisdom flows back to Europe, and will produce a fundamental change in our knowledge and our thought.[161]

In the hands of a different author of the day, such an allusion might reek of Japanese Buddhist triumphalism, but Inoue spelled out his unwillingness to treat Japanese Buddhism in the introduction. In a maneuver strikingly parallel to the Victorian disinclination to rely on "native" Buddhist clergy for instruction about "true Buddhism," Inoue observed that it would be useless to ask Japanese Buddhist clergy for help in navigating through the Buddhist canon, for "the monks all have partialities and are therefore unreliable as a matter of course."[162] With its vast pantheon of gods derived from the Brahmanical tradition, Inoue continued, Japanese Buddhism differed too greatly from "primitive Buddhism" (*genshiteki Bukkyō*) to be taken as the "true form" (*shinmenmoku*) of Buddhism writ large.[163] Whatever kind of "Indian wisdom" might be eventually destined to "flow back to Europe," Inoue therefore implied, unreconstructed Japanese Buddhism would not conduct it.

True to his own urging in the earlier "Concerning Research into Buddhism," Inoue made generous use of the comparative method in his biography of the Buddha. Most of the individual chapters in his study take up discrete phases of the life of the Buddha, their analysis proceeding through citations of European scholarship and scriptures written in Chinese, though Inoue also made lengthy digressions as he saw fit. Throughout these chapters, Inoue made repeated reference to other great men; more precisely, he used both comparison and contrast to associate the Buddha with these figures. Invoked in the mode of comparison, these figures suggest universal standards against which the Buddha is never found wanting. Invoked in the mode of contrast, though, these figures serve to set off what Inoue found superior in the Buddha.

A few examples from the text should suffice to illustrate the tenor of these invocations. Like his European peers, Inoue thought the Buddha to have attempted a reform of Brahmanism like Christ's reform of Judaism (comparison).[164] Unlike Confucius or Jesus, however, the Buddha was of noble birth (contrast).[165] Again, unlike Confucius, he received a proper education as a prince; unlike Jesus, he was not inclined only to the emotional, but also to the intellectual (contrast).[166] The prince had multiple wives—but then again, so did the Japanese emperor of Inoue's day (though Inoue was sufficiently judicious not to refer to the emperor explicitly), and besides, monogamy was an invention of Christianity (both comparison and contrast).[167] The intellectual precocity of the young prince precisely parallelled the great minds of Europe—and here, in a rhetorical device that he used more than once, Inoue itemized a litany of such minds: Gottfried Wilhelm Leibniz (1646–1716), David Hume (1711–1776), George Berkeley (1685–1753), Friedrich Wilhelm Joseph von Schelling (1775–1854), Eduard von Hartmann (1842–1906), Auguste Comte (1798–1857), and Rudolph Hermann Lotze (1817–1881). All these men manifested precocious intellectual accomplishments in their twenties (comparison). "In his youth, the prince, too," Inoue followed, "abundantly evinced the tendencies of his future development."[168] If Jesus had been a short-lived and short-tempered man, prone to harsh outbursts unconducive to sympathy, then the Buddha was the opposite: long-lived, gentle and tolerant, and sympathetic (contrast). An inquiry into the dissimilar, later histories of Christianity and Buddhism could be explained as a result of such differences in the founders whom later followers imitated.[169]

Such techniques of comparison and contrast further enabled Inoue to finesse difficulties in his sources—for instance, to resolve competing claims emerging from different texts. At what age did the precocious prince decide to abandon the world? Some scriptures give the age of nineteen; others, twenty-nine. Not wholly unlike his early modern predecessor Gentei, Inoue addressed the conflict in ages not through study of the texts in question, but through appeal to other universal precedents: "When we consider the achievements of men of religion, past and present, [we see that] many of them expounded their original doctrines around the age of thirty."[170] Here too, Inoue's prose offered up sheer quantity as a kind of evidence in its own right, itemizing the ages of the spiritual awakenings achieved by Confucius, Mencius, Jesus, Muhammad, Kūkai, Saichō, Hōnen, Shinran, Nichiren, Martin Luther, Ignatius of Loyola, the Swiss Reformation leader Huldrych Zwingli, the Jain founder Mahāvīra, the Bengali mystic Caitanya Mahāprabhu (1486–1533), the nineteenth-century Hindu reformer Rammohan Ray (1772–1833), his later follower Keshub Chandra Sen (1838–1884), and the founder of Manichaenism, Mani.[171] Based on this pattern, Inoue held, nineteen would be too young. Like his peers across space and time, the Buddha must have come to his awakening later.

Aligning the life of the Buddha with those of his peers could also help Inoue cope with troubling elements of the life story. Inoue espoused the metaphor of the Meiji Japanese state as the patrilineal family writ large. This may account for the need he felt to explain the reciprocal disregard between the Buddha and his birth family on his return to Kapilavastu after his awakening, when he came on his alms rounds. How could his own family have failed to acknowledge his greatness? Inoue had recourse to no less prominent an authority than Jesus himself, and he quoted the New Testament: "A prophet hath no honour in his own country" (John 4:44).[172] In fact, Inoue contended, the dismissal of great religious figures in their homelands actually *proved* their status as great men. As evidence, Inoue cited the rejection of Jesus on his return to Nazareth, and the rejection of Muhammad by the people of Mecca, who included some of Muhammad's own relatives.[173] The problem, Inoue concluded, turned out to be the inability of surrounding family and acquaintances to understand prophethood:

> When a man of religion reaches a certain period in his life, he undergoes a fundamental transmutation of spirit, and from some place, acquires noble ideals sufficient to initiate a new era for the world. Having distinctly recognized the severity of the gap between the ideal and the real, he therefore comes to the point of attempting to realize those ideals, by removing all obstacles in his way. However, because the people of his native place know all about this man as a child, they are unable to see him as an ideal person who has undergone a fundamental transmutation of spirit. . . . As expected, they consider the man of religion to carry on from his childhood, and as his childhood differed in no respect from that of other children, they are unable to conceive of his present fundamental difference from others. . . . But the man of religion is no longer the sort of person whom they consider him to be; he has thoughts that they cannot even imagine, which is why they cannot treat him in a way appropriate to his true position as a man of religion.[174]

While Inoue was willing to employ such comparative arguments to smooth over certain problems in the account of the Buddha's life, he did not attempt to reconcile the events of that life fully with his own perspective. Ever anxious for the welfare of the state, Inoue was alarmed to see that the Buddha's conversion of his clan was so successful that it deprived Kapilavastu of its princely successor and ultimately deprived its people of the ability to resist the invasion of King Virūḍhaka, thus leading to the destruction of the Śākyas. "On this account," he mused darkly, "we must observe how Buddhism was unable to make the state flourish, and see that it instead brought about the opposite result."[175]

Inoue's admittedly reactionary interest in the protection of the Japanese state undergirded his arguments in this text and its predecessors. Following Inoue's lead, his student Takayama Chogyū was, during his own brief span as a public intellectual, also at one point a staunch defender of nationalism. But Takayama exhibited interest in literature and aesthetics as well, and he made his public reputation as a professional critic active in the national press. After his nationalist phase ended around 1900, Takayama went through a brief phase of promoting individualism and even hedonism, inspired at least in part by his encounter with the writings of Nietzsche. In the last, short stage of his intellectual odyssey, Takayama embraced Nichiren Buddhism, expressing particular admiration for the greatness of Nichiren himself. These two final phases of Takayama's intellectual life shared a common concern for the greatness of individuals, of whom Nichiren was only the most prominent of many instances.

Considering the final two phases in his intellectual career, it is not entirely surprising that Takayama accepted a request to write a biography of the Buddha specifically for young adults for a series published by Hakubunkan, the commercial publisher behind the *Sun* as well. (The same press also produced Takayama's own posthumous *Complete Works*.) His short volume *Śākyamuni* (*Shaka*, published in 1899 but completed in 1898) inaugurated Hakubunkan's longstanding series Tales from World History (Sekai rekishi dan). Printed monthly until the release of its thirty-sixth volume (about Isaac Newton) in March 1902, each installation of the series featured a biography of a different great individual, typically drawn from Euro-American or Chinese history.[176] At the head of this series, the Buddha joined the ranks of such global luminaries as Confucius (volume 2), Jesus (3), Muhammad (6), the Chinese general Yue Fei (9), George Washington (13), the ancient Greek orator and statesman Demosthenes (20), the British explorer James Cook (31), and even Joan of Arc (32).

As was the case with Takayama, many of the authors for this series were elite intellectuals, university graduates, and men of literary talent; few were, in fact, full-time authors of children's books. A number of these volumes were hits with the reading public and underwent multiple impressions. Takayama's biography of Śākyamuni seems to have been the most highly in demand, with its accumulated twenty-three impressions—a number far outstripping the demand for the next most reprinted volume, the biography of Otto von Bismarck (volume 4), with only fifteen impressions.[177] Takayama's book garnered critical praise, too, with one history journal endorsing it as "highly beneficial in the education of youth" who were to be taught of the Buddha's work as a religious reformer.[178]

In keeping with its target readership, Takayama's biography was the first new production of the Meiji years to be illustrated extensively, entirely by Shimomura Kanzan. This is a striking choice, considering the emphasis on historical verisimilitude and critical attitude that Takayama himself had exhibited toward Kanzan's *Cremation* just a few years earlier. However, by the time he was composing *Śākyamuni*, Takayama had reversed his position, and was now arguing that so-called "historical painting" ought not to be subservient to the empiricist standards of historical scholarship.[179] Also compared with its various Japanese predecessors, Takayama's approach to the biography of the Buddha stands out for its self-conscious willingness to admit narratives that more academic texts might discard. His own preface for the text begins:

> Today it is impossible for any scholar to document the biography of the Buddha with precision. Thus, rather than insert my own opinions and arbitrarily rearrange the facts, I believe that it would instead be better to rely on the existing traditions (*densetsu*). This is because I trust that, rather than forcibly excluding the strange and unbelievable episodes as untruths, even such strange episodes will be of some help in comprehending the real spirit (*shin seishin*) of Śākyamuni.[180]

In the introduction to the text proper, Takayama amplified this explanation, expanding his field of vision from the single case of the Buddha to make a general argument about the nature of saintly biography in general. While the passage is not short, it is nonetheless worth quoting at some length:

> Speaking generally, there is nothing in the world harder to know than the biography of someone called the founder of a religion. That is because later generations of believers, through an excess of adulation for his teaching, added strange and unforeseen episodes, and labored as much as possible to make the spiritual body (*reitai*) of their master sacred and extraordinary. This is particularly so in the case of the biography of the Buddha. This being the case, no one today is able to document his biography accurately. For now, then, shall we rely on the ancient traditions and be satisfied to learn about the way in which ancient Indian Buddhists conceived of their founder? This is not the case only for the Buddha, but for Christ and Muhammad as well; leaving aside their miracles and their prophecies, who can narrate

their biographies to us? But even their miracles and their prophecies must often be the obverse side of the facts, and emerge from metaphors and parables. Thus, if we discard their forms and ferret out their intention, then perhaps it will not be unduly troublesome [to use such episodes] to learn about the characters and deeds (*seikaku gyōjō*) of these people.[181]

Based on this reasoning, Takayama informed his readers at the end of this discussion, his decision to follow the existing biographical literature ought not to preclude their own good judgement: "Although I have followed these biographies for the time being, knowledgeable readers should, from the passages themselves, comprehend the true biography of the great sage, Śākyamuni."[182] In keeping with this stated intention, Takayama's narrative does admit of some of the fantastic or supernatural elements from the standard narratives—maintaining the place, for instance, of Māra and his forces in attempting to dissuade the prince from his attempt to attain enlightenment.

In adopting this new framework, Takayama's work here pioneered a popular new series of biographies as well as a new approach to the biography of the Buddha itself. Maintaining the positioning of Śākyamuni within a global pantheon of great men—presumably a position to which he was exposed as an auditor of Inoue's lectures in the mid-1890s—Takayama nonetheless radically repositioned the difficult, "nonhistorical" parts of the Buddha's biography. He did not merely repeat them, nor did he attempt to distinguish the historical from the nonhistorical. Instead, Takayama opted to extend the ambit of "the historical," so that the narrative apotheosis of the Buddha would no longer obstruct historical investigation, but rather enable it. Takayama's innovation did not rely on a new explanation for the formation of the biographical literature. Takayama seems basically to have agreed with Inoue, who attributed the biographical implausibilities to an excess of devotion toward the Buddha's "character" (*jinkaku*). Takayama's innovation lay in his repositioning of those implausibilities as evidence for the greatness of that character itself.

Another, much shorter, piece by Takayama also helped install Śākyamuni among a pantheon of global figures: his two-part essay "Four Sages of the World" ("Sekai no shisei"), written as one of his contributions for the textbook *New Middle-School Reader* (*Chūgaku shin tokuhon*) of 1901. He also contributed a three-part biography of Joan of Arc to the same volume.[183] The "Four Sages" essay—which treats Śākyamuni, Confucius, Socrates, and Jesus—continued to be taught at least into the mid-1930s.[184] Although what is usually translated as "middle school" (*chūgakkō*) ought better to be rendered as "lower secondary school," which was not compulsory, it is still safe to assume that Takayama's piece was widely read over the intervening decades.[185] Among its brief introductions to the lives and teachings of each of the four men, it especially emphasizes the suffering of each, and his determination and perseverance.[186]

In the years after Takayama's death in 1902, other intellectuals would further develop the theme of a group of sages suitable for emulation in the twentieth century, not least among them Takayama's mentor, Inoue Tetsujirō, himself. In an article of 1910, "On Sages" ("Seijin ron"), Inoue discarded the limited Confucian concept of a "sage" as too narrowly applied in China, and he declared instead that the true sage must be "universal" (again, literally "global") and "not limited to a single nation."[187] Inoue's selection of four truly global sages precisely inherits Takayama's, though his piece goes further, also offering reasons for not including Kant or Darwin among their number. It also inherits something of the pedagogical mode of Takayama's piece, for Inoue ends by explicitly asking his readers to take those sages, and others, as "models" (*mohan*) for themselves. "Those persons with an aspiration for improvement and development," wrote Inoue, "must have the intent of taking themselves as the basis, and of completing it by assembling the strengths of these sages."[188]

Writing outside of Buddhist institutions, in the newly created secular spaces of the national university and the national press, Inoue and Takayama endowed the life story of the Buddha with a prestige and societal relevance that only those institutions of Meiji Japan could grant. They insured that the topic of the Buddha's life would be an issue for serious intellectual discussion, and that the Buddha would take his place among the panoply of other sagely figures in works for young readers. They did not, however, attempt to describe the mechanism that would link the mythologized Śākyamuni of the past with the moral exemplar and great man still valuable to the present day. That task fell to the third member of this group, Anesaki Masaharu.

The Buddha as a Man of Character

As contemporary scholarship has only begun to recognize, the concept of "character" (*jinkaku*, also translatable in some instances as "personality" or "personhood") attracted a great deal of attention in late Meiji intellectual circles, including Buddhist intellectuals and intellectuals with an interest in Buddhism.[189] In fact, Inoue Tetsujirō himself popularized this term and developed it into a key pillar of the ethical program that he promoted through the influential textbooks that he authored. His disciple Anesaki Masaharu reacted negatively to some elements of Inoue's thought—particularly his statism—but he inherited and developed Inoue's emphasis on the development of moral "character" (also rendered as *seikaku*).[190] Anesaki then went on to fuse the existing emphasis on great men with this concept of character. In an essay originally written in 1899, the same year as Takayama's book, Anesaki posited:

> The focus of moral education (*dōtokuteki kyōka*) is enriching the content of one's character (*jinkaku*), activating that character (*seikaku*) to adapt to the needs of the day and the society, and thus promoting the progress of social and individual activities. Because the hero (*eiyū*) is one who best expresses the perfection of individual character and aids his era, it should by now go without saying that the sentiments of hero-worship, which rouse up the veneration of that character (*seikaku*), are indispensible tools in moral education.[191]

Development of the learner's character formed a motif in Anesaki's later activities. In the following year, 1900, Takayama was primarily responsible for drafting the manifesto for an ethical society (which Anesaki helped to found), the Teiyū Rinrikai. Notably, one of Anesaki's identifiable contributions to the text, not evident in Takayama's draft, is the phrase "We firmly believe that the cultivation of character (*jinkaku no shūyō*) must be the root of all morality."[192]

In two scholarly monographs published in the first decade after Takayama's death, Anesaki applied the ideas of heroism, character, and moral cultivation to the case of the historical Buddha. The historical association of the Buddha with a supreme *jinkaku* is central to each. The very first words of the first chapter of Anesaki's doctoral study, *The Buddha's Manifestation Body and the Buddha's Dharma-Body* (*Genshinbutsu to hosshinbutsu*, 1904), spell out their confluence: "While religion may be a product of a society's humanistic nature, it goes without saying that the religion's transformation and development often await a single individual's character of genius (*tensai jinkaku*)."[193] The purpose of Anesaki's study—given the presupposition of character as propulsion for the development of any religion—was to trace the links between the two. In the case of the Buddha, this meant Anesaki aimed to show that the metaphysical concept of a transcendent dharma body was nothing more than the way in which the Buddha's later followers conceived of his ideal character.[194] As he titled the chapter in which he concentrated this exposition: "The Metaphorical Description of the Buddha's Character and the Mythologization of the Buddha's Biography: How Did Buddhists Transform the Buddha into a God beyond the Human World?"[195]

As concrete examples of the unfolding of this process, Anesaki cited the increasingly literal understanding of metaphors describing the virtues of the Buddha. For instance, the comparison of the Buddha with a lotus, which emerges from the mud untouched by it, ultimately became one of the minor characteristics of a "great man," which is to say, that he cannot be defiled by dirt. The comparison of the Buddha to a doctor who treats the ills of the world was literalized into a vision of the Buddha as a miraculous healer, the Medicine King, which ultimately developed into the figure of the Buddha as Bhaiṣajyaguru Vaiḍūryaprabha (Jpn. Yakushi Nyorai), the Buddha Radiant Lapis-Lazuli Master of Healing. Again, the comparisons of the Buddha to the sun that illumines the ignorance of all beings were gradually literalized into an account of the Buddha as possessing a visibly golden body. The basic ingredients for all these literalizations, Anesaki stressed, actually emerge from within the Brahmanical tradition, but they were merely efforts to depict the Buddha's magnificent *jinkaku* in a popular and concrete manner. Or, as he more succinctly summarized, they were "confusions between metaphor and fact."[196] But the confusion itself was valuable for Anesaki, because he believed that it could lead later historians back to the fact. In his later *Fundamental Buddhism* (*Konpon Bukkyō*, 1911), Anesaki developed this possibility still further, using textual parallels between the Chinese and Pāli Buddhist canons to document the relationship of the two spheres of Buddhism. In effect, the character of the Buddha had become the central device with which Anesaki attempted to prove the basic unity of all forms of Buddhism in Asia.

Across the span of just a few decades—from the 1880s to the 1910s—leading Japanese intellectuals' understandings of the Buddha transformed radically. The comparison of the Buddha to other philosophical or religious leaders, which had so infuriated the Zen cleric Nōnin Hakugan, became for the new generation of leading lay intellectuals—Inoue Tetsujirō, Takayama Chogyū, Anesaki Masaharu—essential not only for securing the Buddha a place in the new disciplines of history and religious studies, but also for understanding the Buddha himself. Comparison had gone from being a taboo to an essential tool at the cutting edge of scholarship.

Nor could leading Buddhist intellectuals within denominational institutions avoid engagement with these discourses. The April 1909 issue of the journal *Warning to the World* (*Keisei*), affiliated with the Honganji subdenomination of True Pure Land Buddhism, was a special issue devoted to Śākyamuni. Inoue Tetsujirō, Saji Jitsunen, Anesaki Masaharu, and Katō Totsudō were all among the contributors. Another was the high-ranking scholar-cleric Maeda Eun (1855–1930), also of the Honganji subdenomination, who submitted a highly defensive response to the proposition that the Buddha ranked as one great sage among others, in a piece titled "My Reflections Concerning Śākyamuni" ("Shakuson ni tai suru yo no kansō"). He objected to the comparison of the Buddha with such other "sages" as Jesus or Socrates, and stressed that for him, the Buddha was the highest figure to be revered anywhere. On the basis of its claims, Maeda's piece here might seem like a piece of unreconstructed reaction. Significantly, though, it began with a caveat: Maeda wrote that he did not appreciate the Buddha *only* as a historical figure, but that he also had reverence for the Buddha that did not have a source in history. "Do not," he urged his readers, "use only the eye of history to criticize my reflections concerning the Buddha."[197] By the end of the Meiji period, then, the discourse of the Buddha as a historical figure had become so entrenched as to be inescapable even within the intellectual circles of Buddhist institutions.

CONCLUSION

Sage as Story

The history of Buddhism may be understood a history of coping with the loss of its founder, a catalog of efforts to compensate for the loss by locating the Buddha elsewhere than in his historical, human form. In doctrinal terms, this problem gave rise to the notion of multiple bodies of the Buddha. Later substitutes for the Buddha have included his relics; the stupas and reliquaries that enshrine them; images, particularly sculptures revered as alive in their own right; and the Buddha's teaching, whether conceived of in the abstract, or embodied in concrete Buddhist scriptures, or condensed into such compact forms as the verse on dependent origination (Skt. *pratītyasamutpāda gāthā*, Jpn. *engi hōju*), often found on Buddhist images from South Asia and Tibet.[1] In no abstract sense, these and other such replacements do not merely represent or memorialize the Buddha; they actually realize his presence in the present.[2] Such surrogates proliferated in Japan, just as they proliferated throughout the rest of the Buddhist world, and the study of their functions in Japan remains valuable.[3]

In that spirit of substitution, this book has carried out its own sleight of hand, equating the changes made to narratives of the Buddha's life with varying perspectives toward the Buddha himself. By the logic implicit in this study, to reframe the narrative of that life in a new setting or genre is to emplot the Buddha in a new system of meaning. To retell that narrative is to modify or reinvent the "bio-blueprint" of events constitutive of a buddha.[4] By the same token, to undertake historical or text-critical study of that narrative is to assume, or to question, the very conditions of possibility for knowing the Buddha. Whether those narratives be written, or sculpted, or painted, there is one crucial difference between narrative as a substitute-body and the other stand-ins: in part because any narrative unfolds in time, to engage in any narrative operation is to participate in a self-conscious negotiation with the past. Reverence for such holy objects as the relics of the Buddha or images of the timeless Tathāgata Śākyamuni may be read as an effort to annihilate time and change. By contrast, temporal change is at the heart of any telling of the Buddha's life, even if the narrative framework for that telling denies its own ultimate reality (for instance, by portraying the events of the Buddha's life as mere display or expedient means).

Coping with the loss of the Buddha was a particular problem in ancient Japan. Until at least the fourteenth century, Japanese Buddhist intellectuals typically perceived their land as poor and marginal—in one prominent articulation, as one among many "marginal lands [small as] scattered millet seeds" (*zokusan hendo*). Given this kind of self-understanding, it would have appeared all the more urgent to forge a direct connection with the Buddha, believed to reside in a central land propitious to the practice of Buddhism. Perhaps a lasting sense of concern for the vast distance at which the Buddha lived, both temporally and spatially, helps explain why relics and images of the timeless Tathāgata were so much more important to Japanese ritual life than orthodox depictions of his biography, which were inevitably set in a distant place and time. In this sense, it is useful to remember that even narrative depictions of the Buddha's life could serve to animate timeless objects of worship. Examples of this subordination of the narrative to the cults of the realized, eternal Buddha include the eighth-century stupas at the Hōryūji and the Yakushiji, as well as the illustrated scroll of the life of the Buddha, produced in 1515 as a kind of "biography" less of the Buddha himself than of his standing image and substitute at the Seiryōji.

By privileging changing narrative over timeless presence, this book has probed not the collapse of time and space accomplished in ritual, but the consequences of a narrative that always ended with the loss of the Buddha and his utter separation from Japan. In light of this foregone conclusion, assigning significance to and finding a connection with the life of the Buddha posed a problem for all his Japanese biographers. Nor was the larger import of the Buddha's life the only problem that they had to face; as the subtitle of this book suggests, negotiating the question of sources for the Buddha's life was necessary from the start of Buddhism in Japan. While certain Chinese-language scriptures and commentaries exerted more influence in Japan than did others, the biographers of the Buddha in Japan nonetheless had to cope with multiple, contradictory source texts. Typically, the significance assigned to the life of the Buddha helped determine the source texts that were employed (or neglected) in the making of any individual retelling. This book has sought to chart the changing significance of the Buddha's life as reflected in the sources used by his biographers, and by their changing evaluation of his distance.

Meaning and Sources in the Japanese Guises of the Buddha

For roughly the first millennium of writings about the life of the Buddha in Japan, writers and artists tended to hew closely to the accounts and depictions of that life transmitted from the Asian continent. The *Sutra of Past and Present Cause and Effect* was just one particularly influential scriptural source, but Japanese intellectuals also had recourse to the accounts of the Buddha from such Chinese encyclopedic compilations of scriptural material as the *Genealogy of Śākyamuni* and the *Pearl Grove of the Dharma Garden*. Likewise, material representations of the life of the Buddha tended to adhere closely to continental precedents. Such precedents may be identified, or posited, for the dioramas at the pagoda of the Hōryūji; the *Illustrated Sutra of Past and Present Cause and Effect*; the medieval hanging scrolls at the Daifukudenji, the Jikōji, the Jōrakuji, and elsewhere; and the 1515 *Origin Tale of the Hall of Śākyamuni*.

While these works drew on a variety of sources and told various versions of the Buddha's life, they consistently expressed a "will to canonicity." That is to say, the gesture of adducing canonical sources punctuates and supports their narratives. Like their continental models, these retellings explicitly addressed the canon, both as testimony for the correctness of their versions of Buddha's life and, within their stories, as milestones in the Buddha's preaching career, as well as commentative traditions. Doctrinally, these biographies tended to use the life of the Buddha to communicate the uniquely Tendai classification of the scriptures. This Buddha was principally a pedagogue.

By the close of Japan's medieval period at the end of the sixteenth century, the temporal and intellectual dominance of the great temple complexes had been shattered. Accordingly, Buddhist institutions' ascendancy over cultural production began to erode. Within decades, improvements in printing technology, the advent of political peace, and the expansion of urban commercial centers created a new demand for entertaining tales, both published and performed. Works treating broadly religious themes retained an important position in this body of work, but as popular literature, they showed relatively little interest in responding to canonical texts. In the case of the life of the Buddha, these shifts broke the medieval mold for the tale, which had been exemplified by such works as the first volume of the *Tales of Times Now Past* (early twelfth century) and the *Program of the Eight Phases of the Life of the Tathāgata Śākyamuni* (fourteenth century). Produced and marketed across the seventeenth century, the anonymous body of literature taking the title *Original Ground of Śākyamuni*, and its elaboration in the *Tale of Śākyamuni in Eight Phases*, responded more obviously to promotional needs than to any profession of orthodox adherence to a scriptural canon. Such free reinvention of the life of the Buddha—exemplified by Chikamatsu's 1695 play *A Birth Assembly for the Tathāgata Śākyamuni*—went on to dominate Japanese commercial storytelling about the Buddha through the end of the nineteenth century. These works transformed the Buddha's life into an entertaining and moving story, and the Buddha into a suffering hero, in a mode responsive to distinctly local concerns.

On the whole, Buddhist institutions seem to have expressed little interest in this new and decidedly non-canonical body of work. The reassertion of the orthodox biography of the Buddha fell to individual Buddhist clerics. The *vinaya* master and nun Kōgetsu Sōgi, disciple of the reformist cleric Jiun Onkō, produced the most important orthodox retelling of the life of the Buddha for the late Edo period, *The Light of the Three Ages*. Unlike her seventeenth-century predecessor Gentei, Kōgetsu did not have recourse to basically medieval assumptions about the uniformly equal value of the various scriptural accounts of the Buddha's life. Rather, she engaged in the critical adjudication of conflicting texts, and she labored to restore orthography, scriptural quotations, and episodes absent from the Buddha's biography in Japan for hundreds of years. Nor was Kōgetsu's work merely a straightforward rehashing of the life of the Buddha: she used the episodes recounted in it as evidence for her own intermittent remarks, critiquing the practice of Buddhism in the Japan of her day. Kōgetsu's Buddha represents an exemplar, making possible her critical perspective on the world around her. *The Light of the Three Ages*, with its call for a revival of traditional precept practice, was itself revived half a century after her death, even finding its way into the curriculum for young Buddhist nuns.

Although composed at roughly the same time as Kōgetsu's biography, treatises by the nativist scholar Hirata Atsutane used historical research about the Buddha for entirely opposite ends. Convinced that the Buddha was a scoundrel and a trickster, Atsutane cast a critical eye over a massive body of Chinese-language sources for the life of Śākyamuni. Atsutane argued that large parts of the account of the life of the Buddha were fabrications, and he claimed the ability to sift the true from the false in these accounts. In his popular vernacular lectures, *A Mocking Discourse upon Emerging from Meditation* (delivered in 1811), Atsutane excoriated the textual accounts of the Buddha's life for their mendacity. On the other hand, in his vast unfinished compendium of Chinese-language sources and notes, the *Compendium of Indian Records* (1826), Atsutane worked less to debunk those accounts than to extract the hidden historical truths that they obscured. For Atsutane, then, the Buddha amounted to nothing but a fraud—but hardly a harmless one. Precisely because the fantastic tales of the Buddha had obscured the true, ancient way of the Shintō gods, Atsutane was concerned not with the Buddha's distance, but rather with his lingering and powerful influence. Atsutane's vernacular lectures circulated widely in the final decades of the Edo period, alarming his Buddhist clerical readers but leaving them unable to counter his arguments.

After the Meiji Restoration of 1868, Christian missionaries and their Japanese converts added their voices to the chorus of historical objections to the standard accounts of the life of the Buddha. Against these critiques, too, traditional Buddhist intellectuals were powerless to mount a persuasive defense. Both governmental and Buddhist institutions began to assimilate European Buddhological scholarship, even as outward-looking Japanese Buddhist intellectuals, lay and clerical, struggled to reconcile the new methodology of that scholarship with the received literature of the Buddha's life. A thoroughly demythologized and historicized Buddha would not only be insufferably distant from the Meiji-era present, but would also lack any power to inspire reverence—at best, ranking only as one of many past sages and thinkers.

In the end, it was artists and intellectuals outside Buddhist institutions who pressed forward with a compromise, representing the Buddha Śākyamuni as a historical individual who nonetheless remained a locus of timeless value. From the final years of the nineteenth century, up-and-coming artists in the new painting style of Nihonga embraced scenes from the Buddha's life as one important historical motif in their work. Across the first decades of the twentieth century, a number of Nihonga artists traveled to South Asia in search of authentically Indian sources for their original pieces. Around the same time, three pivotal intellectuals connected through the Department of Philosophy at Tokyo Imperial University—Inoue Tetsujirō, Takayama Chogyū, and Anesaki Masaharu—not only researched the Buddha's life in its historical context, but also reframed his life within a pantheon of globally recognized great men.

The source of the Buddha's greatness, their work collectively suggested, lay in his moral "character" (*jinkaku*). Fantastic biographical episodes, unamenable to empirical historical analysis, could nonetheless be taken as evidence for the historical greatness of character that inspired them. At a stroke, the legendary aspects of the many versions of the Buddha's life transformed from liabilities to confirmation of the Buddha's value. Along with other venerable figures from world history, the Buddha and his life could offer suitable models for moral education. The focus on the Buddha's comparability with other great sages rankled some clerical intellectuals, but they could not ignore it.

The preceding discussion should not, of course, imply that the Buddhas of these historical periods were mutually exclusive, and that the Buddha as pedagogue was utterly replaced by the Buddha as hero, who was placed in a historical framework and by turns idealized and denigrated, only to experience another sea change into a figure of global stature. Far from it: the life of the Buddha remains a teaching tool, and processions and lustrations to commemorate the birth of the prince remain well-established staples at kindergartens associated with Buddhist temples throughout Japan. By the same token, the anniversary of the Buddha's *parinirvāṇa* holds its place in the ritual calendar at Japanese Buddhist temples large and small. Myōe's *Ceremonial in Four Sessions* is still performed in the traditional *shōmyō* vocal style, at the great Shingon Buddhist center of Mount Kōya and elsewhere. The literature of the Buddha as Japanese hero coexisted with the rise of empiricist historical scholarship, which continues in Japan through the present. Even after plays like *A Birth Assembly for the Tathāgata Śākyamuni* fell out of the current repertoire for the puppet theater, Japanese dramatists and novelists found new uses for the Buddha across the twentieth century and beyond—and with the cachet of anime and manga, their productions now circulate more globally than ever before. With the glorification of the Buddha's character as a universal and transcendent value, the Buddha's life and teachings became available as sources of "cultivation" (*kyōyō*, from the German *Bildung*) for Japanese audiences without religious commitment, in a steady stream of popular magazine publications, television documentaries, and public lectures.

Reimagining the Buddha in Twentieth-Century Japan and Beyond

New uses for the Buddha—as a creative vehicle for cultural producers, and as a vehicle for education—began in earnest in the 1910s. If *A Storied Sage* focuses on the changing epistemologies by which to know the Buddha, ending with thc triumph of historical thinking and the cult of character, then future study will attempt a cultural history of the Buddha, asking how his human figure was appropriated in creative works and in the new concern for the enrichment and perfection of human character. It is possible to sketch out the parameters of that study here.

Evidence of the appropriation of the Buddha's life story is not hard to find in Japan after the Meiji period, particularly in the visual arts. After 1910, Nihonga artists continued to venture to South Asia and exploit their observations there in depictions of the life of the Buddha. Arai Kanpō (1878–1945) spent nearly a year and a half in India (1916–1918), including long months copying mural art from the cave temples at Ajantā. His fellow Nihonga artist, Kiriya Senrin (1877–1932), who also worked at Ajantā, made a total of three visits to India (1911–1913, 1917–1918, 1929).

Artistic exchange flowed both ways: Kiriya received and accepted an invitation from the Maha Bodhi Society to adorn the interior of its temple at Sarnath with illustrations the life of the Buddha, but died suddenly on the verge of departure. He was replaced by the artist Nousu Kōsetsu (1885–1973), who went on to spend some four years (1932–1936) completing the mural project. The maverick painter Sugimoto Tetsuo (1899–1985)—himself a student of the Buddhological giant Takakusu Junjirō (1866–1945)—spent part of the war years conducting expeditions in continental Asia for Kyoto Imperial University and the temple Higashi Honganji. During the postwar years, he painted sacred figures from religious traditions around the world, affording a prominent place to scenes from the life of the Buddha. After 1945, the Buddha's life story also informed a major program of murals (1959–1960) painted by Nakamura Gakuryō (1890–1969) for the temple Shitennōji in Osaka, and it featured in a series of luminous paintings on silk by Hirayama Ikuo (1930–2009).

Travel was not the monopoly of artists. The period after 1910 saw the production of lavishly illustrated photographic catalogs and book-length travelogues of visits to Buddhist sites in India and Tibet, some produced by prominent Japanese clerics, like Akegarasu Haya (1877–

1954) and Kawaguchi Ekai (1866–1945). A new wave of lay travelers also began to visit and write about sites associated with the Buddha, prominently including the cosmopolitan Okina Kyūin (1888–1973). After enduring more than fifteen years of immigrant life in the United States, Okina returned to Japan in 1924, from which he visited India in 1933. He produced an extensive travelogue about Buddhist sites (1935) and a play about the Buddha's life (1936). Nor was South Asia the only important site of influence on Japanese narratives of the life of the Buddha: versions of the life of the Buddha produced during the 1930s by other figures with international connections include the 1935 play *The Light of the Four Seas* (*Shikai no hikari*) by Hayakawa Sesshū (1889–1973), erstwhile star of American silent films, and the incomplete novel *Śākyamuni* (*Shakuson*), partially written and partially dictated by Ikuta Chōkō (1882–1936), also the first translator of Nietzsche's complete works, after he lost his eyesight in his final years.

Also starting in the 1910s, the life of the Buddha began to influence Japan's European-style prose fiction, theater, and even film. Japanese writers after the Meiji years treated his figure with an increasingly free hand. Not unlike their early modern predecessors, they evinced interest in the vulnerability, struggles, and human conflicts of the Buddha and surrounding characters. Matsui Shōyō's (1870–1933) opera libretto of 1912—written for one of the very first original operatic productions ever mounted in Japan—dramatized the temptations threatening the prince Siddhartha and his wife, Yaśodharā, between his renunciation and homecoming. Other works reflected the era's new interest in humanism. A 1914 drama by Mushanokōji Saneatsu (1885–1976) staged the Buddha's refusal to save his clan of birth from massacre by King Virūḍhaka, stressing Tolstoyan nonviolence rather than the usual moral of inevitable karmic retribution. In 1921, the novelist Naka Kansuke (1885–1965) told the story of Yaśodharā through the eyes of the Buddha's evil cousin Devadatta, who pursued her—a plot device already evident in Edo fiction and drama about the Buddha—but he now imagined that Devadatta's relentless pursuit of her ultimately drove her to suicide.

This liberty with the story of the Buddha's family found its way into the 1961 cinematic extravaganza *Śākyamuni* (*Shaka*), itself a Japanese response to such Hollywood spectacles as *The Ten Commandments* (1956). Unlike the murals that Nousu painted at Sarnath, this filmic innovation to the tale was distinctly not welcomed abroad: offended by the film's treatment of Yaśodharā, governments across South and Southeast Asia protested to the Japanese Foreign Ministry against the film's "historical inaccuracy." When the Japanese government refused to alter the film, the government of Ceylon even forbade its importation and screening.

The period after the 1910s also saw a dramatic rise in the use of the Buddha as an exemplar of secular cultural value. The aspiration for "cultivation," modeled on German Romantic traditions, took root first in the elite Higher Schools of the Taishō era (1912–1925), and spread to become a much broader societal aspiration by the postwar years. In this new context, knowledge of the Buddha and his teachings was repositioned as a mode of enrichment to which a growing body of people could aspire, outside the context of any Buddhist institution. New media played an important role in this recasting. Pivotal in this movement was the erstwhile Buddhist cleric Tomomatsu Entai (1895–1973). As early as 1922, Tomomatsu had written and published his own drama, *The Buddha Suffering on This Earth* (*Chi ni nayameru Shaka*). Tomomatsu's public recognition exploded in 1934, when he was offered the chance to lecture on the Tokyo NHK radio station, JOAK, about a Buddhist text. Tomomatsu himself seems to have chosen to lecture about a compendium of early Buddhist teachings, the *Dhammapada*, which was relatively obscure in Japan.

Tomomatsu's gamble paid off: the fifteen-day lecture given in March 1934 was by all accounts a great hit, and Tomomatsu himself returned to the station in October 1934, with another fifteen-day lecture series about his other specialty, the Āgamas. Tomomatsu's lectures succeeded precisely because they applied ideas from these texts—closely associated with the historical Buddha—to the pressing problems of daily life in 1930s Japan. Tomomatsu went on to found a short-lived but mass social movement that attracted educated urban listeners with its promise of a practical Buddhism. Although his movement collapsed with the war's end, Tomomatsu maintained his distance from the established Buddhist groups, continuing to lecture on these two early Buddhist texts through the end of his life. His translations of them into modern Japanese remain standard and in print even today.

In the postwar years, the Tokyo University scholar Nakamura Hajime (a.k.a. Nakamura Gen, 1912–1999) did the most to promote knowledge of the Buddha as a kind of cultivation in the public eye. Himself a product of the elite First Higher School, Nakamura distinguished himself as an interpreter of early Buddhist texts from South Asian sources. He disseminated these as published vernacular Japanese translations and also appeared extensively in Japan's broadcast media, with such series as *Reading the Heart of the Buddhist Scriptures* (NHK Radio, 1985) and *The Life and Thought of the Buddha* (NHK Educational Television, 1995–1996). In these broadcasts, Nakamura's messages shared space with a range of other religious messages; as NHK has always suggested, learning about the life of the Buddha is part of a well-rounded humanistic education, but certainly not the only part. Further popularizers of the same message have carried on Nakamura's project. Notable among these is Koike Ryūnosuke (1978–), a Tokyo University–educated onetime True Pure Land monk who was excommunicated in 2011. His *Super-Translation: Words of the Buddha* (*Chōyaku: Budda no kotoba*), drawn largely from the *Dhammapada* and the Āgamas, underwent thirteen impressions between its publication in 2011 and February 2013. By now, it should come as no surprise to learn that the same Super-Translation series also includes volumes devoted to the maxims of the Old Testament, Nietzsche, and Confucius.

Remolding the Buddha

As both an epitome of the argument carried forward in the present study and an indication of the kind of materials to feature in future scholarship, it will be useful to consider a set of works created by a mature sculptor active in the 1910s, Shinkai Taketarō (1868–1927). Shinkai had been born into a lineage of *busshi*—sculptors of traditional Buddhist images—in modern Yamagata Prefecture. As was the case in other regions of Japan, Buddhist images in Yamagata also suffered during the forcible, violent "separation" of Shintō from Buddhist images and institutions. Together with his father, the teenage Shinkai was just one of many *busshi* who engaged in the repair of ancient Buddhist sculpture across Japan during the early 1880s. Left in Yamagata, Shinkai could have become a reviver of antique Buddhist statuary.[5] Instead, he left home to join the military, returning to sculpture through a circuitous route. In his mature years, Shinkai revisited Buddhist themes. In the final decades of his life, his output included an imaginative portrait sculpture of the ancient Buddhist philosopher and patriarch Nāgārjuna (1916), as well as a bold (and ultimately, censored) reworking of the traditional Esoteric Buddhist depiction of the elephant-headed Hindu deity Gaṇeśa, as a male-female pair in loving embrace (1923).

In the autumn of 1915, Shinkai—then at the height of his creative and professional career—included a set of reliefs among his submissions to the ninth annual Ministry of Education Fine Arts Exhibition, for which he also served as a judge. Titled *The Eight Phases of the Life of*

Śākyamuni (*Shaka hassō*), the set consisted of eight panels, each measuring about one foot (*shaku*) and a half by two feet and a half. As the title suggests, the topics that Shinkai chose for each of the reliefs reflect a typical set of key events in the Buddha's life familiar in Japan. Lost in the Great Kantō earthquake of 1923, the reliefs survive today only in photographs, which nonetheless suffice to communicate their general composition. At the same time, those photographs suggest the sheer novelty of Shinkai's artistic production, in comparison with previous sculptural representations of the Eight Phases in Japan, a tradition which by Shinkai's time was already over one millennium old. (See fig. 12.)

For his part, Shinkai was more strongly influenced by techniques and models he had absorbed during his stay in France and Germany (1900–1901) than by any traditional iconography. Not unlike Okakura, Shinkai also went so far as to express disdain for received models for the life of the Buddha in his public remarks:

> In Japan, there are no cohesive objects of reference [for the life of the Buddha], apart from popular illustrated storybooks, but I have previously seen that in the temples of Java there are more phases [of the Buddha's life] engraved. But my work steers clear of the excessively strange parts, and therefore differs from [the version]

FIGURE 12 Shinkai Taketarō, from *The Eight Phases of the Life of Śākyamuni* (set of reliefs). *Parinirvāṇa (Nehan), Shaka hassō* (1915; orig. now lost). Photograph courtesy of the Tokyo Research Institute for Cultural Properties.

evident in the Buddhist texts, so persons of religion (*shūkyōka*) might not be too happy about it.[6]

By "popular illustrated storybooks" (*kusazōshi*), Shinkai presumably meant the depictions in the illustrated late Edo literature of the life of the Buddha. They are so poor and fanciful, Shinkai averred in these cutting remarks, that if anything, Buddhist reliefs from other lands—such as the program of reliefs at the temple site of Borobudur—would make for better models.

Thus, Shinkai's sculpted life of the Buddha self-consciously bypassed Japanese or continental Asian models to draw extensively on works by European predecessors, including the early Renaissance sculptor Donatello, whom Shinkai identified as a pioneer of bas-relief.[7] In the idealization of its subject matter and its use of linear perspective, Donatello's early-fifteenth-century relief of the Ascension (now in the collection of the Victoria and Albert Museum) could easily have been one point of reference for Shinkai's reliefs. Like Donatello, Shinkai also structured his scenes of the Eight Phases around linear, single-point perspective. In other respects, Shinkai's reliefs cite different classics of European art: the posture of Māyā in the relief depicting the Buddha's entry into her womb—lying in a richly canopied bed, on her back, with her head to the left, and her left knee raised to point to a window—strongly recalls a mid-sixteenth-century series of paintings depicting Danaë and her impregnation by a shower of gold sent by Zeus, produced by Titian in the sixteenth century.[8] Needless to say, the mythology on which Titian's painting relied marks another instance of divine conception. (Unlike Titian's work, Shinkai's relief does allude to the presence of a human father by placing Śuddhodana in outline next to Māyā, on the side away from the viewer.)

Shinkai made even more strikingly original revisions to the depiction of the Buddha's life. His portrayal of the birth of the Buddha abjured any depiction of the delivery itself, placing a tree in the foreground to block any access to the activity on the other side by viewers. Thus, hidden behind the tree, Māyā and the newborn prince are nowhere in evidence; spectators glimpse only their attendants thronging the site of the birth, along with a figure in the distance who is doing obeisance to the act—presumably, the father-king Śuddhodana. The figure of the prince appears for the first time only in the panel showing the Buddha's renunciation. Here there appear no clouds, no horse, no groom, and no flight through the air; there is only a single lone figure, his back turned to the viewer, walking out of a colonnaded structure. The panel showing the defeat of Māra likewise subverts the viewer's expectations, suggesting the Buddha only through his face at the center top of the visual field, surrounded by cloudlike modeling in the upper half of the panel, and the figures of writhing, fleeing naked women in the lower half. The composition thus draws the viewer into the mental landscape of the Buddha, eschewing any effort at objective representation.

The Buddha's body reappears only in the following panel, the sixth, which depicts his awakening. Here the Buddha sits utterly alone, facing the viewer, on a rock under a tree (presumably inverting the concealment of his figure behind the tree of the third panel), making a mudra of meditation. Strikingly, the Buddha does not retain this seated posture for the Turning of the Wheel of the Dharma in the seventh panel, which depicts the Buddha now standing erect, holding a begging bowl and trailed by his monks to his rear, as he preaches to a crowd suggested by figures in the corners of the panel.

The final panel, depicting the *parinirvāṇa* of the Buddha, breaks still more astonishingly with convention established across many centuries: it shows a highly elongated, distinctly gaunt figure lying on his back under a tree, his pillowed head depicted in profile, his arms by his sides, and his community of followers standing in attendance on him, stretching in a line from the foot of the bed into the distance. These choices by Shinkai could easily have drawn upon late medieval and early Renaissance iconography for the laying out and burial of Jesus. By contrast, typical images of the Buddha's demise surround his figure with vast throngs of mourners, both human and otherwise, and they place his body on its right side, with his head visible to or directly facing the viewer. Like the fourth panel, which does not reveal the Buddha's birth but instead conceals it, the final panel of this series denies viewers a connection that they might otherwise expect.

As the work of a judge at the Ministry exhibition, Shinkai's relief set of the *Eight Phases* was ineligible for consideration for an award, but critics commented on it regardless.[9] Taki Seiichi (1873–1945), professor of art history at Tokyo Imperial University, conceded in a newspaper review of the exhibition that Shinkai's set merited attention, but sniffed that "it would seem that there is still room for polishing." He continued: "In the scene of the [Buddha's] *nirvāṇa*, there is a novel technique of having Śākyamuni lying supine and facing upward, but in such matters as this, it is ultimately proper to follow the practices of old (*kojitsu*)."[10]

For his part, Shinkai had been railing against the criterion of "verification based on practices of old" (*kojitsu kōshō*)—one of the criteria to which the early Nihonga paintings of the Buddha's life were frequently subjected—since his return to Japan from Europe in 1902. In a contribution to *Art News* (*Bijutsu shinpō*) in the following year of 1903, Shinkai bewailed the "excessive honesty" of Japanese sculptors, who, he lamented, had to worry about "how many scales were on the armor of which period, whether folds would not form in the cloth of ceremonial robes of a certain period, whether [European] frock coats were always buttoned up in the front, and what measurements they should have." Shinkai continued, with a further flourish, that when sculptors produce a piece, "unless they can brandish a certificate of authenticity about, they cannot feel at ease, and nobody will accept their work."[11] Shinkai's argument that the artist had a responsibility to history, but also a greater responsibility to art, echoes Takayama Chogyū's public case for the autonomy of art from history.

Shinkai elaborated on these sentiments, explaining precisely what he deemed the "excessively strange parts" of the Buddha's biography, in a short article that he submitted to the first issue of the influential journal *Central Arts Review* (*Chūō bijutsu*), which appeared immediately before the opening of the 1915 exhibition and the display of his *Eight Phases* reliefs. In this article, he commented on the thinking that guided his design for each of the eight panels. For some, he freely admitted, he had elected to follow the conventional iconography, but for others, he had selectively edited out aspects of the conventional iconography that he could not accept.

> As for the fifth scene, of the conquest of Māra: It is said that Māra, who controls the evil of this world, resented the Buddha's attainment of the Way, and attempted to confuse the Buddha's mind by dispatching his various followers, but the Buddha shattered these temptations full well and became awakened. *These monsters are, of course, not creatures that truly exist; they are nothing more than the shadows of the delusions in the mind of Śākyamuni. Therefore, I have decided not to depict the scene of the conquest of Māra, but rather to represent the Buddha's head at the center of the scene, and to depict the demons, surrounding him on all sides, faintly, like smoke.* . . . Finally, the eighth scene, the Buddha's *nirvāṇa*, depicts the death of the Buddha. According to the existing common account, even the birds and the beasts came and congregated around him, and mourned the death of this great man (*ijin*), but *it is impossible that such an unnatural event could occur. Thus, I have decided that it would be proper to exclude the birds and the beasts, in particular.*[12]

The photographs accompanying this article reproduced the depictions of the birth and *parinirvāṇa* of the Buddha, two of the more unconventional among Shinkai's relief scenes.

Shinkai's willingness to break with iconographic convention in his treatment of the life of the Buddha does, in one sense, represent his self-consciously modern stance of distance from the past. It would be easy to follow Shinkai's biographers in attributing such innovations to his commitment to a thoroughgoing naturalism or realism, a commitment assimilated from his study of European art.[13] As this study has shown, however, the processes that ultimately resulted in a naturalized or humanized version of Śākyamuni in Japan actually began centuries before Shinkai was born.

Placed in the context of this study, then, Shinkai's reliefs represent as much continuity as innovation. Shinkai's willingness to restructure his depiction of the Buddha through motifs deriving from other artistic traditions (here, Italian Renaissance art) is a distant echo of the late medieval Japanese incorporation of the tale of the Buddha's life into the body of popular *kanazōshi* tale literature and art. Shinkai's depiction of the Buddha at his death as a mere human being, gaunt and wizened, would surely have earned the approval of Hirata Atsutane, who took the very human demise of the Buddha ("I am now old in age, my body tired, my life nearing its end") as his own article of faith. In his treatment of the scene of the prince's defeat of Māra and attainment of awakening, Shinkai refused the supernatural and reduced Māra and his forces to mere psychological phenomena—decisions that closely mirror the empiricist strain of scholarship concerning the Buddha, pioneered in Japan by Inoue Tetsujirō and his disciples. (Unlike Ōmiya Kōnin, Shinkai made no effort to reconcile this interpretation of the Buddha's awakening with doctrinally authoritative texts.) So too did Shinkai inherit their positioning of the Buddha as a "great man," or *ijin*. As we might expect of a sculptor who had imbibed late-nineteenth-century European techniques and subject matter, many of Shinkai's works were memorial portraits of "great men" of his own time.

Nor were Buddhist intellectuals necessarily as hostile to these innovations as Shinkai had predicted they would be. In his published eulogy for his longtime friend Shinkai, the reformist lay Buddhist leader Takashima Beihō (1875–1949) reserved special praise for Shinkai's reliefs of the life of the Buddha, noting that they "shattered the mold of previous depictions in both their scale and their delicate skill" and lauding Shinkai for "producing from his own unique point of view a *Life of Śākyamuni* with abundant humanity (*ningenmi*)."[14] Takashima had himself been the eldest son of a True Pure Land temple household in modern Niigata Prefecture. While he did not inherit his father's position as chief priest, he was nonetheless educated at Buddhist institutions and remained active in the reform of Buddhism until his death. In addition to his dozens of books and hundreds of articles, he edited the journal *New Buddhism* (*Shin Bukkyō*) throughout its lifespan, and he led the lobbying for the establishment of the chair in Indian Philosophy at Tokyo Imperial University.

In his 1915 lament concerning the lack of coherent artistic models for the life of the Buddha in Japan, Shinkai mentioned that the Eastern Pagoda at the Nara temple Yakushiji—the lone original structure of the temple to survive to Shinkai's day—had previously been adorned with a set of reliefs depicting four scenes of the life of the Buddha, but that they had been long since lost. In the decades after the death of Shinkai, a major effort at the Yakushiji has restored the lost Western Pagoda, along with other major additions to the temple complex.

In early 2010, the sculptor Nakamura Shin'ya, then eighty-three, announced that he would embark on the final work of his life, a vast sculptural program to replace the original eight scenes of the life of Śākyamuni to adorn both the Eastern and Western pagodas. By the start of 2014, he had already completed two of the panels for the Western Pagoda, and the casting of the bronze images began that summer. The first set of four scenes was installed in the Western Pagoda in the spring of 2015. What did Nakamura, who had previously sculpted works in both Christian and Buddhist traditions, see himself doing in this final lifework? In comments made to the press early in 2014, Nakamura revealed that he had been doing research—both by reading texts and by traveling to the sites of the Buddha's life in India—but he suggested that the finished product would not impose any single definitive version of the life of the Buddha. "Various scenes from the life of the Buddha will be distributed [across these sculptures]," he was quoted as saying, but "I would like to make this a work upon which each person can project his or her individual thoughts."[15]

Notes

INTRODUCTION

1. Yamauchi Susumu [Shinkyō], "Kyōso Shaka ni tai-suru kodai Bukkyōto no shisō," *Taiyō* 3, no. 2 (1897): 170.
2. Nara Kokuritsu Hakubutsukan, ed., *Budda Shakuson: Sono shōgai to zōkei* (Nara: Nara Kokuritsu Hakubutsukan, 1984), 14.
3. Kabushiki Kaisha G. B. et al., eds., *Budda no kotoba: Budda to Nihonjin* (Tokyo: Tokuma Shoten, 2012), 95.
4. For a fairly typical indictment of the evils of the excessive "veneration of the founders" from a Buddhist reformer of the mid-twentieth century, see Tomomatsu Entai, *Bukkyō no mirai o hiraku: Shakai to mukiau Bukkyō to wa* (Tokyo: Suzuki Shuppan, 2002), 39–43.
5. Such genres include, but are not limited to, ritual manuals, invocations, and doctrinal scholarship.
6. Kawaguchi Ekai, *Upāsaka Bukkyō*, vol. 1, *Kawaguchi Ekai chosaku senshū* (Tokyo: Keibunsha, 2009), 59.
7. For scholarship about the absence of this mudra, see Ryu Sŭngjin, "Hōkei sanzon senbutsu to Einga kyo: Kodai Nihon ni okeru sokujiin zazō no fuzai o kangaeru tegakari to shite," *Kyōto bigaku bijutsu shigaku* 9 (2010): 35–69.
8. Concerning Takada Dōken, see John S. LoBreglio, "Uniting Buddhism: The Varities of *Tsūbukkyō* in Meiji-Taishō Japan and the Case of Takada Dōken," *Eastern Buddhist* 37, no. 1/2 (2005).
9. Some Japanese New Religious Movements founded after the conclusion of the Pacific War, such as Agonshū and Shinnyoen, have actively adopted imagery associated with the historical Buddha. Shinnyoen even employs a reclin-

ing image of the Buddha at his *parinirvāṇa* as the center of its ritual space. However, both organizations' ritual repertoire and doctrinal formulations generally take inspiration from sources other than the early Buddhist scriptures.

10. See Ryūkoku Daigaku Ryūkoku Myūjiamu, ed., *Shakuson to Shinran: Indo kara Nihon e no kiseki* (Kyoto: Hōzōkan, 2011).
11. Tokiwa Daijō, "Kako genzai ingakyō kaidai," in *Hon'enbu 4*, vol. 32, Kokuyaku issaikyō (Tokyo: Daitō Shuppansha, 1929), 1–10.
12. This is a variant term for more standard Chinese translations of Dīpaṃkara's name.
13. *T* 189:623c23.
14. *T* 189:625a20.
15. *T* 189:634c20.
16. *T* 189:642a17.
17. Robert E. Buswell and Donald S. Lopez, eds., *The Princeton Dictionary of Buddhism* (Princeton, NJ: Princeton University Press, 2014), s.v. "Four Noble Truths." See also chap. 5, note 57 for more on the interpretation of "four noble truths."
18. *T* 189:653b12.
19. John S. Strong, *The Buddha: A Short Biography* (Oxford: Oneworld, 2001), 10–14.
20. Donald S. Lopez Jr., *From Stone to Flesh: A Short History of the Buddha* (Chicago: University of Chicago Press, 2013), 227.
21. See the table in Kurobe Michiyoshi, *Nihon Butsuden bungaku no kenkyū* (Osaka: Izumi Shoin, 1989), 33–34.
22. Donohashi Akio, *Butsudenzu*, vol. 267, *Nihon no bijutsu* (Tokyo: Shibundō, 1988), 80.
23. On the relationship between Prince Shōtoku and Śākyamuni, see especially the first chapter of Kevin Gray Carr, *Plotting the Prince: Shōtoku Cults and the Mapping of Medieval Japanese Buddhism* (Honolulu: University of Hawaii Press, 2012). On reappearance of motifs from the biographies of the Buddha in the *Tale of Genji*, see Araki Hiroshi, *Kakushite Genji monogatari ga tanjō suru: Monogatari ga ryūdō suru genba ni dō tachiau ka* (Tokyo: Kasama Shoin, 2014), 252–309.
24. See the table in Komine Kazuaki, "Higashi Ajia no Butsuden bungaku/Budda no monogatari to kaiga o yomu: Nihon no *Shaka no honji* to Chūgoku no *Shakushi genryū* o chūshin ni," *Ronshō kokugo kyōiku gaku* 3 (2012): 123–26.
25. For some exceptions, see Julia Reinhard Lupton, *Afterlives of the Saints: Hagiography, Typology, and Renaissance Literature* (Stanford, CA: Stanford University Press, 1996); Alison Knowles Frazier, *Possible Lives: Authors and Saints in Renaissance Italy* (New York: Columbia University Press, 2004); Matthew Woodcock, "Crossovers and Afterlife," in *A Companion to Middle English Hagiography*, ed. Sarah Salih (Woodbridge: D. S. Brewer, 2006), 141–

57; and Joni Henry, "Humanist Hagiography in England, c. 1480–c. 1520," *Literature Compass* 10, no. 7 (2013): 535–43.

26. See Jonathan Morris Augustine, *Buddhist Hagiography in Early Japan: Images of Compassion in the Gyōki Tradition* (New York: RoutledgeCurzon, 2005); Kenneth Doo Lee, *The Prince and the Monk: Shōtoku Worship in Shinran's Buddhism* (Albany: State University of New York Press, 2007); Michael I. Como, *Shōtoku: Ethnicity, Ritual, and Violence in the Japanese Buddhist Tradition* (Oxford: Oxford University Press, 2008); and Carr, *Plotting the Prince*. Also see Christopher Thane Callahan, "Kakunyo and the Making of Shinran and Shin Buddhism" (PhD diss., Harvard University, 2011).
27. For a representative example of such new developments in the study of hagiography in South Asia, see Christian Lee Novetzke, *Religion and Public Memory: A Cultural History of Saint Namdev in India* (New York: Columbia University Press, 2008). In the case of hagiography in Japan, a few articles do treat the rediscovery, or repositioning, of saintly figures from the distant past in the nineteenth and twentieth centuries. See Richard M. Jaffe, "Seeing Śākyamuni: Travel and the Reconstruction of Japanese Buddhism," *Journal of Japanese Studies* 30, no. 1 (2004): 65–96; James C. Dobbins, "The Many Faces of Shinran: Images from D. T. Suzuki and *The Eastern Buddhist*," *Eastern Buddhist* 42, no. 2 (2011):1–24; and Orion Klautau, "Between Essence and Manifestation: Shōtoku Taishi and Shinran during the Fifteen-Year War (1931–1945)," *Ryūkoku Daigaku Ajia Bukkyō Bunka Kenkyū Sentā Wākingu Pēpā* 12, no. 5 (2013): 27–94. Among these articles, though, only the piece by Dobbins takes a diachronic perspective by modern visions of Shinran against premodern ones, thus foregrounding the difference between the dominant images in the two periods.
28. Fukushima Kazuto, *Kindai Nihon no Shinran: Sono shisō shi* (Kyoto: Hōzōkan, 1973).
29. Michael Radich, *How Ajātaśatru Was Reformed: The Domestication of "Ajase" and Stories in Buddhist History* (Tokyo: International Institute for Buddhist Studies of the International College for Postgraduate Buddhist Studies, 2011).

CHAPTER ONE

1. The periodization of Japanese history remains controversial, and here a fairly standard version is used somewhat arbitrarily, only for the sake of convenience. For the purposes of this book, "ancient Japan" is understood to begin with the Asuka period, around the turn of the seventh century CE, and to end in the late twelfth century; "medieval Japan" is understood to begin around the turn of the twelfth century and to end around 1600, with the battle of Sekigahara. As this chapter shows, the "ancient" and "medieval" treatments of the life of Śākyamuni actually have more in common than not.

2. Kenneth Doo Lee, *The Prince and the Monk: Shōtoku Worship in Shinran's Buddhism* (Albany: State University of New York Press, 2007), 54. The source in question here is translated in full in William E. Deal, "Hagiography and History: The Image of Prince Shōtoku," in *Religions of Japan in Practice*, ed. George Joji Tanabe (Princeton, NJ: Princeton University Press, 1999): 316–33.
3. Jonathan Morris Augustine, *Buddhist Hagiography in Early Japan: Images of Compassion in the Gyōki Tradition* (New York: RoutledgeCurzon, 2005).
4. Takagi Yutaka, "Soden," in *Nihon Bukkyōshi jiten*, ed. Imaizumi Yoshio (Tokyo: Yoshikawa Kōbunkan, 1999).
5. Carl Bielefeldt, "Expedient Devices, the One Vehicle, and the Life Span of the Buddha," in *Readings of the Lotus Sutra*, ed. Stephen F. Teiser and Jacqueline Ilyse Stone (New York: Columbia University Press, 2009), 77.
6. Jacqueline I. Stone, *Original Enlightenment and the Transformation of Medieval Japanese Buddhism* (Honolulu: University of Hawaii Press, 1999): 26.
7. Concerning early Japanese aspirations to travel to India, see Masuda Katsumi, "Budda no kuni Tenjiku e no gongu: Sono keifu," *Kokubungaku kaishaku to kyōzai no kenkyū* 28, no. 4 (1983): 19–26. See also the relevant chapters in Kasugai Shin'ya, *Indo: Kinkei to enkei* (Kyoto: Dōhōsha Shuppan, 1981).
8. Again, following standard conventions, this book employs "modern" here simply as the marker of a period, typically understood to begin with the Meiji Restoration of 1868.
9. In the same period, Japanese traders began to venture abroad and settled in various parts of Southeast Asia. Early seventeenth-century Japanese graffiti surviving at Angkor Wat, the great temple complex in Cambodia, confirms not only that Japanese visited the temple then, but also that they mistakenly believed it to be the Jetavana Monastery (Jpn. Gion Shōja), reputed to be the first such compound inhabited by the Buddha. On this point, see especially the work of Ishizawa Yoshiaki, beginning with his "Rakugaki to rekishi: 17-seiki ni Ankōru Watto ni sankei shita Nihonjin," *Bunkachō geppō* 309 (1994): 20–21.
10. The earliest text, simply called the *Sutra of the Buddha* (*Futu jing*), is now mostly lost, with the exception of some quotations surviving in other works.
11. This summary is largely adapted from Max Deeg, "Chips from a Biographical Workshop: Early Chinese Biographies of the Buddha," in *Lives Lived, Lives Imagined: Biography in the Buddhist Traditions*, ed. Linda Covill, Ulrike Roesler, and Sarah Shaw (Somerville, MA: Wisdom Publications, 2010), 53–54. See also the more compact discussion in Charles Willemen, "Selected Materials for the Study of the Life of Buddha Śākyamuni," *Pacific World*, no. 13 (2011): 67–80. For this research, Deeg's attributions of dates in which translators lived or were active are accepted as estimates for the dates of translation of individual texts. Hubert Durt chose a different

English translation for the title of an early version of the *Lalitavistara*, the *Puyao jing*, rendering it more literally as the *Sutra of Universal Brilliance*. See Hubert Durt, "The Birth of the Buddha in the Chinese Anthologies of the Early Sixth Century," in *The Birth of the Buddha: Proceedings of the Seminar Held in Lumbini, Nepal, October 2004*, ed. Christoph Cüppers, Max Deeg, and Hubert Durt (Lumbini: Lumbini International Research Institute, 2010), 286.

For useful summaries in Japanese of the various scriptural biographies translated into Chinese, see the following: Tachibana Shundō, "Kan'yaku sho Butsuden to kakugo kakkoku shoden no Butsuden," in *Bukkyōgaku no sho mondai*, ed. Buttan Nisen Gohyaku-nen Kinen Gakkai (Tokyo: Iwanami Shoten, 1935), 253–63; and Hirai Yūkei, "Taishi zuiō hongikyō kaidai," in *Taishi zuiō hongikyō, Bussho gyōsan*, vol. Hon'enbu 1, Shin kokuyaku daizōkyō (Tokyo: Daizō Shuppan, 2002), 7–51. For a chart showing which subnarratives are to be found in which scriptural biographies—primarily, but not all, in Chinese—see Hokazono Kōichi, "Butsuden kyōten no keisei katei ni tsuite," *Kagoshima Keidai ronshū* 24, no. 3 (1983): 47–69. For scholarship touching on early extant Chinese-language biographical scriptures, see Kawano Satoshi, *Kan'yaku Butsuden kenkyū* (Ise: Kōgakkan Daigaku Shuppanbu, 2007); Jan Nattier, *A Guide to the Earliest Chinese Buddhist Translations: Texts from the Eastern Han and Three Kingdoms Periods* (Tokyo: International Research Institute for Advanced Buddhology, Soka University, 2008); and Jonathan A. Silk, ed., *Buddhism in China: Collected Papers of Erik Zürcher* (Leiden: Brill, 2013), 419–45.

12. For the scholarship behind this proposal, see Kawano Satoshi, "Shoki Chūgoku Bukkyō no Butsuden o meguru sho mondai: *Shugyō hongikyō* ni kanren shite," *Tōyō Bunka Kenkyūsho kiyō*, no. 113 (1991): 127–76. See also Hirai, "Taishi zuiō hongikyō kaidai," 32. For a discussion in English of Kawano's reasoning, see Nattier, *Earliest Chinese Buddhist Translations*, 104–09.
13. Funayama Tōru, *Butten wa dō kan'yaku sareta no ka: Sūtora ga kyōten ni naru toki* (Tokyo: Iwanami Shoten, 2013), 173.
14. Yūko Matsuda, "Chinese Versions of the Buddha's Biography," *Indogaku Bukkyōgaku kenkyū* 37, no. 1 (1988): 28–29.
15. Concerning the relationship between the Pāli Āgama literature and its translation into Chinese, see Masaharu Anesaki, *The Four Buddhist Āgamas in Chinese: A Concordance of Their Parts and of the Corresponding Counterparts in the Pāli Nikāyas*, Transactions of the Asiatic Society of Japan (Yokohama: Kelly & Walsh, 1908); and Chizen Akanuma, *The Comparative Catalogue of Chinese Āgamas & Pāli Nikāyas*, Bibliotheca Indo-Buddhica (Nagoya: Hajinkaku Shobō, 1929). While Japanese scholars prepared these two groundbreaking studies, they issued them in English for the benefit of scholars in Western Europe.
16. Kajitani Ryōji, "Butsudenzu no tenkai: Bukkyō setsuwa-e no hyōgen

to tekisuto," in *Engi-e to nise-e*, ed. Nakano Masaki (Tokyo: Kōdansha, 1993), 161.

17. Sen Tansen, *Buddhism, Diplomacy, and Trade: The Realignment of Sino-Indian Relations, 600–1400* (Honolulu: University of Hawaii Press, 2003), 132–41.
18. Hubert Durt, "The *Shijiapu* of Sengyou: The First Chinese Attempt to Produce a Critical Biography of the Buddha," *Kokusai Bukkyō Daigakuin Daigaku kenkyū kiyō* 10 (2006): 74–76.
19. Komine Kazuaki, "Higashi Ajia no Butsuden o tadoru: Hikaku setsuwagaku no kiten," *Bungaku* 6, no. 6 (2005): 31–34.
20. Chandra Lokesh and Sushama Lohia, *Life of Lord Buddha: Compiled by Monk Pao-ch'eng from Chinese Sutras and Illustrated in Woodcuts in the Ming Period* (New Delhi: International Academy of Indian Culture and Aditya Prakashan, 2010), 18–19.
21. Find a short English-language discussion of this text, its woodblock illustrations, and its influence on Chinese temple painting in Juila K. Murray, "The Childhood of Gods and Sages," in *Children in Chinese Art*, ed. Ann Barrott Wicks (Honolulu: University of Hawaii Press, 2002), 120–23. A longer discussion of the influence of the work on fifteenth-century Chinese temple paintings may be found in Emmanuelle Lesbre, "Une vie illustrée du Buddha (Shishi yuanliu, 1425), modèle pour les peintures murales d'un monastère du XVe s. (Jueyuan si, Sichuan oriental)," *Arts asiatiques* 57 (2002): 69–101. Concerning the influence of these depictions in Korean Buddhist temples, see Hayashi Masahiko, "Kankoku ni okeru *Shakushi genryū ōka jiseki* no igi: Hyōshi kaisetsu ni kaete," *Etoki kenkyū* 13 (1997): 64–69.
22. Its artistic style was adapted for an illustrated handscroll produced in 1515. See Tsuchiya Maki, "*Shakadō engi emaki* o meguru ichi kōsatsu," *Bijutsushi* 57, no. 1 (2007): 90–107.
23. On Sengyou's apparent antipathy toward the tale of Sumedha and Dīpaṃkara, see Durt, "The *Shijiapu* of Sengyou," 71–72; see also his "Birth of the Buddha," 291–94.
24. Komine, "Higashi Ajia no Butsuden o tadoru," 36.
25. Durt, "The *Shijiapu* of Sengyou," 64.
26. *T* 2040:70c16–7.
27. On Sengyou's inclination toward the Mahāyāna, see Hubert Durt, "Birth of the Buddha," 284–85.
28. Thus, this section cannot be even a comprehensive overview of the presence of Śākyamuni at Dunhuang, much less a detailed discussion. Other literary representations of the life of the Buddha to have survived at the site include the *Day of the Holy Teaching* (*Shengjiao shi'ershi*), the *Eulogy to the Prince* (*Taizi zan*), the *Eulogy to Prince Siddhartha* (*Xida taizi zan*), and so forth. Treatment of these works in English remains a scholarly desideratum. I am grateful to D. Neil Schmid for bringing such works to my attention.

29. Neither set of works survives intact; even the identification of some surviving scenes in each—much less the determination of the precise number of scenes—has proven problematic. The Kizil scenes, now thought to have originally numbered at least sixty, begin with the Buddha's descent into his mother's womb and end with his *parinirvāṇa*. See Lei Yuhua, "Kezier 110 ku Fozhuan bihua de yiyi," *Sichuan Daxue xuebao (Zhexue shehui kexue ban)*, no. 142 (2006): 102. The thirty-six surviving Yungang reliefs, on the other hand, seem to begin with (or before) the birth of the Buddha, but they conclude shortly after the beginning of his preaching career, with his conversion of the three Kāśyapa brothers through the subjugation of the fire dragon that they worshipped. See Mizuno Seiichi and Nagahiro Toshio, *Dai 10-dō*, vol. 7, *Unkō sekkutsu: Seireki go-seiki ni okeru Chūgoku hokubu Bukkyō kutsuin no kōkogakuteki chōsa hōkoku* (Kyoto: Kyōto Daigaku Jinbun Kagaku Kenkyūjo, 1952), 7–9.
30. Find a brief introduction to this cave in Fan Jinshi, *The Caves of Dunhuang*, trans. Susan Whitfield (Hong Kong: Dunhuang Academy, 2010), 80–83.
31. Eugene Yuejin Wang, *Shaping the Lotus Sutra: Buddhist Visual Culture in Medieval China* (Seattle: University of Washington Press, 2005), 74.
32. In the case of Yungang Cave 6, recent scholarship has cautioned against relying upon any particular scripture for a key to the iconographic program. See Andō Fusae, "Unkō dai-6 kutsu no zuzō kōsei ni tsuite: Butsuden zuzō ni shōten o atete," *Tōhō gakuhō*, no. 85 (2010): 724. On the other hand, the murals of Mogao Cave 290 include a long sequence of thirty-two miracles associated with the birth of the Buddha, a combination not extant in any other visual works of premodern East Asia. Having compared the ordering of these miracles and other events in the murals of Cave 290 to the various Chinese scriptural accounts, Fan Jinshi and Ma Shichang concluded that the *Avadāna of the Practice* was the closest match to the arrangement in the cave, while allowing that events from other texts were used to supplement them in the murals. Because of the early date of the translation of this scripture, they contended, an appeal to it would have been useful in stressing the authenticity and antiquity of the account of these events. See Fan Jinshi and Ma Shichang, "Mogao ku di-290 ku de Fozhuan gushihua," *Dunhuang yanjiu* 1, no. 3 (1983): 79–80. For the corresponding section of the translation of this article into Japanese, see Fan and Ma, "Bakkōkutsu dai-290 kutsu no Butsudenzu," trans. Yasuda Naoki, *Tōyō gakujutsu kenkyū* 25, no. 2 (1986): 168–72. By contrast, Patricia Karetzky argued for the *Sutra of Past and Present Cause and Effect* as a source for the mural program in Cave 290. See Patricia Eichenbaum Karetzky, "A Chinese Illustration of the *Guoqu xianzai yinguo jing* at Dunhuang," *Journal of Chinese Religions*, no. 16 (1988): 55–72, and *Early Buddhist Narrative Art: Illustrations of the Life of the Buddha from Central Asia to China, Korea, and Japan* (Lanham, MD: University Press of America, 2000), 81–97.

33. Fan and Ma, "Mogao ku di-290 ku de Fozhuan gushihua," 58. For the corresponding section of the Japanese translation of this article, see "Bakkōkutsu dai-290 kutsu no Butsudenzu," 138.
34. Li Ru, "Dunhuang Mogaoku di-290 ku Fozhuan gushihua de tushi yishu ji qi yuanliu shishi," *Dunhuangxue jikan*, no. 3 (2009): 80.
35. Arami Hiroshi, *Dunhuang jiangchang wenxue xieben yanjiu* (Beijing: Zhonghua Shuju, 2010), 16–17.
36. Jin Taikuan, "Dunhuang bianwen *Taizi chengdao jing, Baxiang bian, Po mo bianwen, Xiang mo bianwen* yu Fojing bijiao yanjiu" (master's thesis, Guoli Zhengzhi Daxue, 1984), 57–58.
37. Although *Sutra on the Achievement of the Way* does not fulfill strict criteria for the genre, it does resemble normative "transformation texts" in multiple senses: it includes an introductory formula, alternates between verse and vernacular prose (a rarity in Chinese letters of the day), and is strongly linked to wall paintings from the Dunhuang site. Variant titles are listed and discussed in Arami, *Dunhuang jiangchang wenxue xieben yanjiu*, 11–15. On the genre of "transformation text," see Victor H. Mair, *T'ang Transformation Texts: A Study of the Buddhist Contribution to the Rise of Vernacular Fiction and Drama in China* (Cambridge, MA: Harvard University Press, 1989), 9–72. Relatively complete editions of the text survive in the Pelliot collection at the Bibliothèque nationale de France (P. 2299) in Paris, and at Ryukoku University in Kyoto, Japan, among other sites. See the discussion of this text in Seiiki Bunka Kenkyūkai, ed., *Tonkō Bukkyō shiryō*, vol. 1, Seiiki bunka kenkyū (Kyōto: Hōzōkan, 1958), 212–13 in the Japanese text and 44–47 in the English. The Ryukoku University edition, briefly discussed in this piece, has a variant title, translated in the English section of the publication as *Story of Prince Siddhartha's Practice of the Way.* The Chinese term here rendered as "story," *yinyuan*, translates the Sanskrit *hetu-pratyaya* ("cause and condition"). In the East Asian context, it bears a distinctly Buddhist sense of "origin tale," used in descriptions of the life of the Buddha or other sacred figures. Concerning the different genre categories evident in these texts, see D. Neil Schmid, "Yuanqi: Medieval Buddhist Narratives from Dunhuang" (PhD diss., University of Pennsylvania, 2002).
38. Precisely *which* source has been disputed: Jin Taikuan concluded that this text constitutes a condensation, with minor alterations, of the *Sutra of the Collection of Authentic Deeds of the Buddha.* See Jin, "Dunhuang bianwen," 147–50. Liang Weiying made a similar determination. Liang Weiying, "Dunhuang Fozhuan gaiguan ji qi Zhongguohua zhi tedian," in *1990 Dunhuangxue guoji yantaohui wenji: Shiku kaogu bian*, ed. Duan Wenjie, Lin Yingshan, and Liang Weiying (Shenyang: Liaoning Renmin Chubanshe, 1995), 333. On the other hand, Iwamoto Yutaka declared the text to be relatively dissimilar to the *Sutra of the Collection of Authentic Deeds*, instead tracing some of its accounts to predecessors in the *Sutra of the Wise and*

the Foolish and the *Sutra of Past and Present Cause and Effect*. See Iwamoto Yutaka, "Tonkō ni okeru Butsuden, honshōtan," in Kōza Tonkō, ed. Kanaoka Shōkō, vol. 9 (Tokyo: Daitō Shuppansha, 1990), 436–42. More recent work by Arami Hiroshi argued that no single scriptural text constitutes a major source for this vernacular adapation. See Arami, *Dunhuang jiangchang wenxue xieben yanjiu*, 16–24.

39. For a discussion of this parallelism as evidenced in an extant Sanskrit version of the Mūlasarvāstivāda Vinaya, see John S. Strong, "A Family Quest: The Buddha, Yaśodharā, and Rāhula in the Mūlasarvāstivāda Vinaya," in *Sacred Biography in the Buddhist Traditions of South and Southeast Asia*, ed. Juliane Schober (Honolulu: University of Hawaii Press, 1997). For English translations of these episodes from Chinese sources, see the appendix to Deeg, "Chips from a Biographical Workshop," 68–83.
40. Adapted from the translation in Arthur Waley, *Ballads and Stories from Tun-huang: An Anthology* (New York: Macmillan, 1960), 207. For a modern edition of the original text in this passage, see Huang Zheng and Zhang Yongquan, *Dunhuang bianwen jiaozhu* (Beijing: Zhonghua Shuju, 1997), 440. For a modern Japanese translation, see Iriya Yoshitaka, ed., *Bukkyō bungaku shū*, vol. 60, Chūgoku koten bungaku taikei (Tokyo: Heibonsha, 1975), 13–14. See also the summary in Thomas Edward Graham, "The Reconstruction of Popular Buddhism in Medieval China Using Selected *Pien-Wen* from Tun-Huang" (PhD diss., University of Iowa, 1975), 260–61.
41. Iwamoto, "Tonkō ni okeru Butsuden, honshōtan," 442. A late-Chosŏn-dynasty adaptation of this story, recorded in Korean vernacular script in the mid-nineteenth century, retells this episode. It culminates in the escape of mother and son to the mountains where the Buddha is practicing, although it apparently does not indicate that Yaśodharā becomes a man. See the discussion in Cho Une, "Kan-Nichi ni okeru 'Butsuden bungaku' no tenkai: Shaka to Yashudara no monogatari o chūshin ni," *Ilbon munhwa yŏn'gu*, no. 50 (2014): 342–43.
42. For a modern edition of the original text in this passage, see Huang and Zhang, *Dunhuang bianwen jiaozhu*, 437. For a translation of this passage into modern Japanese, see Iriya, *Bukkyō bungaku shū*, 9. See also the summary of the five encounters in Graham, "Reconstruction of Popular Buddhism," 237–38.
43. In the painted versions of the life of the Buddha now held by the Jikōji, the Butsūji, and the Metropolitan Museum, the overall number of encounters remains four. Each of these versions elides the final encounter with the ascetic, and shows instead the prince encountering a woman in childbirth at the beginning of his ventures outside the gates. See Watanabe Satoshi, *Butsudenzu ronkō* (Tokyo: Chūō Kōron Bijutsu Shuppan, 2012), 240. For a discussion of the relation between this alteration in the Dunhuang text and later Japanese writing, see Kurobe Michiyoshi, *Nihon Butsuden bungaku no kenkyū* (Osaka: Izumi Shoin, 1989), 133–48.

44. For a modern edition of the original text in this passage, see Huang and Zhang, *Dunhuang bianwen jiaozhu*, 439. For a modern Japanese translation of this passage, see Iriya, *Bukkyō bungaku shū*, 12.
45. For a modern edition of the original text in this passage, see Huang and Zhang, *Dunhuang bianwen jiaozhu*, 439. For a modern Japanese translation of this passage, see Iriya, *Bukkyō bungaku shū*, 13.
46. See the inscriptions reproduced in Liang, "Dunhuang Fozhuan gaiguan ji qi Zhongguohua zhi tedian," 340–41.
47. Although they never exerted influence in Japan to the same degree as their Chinese counterparts, Korean intellectuals also used classical Chinese to compose their own biographies of the Buddha, even before the celebrated vernacular texts of the early Chosŏn period. These include a prose work issued in 1328, during the Mongol suzerainty over Korea (1270–1356), late in the Koryŏ dynasty (935–1392). This prose work is the anonymous ten-fascicle *Record of the Ten-Stage Practice of the Tathāgata Śākyamuni* (*Sŏkka yŏrae sipchi suhaenggi*). Each of the first nine fascicles records the bodhisattva's perfection of one of the key virtues in a discrete former life; the last fascicle records his final existence, as Śākyamuni. To date, only one study in English considers this work: A. M. Olof, "Sŏkka Yŏrae Sipchi Haengnok: An Attempt to Find Its Place in Buddhist Literature," in *Twenty Papers on Korean Studies Offered to Professor W. E. Skillend*, ed. Daniel Bouchez, Robert C. Provine, and Roderick Whitfield (Paris: Collège de France, Centre d'études coréennes, 1989). The major Korean-language study of this text, which includes a facsimile edition of its Chinese original, is Pak Pyŏngdong, *Pulgyŏng chŏllae sŏrhwa ŭi sosŏljŏk pyŏnmo yangsang: Pyŏnmunjip Sŏkka yŏrae sipchi suhaenggi yŏn'gu* (Seoul: Yŏngnak, 2003). There is also a translation into modern Korean in Chŏng Sŏun, *Pult'a ŭi sipchi haengjŏk* (Seoul: Sanmi, 1970).

   Also in 1328, the Korean Ch'ŏnt'ae (Ch. Tiantai) master Puam Mugi (a.k.a. Unmuk, n.d.) composed his *Ode to the Acts of the Tathāgata Śākyamuni (Sŏkka yŏrae haengjŏk song),* a long verse biography of the Buddha in classical Chinese. By means of this text, he sought to chastise the monastic community of his day for its lax observance of the precepts. Like the *Record of the Ten-Stage Practice of the Tathāgata Śākyamuni*, this text also seems not to have been known in Japan before the modern era, as all the extant premodern editions survive in Korea. See Cho Une, "Kankoku ni okeru Butsuden bungaku: Chōsa to kenkyū no genjō," *Ajia yūgaku*, no. 79 (2005): 34–39. For a modern text of the *Ode*, see Tongguk Taehakkyo Han'guk Pulgyo Chŏnsŏ P'yŏnch'an Wiwŏn, ed., *Koryŏ sidae pyŏn 3,* vol. 6, Han'guk Pulgyo chŏnsŏ (Seoul: Tongguk Taehakkyo Ch'ulp'anbu, 1994), 485–540. For a study of this text in English, see Sem Vermeersch, "An Early Korean Version of the Buddha's Biography," *Journal of the Oxford Centre for Buddhist Studies* 1 (2011): 197–211. In Korean-language scholarship, see Yi Yŏngja, "Mugi ŭi Ch'ŏnt'ae sasang: Sŏkka yŏrae haengjŏk song ŭl chungsim ŭro," *Han'guk Pulgyohak* 3 (1977): 77–103; Chŏng Sŏngu, "*Sŏkka yŏrae haengjŏk song* yŏn'gu: *Puljo t'onggi* wa pigyo hayŏ" (master's thesis, Tongguk Taehakkyo, 2007); and Pak Soyŏng, "Koryŏ hugi Unmuk ŭi *Sŏkka yŏrae haengjŏk song* yŏn'gu" (PhD diss., Tongguk Taehakkyo, 2011). Some of Pak Soyŏng's research concerning this text is also available as individual articles in Japanese publications, including the following: "Unmoku sen *Shaka nyorai gyōseki ju* no 'Kegon Agon ichiji' setsu ni tsuite," *Tendai gakuhō*, no. 50 (2007):118–28; "*Shaka nyorai gyōseki ju* ni mirareru Shaka nyorai ichidaiki: Tendai kyōgaku no shiten kara no kōsatsu," *Eizan Gakuin kenkyū kiyō*, no. 30 (2008): 140–18 [reverse pagination]; and "Unmoku sen *Shaka nyorai gyōseki ju* ni mirareru Tendai kyōhan ni tsuite no ichi kōsatsu," *Indogaku Bukkyōgaku kenkyū* 58, no. 1 (2009): 164–68.

48. Kurobe, *Nihon Butsuden bungaku no kenkyū*, 3.
49. Takemura Shinji, "Shakuson den," *Kokubungaku kaishaku to kanshō* 51, no. 9 (1986): 70–75.
50. These dates derive from the appendices in Miyazaki Kenji, *Nihon kodai no shakyō to shakai* (Tokyo: Hanawa Shobō, 2006), 33–218 in the left-to-right pagination.
51. Kajitani, "Butsuden zu no tenkai," 158.
52. Tomimura Takafumi, "Gedatsu Shōnin Jōkei no Shaka shinkō ni tsuite," *Ryūkyū Daigaku Hōbungakubu kiyō: Shigaku, chirigaku hen* 32 (1989): 143–46.
53. Concerning Myōe's devotion to Śākyamuni, see, for instance, Robert E. Morrell, *Early Kamakura Buddhism: A Minority Report* (Berkeley, CA: Asian Humanities Press, 1987), 61: "I never thought of allying myself with some fine scholar, but sought rather to hold firmly to the Buddha Śākyamuni, if only to his representation on a scrap of paper. Had I been alive in the days of the Blessed Śākyamuni, I would have been among the least worthy of his disciples." For the original text of this passage, see Kubota Jun and Yamaguchi Akiho, eds., *Myōe Shōnin shū* (Tokyo: Iwanami Shoten, 1981), 211–12.
54. Nishimura Ryō, "The Intellectual Development of the Cult of Śākyamuni: What Is 'Modern' about the Proposition That the Buddha Did Not Preach the Mahāyāna?," trans. Micah Auerback, *Eastern Buddhist* 42, no. 1 (2011): 6–11.
55. This ritual, traditionally performed on the eighth day of the fourth month, is now typically called the "Flower Festival," *Hanamatsuri*. However, historically it has been known by such terms as *Busshō-e* ("Assembly of the Birth of the Buddha"), *Kanbutsu-e* ("Lustration Assembly"), *Gōtan-e* ("Birth Assembly"), and so on. Concerning its history, see Marinus Willem de Visser, *Ancient Buddhism in Japan: Sutras and Ceremonies in Use in the Seventh and Eighth Centuries A.D. and Their History in Later Times* (Leiden: E. J. Brill, 1935), 45–57; Yamanaka Yutaka, *Heianchō no nenjū gyōji* (Tokyo: Hanawa Shobō, 1972), 190–96; and Itō Yuishin, "Kanbutsu-e to kuge," in *Bukkyō nenjū gyōji*, ed. Itō Yuishin, vol. 6, Bukkyō minzokugaku

taikei (Tokyo: Meicho Shuppan, 1986), 79–96. *Amacha* here does not mean any kind of "sweetened tea," but refers specifically to a tea brewed from the leaves of a particular kind of hortensia plant, which is naturally sweet.

56. Tanaka Yoshiyasu, *Tanjōbutsu*, vol. 159, Nihon no bijutsu (Shibundō, 1979), 19–20. For a less comprehensive discussion of early images of the newborn Buddha for use in rituals commemorating his birth, see Noma Seiroku, "Busshō-e to tanjō-Butsu," *Myūjiamu*, no. 61 (1956): 2–6. In English, see the early images published in Hiromitsu Washizuka et al., eds., *Transmitting the Forms of Divinity: Early Buddhist Art from Korea and Japan* (New York: Japan Society, 2003), 240–41, 260–61, 292–93. In 1940, an ancient bronze image of a newborn Buddha was discovered at the convent Chūgūji, in Nara Prefecture. After the theft of this image in 1950, it was recast in 1958. See the account in Nara Kokuritsu Hakubutsukan and Bukkyō Bijutsu Kyōkai, eds., *Oshakasama tanjō* (Nara: Bukkyō Bijutsu Kyōkai, 2000), 24–25.
57. Nishikawa Kyōtarō, ed., *Chōkoku*, vol. 2, *Kokuhō daijiten* (Tokyo: Kōdansha, 1985), 69. The technique is traditionally attributed to the Tang-dynasty sculptor Yang Huizhi (n.d.), active in the first half of the eighth century.
58. Concerning the dating of the pagoda and the inset tableaux, see Machida Kōichi, "Kaisetsu: Gojū no tō tōhon sozō," in *Hōryūji*, ed. Nara Rokudaiji Taikan Kankōkai, vol. 3, *Nara Rokudaiji Taikan* (Tokyo: Iwanami Shoten, 2000), 44–45.
59. See Yamagishi Kōki, "Hōryūji saiken o meguru seiji jōkyō to gojū no tō tōhon shimengu," *Mikkyō zuzōgaku* 26 (2007): 1–16. Yamagishi's case relies in part on circumstantial evidence: a sudden spike in state support designated for the pagoda, which by the mid-eighth century dwarfed even the allotment for the temple's main or golden hall (Jpn. *kondō*).
60. Eighth-century editions of this illustrated scroll, all fragmentary, are scattered across a number of institutions and owners, including the collections of the Kyoto temples Jōbonrendaiji and the Daigoji; the Nara National Museum; the Idemitsu Museum; and the University Art Museum, Tokyo University of the Arts. For a partial list, see Tsugio Miya et al., eds., *Kadokawa emakimono sōran* (Tokyo: Kadokawa Shoten, 1995), 28. For a diagram detailing which scenes from the text appear in which of the surviving editions, see Umezu Jirō, "Emakimono zanketsu aiseki no fu 11: Eingakyō," *Nihon bijutsu kōgei*, January 1966, 108–09.
61. Naitō Tōichirō, *Nihon Bukkyō kaiga shi: Nara chō honki hen* (Kyoto: Seikei Shoin, 1934), 43.
62. Ibid., 52–53.
63. Watanabe Satoshi, "Eingakyō Butsudenzu no zuzōteki kenkyū shiron: Kyōto Jōbonrendaiji bon o chūshin ni," in *Bijutsushika, ōi ni warau: Kōno Motoaki sensei no tame no Nihon bijutsushi ronshū*, ed. Kōno Motoaki Sensei Taikan Kinen Ronbunshu Henshu Iinkai (Kunitachi: Buryukke, 2006), 212.

64. *T* 189:620c25.
65. Umezu, "Emakimono zanketsu," 106–07.
66. Tanaka Ichimatsu, "Chūsei ni okeru Eingakyō no sho sakuhin," in *Eingakyō*, ed. Kadokawa Shoten Henshūbu, vol. 16, Nihon emakimono zenshū (Tokyo: Kadokawa Shoten, 1969), 64–65.
67. The full scroll is reproduced in black and white in Nara Kokuritsu Hakubutsukan, ed., *Shaji engi e* (Tokyo: Kadokawa Shoten, 1975), 274–308. The scroll text, which alternates with the paintings, is reproduced in Bussho Kankōkai, ed., *Jishi sōsho dai-1*, vol. 117, *Dai-Nihon Bukkyō zensho* (Tokyo: Bussho Kankōkai, 1913), 465–88. This transcription, however, is not always reliable. A preferred transcription appears in Tōhō Shoin, ed., *Nihon emaki zenshū*, vol. 1 (Tokyo: Tōhō Shoin, 1928), 1–18. In English, the scroll is briefly discussed and partially reproduced in Miyeko Murase, *Emaki: Narrative Scrolls from Japan* (New York: Asia Society, 1983), 169–73. Also in English, see the brief discussion in Eugene Phillips Quitman, "Kano Motonobu and Early Kano Narrative Painting" (PhD diss., University of California at Berkeley, 1992), 107–16.
68. Namiki Seishi, "Shakadō engi: Shaka shinkō no zōfuku," *Bijutsu fōramu 21*, no. 15 (2007): 126.
69. For a detailed survey of copies of the Seiryōji image of Śākyamuni scattered across multiple regions of Japan, see the following set of articles by Ikawa Kazuko: "Kantō no Seiryōji-shiki Shaka zō," *Bijutsu kenkyū*, no. 237 (1964): 145–57; "Saikoku no Seiryōji-shiki Shaka Nyorai zō jō," *Bijutsu kenkyū*, no. 324 (1984): 39–46; "Saikoku no Seiryōji-shiki Shaka Nyorai zō ge," *Bijutsu kenkyū*, no. 327 (1984):17–84; and "Ehime no Seiryōji-shiki Shaka Nyorai zō," *Bijutsu kenkyū*, no. 330 (1984): 37–42. For studies in English concerning the duplication of the image, see Donald F. McCallum, "The Replication of Miraculous Icons: The Zenkoji Amida and the Seiryoji Shaka," in *Images, Miracles, and Authority in Asian Religious Traditions*, ed. Richard H. Davis (Boulder, CO: Westview Press, 1988), 207–26; McCallum, "The Saidaiji Lineage of the Seiryōji Shaka Tradition," *Archives of Asian Art* 49 (1996): 51–67, and Paul Groner, "Icons and Relics in Eison's Religious Activities," in *Living Images: Japanese Buddhist Icons in Context*, ed. Robert H. Sharf and Elizabeth Horton Sharf (Stanford, CA: Stanford University Press, 2001), 121–26.
70. Needless to say, however, other images elsewhere in the Buddhist world are also claimed as the Udāyana image. See Robert E. Buswell and Donald S. Lopez, eds., *The Princeton Dictionary of Buddhism* (Princeton, NJ: Princeton University Press, 2014), s.v. "Udāyana Buddha."
71. In English alone, see the following discussions of the Seiryōji image: Gregory Henderson and Leon Hurvitz, "The Buddha of Seiryōji: New Finds and New Theory," *Artibus Asiae* 19, no. 1 (1956): 4–55; McCallum, "The Replication of Miraculous Icons"; and chap. 2 of Sarah J. Horton, *Living Buddhist Statues in Early Medieval and Modern Japan* (New York: Palgrave

Macmillan, 2007). Among the publications of the Seiryōji image in Japanese, the following exhibition catalogue is particularly noteworthy: Kyōto Kokuritsu Hakubutsukan, *Shaka shinkō to Seiryōji: Tokubetsu tenrankai* (Kyoto: Kyoto Shinbunsha, 1982).

72. Tōhō, *Nihon emaki zenshū*, 6. The Japanese term *zuizō* typically refers to the Seiryōji's "auspicious image."
73. Find a detailed description of the contents in Henderson and Hurvitz, "The Buddha of Seiryōji."
74. Tsuchiya, "*Shakadō engi emaki* o meguru ichi kōsatsu."
75. Find a categorization of the modes by which the *Origin Tale* images draw upon the *Origins and Transmission* in ibid., 92–98.
76. This is the ink painting, probably missing its companion image, held at the Mibudera in Kyoto (a.k.a. Hōdōzanmaiin, etc.). Ibid., 98. The painting is reproduced in Ueyama Shigeru and Ōtsuka Katsumi, eds., *Mibudera ten: Dainenbutsu kyōshin to Jizō shinkō no tera, sōken 1000-nen kinen* (Kyoto: Kyōto Bunka Hakubutsukan, 1992). See also the discussion in Watanabe Satoshi, *Butsudenzu ronkō*, 232–34.
77. Komine Kazuaki, "Nihon to Higashi Ajia no 'Bukkyō bungaku': *Shakushi genryū* o chūshin ni," *Bukkyō bungaku*, no. 39 (2014): 27. The 1684 edition that Komine mentions here is the only Japanese reprinting (*Wakokubon*) listed in the Union Catalogue of Early Japanese Books (*Nihon kotenseki sōgō mokuroku dētabēsu*).
78. Concerning the Korean and Vietnamese reprintings of the illustrated text, see ibid., 23–29. See also the discussion in Komine, "Higashi Ajia no Butsuden o tadoru."
79. Ming-dynasty Chinese temples whose mural programs were influenced by the *Origins and Transmission* include the Jueyuansi, in Sichuan Province; halls in the Nanshansi complex, on Mount Wutai in Shanxi Province; and the Chongshansi, in Shanxi Province. (Now lost, the Chongshansi murals are known today only through reproductions in an album of drawings.) For a comprehensive study of such influence, see Xing Lili, *Mingdai Fozhuan gushihua yanjiu* (Beijing: Xianzhuang Shuju, 2010). In French, see also Lesbre, "Une vie illustrée du Buddha." For a brief discussion in English, see Murray, "The Childhood of Gods and Sages," 120–23. Scholarship in the Anglophone world has yet to give adequate consideration to late imperial Chinese Buddhist temple murals of the life of the Buddha. Nor has it noted the existence of a late Ming-dynasty version in *bisu*—wall-mounted diorama images—still extant in the Shijiadian (Hall of Śākyamuni) at the temple Shuanglinsi, also in Shanxi Province. Photographic reproductions of some of the wall-mounted clay images depicting the life of the Buddha, installed at the Shuanglinsi, may be found in Jin Weinuo, *Shuanglinsi caisu*, 2nd ed. (Tianjin: Tianjin Renmin Chubanshe, 2007), 27–61. These presumably descend from the Chinese clay-sculpting technique represented by the

dioramas in the five-story pagoda at the Hōryūji, and the fragments from the site of the Western Pagoda at the Yakushiji.

Paintings of the life of the Buddha in Korean temples of the late Chosŏn-dynasty period (from the eighteenth century through the early twentieth) were also influenced, albeit to varying degrees, by the iconography of the woodblock illustrations in the *Origins and Transmission*. Such temples include the Songgwangsa, in South Chŏlla Province, and the Ssanggyesa, in South Kyŏngsang Province. Like the Japanese *Origin Hall* handscroll paintings, these Korean programs of painting make selective use of the iconography of the *Origins and Transmission*, combining it with previously established iconographic patterns. In the case of late Chosŏn-dynasty Korea, such existing patterns developed from the woodblock print illustrations of the early Chosŏn published texts, *The Detailed Record of the Life of Śākyamuni* (*Sŏkpo sangjŏl*, originally composed in 1447) and its reworking in *The Moon's Reflection and the Life of Śākyamuni* (*Wŏrin Sŏkpo*, originally composed in 1459). In the history of Korean temple paintings, the most fully researched instance of borrowing from the *Origins and Transmission* is to be found in the case of forty-eight of the fifty-two wall murals in the eighteenth-century Hall of Vulture Peak (Kor. Yŏngsanjŏn) at the T'ongdosa, also in South Kyŏngsang Province, as well the same temple's eight hanging paintings of the Buddha's life. Concerning these works, see Yi Yŏngjong, "Chosŏn sidae p'alsangdo tosang ŭi yŏnwŏn gwa chŏngae," *Misul sahak yon'gu*, no. 215 (1997): 27–56; Ch'oe Yŏnsik, "Chosŏn hugi *Sŏkssi wŏllyu* ŭi suyong gwa Pulgyogye e mich'in yŏnghyang," *Pojo sasang*, no. 11 (1998): 324–29; Yang Ungi, "T'ongdosa p'alsangdo wa *Sŏkssi wŏllyu* ŭi kwangye pigyo," *Pulgyo misul sahak*, no. 3 (2005): 214–36; and Yi Yŏngjong, "T'ongdosa Yongsanjŏn ŭi *Sŏkssi wŏllyu ŭnghwa sajŏk* pyŏk'hwa yŏn'gu," *Misul sahak yon'gu*, no. 250–251 (2006):253–86. Color photographic reproductions of the T'ongdosa's set of eight paintings of the Buddha are available in T'ongdosa Sŏngbo Pangmulgwan, *T'ongdosa Sŏngbo Pangmulgwan myŏngp'um torok: T'ongdosa Sŏngbo Pangmulgwan kaegwan kinyŏm* (Yangsan: T'ongdosa Sŏngbo Pangmulgwan, 1999), 54–61.

80. Suey-Ling Tsai, *The Life of the Buddha: Woodblock Illustrated Books in China and Korea* (Wiesbaden: Harrassowitz, 2012), 13.
81. Komine, "Imēji no kairō (6)," 55. In the discussion here, Komine distinguishes between Japan and "East Asia," which presumably does not include Japan, where the *Origins and Transmission* represented the dominant version. The *Original Ground of Śākyamuni* will be discussed in chap. 2.
82. Kurobe, *Nihon Butsuden bungaku no kenkyū*, 327.
83. Tōhō, *Nihon emaki zenshū*, 1–2.
84. Notably, the Japanese reprint edition of the *Origins and Transmission* excludes this second half. See Komine, "Higashi Ajia no Butsuden o tadoru," 35.

85. The book to offer the largest and most comprehensive collection of photographic reproductions of paintings of the life of the Buddha still extant in Japan—including paintings originating on the Asian continent—is Shinbo Tōru, *Butsudenzu* (Tokyo: Mainichi Shinbunsha, 1978). Photographic reprints of multiple Japanese biographical paintings are also available in more recent works, including Nara Kokuritsu Hakubutsukan, ed., *Budda Shakuson: Sono shōgai to zōkei* (Nara: Nara Kokuritsu Hakubutsukan, 1984); Donohashi Akio, *Butsudenzu*, vol. 267, *Nihon no bijutsu* (Tokyo: Shibundō, 1988); and Tōbu Bijutsukan et al., eds., *Budda ten: Ōinaru tabiji* (Tokyo: NHK Promōshon, 1998).
86. See the summary table in Watanabe Satoshi, *Butsudenzu ronkō*, 235–37. The paintings on the interior of the doors of the Kōdaiji shrine are photographically reproduced in Santorī Bijutsukan et al., eds., *Kōdaiji no meihō: Hideyoshi to Nene no tera* (Kyoto: Jubusen Kōdaiji and Asahi Shinbunsha, 1995), 46, 49.
87. The most detailed discussion of this set is to be found in this series of articles by Sekiguchi Masayuki: "Onomichi-shi Jikōji shozō Shaka hassō zu ni tsuite (1)," *Bijutsu kenkyū*, no. 317 (1981): 21–32; "Onomichi-shi Jikōji shozō Shaka hassō zu ni tsuite (2)," *Bijutsu kenkyū*, no. 319 (1982):23–31; "Onomichi-shi Jikōji shozō Shaka hassō zu ni tsuite (3)," *Bijutsu kenkyū*, no. 321 (1984): 15–24; "Onomichi-shi Jikōji shozō Shaka hassō zu ni tsuite (4)," *Bijutsu kenkyū*, no. 333 (1985): 11–19; and "Onomichi-shi Jikōji shozō Shaka hassō zu ni tsuite (5)," *Bijutsu kenkyū*, no. 344 (1989): 13–18.
88. Concerning the set held by the Metropolitan Museum, see Masako Watanabe, "A Preliminary Study of 'Life of the Buddha' in Mediaeval Japan: The Metropolitan Museum Paintings," *Orientations* 27, no. 8 (1996): 46–56. To date, this is the only extensive publication in English to address any medieval Japanese depiction of the life of the Buddha. For an argument that this study might have misidentified one of the scenes depicted in the Metropolitan Museum set of paintings, see Watanabe Satoshi, *Butsudenzu ronkō*, 230–32.
89. Concerning the dating of this hanging scroll, see Watanabe Satoshi, *Butsudenzu ronkō*, 118.
90. Concerning the dating of this hanging scroll, see Izumi Takeo, "Kojin zō Shaka hassō zu," *Kokka*, no. 1263 (2001): 50.
91. Nor is the mural the only format in which images from the Buddha's life were crafted for only a short period, early in the assimilation of Buddhism in Japan. Other formats that were largely abandoned include repoussé and clay tiles. For a discussion of a rare Nara-period bronze repoussé relief depicting the birth of the Buddha from his mother's side, see Umehara Sueji, "Oshidashi Shaka tanjō Maya bunin oyobi suinyo zō," *Shiseki to bijutsu*, no. 389 (1968): 322–26. Like their continental counterparts and models, early Buddhist temples in Japan employed mold-produced images on unglazed clay tiles (*senbutsu*) as a form of "adornment" (*shōgon*) for use

on interior walls. For the argument that some of these tiles might depict the Buddha's moment of awakening, see Ryu Sŭngjin, "Hōkei sanzon senbutsu to Einga kyō: Kodai Nihon ni okeru sokujiin zazō no fuzai o kangaeru tegakari to shite," *Kyōto bigaku bijutsu shigaku* 9 (2010): 35–69. Neither of these media continued to be used widely in Japanese temples beyond the ninth century.

92. This is a slight adaptation of the translation in William H. McCullough and Helen Craig McCullough, trans., *A Tale of Flowering Fortunes: Annals of Japanese Aristocratic Life in the Heian Period*, vol. 2 (Stanford: Stanford University Press, 1980), 554. For the original text of this passage, see Yamanaka Yutaka, ed., *Eiga monogatari*, vol. 32, Shinpen Nihon koten bungaku zenshū (Tokyo: Shōgakkan, 1995), 176–77.
93. Japanese thinkers made reference to the same historical records used by their Chinese predecessors—generally in relatively uncritical ways, at least until the early eighteenth century.
94. For comments on the iconography of the main hall at the Hōjōji, see Donohashi, *Butsudenzu*, 95.
95. However, the scrolls in this set are numbered. See Sekiguchi, "Onomichi-shi Jikōji shozō Shaka hassō zu ni tsuite (1)," 23.
96. See Komine Kazuaki, "Butsuden to etoki II: Chūsei Butsuden no yōsō," *Etoki kenkyū*, no. 9 (1991): 25; Watanabe Masako, "Nihon chūsei Butsudenzu no hen'yō: Shimon shutsuyū o chūshin ni shite," in *Bukkyō bijutsu to rekishi bunka*, ed. Manabe Shunshō (Kyoto: Hōzōkan, 2005), 504; and Watanabe Satoshi, *Butsudenzu ronkō*, 11–12. For a more general discussion of *etoki* in English, see Ikumi Kaminishi, *Explaining Pictures: Buddhist Propaganda and Etoki Storytelling in Japan* (Honolulu: University of Hawaii Press, 2006).
97. The original text for this passage is reproduced in Kodaigaku Kyōkai, ed., *Rihō Ō ki*, vol. 3, Shiryō shūi (Kyoto: Rinsen Shoten, 1969), 47. For a discussion and translation of this diary entry, see Kaminishi, *Explaining Pictures*, 20. Recent scholarship has raised the possibility that objects used in "preaching with, or by means of" pictures (*etoki*) might have functioned less as visual narratives than as a kind of "adornment" for a ritual space in their own right. See Kevin Gray Carr, "The Material Facts of Ritual: Revisioning Medieval Viewing through Material Analysis, Ethnographic Analogy, and Architectural History," in *A Companion to Asian Art and Architecture*, ed. Rebecca M. Brown and Deborah S. Hutton (Chichester, UK: Wiley-Blackwell, 2011), 23–47.
98. Archaeological excavations were conducted at the site of the Western Pagoda in 1934, 1969, and 1976. (The pagoda was rebuilt in 1981 using original techniques, but without reproductions of the original dioramas.) For photographic reproductions and a discussion of the recovered fragments of the sculptures, see Nara Kokuritsu Hakubutsukan, ed., *Yakushiji saitō ato shutsudo sozōgun* (Nara: Nara Kokuritsu Hakubutsukan, 1981). For a brief illustrated account of these fragments, written for general readers,

see Yamakawa Midori, "Kireppashi ni shinobu ōji no eikō," *Geijutsu shinchō*, November 1, 1997, 53–55.

99. The original text for this passage is reproduced in Nara Kokuritsu Bunkazai Kenkyūjo, ed., *Shichidaiji junrei shiki: Nara Kokuritsu Bunkazai Kenkyūjo sōritsu sanjisshūnen kinen* (Nara: Nara Kokuritsu Bunkazai Kenkyūjo, 1982), 214.
100. Watanabe Satoshi, *Butsudenzu ronkō*, 181. Although "birth, old age, sickness, and death" form a list common in Buddhist scriptures, no scriptural account of the life of the Buddha counts a scene of birth among his Four Encounters. See the discussion in Sekiguchi, "Onomichi-shi Jikōji shozō Shaka hassō zu ni tsuite (4)," 15–18.
101. Watanabe Satoshi, *Butsudenzu ronkō*, 238.
102. This is an adaptation of the translation in Leon Hurvitz, *Scripture of the Lotus Blossom of the Fine Dharma* (New York: Columbia University Press, 1976), 195. For the original text, see *T* 262:34b24–c8.
103. Watanabe Satoshi, *Butsudenzu ronkō*, 202.
104. Kevin Gray Carr, *Plotting the Prince: Shōtoku Cults and the Mapping of Medieval Japanese Buddhism* (Honolulu: University of Hawaii Press, 2012), 87.
105. Detailed entries for each of these are available in Miya et al., *Kadokawa emakimono sōran*, 202–31.
106. For a quick summary of the composition of these sets, see the chart in Kobayashi Tatsurō, *Shinran Shōnin eden*, vol. 415, Nihon no bijutsu (Tokyo: Shibundō, 2000), 98.
107. Watanabe Shōgo, "Shūso kakefuku eden etokishi no shoron," *Ōtsuma kokubun*, no. 30 (1999): 136.
108. Watanabe Satoshi, "Nihon no butsuden bijutsu (Muromachi jidai made)," in *Butsuden bijutsu no denpan to hen'yō: Shiruku Rōdo ni sotte*, ed. Shiruku Rōdo Gaku Kenkyū Sentā (Nara: Shiruku Rōdo Gaku Kinen Kokusai Kōryū Zaidan, 1997), 88. Find reproductions of some of these hybrid paintings in Nara Kokuritsu Hakubutsukan, *Budda Shakuson: Sono shōgai to zōkei*, 230–34; Nakano Genzō, *Nehanzu*, vol. 268, Nihon no bijutsu (Tokyo: Shibundō, 1988), 64–69; and Tōbu Bijutsukan et al., *Budda ten*, 144–47.
109. The exemplary work in this regard is held by the Ryūganji in Kumamoto Prefecture. See Kyōto Kokuritsu Hakubutsukan, ed., *Nehanzu no meisaku: Tokubetsu chinretsu* (Kyoto: Seifūkai, 1978), 55.
110. Concerning the European medieval vita icon, see Glenn Peers, *Sacred Shock: Framing Visual Experience in Byzantium* (University Park: Pennsylvania State University Press, 2004); and Paroma Chatterjee, *The Living Icon in Byzantium and Italy: The Vita Image, Eleventh to Thirteenth Centuries* (Cambridge: Cambridge University Press, 2014). I am obliged to Elizabeth (Betsy) Sears for this reference.
111. On this iconography in Pāla art, see Alvan C. Eastman, "Some Steles of the Pala Period Containing the Eight Miracles of Buddha with Notes on the Variations: Part One," *Art in America and Elsewhere* 18, no. 6 (1930):

271–83; John C. Huntington, "Pilgrimage as Image: The Cult of the *Aṣṭamahāprātihārya*, Part II," *Orientations* 18, no. 8 (1987): 56–68; Janice Leoshko, "Scenes of the Buddha's Life in Pāla-Period Art," *Silk Road Art and Archaeology*, no. 3 (1993–1994): 261–63; and Jacob N. Kinnard, "Reevaluating the Eighth-Ninth Century Pāla Milieu: Icono-Conservatism and the Persistence of Śākyamuni," *Journal of the International Association of Buddhist Studies* 19, no. 2 (1996): 281–300. From the Chinese cultural sphere, Cave 33 at the Yulin Grotto site includes a mural of generally similar iconography, as does an eleventh-century silk painting recovered from Dunhuang and now held by the Guimet Museum in Paris. See Watanabe Satoshi, *Butsudenzu ronkō*, 361–62.

112. Compare the provenances assigned to the same paintings (i.e., nirvana transformation paintings held by the Eifukuji, the Jōfukuji, and the Saikyōji) in Kikutake Jun'ichi, "Kōrai jidai no Nehan hensōzu: Kagawa Jōtokuji o chūshin ni," *Yamato bunka*, no. 80 (1988): 17–35, with those assigned in Takeda Kazuaki, "Kagawa Jōtokuji no Nehan hensōzu ni tsuite: Sono seiritsu to Chōfukuji Nehanzu to no kankei o chūshin to shite," *Bukkyō geijutsu*, no. 196 (1991): 11–36.
113. Concerning the sources of the *Nirvana Ceremonial*, see Inoue Tadashi, "Kenkyū zadankai '"Tanjō to nehan" no bijutsu,'" in *Tanjō to Nehan no bijutsu: Kenkyū happyō to zadankai*, ed. Hayashiya Tatsusaburō (Kyoto: Bukkyō Bijutsu Kenkyū Ueno Kinen Zaidan, 1980), 31.
114. Enoki Katsurō, *Nihon Bukkyō bungaku to kayō* (Tokyo: Kasama Shoin, 1994), 32–33.
115. Sawada Atsuko, "Kōshiki," in *Nihon ongaku daijiten*, ed. Hirano Kenji, Kamisangō Yūkō, and Gamō Satoaki (Tokyo: Heibonsha, 1989), 434.
116. *T* 2731:900c4–c5.
117. On the dissemination of Myōe's *Nirvana Ceremonial*, see Arai Kōjun, "Nehan-e no hensen: Hōyō shidai o chūshin ni," in *Nehan-e no kenkyū: Nehan-e to Nehanzu*, ed. Gangōji Bunkazai Kenkyūjo (Nara: Gangōji Bunkazai Kenkyūjo, 1981), 26–29.
118. The name of the assembly derives from the first two of the four qualities of *nirvana* identified in the *Mahāyāna* version of the *Nirvana Sutra*: (1) permanence, (2) bliss, (3) self, and (4) purity (in Japanese, these four combine to form the phrase *jōraku gajō*).
119. An audio recording of the *Dharma Assembly of Permanence and Bliss* is available on CD, as Kōyasan Shōmyō no Kai, *Jōrakue: Kōyasan no shōmyō* (Tokyo: Bikutā Dentō Bunka Shinkō Zaidan, 2004), VZCG-346. There is also an abridged videorecording of the ritual available on DVD, as Matsunaga Yūkei, *Kōyasan no inori*, vol. 3, *Kōyasan Kōbō Daishi Kūkai no mandara sekai* (Kyoto: Dōhōsha Media Puran, 2005). Although it is now out of print, the following book and audiocassette combination is highly recommended: Ōguri Dōei and Kindaichi Haruhiko, *Shiza kōshiki: Shōmyō de katarareta Shaka no monogatari* (Tokyo: Shinchōsha, 1992).

120. See the comments in Inoue Tadashi, "Kenkyū zadankai" 35. The most complete treatment of Myōe's relationship to nirvana paintings in English, which includes a summary treatment of this scholarship, remains Jean Hunter Harriet, "The Japanese *Hasso* Nirvana Tradition of Paintings: An Iconological Study" (master's thesis, University of British Columbia, 1986).
121. Takeda, "Kagawa Jōtokuji no Nehan hensōzu ni tsuite," 31–32.
122. Kujirai Kiyotaka, "Kamakura jidai ni okeru Nehan hensōzu no tenkai ni tsuite: Jishōin, An'yōin bon to *Shiza kōshiki* no kanren o chūshin ni," *Bukkyō bijutsu*, no. 323 (2012): 54–55.
123. Donohashi Akio, "Tsurugi Jinja zō hassō nehan zu," *Kokka*, no. 1263 (2001): 48.
124. Watanabe Satoshi, *Butsudenzu ronkō*, 363.
125. Donohashi, "Tsurugi Jinja zō hassō nehan zu," 48.
126. *T* 2731:903–c24.
127. Watanabe Satoshi, *Butsudenzu ronkō*, 41.
128. Kajitani, "Butsudenzu no tenkai," 161–62.
129. Tsukishima Hiroshi, "*Tōdaiji fujumon kō* shōkō," *Kokugo kokubun* 21, no. 5 (1952): 342.
130. This passage is reproduced via lithography and transcription in Nakada Norio, ed., *Tōdai-ji fujumonkō no kokugogakuteki kenkyū* (Tokyo: Kazama Shobō, 1969), 44–45. The *yomikudashi* reading of the passage via the grammar of classical Japanese appears in ibid., 132–33.
131. This passage is reproduced via lithography and transcription in ibid., 96–97. The *yomikudashi* reading of the passage in the grammar of classical Japanese appears in ibid., 174.
132. For variant sets of these Eight Phases within East Asia, see Mochizuki Shinkō and Tsukamoto Zenryū, *Mochizuki Bukkyō daijiten* (Tokyo: Sekai Seiten Kankō Kyōkai, 1954), 4215–16. The relationship of these East Asian lists of the Eight Phases to the events commemorated in post-Gupta India with the Eight Great Pilgrimage Sites (Skt. *Aṣṭamahāprātihārya*) remains unclear. The earliest scriptural introduction into China of the Eight Great Pilgrimage Sites may be traced to a Northern Song–era translation whose title Nanjō Bun'yū rendered into English as the *Sutra on the Names of the Eight Great and Auspicious Caityas* (Ch. *Bada lingta minghao jing*, Skt. **Aṣṭā mahāsthānacaityastotra*). See no. 898 in Nanjio Bunyiu, *A Catalogue of the Chinese Translation of the Buddhist Tripitaka: The Sacred Canon of the Buddhists in China and Japan* (Oxford: Clarendon Press, 1883), 202. Like other translations of the period, this sutra had comparatively little influence in either China or Japan. For English translations of this very short sutra, along with renderings of related texts in Tibetan, see P. C. Bagchi, "The Eight Great Caityas and Their Cult," *Indian Historical Quarterly* 17, no. 1 (1947): 223–35; and Hajime Nakamura, "The Aṣṭāmahāsthānacaityastotra and the Chinese and Tibetan Versions of a Text Similar to It," in *Indi-*

anisme et bouddhisme: Mélanges offerts à Mgr Étienne Lamotte (Louvain: Institut Orientaliste, 1980), 259–65.

133. For a later example, we could look to a similarly compact summary of the life of the Buddha, part of the so-called "*gāthā* on hearing the bell [for meals]" (Jpn. *montsui no ge*), to be chanted before mealtime in the Sōtō denomination of Buddhism: "The Buddha was born at Kapilavastu, attained the way at Maghada, taught the Dharma at Vārāṇasī, and entered nirvana at Kuśinagara." These verses ultimately derive from the *Imperially Commissioned Rules for Purity by Baizhang* (*Chixiu Baizhang qinggui*, completed 1338), *T* 2025:1144c28. Concerning this monastic code, see Yifa, *The Origins of Buddhist Monastic Codes in China: An Annotated Translation and Study of the Chanyuan qinggui* (Honolulu: University of Hawaii Press, 2002), 48–51.

134. Like the *Tōdaiji Notes for Sermons*, this text too survives in just one manuscript edition, held by the Hōryūji. See Satō Ryōyū, ed., *Hyakuza hōdan kikigaki shō* (Tokyo: Nan'undō Ōfūsha, 1963), 158–59.

135. Ibid., 99.

136. Gotō Akio, "Kyōjiden: Ichi Tendai sō no kaita Butsuden," in *Eizan no waka to setsuwa*, ed. Arai Eizō, Watanabe Sadamaro, and Terakawa Michio (Kyoto: Sekai Shisōsha, 1991), 102–03.

137. For a summary from the mid-1970s of Japanese- and English-language scholarship concerning this doctrinal classification, see David Chappell, "Introduction to the 'T'ien-t'ai ssu-chiao-i,'" *Eastern Buddhist* 9, no. 1 (1976): 72–86.

138. Ibid., 83.

139. Paul Groner, "Vicissitudes in the Ordination of Japanese 'Nuns' during the Eighth through Tenth Centuries," in *Engendering Faith: Women and Buddhism in Premodern Japan*, ed. Barbara Ruch (Ann Arbor: Center for Japanese Studies, University of Michigan, 2002), 79–80.

140. Edward Kamens, *The Three Jewels: A Study and Translation of Minamoto Tamenori's Sanbōe* (Ann Arbor: Center for Japanese Studies, University of Michigan, 1988), 15–16.

141. I have followed the translation in ibid., 101. See the Japanese text of this passage, transcribed from two of the various extant editions, in Koizumi Hiroshi et al., *Sanbō-e shūsei: Shohon taishō* (Tokyo: Kasama Shoin, 1980), 9.

142. I have followed the translation in Kamens, *The Three Jewels*, 165. See the Japanese text of this passage, transcribed from three of the various extant editions, in Koizumi et al., *Sanbō-e shūsei*, 90–91.

143. As is often the case for scriptural citation in East Asia, the citation of scripture in the *Three Jewels* cannot always be taken at face value. Kamens cautions: "Some citations of primary sources are offered even where Tamenori may have used a text other than that cited, or where he may have written his own version independently, without close reliance on the original or any other recension. It has been shown that in many instances, where

Tamenori cited a work of scripture as his source, or paraphrased one without identification, his model text may not, in fact, have been the original scripture but, rather, the version of it that appears in Chinese Buddhist encyclopedias." *The Three Jewels*, 43. Concerning the *Biography*'s use of citation, see Gotō, "Kyōjiden," 114–15.

144. The following summaries of episodes covered in the *Biography* draws upon ibid., 107–112.
145. Ibid., 112.
146. Ibid., 115–16.
147. Ibid., 120.
148. Ibid., 118–19.

CHAPTER TWO

1. Kurobe Michiyoshi, *Nihon Butsuden bungaku no kenkyū* (Osaka: Izumi Shoin, 1989), 116–17.
2. For the purpose of this research, I am treating what have been called "sermon-ballads" (*sekkyōbushi*) as texts for the puppet theater as well. Concerning the use of puppets in the "sermon-ballad" theatrical form and the strong similarities between *sekkyōbushi* and "older puppet dramas" (*ko jōruri*) see Nobuko Ishi, "Sekkyō-bushi," *Monumenta Nipponica* 44, no. 3 (1989): 283–307; and Araki Shigeru, "Sekkyō no seisui," in *Jōruri no tanjō to ko jōruri*, ed. Torigoe Bunzō, Yamauchi Mikiko, and Watanabe Tamotsu, vol. 7, Iwanami kōza kabuki, Bunraku (Tokyo: Iwanami Shoten, 1998), 71–93.
3. Kokubungaku Kenkyū Shiryōkan, ed., *Chūsei butsuden shū*, vol. 5, Shinpukuji zenpon sōkan (Kyōto: Rinsen Shoten, 2000), 476.
4. Known as *shōhon* or "true texts," these are not dramatic scripts in the contemporary sense. Rather, they purport to record the actual words spoken by a master chanter, whose voice would animate all the characters in the play, as well as narrate the action. Since these texts circulated widely (and often without the permission of the chanter in question) and reached many readers who could never have seen an actual performance, they effectively were the mass, public face of the puppet theater. See R. Keller Kimbrough and Satoko Shimazaki, eds., *Publishing the Stage: Print and Performance in Early Modern Japan* (Boulder: Center for Asian Studies, University of Colorado, Boulder, 2011), 1–14.
5. Many of these are reproduced in Kokubungaku Kenkyū Shiryōkan, *Chūsei butsuden shū*. As not all variations of this body of literature have yet been studied comprehensively, much less printed in scholarly editions, the conclusions regarding the *Original Ground* literature in the present study reflect only a limited part of the corpus.
6. Yoshiko Kurata Dykstra, "Shinto Tales," *Journal of Intercultural Studies*, no. 5 (1978): 68.

7. "Shaka no gohonji," in *Sekkyōbushi shōhon shū*, ed. Yokoyama Shigeru and Fujiwara Hiroshi, vol. 1 (Tokyo: Ōokayama Shoten, 1936), 195.
8. Kurobe, *Nihon Butsuden bungaku no kenkyū*, 228.
9. Hank Glassman, "Shaka no Honji: Preaching, Intertextuality, and Popular Hagiography," *Monumenta Nipponica* 62, no. 3 (2007): 315.
10. Komine Kazuaki, "Shinpukuji zō *Shaka nyorai hassō shidai* ni tsuite: Chūsei Butsuden no shin shiryō," *Kokubungaku Kenkyū Shiryōkan kiyō*, no. 17 (1991): 110.
11. Ibid., 107.
12. Kokubungaku Kenkyū Shiryōkan, *Chūsei butsuden shū*, 357.
13. Ibid., 360.
14. Glassman, "Shaka no Honji," 309–310.
15. Kokubungaku Kenkyū Shiryōkan, *Chūsei butsuden shū*, 386.
16. For "the infinite sea of samsara," the original text has "for infinite *asaṃkhya* [kalpas]." *T* 190:791a7.
17. Peter Skilling, "Dharma, Dhāraṇī, Abhidharma, Avadāna: What Was Taught in Trayastriṃśa?" *Sōka Daigaku Kokusai Bukkyōgaku Kōtō Kenkyūsho nenpō*, no. 11 (2007): 43–44.
18. *T* 383: 1009a.
19. *T* 383: 1005c.
20. Kokubungaku Kenkyū Shiryōkan, *Chūsei butsuden shū*, 402.
21. Ruth Fuller Sasaki, trans., and Thomas Kirchner, ed., *The Record of Linji* (Honolulu: University of Hawaii Press, 2009), 31. For the Chinese text of this passage, with annotations in English, see ibid., 279.
22. "Shaka no gohonji," 180.
23. Ibid., 181.
24. Alan Cole, *Mothers and Sons in Chinese Buddhism* (Stanford, CA: Stanford University Press, 1998), 250–51.
25. For a vivid retelling of Devadatta's offences against the Buddha, and his ultimate fate, as described in the Pāli canon, see Donald S. Lopez Jr., *From Stone to Flesh: A Short History of the Buddha* (Chicago: University of Chicago Press, 2013), 81–84.
26. "Shaka no gohonji," 191.
27. "Shaka no honji (Kan'ei 20-nen kanpon)," in *Muromachi jidai monogatari taisei*, vol. 7, ed. Yokoyama Shigeru and Matsumoto Ryūshin (Tokyo: Kadokawa Shoten, 1979), 143.
28. This *jātaka* account is ultimately to be found in the first fascicle of the *Sutra of the Wise and the Foolish* (*Xianyu jing*). See the discussion in Motoi Makiko, "*Shaka no honji* to sono engen: *Hokekyō* no sennin kyūshi o meguru," in *Chūsei no monogatari to kaiga*, ed. Ishikawa Tōru (Tokyo: Chikurinsha, 2013), 225–26, which suggests that this tale entered the *Original Ground* literature through the mediation of the *Tales of the Three Lands* (*Sangoku denki*, first half of the fifteenth century). The scriptural passage can be found in *T* 202:350a–b.

29. "Shaka no honji (Kan'ei 20-nen kanpon)," 144.
30. Ibid., 146.
31. Ibid., 146.
32. "Shaka no gohonji," 190.
33. For this scene in the original Japanese manga version, see Tezuka Osamu, *Budda 4*, vol. BT-111, Tezuka Osamu bunko zenshū (Tokyo: Kōdansha, 2011), 260–62. For this scene in English translation, see Tezuka, *Buddha 4: The Forest of Uruvela* (New York: Vertical, 2006), 368–70.
34. Sng S. A., "This 'Buddha' Should Be Forgotten," *The Daily Enlightenment*, last modified December 3, 2014, http://thedailyenlightenment.com/2014/12/this-buddha-should-be-forgotten/comment-page-1/.
35. Zhao Ng Xin, "Review of Osamu Tezuka's 'Buddha 1 & 2,'" *The Daily Enlightenment*, last modified December 1, 2014, http://thedailyenlightenment.com/2014/12/review-of-osamu-tezukas-buddha-1–2/.
36. Yomota Inuhiko, "Genzai shakai ni motomerareru *Budda* no sekaikan," *Ushio*, June 2011, 228.
37. "Shaka no gohonji," 192–93.
38. This English rendition is taken from Shinran, *The Kyogyoshinsho, or the "Teaching, Practice, Faith, and Attainment,"* trans. Yamamoto Kosho (Tokyo: Karin Bunko, 1958), 32.
39. The dating of Chikamatsu's play is controversial. Generally, older scholarship—represented by the following sources—favors an earlier date for the play's premiere, 1695 (the eighth year of the Genroku era): Fujii Otoo, *Chikamatsu Monzaemon* (Tokyo: Kinkōdō Shoseki Kabushiki Kaisha, 1904), 114; Tōkyō Ongaku Gakkō, ed., *Kinsei hōgaku nenpyō: Gidayū bushi no bu* (Tokyo: Rikugōkan, 1927), 9; Takano Masami, "Shaka Nyorai tanjō-e," in *Nihon bungaku daijiten*, ed. Fujimura Tsukuru (Tokyo: Shinchōsha, 1950), 445–47; and Hayashi Kyōhei, "Shaka Nyorai tanjō-e," in *Sōgō Nihon gikyoku jiten*, ed. Kawatake Shigetoshi (Tokyo: Heibonsha, 1964), 291. In tentatively dating the play to 1714, the present study follows more recent scholarship, including Yūda Yoshio, "Chikamatsu nenpu," *Kokubungaku kaishaku to kanshō* 30, no. 3 (1965): 112–21; and Chikamatsu Monzaemon, "Shaka nyorai tanjō-e," in *Chikamatsu zenshū*, ed. Chikamatsu Zenshū Kankōkai, vol. 8 (Tokyo: Iwanami Shoten, 1988), 508.
40. For a photographic reproduction of the illustrated digest book, see Kansai Daigaku Toshokan, ed., *Aohon kurohon shū*, vol. 7, Kansai Daigaku Toshokan eiin sōsho Dai 1-ki (Suita: Kansai Daigaku Shuppanbu, 1997), 1–44. The dating of 1749 is an inference made by the editors of this text, based on the style of illustrations by Torii Kiyomitsu.
41. See the entry for the performance of excerpts from this play at the Bunrakuza in Osaka in July 1930, in Hibi Shigejirō, ed., *Shōchiku Kansai engeki shi* (Osaka: Shōchiku Hensanbu, 1940), 376.
42. For selected reproductions of Kyōsai's illustrations from this text—some

of which he rendered in the style of the Noh and *kyōgen* theaters—see Yamaguchi Seiichi, ed., *Kawanabe Kyōsai sashie 1: Shōsetsu, kokkei fūshibon yori*, vol. 7, Kyōsai shiryō (Warabi: Kyōsai Kinenkan, 1985), 17–24, 252–54. In English, the most comprehensive introduction to Kyōsai's life and art is Timothy Clark, *Demon of Painting: The Art of Kawanabe Kyōsai* (London: British Museum Press, 1993).

43. A printed version of the Kabuki script is available in Atsumi Seitarō, ed., *Bakumatsu Edo kyōgen hen*, vol. 22, Nihon gikyoku zenshū (Tokyo: Shun'yōdō, 1930), 1–62.
44. See the entry for the all-female (*onna shibai*) performance in Kokuritsu Gekijō Chōsa Yōseibu Geinō Chōsashitsu and Kindai Kabuki Nenpyō Hensanshitsu, eds., *Kindai kabuki nenpyō Kyōto hen*, vol. 4 (Tokyo: Yagi Shoten, 1998), 117.
45. The erotic adaptation is available online through the website of the Museum of Fine Arts, Boston: "Shaka hassô zoku Yamato bunko," Museum of Fine Arts, Boston, last modified May 14, 2015, http://educators.mfa.org/shaka-hass%C3%B4-zoku-yamato-bunko-162518.
46. Reitei [Umebori] Kokuga, *Hasshū kigen Shaka jitsuroku* (Tokyo: Seiundō, 1854).
47. Uchimura Katsushi, "Hagiwara Otohiko no gesaku rui ni tsuite," *Bungei kenkyū*, no. 116 (2012): 10.
48. Ernest Mason Satow and A. G. S. Hawes, *A Handbook for Travellers in Central & Northern Japan, Being a Guide to Tōkiō, Kiōto, Ōzaka* [*sic*], *Hakodate, Nagasaki, and Other Cities; the Most Interesting Parts of the Main Island; Ascents of the Principal Mountains; Descriptions of Temples; and Historical Notes and Legends*, 2nd ed., Murray's Hand-book, Japan (London: Murray, 1884), 70–84.
49. John Laidlaw Atkinson, *Prince Siddartha: The Japanese Buddha* (Boston: Congregational Sunday-School and Pub. Society, 1893), 307.
50. Asakura Haruhiko, ed., *Kanazōshi shūsei*, vol. 35 (Tokyo: Tōkyōdō Shuppan, 2004), 18.
51. Ibid., 20.
52. Ibid., 37.
53. Ibid., 39.
54. It comprises one of the scenes depicted on the seventh-century Tamamushi Shrine at the temple Hōryūji; it ranks among the former lives in *The Three Jewels* (984); and in the final chapter of the semi-historical *Tale of Flowering Fortunes*, the chief abbot of the great temple Enryakuji takes it as the theme for his sermon at the funeral of the protagonist, Fujiwara no Michinaga (966–1027), the aristocrat who wielded unprecedented power at the late Heian imperial court. It is surely no coincidence that this chapter of the *Tale of Flowering Fortunes* repeatedly aligns Michinaga's death with the death of Śākyamuni himself.

55. I have adopted the translation from William H. McCullough and Helen Craig McCullough, trans., *A Tale of Flowering Fortunes: Annals of Japanese Aristocratic Life in the Heian Period*, vol. 2 (Stanford: Stanford University Press, 1980), 766.
56. Asakura, *Kanazōshi shūsei*, 185–88.
57. Ibid., 189.
58. T. Griffith Foulk, "Sung Controversies Concerning the 'Separate Transmission' of Ch'an," in *Buddhism in the Sung*, ed. Peter N. Gregory and Daniel A. Getz Jr. (Honolulu: University of Hawaii Press, 1999), 257.
59. Aoyama Tadakazu, *Kinsei Bukkyō bungaku no kenkyū* (Tokyo: Ōfū, 1999), 983.
60. Izumoji Osamu, "Gōtama Budda no tanjō: Butsuden no hen'yō o megutte," *Setsuwa denshōgaku*, no. 7 (1999): 4.
61. Nagai Kazuaki, *Hangi wa kataru* (Tokyo: Kasama Shoin, 2014), 525–527.
62. "Edo-ki no hangi 3500-mai hakken: Kyōto Bukkōji, Inga monogatari mo," *Asahi shinbun*, October 11, 2003, 1.
63. "'Kanazōshi' 'otogizōshi' hangi hatsu hakken: Kyōto no tera, danka e no seppō ni shiyō?" *Sankei shinbun*, October 12, 2003, 29.
64. Chikamatsu, "Shaka nyorai tanjō-e," 533.
65. Ibid., 554.
66. These translations are taken from Leon Hurvitz, *Scripture of the Lotus Blossom of the Fine Dharma* (New York: Columbia University Press, 1976), 34 and 37.
67. Carl Bielefeldt, "Expedient Devices, the One Vehicle, and the Life Span of the Buddha," in *Readings of the Lotus Sutra*, ed. Stephen F. Teiser and Jacqueline Ilyse Stone (New York: Columbia University Press, 2009), 73.
68. Chikamatsu, "Shaka nyorai tanjō-e," 602.
69. Ibid., 590.
70. Kaewrithidej Ladda, "*Shaka nyorai tanjō-e*: Jōruriteki shukō ni yoru Shaka denki no hen'yō," *Kokugo kokubun* 72, no. 2 (2003): 161–83.
71. Chikamatsu, "Shaka nyorai tanjō-e," 615.
72. Ibid., 619.
73. Ibid., 623; Ladda, "*Shaka nyorai tanjō-e*," 161–83.
74. For some of the Buddhist material to which Chikamatsu made reference in this play, see Ueda Kazutoshi and Higuchi Yoshichiyo, *Chikamatsu goi* (Tokyo: Fuzanbō, 1930), 560, 565–66, 570, 576, 579, and 581.
75. Michael Emmerich, *The Tale of Genji: Translation, Canonization, and World Literature* (New York: Columbia University Press, 2013).
76. Yamagata Genjō, *Hyakuren no tetchō* (Kyoto: Dentōsha, 1897), 19.
77. For an account of the importance of these popular tales in inspiring Kawaguchi Ekai's commitment to Buddhism, see Okuyama Naoji, *Hyōden Kawaguchi Ekai* (Tokyo: Chūō Kōron Shinsha, 2003), 29–36.
78. See "Indo Busseki gentō kyōji kai," *Yomiuri shinbun*, March 20, 1886.

79. See Ikeda Toraku, *Daishō Shakuson go-ichidai ki* (Tokyo: Ikeda, Kenkichi, 1903).

CHAPTER THREE

1. Mary Elizabeth Berry, *Japan in Print: Information and Nation in the Early Modern Period* (Berkeley: University of California Press, 2006), 32.
2. Mannami Hisako, "Edo jidai no Nishi Honganji to shuppan," *Ajia yūgaku*, no. 155 (2012): 154–63.
3. See Tamura Maiko, "Kinsei/Kindai ni okeru 'Nichiren-ki mono' no ichi kōsatsu," *Nichiren kyōgaku kenkyūsho kiyō*, no. 31 (2004): 121–28; and Kanmuri Ken'ichi, *Kinsei Nichirenshū shuppanshi kenkyū* (Kyoto: Heirakuji Shoten, 1983), 164–75.
4. See En'ya Kikumi, *Katarareta Shinran* (Kyoto: Hōzōkan, 2011), 170–77. Efforts to restrict the circulation of biographies to the orthodox version continued through the nineteenth century, but ultimately failed to stamp out peripheral and "heretical" competitors. See also Tsutsumi Kunihiko, *Edo no kōsō densetsu* (Tokyo: Miyai Shoten, 2008), 282–86.
5. Sakado Hiromu, *Shinshū kankei jōruri tenkaishi josetsu: Sozai no jidai* (Kyoto: Hōzōkan, 2008), 158–59.
6. For the scene of Prince Siddhartha's fulfillment of his promise to his father to leave an heir, see "Shaka monogatari (Keichō 16-nen shahon)," in *Muromachi jidai monogatari shūsei*, ed. Yokoyama Shigeru and Ōta Takeo, vol. 4, 23–52 (Tokyo: Inoue Shobō, 1962), 37. For the distribution of the Buddha's relics, see ibid., 52.
7. Ibid., 45.
8. Araki Shigeru, "Sekkyōbushi no katarimono no keisei katei o meguru mondai: Bukkyō setsuwa-kei no katarimono no baai," *Bungaku* 42, no. 9 (1974): 26.
9. This linkage was especially important within Japanese Tendai. See Kevin Gray Carr, *Plotting the Prince: Shōtoku Cults and the Mapping of Medieval Japanese Buddhism* (Honolulu: University of Hawaii Press, 2012), 51–58.
10. Kurobe Michiyoshi, "Shaka ichidai denki kosui kan 3 (honkoku)," *Aichi Gakuin Daigaku Kyōyōbu kiyō* 43, no. 1 (1995): 187.
11. Kurobe Michiyoshi, "Shaka ichidai denki kosui kan 7 (honkoku)," *Aichi Gakuin Daigaku Kyōyōbu kiyō* 44, no. 3 (1995): 130.
12. Ibid.
13. Jacqueline I. Stone, *Original Enlightenment and the Transformation of Medieval Japanese Buddhism* (Honolulu: University of Hawaii Press, 1999), 167.
14. Tetsuo Najita, *Visions of Virtue in Tokugawa Japan: The Kaitokudō Merchant Academy of Osaka* (Chicago: University of Chicago Press, 1987), 25–45.
15. Paul Watt, "Jiun Sonja (1718–1804): Life and Thought" (PhD diss., Columbia University, 1982), 85–97.

16. Jiun Sonja 200-kai Onki no Kai, ed., *Shinjitsu no hito Jiun Sonja: Shakuson hitosuji no shōgai to sono oshie* (Tokyo: Daihōrinkaku, 2004), 49.
17. Ibid., 48.
18. Paul Watt, "Body, Gender, and Society in Jiun Sonja's (1718–1804) Buddhism," in *Engendering Faith: Women and Buddhism in Premodern Japan*, ed. Barbara Ruch (Ann Arbor: Center for Japanese Studies, University of Michigan, 2002).
19. Jiun Sonja 200-kai Onki no Kai, *Shinjitsu no hito Jiun Sonja*, 58–59.
20. Regan Eileen Murphy, "The Urgency of History: Language and Ritual in Japanese Buddhism and Kokugaku" (PhD diss., Harvard University, 2010), 143–48.
21. Kinami Takuichi, ed., *Miyo no hikari: Shakuson den* (Osaka: Kinami Takuichi, 1980), 363; Tsukuba Daigaku Toshokan, ed., *Jiun Sonja to Shittan gaku: Jihitsubon Hokke darani ryakuge to Bongaku shinryō no sekai* (Ibaraki: Tsukuba Daigaku Fuzoku Toshokan, 2010), 19.
22. Beginning in 1905, the Christian missionary John Atkinson—the very translator of *Shaka hassō monogatari* into *Prince Siddartha: The Japanese Buddha*—began to serialize an English translation of the *Jūzen hōgo* in the *Transactions of the Asiatic Society of Japan.* Atkinson died in 1908, before he could complete the project of translation. The final installment of his work was published posthumously, in 1913. Although through no fault of his own, Atkinson lacked knowledge of the Buddhist vocabulary and ideas invoked in Jiun's text, meaning that the resulting English version is sometimes obscure to the point of unintelligibility. It is regrettable that a text so important for the later Japanese Buddhist tradition as the *Jūzen hōgo* still lacks a published, accurate translation in full.
23. Concerning this Chōfukuji, see Kyōto-shi, *Ukyō-ku*, vol. 14, Shiryō Kyōto no rekishi (Tokyo: Heibonsha, 1994), 83–84; Kawabata Yasunari et al., eds., *Kyōto jiten* (Tokyo: Jinbutsu Ōraisha, 1967), 327; and Sawa Ryūken et al., *Kyōto daijiten* (Kyoto: Tankōsha, 1984), 625.
24. Kinami, *Miyo no hikari*, 364.
25. Katō Jun, *Bussokuseki no tame ni: Nihon kenzai bussokuseki yōran* (Tokyo: Tsukiji Shokan, 1980), 198–99.
26. Concerning the Sekihōji stone diorama—which is often misleadingly characterized as a depiction only of the Buddha's arhat followers who surround the scenes from his life—see Doi Tsugiyoshi, *Kinsei Nihon kaiga no kenkyū* (Tokyo: Bijutsu Shuppansha, 1970), 591–94; Yoshiaki Shimizu, "On Spirituality in the Work of Itō Jakuchū (1716–1800)," in *Homage to All Creatures Great and Small: The Visionary World of Itō Jakuchū (1716–1800)*, ed. United States-Japan Foundation (New York: United States–Japan Foundation, 2009), 68–81; and Mizuno Katsuhiko, *Sekihōji: Jakuchū 500 rakan* (Kyoto: Unsōdō, 2013).
27. Kinami, *Miyo no hikari*, unpaginated preface.
28. Ibid., unpaginated preface.

29. Ibid., 227.
30. Shibata Mitsuhiko, *Honbun hen*, vol. 1, *Daisō zōsho mokuroku to kenkyū: Kashihon Ōnoya Sōbē kyūzō shomoku* (Musashimurayama: Seishōdō Shoten, 1983), 702.
31. Concerning women's travelogues from the Edo period, see Laura Nenzi, *Excursions in Identity: Travel and the Intersection of Place, Gender, and Status in Edo Japan* (Honolulu: University of Hawaii Press, 2008).
32. Yamada no Kakashi's work is reproduced in moveable type in Furuya Chishin, ed., *Shaka go-ichidaiki zue (Kōkadō cho, Katsushika Hokusai ga), Nichiren shōnin ichidai zue (Nakamura Keinen cho, Katsushika Hokusai ga)*, vol. 8, *Nihon rekishi zue* (Tokyo: Kokumin Tosho, 1920).
33. For Mahāprajāpatī's role in the creation of the nuns' *saṅgha*, see Yamada Yoshio, ed., *Konjaku monogatari shū 1*, vol. 22, Nihon koten bungaku taikei (Tokyo: Iwanami Shoten, 1959), 92–93. For an English translation of this episode, see Yoshiko Kurata Dykstra, ed., *The Konjaku Tales, Indian Section (1)* (Hirakata: Maruzen, 1986), 114–17. For the tale of the eradication of the Śākya clan, see Yamada Y., *Konjaku monogatari shū 1*, 170–76. For an English translation of this episode, see Dykstra, *The Konjaku Tales*, 209–16.
34. See Asakura Haruhiko, ed., *Kanazōshi shūsei*, vol. 35 (Tokyo: Tōkyōdō Shuppan, 2004), 148–49.
35. Kinami, *Miyo no hikari*, 216.
36. Ibid., 269.
37. Reproduced in Furuya, *Shaka go-ichidaiki zue*, 258–59.
38. Kinami, *Miyo no hikari*, 274.
39. Ibid., 327.
40. Ibid., 224.
41. Ibid., 348.
42. Ibid., 350, 353.
43. See Jōdoshū Daijiten Hensan Iinkai, ed., *Jōdoshū daijiten*, vol. 3 (Tokyo: Jōdoshū Daijiten Kankōkai, 1974), s.v. "Hiroyasu Shinzui."
44. Kinami, *Miyo no hikari*, 351.
45. Ibid., 354.
46. Tokumitsu Shōryū, *Shakuson shinjitsu denki* (Nagasaki: Hōtokukai, 1882), unpaginated conventions.
47. Ibid., 61.
48. Itō Shundō, *Shaka jitsu denki* (Tokyo: Morie Shoten, 1902), 1.
49. Ibid.

CHAPTER FOUR

1. Basil Hall Chamberlain, *Things Japanese: Being Notes on Various Subjects Connected with Japan for the Use of Travellers and Others*, 2nd ed. (London: K. Paul, Trench, Trübner, 1891), 271.

2. Masaharu Anesaki, *History of Japanese Religion with Special Reference to the Social and Moral Life of the Nation* (London: K. Paul, Trench, Trübner, 1930), 308.
3. Donald Keene, "Hirata Atsutane and Western Learning," *T'oung Pao* 42, no. 5 (1954): 356.
4. Klaus Antoni, "Does Shinto History 'Begin at Kuroda'? On the Historical Continuities of Political Shinto," in *Politics and Religion in Modern Japan: Red Sun, White Lotus*, ed. Roy Starrs (New York: Palgrave Macmillan, 2011), 95.
5. Mark McNally, *Proving the Way: Conflict and Practice in the History of Japanese Nativism* (Cambridge, MA: Harvard University Asia Center, 2005), 179. McNally's biographical account positions Atsutane's composition of *The Sacred Pillar of the Soul* (*Tama no mihashira*, 1811) at the end of the earliest phase of Atsutane's intellectual development. The English translation of the title of this work is adopted from Anne Walthall, *The Weak Body of a Useless Woman: Matsuo Taseko and the Meiji Restoration* (Chicago: University of Chicago Press, 1998), 122.
6. McNally, *Proving the Way*, 180–81.
7. Wilburn Hansen, *When Tengu Talk: Hirata Atsutane's Ethnography of the Other World* (Honolulu: University of Hawaii Press, 2008), 72.
8. For an English-language study of Atsutane's use of Christian sources, see Keene, "Hirata Atsutane and Western Learning."
9. For a rare exception to the general neglect in English of Atsutane's research into materials from China, see Wai-ming Ng, "The Shintoization of the *Yijing* in Hirata Atsutane's *Kokugaku*," *Sino-Japanese Studies* 19 (2012): 32–47.
10. S. K. Chaudhuri, "India in Japanese Literature: A Case Study of Hirata Atsutane," *China Report* 21 (1985): 65–75.
11. Nobumi Iyanaga, "Medieval Shintō as a Form of 'Japanese Hinduism': An Attempt at Understanding Early Medieval Shintō," *Cahiers d'Extrême-Asie* 16 (2006–2007): 291.
12. Sources in Japanese concerning Hirata Atsutane's scholarship on Buddhism alone include the following: Yamamoto Shindō, "Hirata Atsutane no Bukkyō-kan," *Kenshin gakuhō* 32 (1941): 17–41; Matsunaga Motoki, *Hirata Atsutane no Bukkyō-kan* (Tokyo: Kazama Shobō, 1944); Kashiwahara Yūsen, "Hirata Atsutane ni okeru hai-Butsu ron no honshitsu ni tsuite," *Ōtani shigaku* 4 (1955): 1–13; Nishida Nagao, "Hirata Atsutane no gakumon: Jihitsubon *Daibibasharon bassui* o chūshin to suru sono Indogaku/Bukkyōgaku kenkyū o tsūjite," *Kokugakuin zasshi* 64, no. 11/12 (1963): 1–53; Miki Shōtarō, "Hirata Atsutane no Bukkyō kenkyū," *Kōgakukan Daigaku kiyō* 6 (1968): 24–87; Haga Noboru, "Hirata Atsutane no Bukkyō hihan: Toku ni Shinteki nishū hihan o chūshin ni suete," in *Nihon bunkashi kenkyū: Haga Kōshirō Sensei koki kinen*, ed. Haga Kōshirō Sensei

Koki Kinen Ronbunshū Henshū Iinkai (Tokyo: Kasama Shoin, 1980), 263–92; Kanno Hiroshi, "Hirata Atsutane no *Indo zōshi* to Bukkyō kenkyū no igi," in *Kinsei no seishin seikatsu*, ed. Ōkura Seishin Bunka Kenkyūjo (Tokyo: Zoku Gunsho Ruijū Kanseikai, 1996), 697–734; Tamamuro Fumio, "Hirata Atsutane no hai-Butsu ron ni tsuite," in *Hirata Atsutane no gakumon to shisō*, vol. 5, *Haga Noboru chosaku senshū* (Tokyo: Yūzankaku, 2002), 355–64; Iyanaga Nobumi, "Yuiitsu no kami to hitotsu no sekai: Kindai shoki Nihon to Furansu ni okeru hikaku shinwagaku no hajimari," in *"Hitotsu no sekai" no seiritsu to sono jōken*, ed. Nakagawa Hisayasu (Kizugawa: Kokusai Kōtō Kenkyūjo, 2007), 165–240; and Yoshida Masaki, "Kinsei shomin Bukkyō to *Shutsujō shōgo*," in *Hirata Atsutane: Reikon no yukue* (Tokyo: Kōdansha, 2009), 131–49.

13. Kashiwahara, "Hirata Atsutane ni okeru hai-Butsu ron," 11.
14. For a classic study of the philosophical and religious rivals to the Buddha, see Beni Madhab Barua, *A History of Pre-Buddhistic Indian Philosophy* (Calcutta: University of Calcutta, 1921).
15. Quoted in Livia Kohn, *Laughing at the Tao: Debates among Buddhists and Taoists in Medieval China* (Princeton, NJ: Princeton University Press, 1995), 131. For the original text, see *T* 2103: 151a4–a5.
16. They resumed briefly in the thirteenth century, during the period of Mongol rule over China, in a series of debates held at the court of the khans, pitting Taoist masters of the Complete Perfection (Quanzhen) school against Buddhists, including both Chinese and Tibetan representatives.
17. William Theodore De Bary et al., *Sources of Chinese Tradition*, 2nd ed., vol. 1, *Introduction to Asian Civilization* (New York: Columbia University Press, 1999), 569.
18. Translated in Wing-tsit Chan, *A Source Book in Chinese Philosophy* (Princeton, NJ: Princeton University Press, 1963), 554. For the original text of this passage, see Pan Fu'en, ed., *Er Cheng yishu*, Tiandiren congshu (Shanghai: Shanghai Guji Chubanshe, 2000), 195. For a translation into Japanese, see Fumoto Yasutaka, ed., *Shushi no senku (jō)*, vol. 2, *Shushigaku taikei* (Tokyo: Meitoku Shuppansha, 1978), 343.
19. This translation is adapted from the version in Mark Picco, "A Critical Exegesis and Translation of Zhu Xi's Critique of Buddhism, as Found in the 126th Chapter of the 'Zhuzi Yulei'" (master's thesis, University of Calgary, 2005), 72. For the original text of this passage, from fascicle 126 of the *Classified Conversations of Master Zhu*, see Li Jingde and Wang Xingxian, eds., *Zhuzi yulei*, vol. 8, Lixue congshu (Beijing: Zhonghua Shuju, 1986), 3010.
20. Translated in Picco, "A Critical Exegesis and Translation of Zhu Xi's Critique of Buddhism," 80. For the original text of this passage, also from fascicle 126 of the *Classified Conversations of Master Zhu*, see Li and Wang, *Zhuzi yulei*, 3013.

21. Robert H. Sharf, "The Scripture in Forty-Two Sections," in *Religions of China in Practice*, ed. Donald S. Lopez Jr. (Princeton, NJ: Princeton University Press, 1996), 362–63.
22. Julia Ching, *The Religious Thought of Chu Hsi* (New York: Oxford University Press, 2000), 178.
23. Wing-tsit Chan, *Chu Hsi: New Studies* (Honolulu: University of Hawaii Press, 1989), 525.
24. Ishida Ichirō, "Hayashi Razan no shisō," in *Fujiwara Seika, Hayashi Razan*, ed. Ishida Ichirō and Kataya Osamu, vol. 28, Nihon shisō taikei (Tokyo: Iwanami Shoten, 1975), 476.
25. As is often observed, Seika's break with Zen Buddhism was less than total: a lingering attachment to the Shōkokuji is suggested by his burial in the graveyard attached to one of its subtemples (*tatchū*), the Rinkōin.
26. Of uncertain editorial provenance, the *Dialogue* came into print no later than 1668. It represents an edited adaptation of an exchange of letters between Razan and his erstwhile friend, the master of *haikai* verse and scholar of literature Matsunaga Teitoku (1571–1654), probably in or around 1606. As a lay follower of an intensely exclusivist version of Nichiren Buddhism, Teitoku took the Buddhist side in refuting Razan's charges in this written debate.
27. The Confucians in these debates were not bureaucrats in the service of a ruler (as in China) but private scholars, who depended on patronage or tuition fees. Therefore, the repercussions of the debates were correspondingly attenuated; as observed by the scholar of Japanese Neo-Confucianism Joseph Spae, "the feud" between the two sides in Japan "was before long more or less limited to academic disputations not always backed up by inner conviction." Joseph Spae, "Buddhism as Viewed by Two Tokugawa Confucianists: Itô Jinsai's Letter to Dôkô and Its Refutation by Satô Naokata," *Monumenta Nipponica* 5, no. 1 (1942): 167.
28. For a modern annotated edition of Razan's arguments along these lines and their rebuttal, see Ōkuwa Hitoshi and Maeda Ichirō, eds., *Razan, Teitoku Ju-Butsu mondō: Chūkai to kenkyū* (Tokyo: Perikansha, 2006), 124–40.
29. Hirata Atsutane, "Zoku Shintō taii," in *Shinshū Hirata Atsutane zenshū*, ed. Hirata Atsutane Zenshū Kankōkai (Tokyo: Meicho Shuppan, 1977), vol. 8, 141
30. Tahara Tsuguo, *Hirata Atsutane*, vol. 111, Jinbutsu sōsho (Tokyo: Yoshikawa Kōbunkan, 1963), 232.
31. Hirata Atsutane, "Shutsujō shōgo," in *Shinshū Hirata Atsutane zenshū*, ed. Hirata Atsutane Zenshū Kankōkai (Tokyo: Meicho Shuppan, 1977), vol. 10, 389–90, 393.
32. Ibid., 374.
33. Ibid.
34. Ibid., 375.

35. This is the well-known text *Essentials of the Eight Traditions* (*Hasshū kōyō*, 1268), by the Kegon master Gyōnen (1240–1321).
36. Hirata Atsutane, "Indo zōshi," in *Shinshū Hirata Atsutane zenshū*, ed. Hirata Atsutane Zenshū Kankōkai (Tokyo: Meicho Shuppan, 1977). vol. 11, 369. The section in parenthesis refers here and elsewhere to interlinear notes in the original.
37. Hirata, "Shutsujō shōgo," 372.
38. Ibid., 281.
39. Ibid., 362.
40. Hirata Atsutane, "Indo zōshi," 370.
41. Hirata, "Shutsujō shōgo," 299.
42. The most comprehensively annotated reproduction and translation of this text into modern Japanese is available as Tominaga Nakamoto, *Shutsujō kōgo* (Tokyo: Ryūbunkan, 1982). Other annotated or translated modern Japanese versions are available as Mizuta Norihisa, ed., *Tominaga Nakamoto, Yamagata Bantō*, vol. 43, Nihon shisō taikei (Tokyo: Iwanami Shoten, 1976), and Katō Shūichi, ed., *Tominaga Nakamoto, Ishida Baigan*, vol. 18, *Nihon no meicho* (Tokyo: Chūō Kōronsha, 1978). For an English translation, see Michael Pye, *Emerging from Meditation* (Honolulu: University of Hawaii Press, 1990). Postwar comprehensive monograph-length studies of Nakamoto in Japanese include Miyagawa Yasuko, *Tominaga Nakamoto to Kaitokudō: Shisōshi no zenshō* (Tokyo: Perikansha, 1998). For secondary scholarship in English, see Katō Shūichi, "Tominaga Nakamoto, 1715–46: A Tokugawa Iconoclast," *Monumenta Nipponica* 22, no. 1/2 (1967): 177–93; Tetsuo Najita, *Visions of Virtue in Tokugawa Japan: The Kaitokudō Merchant Academy of Osaka* (Chicago: University of Chicago Press, 1987); James Edward Ketelaar, *Of Heretics and Martyrs in Meiji Japan: Buddhism and Its Persecution* (Princeton, NJ: Princeton University Press, 1990), 19–28; Hubert Durt, *Problems of Chronology and Eschatology: Four Lectures on the Essay on Buddhism by Tominaga Nakamoto* (Kyoto: Istituto Italiano di Cultura, Scuola di Studi sull'Asia Orientale, 1994); and Regan Eileen Murphy, "The Urgency of History: Language and Ritual in Japanese Buddhism and Kokugaku" (PhD diss., Harvard University, 2010), 71–128.
43. Katō, "Tominaga Nakamoto, 1715–46."
44. Ketelaar, *Of Heretics and Martyrs*, 31.
45. Ibid., 22.
46. Hirata, "Shutsujō shōgo," 349–50.
47. Ibid., 295.
48. Ibid., 291.
49. Ibid., 311.
50. Ibid.
51. It is worth mentioning that Atsutane's contemporary, the Osaka merchant-class scholar Yamagata Banto (1748–1821), was during the same period writing his own life's masterwork, *In Place of Dreams* (*Yume no shiro*,

completed in 1820). A Confucian by training with a great interest in European science as transmitted to Japan in Dutch sources, Bantō included in his work a thoroughgoing denial of any supernatural forces. At the least, from such divergence, it seems clear that Atsutane and Bantō found differing uses for rationality.

52. Hirata, "Shutsujō shōgo," 318.
53. Ibid., 293.
54. Ibid., 316.
55. Ibid., 296.
56. This translation is adapted from Nobuyoshi Yamabe, "*The Sūtra on the Ocean-Like Samādhi of the Visualization of the Buddha*: The Interfusion of the Chinese and Indian Cultures in Central Asia as Reflected in a Fifth Century Apocryphal Sūtra" (PhD diss., Yale University, 1999), 379.
57. Hirata, "Shutsujō shōgo," 299 and 297.
58. Ibid., 308.
59. Ibid., 314.
60. Ibid., 316.
61. Ibid., 322. In the translation by Étienne Lamotte: "En outre, il y a des hommes mauvais, livrés à des sentiments d'envie (*īrṣyā*), qui calomnient le Buddha en disant: « La sagesse (*prajñā*) du Buddha ne dépasse pas [celle] des hommes, c'est seulement sa magie (*māyā*) qui trompe le monde»." Lamotte, trans., *Le traité de la grande vertu de sagesse de Nāgārjuna (Mahāprajñāpāramitāśāstra)*, vol. 1 (Louvain: Bibliothèque du Muséon, 1944), 15.
62. Hirata, "Shutsujō shōgo," 322.
63. Ibid., 332.
64. Ibid., 335.
65. Ibid., 336.
66. Ibid., 339. In the translation by Étienne Lamotte: "Le Grand Kasyapa dit encore : « Tu as montré aux femmes la marque de cryptorchidie (*kosagatavastiguhya*) du Buddha après qu'il fut entré dans le Parinirvāṇa. N'est-ce pas honteux? En cela tu as commis une faute duṣkṛta » Ânanda dit: « A ce moment-là j'ai pensé: si les femmes voyaient la marque de la cryptorchidie du Buddha, elles se sentiraient honteuses de leur corps de femme et voudraient obtenir un corps d'homme pour planter des racines de mérite en vue de réaliser la condition de Buddha. C'est pour cette raison que j'ai montré aux femmes [ces organes]. Ce n'est pas par impudence que j'ai enfreint les défenses (śila) »." Lamotte, *Le traité de la grande vertu de sagesse*, 96–97.
67. Kanno, "Hirata Atsutane no *Indo zōshi*," 713–18.
68. Hirata Atsutane, "Indo zōshi kō," in *Shinshū Hirata Atsutane zenshū*, ed. Hirata Atsutane Zenshū Kankōkai (Tokyo: Meicho Shuppan, 1977), vol. 11, 421.
69. Ibid.
70. Ibid., 421–22.

71. Here, Atsutane again worked on the basis of passages in the *Pearl Grove of the Dharma Garden*: These concern the reverence of the images of the gods for the newborn prince, as found in the early Chinese adaptation of the *Lalitavistara* (*T* 2122: 345a20–b20); the discussion of the Sarvāstivādin position on the death of Māyā (*T* 2122: 346a29–b2); and the list of other wondrous births that accompanied the delivery of the Buddha (*T* 2122: 345b21–c22).
72. Hirata, "Indo zōshi kō," 396–97.
73. Hashiguchi Kōnosuke, *Edo no hon'ya to honzukuri: Zoku Wahon nyūmon* (Tokyo: Heibonsha, 2011), 69.
74. This argument is developed in the introduction to Yoshida Asako, *Chi no kyōmei: Hirata Atsutane o meguru shomotsu no shakaishi* (Tokyo: Perikansha, 2012).
75. Tahara, *Hirata Atsutane*, 272–77.
76. For a hagiographic account of this episode, see Mochizuki Shigeru, *Sakura Azumao* (Tokyo: Dai Nihon Yūbenkai Kōdansha, 1943), 127–35.
77. Hashiguchi, *Edo no hon'ya to honzukuri*, 86.
78. Yoshida A., *Chi no kyōmei*, 237.
79. Mochizuki, *Sakura Azumao*, 198.
80. Yoshida A., *Chi no kyōmei*, 238.
81. For bibliographical details concerning these various editions, plus one produced in the Meiji period, see Tajihi Ikuo and Nakano Mitsutoshi, eds., *Kinsei katsujiban mokuroku* (Musashi Murayama: Seishōdō, 1990), vol. 50, Nihon shoshigaku taikei, 126–30. For reproductions of pages from some of these editions, see Gotō Kenji, ed., *Kinsei katsujiban zuroku*, vol. 61, Nihon shoshigaku taikei (Musashi Murayama: Seishōdō, 1990), 296–303.
82. Hashiguchi, *Edo no hon'ya to honzukuri*, 87.
83. Takami Inoue, "Local Buddhism and Its Transformation in Nineteenth Century Japan: *Shinbutsu Bunri* in Shinano Province" (PhD diss., University of California Santa Barbara, 2010), 109. Inoue's study also notes that this farmer, Kitahara Inao, held a copy of the *Compendium of Indian Records*, though without specifying which volumes.
84. That is, the Zen mode of Buddhism, often referred to as a "separate transmission outside the teachings."
85. Hirata Atsutane Zenshū Kankokai, ed., *Shinshū Hirata Atsutane zenshū* (Tokyo: Meicho Shuppan, 1977), vol. 11, 3–6. The Chinese text of this encomium is reproduced and punctuated to facilitate *kundoku* reading in Shigeki Denhachirō, "Hirara Sensei no Indo zōshi o yomite Hirata Atsutane o ronzu," *Myōkōge* 161, no. 10 (1916): 16.
86. Watanabe Kinzō, *Hirata Atsutane kenkyū* (Tokyo: Rokkō Shobō, 1942), 222.
87. Shigeki, "Hirara Sensei no Indo zōshi o yomite," 25.
88. Ibid., 26–27.
89. Ibid., 29.
90. Nishida, "Hirata Atsutane no gakumon," 52.

91. Ibid., 53.
92. Ibid.
93. Relevant entries from Atsutane's diary are reproduced in Watanabe Kinzō, *Hirata Atsutane kenkyū*, 913, 939, and 942.
94. Hirata Atsutane, "Shinji hifumi den," in *Hirata Atsutane zenshū*, ed. Kankōkai Hirata Atsutane Zenshū, vol. 15 (Meicho Shuppan, 1978), 183.
95. Yasumaru Yoshio, *Kamigami no Meiji Ishin: Shinbutsu bunri to haibutsu kishaku* (Tokyo: Iwanami Shoten, 1979), 38.
96. Concerning these critiques, see Kashiwahara Yūsen, "Kinsei hai-Butsu no shisō," in *Kinsei Bukkyō no shisō*, ed. Kashiwahara Yūsen and Fujii Manabu (Tokyo: Iwanami shoten, 1973), 522–24. The English translation for the title of *Sōbō kigen* is adopted from Najita, *Visions of Virtue*, 171, and the translation for the title of *Keizai mondō hiroku* from Janine Anderson Sawada, *Confucian Values and Popular Zen: Sekimon Shingaku in Eighteenth-Century Japan* (Honolulu: University of Hawaii Press, 1993), 206n236.
97. The text is reproduced as "Shiryūgoto," in *Kinsei zuisō shū*, ed. Odaka Michiko and Suzuki Makoto, vol. 82, Shinpen Nihon koten bungaku zenshū (Tokyo: Shōgakukan, 2000). It may also be found as "Shiryūgoto," ed. Sekine Masanao, Wada Hidematsu, and Tanabe Katsuya, vol. 11, Nihon zuihitsu taisei dai 3-ki (Tokyo: Yoshikawa Kōbunkan, 1976).
98. An organizational chart for the Takakura Academy, as well as portraits of its first generations of lecturers, may be found in Otani Daigaku Shinshū Sōgō Kenkyujo Daigakushi Hensan Kenkyūshitsu, ed., *Ōtani Daigaku kindai 100-nen no ayumi* (Kyoto: Ōtani Daigaku, 1997), 16–17.
99. Kashiwahara Yūsen, ed., *Ishinki no Shinshū*, vol. 11, Shinshū shiryō shūsei (Kyoto: Dōhōsha Shuppan, 1983), 59.
100. Ibid., 58.
101. Ibid., 60.
102. Ibid., 67.
103. Ibid., 68.
104. Elsewhere the name of the organization has been rendered as "Institute for Apologetic Studies," which is also plausible. "Defense of the Dharma" is chosen here only for the sake of literalness. See Notto R. Thelle, *Buddhism and Christianity in Japan: From Conflict to Dialogue, 1854–1899* (Honolulu: University of Hawaii Press, 1987), 29.
105. Kashiwahara Yūsen and Fujii Manabu, eds., *Kinsei Bukkyō no shisō*, vol. 57, Nihon shisō taikei (Tokyo: Iwanami Shoten, 1973), 118.
106. Kashiwahara, *Ishinki no Shinshū*, 61.
107. Ibid., 72.
108. Mori Kazuya, "Kindai Bukkyō no jigazō to shite no gohōron," *Shūkyō kenkyū* 81, no. 2 (2007): 413.
109. Quoted in Ono Bunkō, "Udana Nichiki: Kindai Nichirenshū no senkakusha," in *Kindai Nichiren kyōgaku no shisōka: Kindai Nichiren kyōdan, kyōgakushi shiron*, ed. Nakano Kyōtoku (Tokyo: Kokusho Kankōkai, 1977), 58.

110. Quoted in Miyakawa Ikkyō, "Udana Nichiki ni okeru hai-Butsu ron ni tai suru shisei," *Indogaku Bukkyōgaku kenkyū* 21, no. 2 (1973): 192.
111. Ono, "Udana Nichiki," 56–57.
112. Miyakawa, "Udana Nichiki ni okeru hai-Butsu ron," 192.
113. Ono, "Udana Nichiki," 59.
114. One scholar has suggested that one work of Nichiki's could be read as a treatment of the same material as the *Mocking Discourse*. To be sure, this work by Nichiki's does address some of the same issues, but it does not seem to touch on the life of the Buddha. See Miyakawa, "Udana Nichiki ni okeru hai-Butsu ron," 192–93.
115. The one extant printed edition bears the marks of hasty production, including a considerable number of misprints and the extensive use of substitute characters in its final pages. A note attached to its conclusion explains that by the end, the printer had run out of the standard moveable type for some common terms. Jichōshi [Ryōgetsu], "Tsuiyō harae," in *Nihon shisō tōsō shiryō*, vol. 8, ed. Washio Junkyō (Tokyo: Meicho Kankōkai, 1975), 126.
116. Ibid., 302.
117. Ibid., 301.
118. Ibid., 307.
119. Ibid., 322.
120. Ibid., 309–10.
121. Ibid., 313.
122. Ibid., 316.
123. Ibid., 330.
124. Ibid., 320.
125. Ibid., 321.
126. Ibid., 327.
127. Ibid., 328.

CHAPTER FIVE

1. For the best study of these events in English, see Notto R. Thelle, *Buddhism and Christianity in Japan: From Conflict to Dialogue, 1854–1899* (Honolulu: University of Hawaii Press, 1987).
2. Joseph Edkins and Ukai Tetsujō, "Shakkyō shōmu shoha, Shakkyō shōmu saiha," in *Meiji Bukkyō shisō shiryō shūsei*, vol. 1, ed. Meiji Bukkyō Shisō Shiryō Shūsei Henshū Iinkai (Kyoto: Dōhōsha, 1980), 327.
3. Ibid., 328.
4. Ibid., 332.
5. Ibid., 323.
6. Ibid.
7. Ibid., 326.
8. Joseph Edkins, *Chinese Buddhism: A Volume of Sketches, Historical, Descriptive, and Critical* (London: Tribner, 1880), 99–100.

9. "Review: Chinese Buddhism: A Volume of Sketches," *The North China Herald and South China & Consular Gazette*, December 2, 1880, 512.
10. For an account of the course of this debate, see Hoshino Seiji, "Meiji 10-nendai ni okeru aru Buk-Ki ronsō no isō," *Shūkyōgaku ronshū*, no. 26 (2007): 37–65.
11. Little has been published about Takahashi in English, but see "Mr. Takahashi Goro," *The Churchman*, September 6, 1890, 290–91.
12. Takahashi Gorō, "Butsudō shinron," in *Kyōgihen: Tai-gairai shisō*, ed. Ishikawa Rikizan, vol. 6, Sōtōshū sensho (Kyoto: Dōhōsha, 1981), 80.
13. Ibid., 83.
14. Ibid., 84.
15. Ibid., 86.
16. Ibid., 55. Emphasis in the original.
17. Miura Shū, "Bukkyō kindaika no ichi sokumen: *Shakkyō shōmu shoha narabi ni saiha* o chūshin ni," *Taishō Daigaku Daigakuin kenkyū ronshū*, no. 27 (2003): 42.
18. Edkins and Ukai, "Shakkyō shōmu shoha," 325.
19. Fukuda Gyōkai, "Shakkyō shōmu saiha hi," in *Ronkōhen*, ed. Taishō Daigaku Fukuda Gyōkai Shōnin Zenshū Kankōkai, vol. 2, *Heisei shinshū Fukuda Gyōkai Shōnin zenshū* (Tokyo: USS Shuppan, 2009), 244.
20. "Shakkyō shōmu tenda," in *Nihon shisō tōsō shiryō*, ed. Washio Junkyō, vol. 10 (Tokyo: Meicho Kankōkai, 1969), 233.
21. Nōnin Hatsugan, "Bukai nanshin," in *Kyōgihen: Tai-gairai shisō*, ed. Ishikawa Rikizan, vol. 6, *Sōtōshū sensho* (Kyoto: Dōhōsha, 1981), 104.
22. Ibid., 112.
23. Ibid., 100.
24. Ibid., 167.
25. Ibid., 173.
26. Takahashi Gorō, "*Bukai nanshin* benmō," in Kyōgihen, vol. 6, 194.
27. Ibid., 207–8.
28. Murakami Senshō, *Daijō Bussetsu ron hihan* (Tokyo: *Kyōgihen*, 1903), 141.
29. Kawaguchi Kōfū, *Meiji zenki Sōtōshū no kenkyū* (Kyōto: Hōzōkan, 2002), 474.
30. This translation is adapted from Kathleen M. Staggs, "In Defense of Japanese Buddhism: Essays from the Meiji Period by Inoue Enryō and Murakami Senshō" (PhD diss., Princeton University, 1979), 351
31. Takahashi Gorō, "Tetsugakkan no kaikōshiki ni nozomite kanzuru tokoro ari isasaka sho shite kōko ni shisshi, awasete sokusei tetsugaku no ikan o ronben su," *Rikugō zasshi*, no. 81 (1886): 335.
32. Ibid.
33. Nōnin Hakugan, "Mukai nanshin," in *Kyōgihen: Tai-gairai shisō*, ed. Ishikawa Rikizan, vol. 6, Sōtōshū sensho (Kyoto: Dōhōsha, 1981), 174.
34. Revisionist scholarship by Bob Wakabayashi and Julia Adeney Thomas, among others, has complicated this conventional view. See Bob Tadashi Wakabayashi, "Katō Hiroyuki and Confucian Natural Rights, 1861–1870,"

Harvard Journal of Asiatic Studies 44, no. 2 (1984): 469–92; and Julia Adeney Thomas, *Reconfiguring Modernity: Concepts of Nature in Japanese Political Ideology* (Berkeley: University of California Press, 2001).

35. Yamamuro Shin'ichi, "Nihon gakumon no jizoku to tenkai," in *Gakumon to chishikijin*, ed. Matsumoto Sannosuke and Yamamuro Shin'ichi, vol. 10, Nihon kindai shisō taikei (Tokyo: Iwanami Shoten, 1988), 495–96.
36. Concerning the debate over historicism as a kind of relativism, see *A Companion to the Philosophy of History and Historiography*, ed. Aviezer Tucker (Chichester: Wiley-Blackwell, 2009), s.v. "Historicism," by Robert D'Amico.
37. For a sketch of the turn away from social Darwinism in late Meiji Japan, see Thomas, *Reconfiguring Modernity*, 176–78.
38. Concerning this text, see Orion Klautan, *Kindai Nihon shisō to shite no Bukkyō shigaku* (Kyōto: Hōzōkan, 2012), 86–87.
39. Until 1916, when Takakusu Junjirō (1866–1945) took the newly established chair of Sanskrit Studies within the Department of Philosophy, the content of "Indian Philosophy" lectures at the university actually centered on Buddhist materials recorded in Chinese, not in South Asian languages. See Sueki Fumihiko, *Kindai Nihon to Bukkyō* (Tokyo: Toransubyū, 2004), 219. The choice of name for the lecture series deferred to Christian sensibilities concerning instruction in Buddhism in Japan's national university. The Anglophone Christian community did indeed monitor the goings-on at the Department of Philosophy. A Christian student enrolled in the department offered an exhaustive discussion of the department's curriculum, its structure, its faculty, and their areas of specialty, in the September 1898 issue of the missionary journal *The Japan Evangelist*. "Out of 84 graduates (1886–1898) of the Philosophical [*sic*] Department," he noted, "only 4 are baptized Christians." Again: "The number of Buddhist graduates is three times more than the Christians." Okada Tetsuzō, "The Department of Philosophy in the Imperial University of Tokyo," *The Japan Evangelist* 5, no. 9 (September 1898), 280.
40. Ejima Naotoshi, "Tetsugakuteki Bukkyō kenkyū kara rekishiteki Bukkyō kenkyū e: Inoue Enryō to Murakami Senshō o rei to shite," *Taishō Daigaku Daigakuin kenkyū ronshū* 34 (2010): 244–57.
41. For a discussion of the various attempts in the Meiji period to determine the dates of the Buddha's life, see James Edward Ketelaar, "The Non-Modern Confronts the Modern: Dating the Buddha in Japan," *History and Theory*, no. 45 (2006): 62–79.
42. For the affirmation of the traditional dates, see Murakami Senshō, "Shakamuni Butsu shuttan nyūmetsu no gappi kō," *Bukkyō shirin* 1, no. 5: 316.
43. As was common practice, this journal normally serialized long pieces. The following list of citations gives only the bibliographic information for the first installment of each of these article series. Concerning the geography of ancient India, see Nanjō Bun'yū, "Indo kodai chiri," *Bukkyō shirin* 1, no. 1 (1894): 36–47; concerning King Aśoka, see Hata Toshiyuki,

"Asoka-ō," *Bukkyō shirin* 2, no. 19 (1895): 447–62; concerning King Kanishka, see Tokiwa Daijō, "Kanishika-ō," *Bukkyō shirin* 3, no. 26 (1896): 73–94; concerning Gaṇeśa, see Miyoshi Aikichi, "Daishō Kangiten kō," *Bukkyō shirin* 2, no. 22 (1896): 674–83.

44. See, for example, the treatment of Nanjō Bun'yū in the *Encyclopedia of Religion*, as the "Japanese Buddhist scholar who first introduced Sanskrit into Japan from Europe and laid the foundation for Western-style Sanskrit and Buddhist studies in Japan." *Encyclopedia of Religion*, ed. Lindsay Jones, Mircea Eliade, and Charles J. Adams (Detroit: Macmillan Reference USA, 2005), s.v. "Nanjō Bunyū," by Sengaku Mayeda.
45. Nanjō Bun'yū, *Kaikyūroku* (Tokyo: Daiyūkaku Shobō, 1927), 277–78.
46. "Hassō jōdō," *Tōyō tetsugaku* 3, no. 7 (1896); quote, ibid., 345.
47. Concerning Hori, see the following by Kasugai Shin'ya: "Indo to Nihon (4): Hori Shitoku no shisō to shōgai (1)," *Bukkyō Daigaku kenkyū kiyō*, no. 55 (1971): 63–132; "Indo to Nihon (5): Hori Shitoku no shisō to shōgai (2)," *Bukkyō Daigaku kenkyū kiyō*, no. 56 (1972): 59–118; "Ōnishi Ryōkei to Hori Shitoku: Ōnishi Ryōkei shokan o chūshin to shite," *Kōnan Joshi Daigaku kenkyū kiyō*, no. 11/12 (1975): 443–58; and *Indo: Kinkei to enkei* (Kyoto: Dōhōsha Shuppan, 1981), 192–222; see also Nakajima Takeshi, "Hori Shitoku: 20-seiki shotō no Indo netsu," in *Kindai Nihon no Bukkyōsha: Ajia taiken to shisō no hen'yō*, ed. Ogawara Masamichi (Tokyo: Keiō Gijuku Daigaku Shuppankai, 2010), 315–45. By comparison, Fujii's and Shimizu's lives remain incompletely documented by secondary scholarship in any language.
48. For the preceding information, see "Ōmiya Kōnin Bonji ten/Nichi-In kokkyō juritsu 60-shūnen, Ōmiya Kōnin seitan 140-nen," http://www.buddha-world.jp/file/pickup/vol012/index.html.
49. The list of works he cited is in Ōmiya Kōnin, "Shakamuni den," *Shimei yoka* 22, no. 1 (1909): 11–13.
50. Ibid., 9–11.
51. Ōmiya Kōnin, "Shakamuni den furoku (teihon)," *Shimei yoka* 22, no. 4 (1909): 7.
52. Ibid., 5. For the original Chinese text paraphrased here, see *T* 1509: 534a.
53. They used the fourth (1857) and fifth (1874–1875) British editions.
54. Fukukama Tatsuo, *Meiji shoki hyakka zensho no kenkyū* (Tokyo: Kazama Shobō, 1968), 45.
55. See the table in ibid., 49–53.
56. *Chambers's Information for the People* (Edinburgh: W. and R. Chambers, 1856–1858), s.v. "Mohammedanism—Hinduism—Buddhism," by William Chambers and Robert Chambers.
57. The original English prose used a number of South Asian names and terms, which Ōshima often left in phonetic transcription in the *kana* script. Thus he did not employ established Japanese equivalents for such proper nouns as "Kapilavastu," "Śuddhodana," or "Aśoka," but instead

transcribed them as the unfamiliar *Karirahasutsu, Shudodana*, and *Asoka*. In his attempts to translate English terms that themselves gloss Buddhist concepts, he tended to translate directly from the English instead of using established translations known in Japan. Thus the English "Four Sublime Verities"—still familiar today, however misleadingly, as the "Four Noble Truths"—became simply the "four great items" (*shidai setsumoku*), rather than the conventional "four sage truths" (*shi shōdai*). The English term "transmigration" became not *rinne, ruten*, or other standard Japanese equivalents for the Sanskrit *saṃsāra*, but merely "the movement of souls" (*konpaku iten*). In some cases, though, Ōshima did match English transcriptions of South Asian terms to their equivalents, and in other cases, he made (generally correct) guesses in interlinear notes; these names and terms included the standard Japanese equivalents for such terms as "Gautama," "Siddhartha," *preta* (hungry ghost), and *bhikṣu* (monk).

58. William Chambers and Robert Chambers, *Kaikyō oyobi Indokyō Bukkyō*, trans. Ōshima Sadamasu, Hyakka zensho (Tokyo: Monbushō, 1877), 85.
59. Lopez, *From Stone to Flesh*, 206.
60. James Clarke, "Bukkyō ronpyō," in *Meiji Bukkyō shisō shiryō shūsei*, vol. 4, ed. Meiji Bukkyō Shisō Shiryō Shūsei Henshū Iinkai (Kyōto: Dōhōsha Shuppan, 1980), 368.
61. Tomoko Masuzawa, *The Invention of World Religions: Or, How European Universalism Was Preserved in the Language of Pluralism* (Chicago: University of Chicago Press, 2005), 79.
62. Clarke, "Bukkyō ronpyō," 368.
63. Ibid.
64. James Freeman Clarke, *Ten Great Religions: An Essay in Comparative Theology* (Boston: James R. Osgood and Company, 1872), 139–140.
65. Clarke, "Bukkyō ronpyō," 369.
66. See Martin Collcutt, "The Image of Kannon as Compassionate Mother in Meiji Art and Culture," in *Challenging Past and Present: The Metamorphosis of Nineteenth-Century Japanese Art*, ed. Ellen P. Conant (Honolulu: University of Hawaii Press, 2006)
67. Clarke, "Bukkyō ronpyō," 370.
68. Clarke, *Ten Great Religions*, 149.
69. Clarke, "Bukkyō ronpyō," 381.
70. Ibid.
71. In the puppet-theater text for the *Original Ground of Śākyamuni*, the protagonist must be informed that he has attained awakening and become the Buddha. It is interesting to speculate about Ishikawa's reaction to that presentation.
72. T. W. Rhys Davids, *Bodai no hana*, trans. Kuwahara Keiichi (Kyoto: Kyoten Shoin, 1887), unpaginated preface.
73. Ibid., 13.
74. Judith Snodgrass, "Defining Modern Buddhism: Mr. and Mrs. Rhys Davids

and the Pāli Text Society," *Comparative Studies of South Asia, Africa and the Middle East* 27, no. 1 (2007): 191.

75. T. W. Rhys Davids, *Buddhism: Being a Sketch of the Life and Teachings of Gautama, the Buddha* (London: Society for Promoting Christian Knowledge, 1877), 16.
76. T. W. Rhys Davids, *Shakuson no shōgai oyobi sono kyōri*, trans. Akanuma Chizen (Tokyo: Muga Sanbō, 1911), 15.
77. Indeed, in 1885, the author and critic Tsubouchi Shōyō (1859–1935) would publish a treatise, *The Essence of the* Shōsetsu (*Shōsetsu shinzui*), in which he sought to redefine the *shōsetsu* along the lines of the nineteenth-century European novel.
78. Fujishima Ryōon [Tangaku], "Shōsetsuteki Shakuson," *Tōyō tetsugaku* 1, no. 6 (1894): 239.
79. Sakaino Kōyō, "Rekishiteki Bukkyō," *Bukkyō shirin* 1, no. 8 (1894): 509. For a discussion of later (1920s and 1930s) formulations of Japan's role in the academic study of Buddhism around the world, see Jacqueline Stone, "A Vast and Grave Task: Interwar Buddhist Studies as an Expression of Japan's Envisioned Global Role," in *Culture and Identity: Japanese Intellectuals during the Interwar Years*, ed. J. Thomas Rimer (Princeton, NJ: Princeton University Press, 1990), 217–33.
80. Reprinted in Akamatsu Tesshin and Fukushima Kanryū, eds., *Shin Bukkyō ronsetsushū hoi* (Kyoto: Nagata Bunshōdō, 1982), 759.
81. Reprinted in ibid., 778.
82. See Machimoto Tonkū, *Gōtō jūnishū kōyō: Ichimei Tōyō tetsugaku hikkei* (Kyoto: Nagata Bunshōdō, 1887). Despite recent scholarship on the *Bijou*, Matsuyama Matsutarō's biographical details remain obscure. See the discussion in Nakanishi Naoki and Yoshinaga Shin'ichi, *Bukkyō kokusai nettowāku no genryū: Kaigai Senkyōkai (1888-nen—1893-nen) no hikari to kage* (Kyoto: Sanninsha, 2015): 28–29.
83. Furukawa Isamu, "Kaigi jidai ni ireri," repr. in *Shinshū shisō no kindaika*, ed. Mori Ryūkichi, Shinshū shiryō shūsei, vol. 13 (Kyōto: Dōhōsha Shuppan, 1983), 485.
84. Ibid., 486.
85. For an overview of Saji's early career, see chap. 8 of Michel Mohr, *Buddhism, Unitarianism, and the Meiji Competition for Universality* (Cambridge, MA: Harvard University Asia Center, 2014).
86. These were Jesus Christ, Śākyamuni, Confucius, and Socrates. See Tsuchiya Hiromasa, "Naze Nihon Yuniterian Misshon wa shinten shinakatta no ka: Kurei Makōrī to Nihon Yuniterian Misshon (1)," *Keiō Gijuku Daigaku hiyoshi kiyō: Eigo Ei-Bei bungaku* 39 (2001), 113.
87. Saji Jitsunen, "Shakamuni Butsu ryakuden gairon," *Shūkyō*, no. 19 (1893): 15.
88. Ibid., 17.
89. Ibid., 18.

90. Katō Totsudō, *Daishō shaka* (Tokyo: Katō Kumaichirō, 1891), 1. For the English text, see John Young, *The Christ of History: An Argument Grounded in the Facts of His Life on Earth* (London: Longman, Brown, Green, and Longmans, 1855), B2.
91. Katō T., *Daishō shaka*, 1.
92. Ibid., 18–19.
93. Ibid., 39.
94. Concerning the exclusion of the gods, see ibid., 36. Concerning Māra's attack, see ibid., 54.
95. Ibid., 70.
96. For Fujii's place as the first graduate from the Honganji subdenomination, see Honda Tatsujirō, *Kinsei kōsō itsuden* (Tokyo: Morie Shoten, 1906), s.v. "Fujii Senshō."
97. On the marriage ceremony, see the reminiscence by Shimaji Mokurai, who served as the "matchmaker" or "go-between" (*nakōdo*) for Fujii and his bride, Inoue Mieko: Shimaji Morkuai, "Busshiki konrei," in *Shimaji Mokurai zenshū*, vol. 4 , ed. Futaba Kenkō and Fukushima Kanryū (Kyōto: Honganji Shuppanbu, 1976), 159.
98. Shimazaki Tōson, "Yashi no hakage," in *Tōson zenshū*, vol. 2 (Tokyo: Chikuma Shobō, 1966), 455–67.
99. See the account in his student Shimaji Daitō's (1875–1927) preface to the 1921 reprint of the *Short History*: Fujii Senshō and Shimaji Daitō, *Shūho Bukkyō shōshi* (Tokyo: Morie Shoten, 1921).
100. Fujii Senshō, "Bukkyō shōshi," in *Gendai Bukkyō meicho zenshū*, ed. Nakamura Hajime and Masutani Fumio, vol. 4 (Tokyo: Ryūbunkan, 1972), 85.
101. Ibid.
102. Ibid.
103. Ibid, 89.
104. Ibid.
105. Ibid., 90.
106. Ibid., 114.
107. Ibid.
108. Anesaki Masaharu, "Fujii-shi no Bukkyō shōshi," *Tetsugaku zasshi* 12, no. 120 (1897): 148.
109. Ibid., 157.
110. Shimaji Daitō, ed., *Aibai zenshū* (Tokyo: Morie Shoten, 1906), 675.
111. Edwin Arnold, *Ajia no kōki*, trans. Nakagawa Tarō (Tokyo: Kōkyō Shoin, 1890).
112. Edwin Arnold, *Daishō Shakamuni Butsu*, trans. Nakagawa Tarō et al. (Tokyo: Kōbunkan, 1911).
113. Judith Snodgrass, "*Budda no fukuin*: The Deployment of Paul Carus's *Gospel of Buddha* in Meiji Japan," *Japanese Journal of Religious Studies* 25, no. 3/4 (1998): 319–44.
114. "Kenshō Butsuga boshū, *Kaiga sōshi*, no. 105 (October 25, 1895), 3.

115. Furuta Ryō, ed., *Okakura Tenshin: Kindai bijutsu no shi*, vol. 209, *Bessatsu Taiyō Nihon no kokoro* (Tokyo: Heibonsha, 2013), 130; Izumi Takeo, "Kojin zō Shaka hassō zu," *Kokka*, no. 1263 (2001): 49.
116. An edition incorporating Japanese illustrations intended for use in Carus's book has been published as Paul Carus, *The Gospel of Buddha: According to Old Records*, rev. ed. (Chicago: Open Court, 2004).
117. Yamada Keichyu [Keichū], *Scenes from the Life of Buddha* (Chicago: Open Court, 1898).
118. Art Institute of Chicago, *Twenty-First Annual Report of the Trustees, for the Year Ending June 1, 1900* (Chicago: Art Institute, 1900) , 28.
119. Paul Carus, *Catalogue: Collection of Modern Japanese Water-Color Paintings by Keichyu Yamada: Illustrative Scenes from the Life of Buddha after "The Gospel of Buddha"* (Chicago: Open Court, 1899), 5.
120. Jeff Huebner, "Mystery of the Buddhas," *Chicago Reader* (April 20, 2006), 20–21.
121. Yamanashi Toshio, *Egakareta rekishi: Nihon kindai to "rekishiga" no jiba* (Kunitachi: Buryukke, 2005), 69.
122. Paul Carus, *The Gospel of Buddha According to Old Records*, 3rd rev. ed. (Chicago: Open Court, 1895, c1894), 17.
123. Aśvaghoṣa, *Life of the Buddha by Aśvaghoṣa*, trans. Patrick Olivelle, vol. 33, Clay Sanskrit Library (New York: New York University Press, 2008), 131.
124. Victoria Louise Weston, *Japanese Painting and National Identity: Okakura Tenshin and His Circle* (Ann Arbor: Center for Japanese Studies, University of Michigan, 2004), 147.
125. Ibid., 166.
126. For a compact summary of these critical remarks, see Narihara Yuki, "Katsuta Shōkin 'Shutsujo Shaka' no tokushitsu to imi ni kan-suru kōsatsu," in *Bukkyō bijutsu to rekishi bunka*, ed. Manabe Shunshō (Kyoto: Hōzōkan, 2005), 562.
127. Quoted in Nihon Bijutsuin Hyakunenshi Henshūshitsu, ed., *Nihon Bijutsuin hyakunenshi 1-kan jō (zuhan hen)* (Tokyo: Nihon Bijutsuin, 1989), 533.
128. Quoted in ibid.
129. Quoted in ibid., 530.
130. Quoted in ibid.
131. Quoted in Nihon Bijutsuin Hyakunenshi Henshūshitsu, ed., *Nihon Bijutsuin hyakunenshi 2-kan jō (zuhan hen)* (Tokyo: Nihon Bijutsuin, 1990), 499.
132. Quoted in ibid., 499–500.
133. Quoted in ibid., 500.
134. Satō Shino, "Yokoyama Taikan to Ajantā hekiga: 1903-nen saku *Shaka chichi ni au* o chūshin ni," *Indo kōko kenkyū*, no. 32 (2010–2011): 57–70.
135. Satō Shino, "Shaka to Sujātā," *Ajia yūgaku*, no. 21 (1999): 47–58.
136. Narihara, "Katsuta Shōkin 'Shutsujo Shaka.'"

137. Quoted in Nihon Bijutsuin Hyakunenshi Henshūshitsu, *Nihon Bijutsuin hyakunenshi 2-kan jō (zuhan hen)*, 816.
138. Quoted in Nitten Shi Hensan Iinkai, ed., *Bunten hen*, vol. 1, *Nitten shi* (Tokyo: Nitten, 1980), 89.
139. Quoted in Nihon Bijutsuin Hyakunenshi Henshūshitsu, ed., *Nihon Bijutsuin hyakunenshi 3-kan jō (zuhan hen)* (Tokyo: Nihon Bijutsuin, 1992), 753.
140. Among the first wave of enthusiasts for Carlyle was Takayama Chogyū, but the pool of readers grew as the Meiji period continued. Excluding commentaries and excerpts in magazines, six full or partial translations into Japanese of Carlyle's *On Heroes, Hero-Worship, and the Heroic in History* were published between 1893 and 1909. See Kawato Michiaki, "Tomasu Kārairu to Meiji no chishikijin: *Eiyū sūhairon* no juyō o megutte," *Eigo Ei-Bei bungaku*, no. 35 (1995): 395–96. For scholarship in English concerning the reception of Nietzsche in Meiji Japan, see Randolph Spencer Petralia, "Nietzsche in Meiji Japan: Culture Criticism, Individualism and Reaction in the 'Aesthetic Life' Debate of 1901–1903" (PhD diss., Washington University in St. Louis, 1981); and Graham Parkes, "The Early Reception of Nietzsche's Philosophy in Japan," in *Nietzsche and Asian Thought*, ed. Graham Parkes (Chicago: University of Chicago Press, 1991), 177–99.
141. Thomas Carlyle, *On Heroes, Hero-Worship, and the Heroic in History* (London: Chapman and Hall, Strand, 1842), 1.
142. See the series of articles beginning with Imanishi Junkichi, "Waga kuni saisho no 'Indo tetsugaku shi' kōgi (1): Inoue Tetsujirō no mikōkan sōkō," *Hokkaidō Daigaku Bungakubu kiyō* 39, no. 1 (1990): 1–82.
143. Inoue Tetsujirō, "Bukkyō no kenkyū ni tsukite," *Bukkyō*, no. 85 (1894): 17–22.
144. Lopez, *From Stone to Flesh*, 210. Concerning the European "discovery" of Buddhism as a "world religion," see chap. 4 of Masuzawa, *The Invention of World Religions*.
145. Inoue Tetsujirō, "Indo rekishi jō ni okeru Shaka no chii," *Zenshū*, no. 8 (1895): 10.
146. Inoue Tetsujirō, "Budda ron," *Dentō*, no. 186 (1897): 21.
147. Concerning this "African hypothesis," see chap. 3 of Lopez, *From Stone to Flesh*.
148. Concerning Müller's objections to racialized "Aryanism," see chap. 7 of Masuzawa, *The Invention of World Religions*.
149. Müller did not invent the term, but he did use it in a particular way as a category in his linguistic analyses. See chap. 7 of ibid.
150. Inoue Tetsujirō, "Shaka wa ikanaru shuzoku naru ka," *Taiyō* 1, no. 10 (1895): 157.
151. Ibid. For the abridged English-language version, see Inoue Tetsujirō, "To What Race Does Buddha Belong?," *Taiyō* 1, no. 12 (1895): 3–4.
152. See Naka Michiyo, "Shakashu no setsu ni tsukite Inoue Bungaku Hakushi ni shissu," *Shigaku zasshi* 6, no. 11 (1895): 58–68. This article was reprinted

as "Shakashu no setsu ni tsukite Inoue Bungaku Hakushi ni shissu," *Taiyō* 2, no. 2 (1896): 184–87.

153. Naka, "Shakashu no setsu ni tsukite," 60–65.
154. Ibid., 59.
155. Inoue Tetsujirō, "Shaka no sosen ni tsukite (Naka Michiyo shi ni kotau)," *Shigaku zasshi* 8, no. 4 (1897): 7–24. The article was also printed under a different title, whose first installment was "Shaka shu no kigen ni kansuru kōshō," *Taiyō* 3, no. 6 (1897): 41–46.
156. Inoue Tetsujirō, "Shaka no sosen ni tsukite (Naka Michiyo shi ni kotau) (kanketsu)," *Shigaku zasshi* 8, no. 5 (1897): 17.
157. Inoue Tetsujirō, "Shaka no sosen ni tsukite (Naka Michiyo shi ni kotau)," 8.
158. Inoue Tetsujirō, *Shakamuni den*, rprt. ed. (Tokyo: Bunmeidō, 1902), 2.
159. Ibid., 3.
160. Ibid., 4.
161. Ibid., unpaginated. This English translation of Schopenhauer's German derives from Arthur Schopenhauer, *The World as Will and Representation*, trans. E. F. J. Payne (New York: Dover Publications, 1966), vol. 1, 357.
162. Ibid., 10.
163. Ibid., 25.
164. Ibid., 41.
165. Ibid., 55.
166. Ibid., 70–71.
167. Ibid., 75.
168. Ibid., 79.
169. Ibid., 208–12.
170. Ibid., 83.
171. Ibid., 84–85.
172. Ibid., 187.
173. Ibid., 187–90.
174. Ibid., 190–91
175. Ibid., 206.
176. For a complete list of the titles and authors published through this series, see Tsuboya Zenshirō, *Hakubunkan gojū-nen shi* (Tokyo: Hakubunkan, 1937), 158–59.
177. Katsuo Kin'ya, *Denki jidō bungaku no ayumi: 1891 kara 1945-nen* (Kyoto: Mineruva Shobō, 1999), 102.
178. Quoted in ibid., 101.
179. Concerning Takayama's critique and his about-face, see Hanazawa Tetsufumi, *Takayama Chogyū: Rekishi o meguru geijutsu to ronsō* (Tokyo: Kanrin Shobō, 2013), 160–62.
180. Takayama Chogyū, *Shaka* (Tokyo: Hakubunkan, 1899), unpaginated preface.
181. Ibid., 2–3.

182. Ibid., 4.
183. Inoue Toshio, ed., *Kyōkasho shi*, vol. 2, Kokugo kyōiku shi shiryō (Tokyo: Tōkyō Hōrei Shuppan Kabushiki Kaisha, 1981), 252.
184. See the discussion of this book in the following teaching manual: Kōfūkan Henshūsho, ed. *Shihan kokubun: Daiichi buyō kyōju bikō*, 3rd rev. ed. (Tokyo: Kōfūkan Shoten, 1935), 101–16.
185. Concerning its lasting influence, see the remarks in Kimura Ki, "'Mono no aware' to tōzai Shakaden: Sekaiteki shiya ni oite no Meiji bungaku kōsatsu shiron," *Bunrin*, no. 10 (1976): 10–11.
186. Inoue, *Kyōkasho shi*, 266.
187. Inoue Tetsujirō, "Seijin ron," *Tō-A no hikari* 5, no. 9 (1910): 4–5.
188. Ibid., 16.
189. For a discussion of this point, see chap. 4 of Ōmi Toshihiro, *Kindai Bukkyō no naka no Shinshū: Chikazumi Jōkan to gudōshatachi* (Kyoto: Hōzōkan, 2014).
190. See the discussion in Wasaki Kōtarō, "Shoki Teiyū Rinrikai ni okeru rinriteki 'shūyō': Anesaki Masaharu to Ukita Kazutami ni chakumoku shite," *Kyōikushi fōramu*, no. 7 (2012): 3–17.
191. Anesaki Masaharu, *Fukkatsu no shokō* (Tokyo: Yūhōkan, 1904), 211–12.
192. Wasaki, "Shoki Teiyū Rinrikai," 5.
193. Anesaki Masaharu, *Genshinbutsu to hosshinbutsu* (Tokyo: Yūhōkan, 1904), 3.
194. Ibid., 13.
195. Ibid., 209.
196. Ibid., 223.
197. Maeda Eun, "Shakuson ni tai suru yo ga kansō," *Keisei* 160 (1909): 5.

CONCLUSION

1. See Daniel Boucher, "The *Pratītyasamutpādagāthā* and Its Role in the Medieval Cult of the Relics," *Journal of the International Association of Buddhist Studies* 14, no. 1 (1991): 1–27.
2. For a forceful exposition of this notion, see the introduction to Robert H. Sharf and Elizabeth Sharf, eds., *Living Images: Japanese Buddhist Icons in Context* (Palo Alto, CA: Stanford University Press, 2002).
3. For a pioneering study of the roles of relics of the Buddha in medieval Japan, see Brian Douglas Ruppert, *Jewel in the Ashes: Buddha Relics and Power in Early Medieval Japan* (Cambridge, MA: Harvard University Asia Center, 2000).
4. On the notion of the life of the Buddha Śākyamuni as a blueprint for all buddhas' lives, see John S. Strong, *The Buddha: A Short Biography* (Oxford: Oneworld, 2001).
5. Even the field of the repair of Buddhist sculpture transformed in the Meiji

period, a transfiguration exemplified in the person of Niiro Chūnosuke (1868–1954), a follower of Okakura's who became a key figure in the preservation of Buddhist images declared national treasures (*kokuhō*).

6. "Mozaiku," *Bijutsu shukan*, no. 80 (1915): 5.
7. Shinkai Taketarō, "Rerīfu (Taiheiyō Kaiga Tsukinamikai nite) shōzen," *Bijutsu Shinpō* 3, no. 21 (1905): 2.
8. I am indebted to my colleague Nachiket Chanchani for this observation.
9. The relevant regulation is in the third clause of Ministry of Education Directive No. 190, promulgated in 1909. Find it reproduced in Nihon Geijutsuin Jimukyoku, ed., *Nihon Geijutsuin shi* (Tokyo: Nihon Geijutsuin Jimukyoku, 1963), 275.
10. Taki Seiichi [Setsuan], "Tenrankai shokan (chū)," *Tōkyō Asahi shinbun*, October 27, 1915, 6.
11. Shinkai Taketarō, "Genkon no chōkoku ni tsuite," *Bijutsu shinpō*, January 5, 1903, 3.
12. Shinkai Taketarō, "Shaka hassō," *Chūō bijutsu* 1, no. 1 (1915): 35. Emphasis added.
13. See Tanaka Shūji, *Chōkokuka Shinkai Taketarō ron* (Tsuruoka: Tōhoku Shuppan Kikaku, 2002), 358–359.
14. Takashima Beihō, "Chōkokukai no senkusha," *Chūō bijutsu* 13, no. 4 (1927): 219.
15. Quoted in Migita Yūji, "Shaka no shōgai sōdai ni: Chōkokuka Nakamura Shin'ya san ga 'Hassō zuzō': Nara Yakushiji e 18-nendo hōnō," *Minami Nihon Shinbun*, January 5, 2014, 2.

Works Cited

Akamatsu Tesshin 赤松徹真 and Fukushima Kanryū 福嶋寛隆, eds. *Shin Bukkyō ronsetsushū hoi* 『新仏教』論説集補遺. Kyoto: Nagata Bunshōdō, 1982.

Akanuma, Chizen. *The Comparative Catalogue of Chinese Āgamas & Pāli Nikāyas*. Bibliotheca Indo-Buddhica. Nagoya: Hajinkaku Shobō, 1929.

Andō Fusae 安藤房枝. "Unkō dai-6 kutsu no zuzō kōsei ni tsuite: Butsuden zuzō ni shōten o atete 雲岡第6窟の圖像構成について: 佛傳圖像に焦點を當てて." *Tōhō gakuhō*, no. 85 (2010): 704–30.

Anesaki, Masaharu. *The Four Buddhist Āgamas in Chinese: A Concordance of Their Parts and of the Corresponding Counterparts in the Pāli Nikāyas*. Transactions of the Asiatic Society of Japan. Yokohama: Kelly & Walsh, 1908.

———. 姉崎正治. "Fujii-shi no Bukkyō shōshi 藤井氏の仏教小史." *Tetsugaku zasshi* 12, no. 120 (1897): 147–58.

———. *Fukkatsu no shokō* 復活の曙光. Tokyo: Yūhōkan, 1904.

———. *Genshinbutsu to hosshinbutsu* 現身仏と法身仏. Tokyo: Yūhōkan, 1904.

———. *History of Japanese Religion with Special Reference to the Social and Moral Life of the Nation*. London: K. Paul, Trench, Trübner, 1930.

Antoni, Klaus. "Does Shinto History 'Begin at Kuroda'? On the Historical Continuities of Political Shinto." In *Politics and Religion in Modern Japan: Red Sun, White Lotus*, edited by Roy Starrs, 84–103. New York: Palgrave Macmillan, 2011.

Aoyama Tadakazu 青山忠一. *Kinsei Bukkyō bungaku no kenkyū* 近世仏教文学の研究. Tokyo: Ōfū, 1999.

Arai Kōjun 新井弘順. "Nehan-e no hensen: Hōyō shidai o chūshin ni 涅槃会の変遷: 法要次第を中心に." In *Nehan-e no kenkyū: Nehan-e to Nehanzu*, edited by Gangōji Bunkazai Kenkyūjo, 21–32. Nara: Gangōji Bunkazai Kenkyūjo, 1981.

Araki Hiroshi 荒木浩. *Kakushite* Genji monogatari *ga tanjō suru: Monogatari ga ryūdō suru genba ni dō tachiau ka* かくして『源氏物語』が誕生する: 物語が流動する現場にどう立ち会うか. Tokyo: Kasama Shoin, 2014.

Araki Shigeru 荒木繁. "Sekkyō no seisui 説経の盛衰." In *Jōruri no tanjō to ko jōruri*, edited by Torigoe Bunzō, Yamauchi Mikiko and Watanabe Tamotsu, Iwanami kōza kabuki, Bunraku, vol. 7, 71–93. Tokyo: Iwanami Shoten, 1998.

———. "Sekkyōbushi no katarimono no keisei katei o meguru mondai: Bukkyō setsuwa-kei no katarimono no baai 説経節の語り物の形成過程をめぐる問題: 仏教説話系の語り物の場合." *Bungaku* 42, no. 9 (1974): 18–32.

Arami Hiroshi 荒見泰史. *Dunhuang jiangchang wenxue xieben yanjiu* 敦煌講唱文學寫本研究. Beijing: Zhonghua Shuju, 2010.

Arnold, Edwin. *Ajia no kōki* 亜細亜の光輝. Translated by Nakagawa Tarō. Tokyo: Kōkyō Shoin, 1890.

———. *Daishō Shakamuni Butsu* 大聖釈迦牟尼仏. Translated by Nakagawa Tarō et al. Tokyo: Kōbunkan, 1911.

Art Institute of Chicago, *Twenty-First Annual Report of the Trustees, for the Year Ending June 1, 1900*. Chicago: Art Institute, 1900. Exhibition catalog.

Asakura Haruhiko 朝倉治彦, ed. *Kanazōshi shūsei* 仮名草子集成. Vol. 35. Tokyo: Tōkyōdō Shuppan, 2004.

Aśvaghoṣa. *Life of the Buddha by Aśvaghoṣa*. Translated by Patrick Olivelle. Vol. 33. Clay Sanskrit Library. New York: New York University Press, 2008.

Atkinson, John Laidlaw. *Prince Siddartha: The Japanese Buddha*. Boston: Congregational Sunday-School and Pub. Society, 1893.

Atsumi Seitarō 渥美清太郎, ed. *Bakumatsu Edo kyōgen hen* 幕末江戸狂言篇. Nihon gikyoku zenshū, vol. 22. Tokyo: Shun'yōdō, 1930.

Augustine, Jonathan Morris. *Buddhist Hagiography in Early Japan: Images of Compassion in the Gyōki Tradition*. New York: RoutledgeCurzon, 2005.

Bagchi, P. C. "The Eight Great Caityas and Their Cult." *Indian Historical Quarterly* 17, no. 1 (1947): 223–35.

Barua, Beni Madhab. *A History of Pre-Buddhistic Indian Philosophy*. Calcutta: University of Calcutta, 1921.

Berry, Mary Elizabeth. *Japan in Print: Information and Nation in the Early Modern Period*. Berkeley: University of California Press, 2006.

Bielefeldt, Carl. "Expedient Devices, the One Vehicle, and the Life Span of the Buddha." In *Readings of the Lotus Sutra*, edited by Stephen F. Teiser and Jacqueline Ilyse Stone, 62–82. New York: Columbia University Press, 2009.

Boucher, Daniel. "The *Pratītyasamutpādagāthā* and Its Role in the Medieval Cult of the Relics." *Journal of the International Association of Buddhist Studies* 14, no. 1 (1991): 1–27.

Bussho Kankōkai 仏書刊行会, ed. *Jishi sōsho dai-1* 寺誌叢書第一. Dai-Nihon Bukkyō zensho, vol. 117. Tokyo: Bussho Kankōkai, 1913.

Buswell, Robert E., and Donald S. Lopez, eds. *The Princeton Dictionary of Buddhism*. Princeton, NJ: Princeton University Press, 2014.

Callahan, Christopher Thane. "Kakunyo and the Making of Shinran and Shin Buddhism." PhD diss., Harvard University, 2011.
Carlyle, Thomas. *On Heroes, Hero-Worship, and the Heroic in History*. London: Chapman and Hall, Strand, 1842.
Carr, Kevin Gray. "The Material Facts of Ritual: Revisioning Medieval Viewing through Material Analysis, Ethnographic Analogy, and Architectural History." In *A Companion to Asian Art and Architecture*, edited by Rebecca M. Brown and Deborah S. Hutton, 23–47. Chichester: Wiley-Blackwell, 2011.
———. *Plotting the Prince: Shōtoku Cults and the Mapping of Medieval Japanese Buddhism*. Honolulu: University of Hawaii Press, 2012.
Carus, Paul. *Catalogue: Collection of Modern Japanese Water-Color Paintings by Keichyu Yamada: Illustrative Scenes from the Life of Buddha after "The Gospel of Buddha."* Chicago: Open Court, 1899.
———. *The Gospel of Buddha According to Old Records*. 3rd rev. ed. Chicago: Open Court, 1895 (c1894).
———. *The Gospel of Buddha: According to Old Records*. Rev. ed. Chicago: Open Court, 2004.
Chamberlain, Basil Hall. *Things Japanese: Being Notes on Various Subjects Connected with Japan for the Use of Travellers and Others*. 2nd ed. London: K. Paul, Trench, Trübner, 1891.
Chambers, William, and Robert Chambers. "Mohammedanism—Hinduism—Buddhism." In *Chambers's Information for the People*. Edinburgh: W. and R. Chambers, 1856–1858.
———. *Kaikyō oyobi Indokyō Bukkyō* 回教及印度教仏教. Translated by Ōshima Sadamasu. Hyakka zensho. Tokyo: Monbushō, 1877.
Chan, Wing-tsit. *Chu Hsi: New Studies*. Honolulu: University of Hawaii Press, 1989.
———. *A Source Book in Chinese Philosophy*. Princeton, NJ: Princeton University Press, 1963.
Chappell, David. "Introduction to the 'T'ien-t'ai ssu-chiao-i.'" *Eastern Buddhist* 9, no. 1 (1976): 72–86.
Chatterjee, Paroma. *The Living Icon in Byzantium and Italy: The Vita Image, Eleventh to Thirteenth Centuries*. Cambridge: Cambridge University Press, 2014.
Chaudhuri, S. K. "India in Japanese Literature: A Case Study of Hirata Atsutane." *China Report* 21 (1985): 65–75.
Chikamatsu Monzaemon 近松門左衛門. "Shaka nyorai tanjō-e 釈迦如来誕生会." In *Chikamatsu zenshū*, edited by Chikamatsu Zenshū Kankōkai, vol. 8. Tokyo: Iwanami Shoten, 1988.
Ching, Julia. *The Religious Thought of Chu Hsi*. New York: Oxford University Press, 2000.
Cho Une 趙恩馤. "Kan-Nichi ni okeru 'Butsuden bungaku' no tenkai: Shaka to Yashudara no monogatari o chūshin ni 韓日における「仏伝文学」の展開: 釈迦と耶輸陀羅の物語を中心に." *Ilbon munhwa yŏn'gu*, no. 50 (2014): 331–46.

———. "Kankoku ni okeru Butsuden bungaku: Chōsa to kenkyū no genjō 韓国における仏伝文学: 調査と研究の現状." *Ajia yūgaku*, no. 79 (2005): 33–45.

Ch'oe Yŏnsik. "Chosŏn hugi *Sŏkssi wŏllyu* ŭi suyong gwa Pulgyogye e mich'in yŏnghyang 朝鮮後期『釋氏源流』의 수용과 佛教界에 미친 영향." *Pojo sasang*, no. 11 (1998): 303–66.

Chŏng Sŏngu. "*Sŏkka yŏrae haengjŏk song* yŏn'gu: *Puljo t'onggi* wa pigyo hayŏ." Master's thesis, Tongguk Taehakkyo, 2007.

Clark, Timothy. *Demon of Painting: The Art of Kawanabe Kyōsai*. London: British Museum Press, 1993.

Clarke, James. "Bukkyō ronpyō 仏教論評." Translated by Yamazaki Hisatarō. In *Meiji Bukkyō shisō shiryō shūsei*, edited by Meiji Bukkyō Shisō Shiryō Shūsei Henshū Iinkai, vol. 4, 367–406. Kyoto: Dōhōsha Shuppan, 1980.

———. *Ten Great Religions: An Essay in Comparative Theology*. Boston: James R. Osgood, 1872.

Cole, Alan. *Mothers and Sons in Chinese Buddhism*. Stanford, CA: Stanford University Press, 1998.

Collcutt, Martin. "The Image of Kannon as Compassionate Mother in Meiji Art and Culture." In *Challenging Past and Present: The Metamorphosis of Nineteenth-Century Japanese Art*, edited by Ellen P. Conant, 197–224. Honolulu: University of Hawaii Press, 2006.

Como, Michael I. *Shōtoku: Ethnicity, Ritual, and Violence in the Japanese Buddhist Tradition*. Oxford: Oxford University Press, 2008.

D'Amico, Robert. "Historicism." In *A Companion to the Philosophy of History and Historiography*, edited by Aviezer Tucker. Chichester: Wiley-Blackwell, 2009.

Davids, T. W. Rhys. *Bodai no hana* 菩提の花. Translated by Kuwahara Keiichi. Kyoto: Kyoten Shoin, 1887.

———. *Buddhism: Being a Sketch of the Life and Teachings of Gautama, the Buddha*. London: Society for Promoting Christian Knowledge, 1877.

———. *Shakuson no shōgai oyobi sono kyōri* 釈尊の生涯及其教理. Translated by Akanuma Chizen. Tokyo: Muga Sanbō, 1911.

De Bary, William Theodore, et al. *Sources of Chinese Tradition*. Introduction to Asian Civilization. 2nd ed. 2 vols. New York: Columbia University Press, 1999.

Deal, William E. "Hagiography and History: The Image of Prince Shōtoku." In *Religions of Japan in Practice*, edited by George Joji Tanabe, 316–33. Princeton, NJ: Princeton University Press, 1999.

Deeg, Max. "Chips from a Biographical Workshop: Early Chinese Biographies of the Buddha." In *Lives Lived, Lives Imagined: Biography in the Buddhist Traditions*, edited by Linda Covill, Ulrike Roesler, and Sarah Shaw, 49–87. Somerville: Wisdom Publications, 2010.

Dobbins, James C. "The Many Faces of Shinran: Images from D. T. Suzuki and *The Eastern Buddhist*." *Eastern Buddhist* 42, no. 2 (2011): 1–24.

Doi Tsugiyoshi 土居次義. *Kinsei Nihon kaiga no kenkyū* 近世日本絵画の研究. Tokyo: Bijutsu Shuppansha, 1970.

Donohashi Akio 百橋明穂. *Butsudenzu* 仏伝図. Nihon no bijutsu, vol. 267. Tokyo: Shibundō, 1988.

———. "Tsurugi Jinja zō hassō nehan zu 剱神社蔵 八相涅槃図." *Kokka*, no. 1263 (2001): 46–48.

Durt, Hubert. "The Birth of the Buddha in the Chinese Anthologies of the Early Sixth Century." In *The Birth of the Buddha: Proceedings of the Seminar Held in Lumbini, Nepal, October 2004*, edited by Christoph Cüppers, Max Deeg, and Hubert Durt, 277–304. Lumbini: Lumbini International Research Institute, 2010.

———. *Problems of Chronology and Eschatology: Four Lectures on the Essay on Buddhism by Tominaga Nakamoto*. Kyoto: Istituto Italiano di Cultura, Scuola di Studi sull'Asia Orientale, 1994.

———. "The *Shijiapu* of Sengyou: The First Chinese Attempt to Produce a Critical Biography of the Buddha." *Kokusai Bukkyō Daigakuin Daigaku kenkyū kiyō* 10 (2006): 51–85.

Dykstra, Yoshiko Kurata, ed. *The Konjaku Tales, Indian Section (1)*. Hirakata: Maruzen, 1986.

———. "Shinto Tales." *Journal of Intercultural Studies*, no. 5 (1978): 67–88.

Eastman, Alvan C. "Some Steles of the Pala Period Containing the Eight Miracles of Buddha with Notes on the Variations: Part One." *Art in America and Elsewhere* 18, no. 6 (1930): 271–83.

Edkins, Joseph, and Ukai Tetsujō 養鸕徹定. "Shakkyō shōmu shoha, Shakkyō shōmu saiha 釈教正謬初破·釈教正謬再破." In *Meiji Bukkyō shisō shiryō shūsei*, edited by Meiji Bukkyō Shisō Shiryō Shūsei Henshū Iinkai, vol. 1. Kyoto: Dōhōsha, 1980.

"Edo-ki no hangi 3500-mai hakken: Kyōto Bukkōji, Inga monogatari mo 江戸期の版木3500枚発見: 京都·佛光寺、因果物語も." *Asahi shinbun*, October 11, 2003, 1.

Ejima Naotoshi 江島尚俊. "Tetsugakuteki Bukkyō kenkyū kara rekishiteki Bukkyō kenkyū e: Inoue Enryō to Murakami Senshō o rei to shite 哲学的仏教研究から歴史的仏教研究へ: 井上円了と村上専精を例として." *Taishō Daigaku Daigakuin kenkyū ronshū* 34 (2010): 244–57.

Emmerich, Michael. *The Tale of Genji: Translation, Canonization, and World Literature*. New York: Columbia University Press, 2013.

Enoki Katsurō 榎克朗. *Nihon Bukkyō bungaku to kayō* 日本仏教文学と歌謡. Tokyo: Kasama Shoin, 1994.

En'ya Kikumi 塩谷菊美. *Katarareta Shinran* 語られた親鸞. Kyoto: Hōzōkan, 2011.

Fan, Jinshi. *The Caves of Dunhuang*. Translated by Susan Whitfield. Hong Kong: Dunhuang Academy, 2010.

Fan Jinshi 樊錦詩 and Ma Shichang 馬世長. "Bakkōkutsu dai-290 kutsu no Butsudenzu 莫高窟第二九〇窟の仏伝図." Translated by Yasuda Haruki. *Tōyō gakujutsu kenkyū* 25, no. 2 (1986): 134–76.

———. "Mogao ku di-290 ku de Fozhuan gushihua 莫高窟第290窟的佛传故事画." *Dunhuang yanjiu* 1, no. 3 (1983): 56–82.

Foulk, T. Griffith. "Sung Controversies Concerning the 'Separate Transmission' of Ch'an." In *Buddhism in the Sung*, edited by Peter N. Gregory and Daniel A. Getz Jr., 220–94. Honolulu: University of Hawaii Press, 1999.

Frazier, Alison Knowles. *Possible Lives: Authors and Saints in Renaissance Italy.* New York: Columbia University Press, 2004.

Fujii Otoo 藤井乙男. *Chikamatsu Monzaemon* 近松門左衛門. Tokyo: Kinkōdō Shoseki Kabushiki Kaisha, 1904.

Fujii Senshō 藤井宣正. "Bukkyō shōshi 仏教小史." In *Gendai Bukkyō meicho zenshū*, edited by Nakamura Hajime and Masutani Fumio, vol. 4, 81–304. Tokyo: Ryūbunkan, 1972.

Fujii Senshō 藤井宣正 and Shimaji Daitō 島地大等. *Shūho Bukkyō shōshi* 修補仏教小史. Tokyo: Morie Shoten, 1921.

Fujishima Ryōon [Tangaku] 藤島了穏［胆岳］. "Shōsetsuteki Shakuson 小説的釈尊." *Tōyō tetsugaku* 1, no. 6 (1894): 238–39.

Fukuda Gyōkai 福田行誡. "Shakkyō shōmu saiha hi 釈教正謬再破批." In *Ronkōhen*, edited by Taishō Daigaku Fukuda Gyōkai Shōnin Zenshū Kankōkai, Heisei shinshū Fukuda Gyōkai Shōnin zenshū, vol. 2, 244–51. Tokyo: USS Shuppan, 2009.

Fukukama Tatsuo 福鎌達夫. *Meiji shoki hyakka zensho no kenkyū* 明治初期百科全書の研究. Tokyo: Kazama Shobō, 1968.

Fukushima Kazuto 福島和人. *Kindai Nihon no Shinran: Sono shisō shi* 近代日本の親鸞: その思想史. Kyoto: Hōzōkan, 1973.

Fumoto Yasutaka 麓保孝, ed. *Shushi no senku (jō)* 朱子の先駆（上）. Shushigaku taikei, vol. 2. Tokyo: Meitoku Shuppansha, 1978.

Funayama Tōru 舟山徹. *Butten wa dō kan'yaku sareta no ka: Sūtora ga kyōten ni naru toki* 仏典はどう漢訳されたのか: スートラが経典になるとき. Tokyo: Iwanami Shoten, 2013.

Furukawa Isamu 古河勇. "Kaigi jidai ni ireri 懐疑時代に入れり." Reprinted in *Shinshū shisō no kindaika*, edited by Mori Ryūkichi, Shinshū shiryō shūsei, vol. 13, 485–88. Kyoto: Dōhōsha Shuppan, 1983.

Furuta Ryō 古田亮, ed. *Okakura Tenshin: Kindai bijutsu no shi* 岡倉天心: 近代美術の師. Vol. 209, Bessatsu Taiyō Nihon no kokoro. Tokyo: Heibonsha, 2013.

Furuya Chishin 古谷知新, ed. *Shaka go-ichidaiki zue (Kōkadō cho, Katsushika Hokusai ga), Nichiren shōnin ichidai zue (Nakamura Keinen cho, Katsushika Hokusai ga)* 釈迦御一代記図会（好華堂著 葛飾北斎画）日蓮上人一代図会（中村経年著 葛飾北斎画） Nihon rekishi zue, vol. 8. Tokyo: Kokumin Tosho, 1920.

Glassman, Hank. "Shaka no Honji: Preaching, Intertextuality, and Popular Hagiography." *Monumenta Nipponica* 62, no. 3 (2007): 299–321.

Gotō Akio 後藤昭雄. "Kyōjiden: Ichi Tendai sō no kaita Butsuden 教児伝: 一天台僧の書いた仏伝." In *Eizan no waka to setsuwa*, edited by Arai Eizō, Watanabe Sadamaro, and Terakawa Machio, 102–20. Kyoto: Sekai Shisōsha, 1991.

Gotō Kenji 後藤憲二, ed. *Kinsei katsujiban zuroku* 近世活字版図録. Nihon shoshigaku taikei, vol. 61. Musashi Murayama: Seishōdō, 1990.

Graham, Thomas Edward. "The Reconstruction of Popular Buddhism in Medieval China Using Selected *Pien-Wen* from Tun-Huang." PhD diss., University of Iowa, 1975.

Groner, Paul. "Icons and Relics in Eison's Religious Activities." In *Living Images: Japanese Buddhist Icons in Context*, edited by Robert H. Sharf and Elizabeth Horton Sharf, 114–50. Stanford, CA: Stanford University Press, 2001.

———. "Vicissitudes in the Ordination of Japanese 'Nuns' during the Eighth through Tenth Centuries." In *Engendering Faith: Women and Buddhism in Premodern Japan*, edited by Barbara Ruch, 65–108. Ann Arbor: Center for Japanese Studies, University of Michigan, 2002.

Haga Noboru 芳賀登. "Hirata Atsutane no Bukkyō hihan: Toku ni Shinteki nishū hihan o chūshin ni suete 平田篤胤の仏教批判: とくに神敵二宗批判を中心にすえて." In *Nihon bunkashi kenkyū: Haga Kōshirō Sensei koki kinen*, edited by Haga Kōshirō Sensei Koki Kinen Ronbunshū Henshū Iinkai, 263–92. Tokyo: Kasama Shoin, 1980.

Hanazawa Tetsufumi 花澤哲文. *Takayama Chogyū: Rekishi o meguru geijutsu to ronsō* 高山樗牛: 歴史をめぐる芸術と論争. Tokyo: Kanrin Shobō, 2013.

Hansen, Wilburn. *When Tengu Talk: Hirata Atsutane's Ethnography of the Other World*. Honolulu: University of Hawaii Press, 2008.

Hashiguchi Kōnosuke 橋口侯之介. *Edo no hon'ya to honzukuri: Zoku Wahon nyūmon* 江戸の本屋と本づくり: 〈続〉和本入門. Tokyo: Heibonsha, 2011.

Hata Toshiyuki 秦敏之. "Asoka-ō 阿恕伽王." *Bukkyō shirin* 2, no. 19 (1895): 17–32.

Hayashi Kyōhei 林京平. "Shaka Nyorai tanjō-e 釈迦如来誕生会." In *Sōgō Nihon gikyoku jiten*, edited by Kawatake Shigetoshi, 291. Tokyo: Heibonsha, 1964.

Hayashi Masahiko 林雅彦. "Kankoku ni okeru *Shakushi genryū ōka jiseki* no igi: Hyōshi kaisetsu ni kaete 韓国における『釈氏源流応化事蹟』の意義: 表紙解説にかえて." *Etoki kenkyū* 13 (1997): 64–69.

Henderson, Gregory, and Leon Hurvitz. "The Buddha of Seiryōji: New Finds and New Theory." *Artibus Asiae* 19, no. 1 (1956): 4–55.

Henry, Joni. "Humanist Hagiography in England, c. 1480–c. 1520." *Literature Compass* 10, no. 7 (2013): 535–43.

Hibi Shigejirō 日比繁治郎, ed. *Shōchiku Kansai engeki shi* 松竹関西演劇誌. Osaka: Shōchiku Hensanbu, 1940.

Hirai Yūkei 平井宥慶. "Taishi zuiō hongikyō kaidai 太子瑞応本起経　解題." In *Taishi zuiō hongikyō, Bussho gyōsan*, Shin kokuyaku daizōkyō, vol. Hon'enbu 1, 7–51. Tokyo: Daizō Shuppan, 2002.

Hirata Atsutane 平田篤胤. "Indo zōshi 印度蔵志." In *Shinshū Hirata Atsutane zenshū*, edited by Hirata Atsutane Zenshū Kankōkai, vol. 11, 7–385. Tokyo: Meicho Shuppan, 1977.

———. "Indo zōshi kō 印度蔵志稿." In *Shinshū Hirata Atsutane zenshū*, edited by Hirata Atsutane Zenshū Kankōkai, vol. 11, 387–571. Tokyo: Meicho Shuppan, 1977.

———. "Shinji hifumi den 神字日文伝." In *Hirata Atsutane zenshū*, edited by

Hirata Atsutane Zenshū Kankōkai, vol. 15, 175–242. Tokyo: Meicho Shuppan, 1978.

———. “Shutsujō shōgo 出定笑語.” In *Shinshū Hirata Atsutane zenshū*, edited by Hirata Atsutane Zenshū Kankōkai, vol. 10, 277–410. Tokyo: Meicho Shuppan, 1977.

———. “Zoku Shintō taii 俗神道大意.” In *Shinshū Hirata Atsutane zenshū*, edited by Hirata Atsutane Zenshū Kankōkai, vol. 8. Tokyo: Meicho Shuppan, 1977.

Hirata Atsutane Zenshū Kankokai 平田篤胤全集刊行会, ed. *Shinshū Hirata Atsutane zenshū* 新修平田篤胤全集. 21 vols. Tokyo: Meicho Shuppan, 1977.

Hokazono Kōichi 外薗幸一. “Butsuden kyōten no keisei katei ni tsuite 仏伝経典の形成過程について.” *Kagoshima Keidai ronshū* 24, no. 3 (1983): 47–69.

Honda Tatsujirō 本多辰次郎. “Fujii Senshō 藤井宣正.” In *Kinsei kōsō itsuden* 近世高僧逸伝. Tokyo: Morie Shoten, 1906.

Horton, Sarah J. *Living Buddhist Statues in Early Medieval and Modern Japan*. New York: Palgrave Macmillan, 2007.

Hoshino Seiji 星野靖二. “Meiji 10-nendai ni okeru aru Buk-Ki ronsō no isō 明治十年代におけるある仏基論争の位相.” *Shūkyōgaku ronshū*, no. 26 (2007): 37–65.

Huang Zheng 黃征 and Zhang Yongquan 張涌泉. *Dunhuang bianwen jiaozhu* 敦煌變文校注. Beijing: Zhonghua Shuju, 1997.

Huebner, Jeff. “Mystery of the Buddhas.” *Chicago Reader*, April 20, 2006, 20–21.

Hunter, Harriet Jean. “The Japanese *Hasso* Nirvana Tradition of Paintings: An Iconological Study.” Master’s thesis, University of British Columbia, 1986.

Huntington, John C. “Pilgrimage as Image: The Cult of the *Aṣṭamahāprātihārya*, Part II.” *Orientations* 18, no. 8 (August 1987): 56–68.

Hurvitz, Leon. *Scripture of the Lotus Blossom of the Fine Dharma*. New York: Columbia University Press, 1976.

Ikawa Kazuko 猪川和子. “Ehime no Seiryōji-shiki Shaka Nyorai zō 愛媛の清涼寺式釈迦如来像.” *Bijutsu kenkyū*, no. 330 (1984): 37–42.

———. “Kantō no Seiryōji-shiki Shaka zō 関東の清涼寺式釈迦如来像.” *Bijutsu kenkyū*, no. 237 (1964): 145–57.

———. “Saikoku no Seiryōji-shiki Shaka Nyorai zō ge 西国の清涼寺式釈迦如来像下.” *Bijutsu kenkyū*, no. 327 (1984): 174–84.

———. “Saikoku no Seiryōji-shiki Shaka Nyorai zō jō 西国の清涼寺式釈迦如来像上.” *Bijutsu kenkyū*, no. 324 (1984): 39–46.

Ikeda Toraku 池田都楽. *Daishō Shakuson go-ichidai ki* 大聖釈尊御一代記. Tokyo: Ikeda, Kenkichi, 1903.

Imanishi Junkichi 今西順吉. “Waga kuni saisho no ‘Indo tetsugaku shi’ kōgi (1): Inoue Tetsujirō no mikōkan sōkō わが国最初の「印度哲学史」講義 (一) : 井上哲次郎の未公刊草稿.” *Hokkaidō Daigaku Bungakubu kiyō* 39, no. 1 (1990): 1–82.

“Indo Busseki gentō kyōji kai 印度仏跡幻燈教示会.” *Yomiuri shinbun*, March 20, 1886.

Inoue Tadashi 井上正. “Kenkyū zadankai ‘“Tanjō to nehan” no bijutsu’ 研究座談会「“誕生と涅槃”の美術」.” In *Tanjō to Nehan no bijutsu: Kenkyū happyō to zadankai*, edited by Hayashiya Tatsusaburō. Kyoto: Bukkyō Bijutsu Kenkyū Ueno Kinen Zaidan, 1980.

Inoue, Takami. "Local Buddhism and Its Transformation in Nineteenth Century Japan: *Shinbutsu Bunri* in Shinano Province." PhD diss., University of California, Santa Barbara, 2010.

Inoue Tetsujirō 井上哲次郎. "Budda ron 仏陀論." *Dentō*, no. 186 (1897): 20–23.

———. "Bukkyō no kenkyū ni tsukite 仏教の研究に就て." *Bukkyō*, no. 85 (1894): 17–22.

———. "Indo rekishi jō ni okeru Shaka no chii 印度歴史上に於ける釈迦の地位." *Zenshū*, no. 8 (1895): 5–12.

———. "Seijin ron 聖人論." *Tō-A no hikari* 5, no. 9 (1910): 1–17.

———. "Shaka no sosen ni tsukite (Naka Michiyo shi ni kotau) 釈迦の祖先に就きて（那珂通世氏に答ふ）." *Shigaku zasshi* 8, no. 4 (1897): 7–24.

———. "Shaka no sosen ni tsukite (Naka Michiyo shi ni kotau) (kanketsu) 釈迦の祖先に就きて（那珂通世氏に答ふ）（完結）." *Shigaku zasshi* 8, no. 5 (1897): 1–18.

———. "Shaka shu no kigen ni kansuru kōshō 釈迦種の起原に関する考証." *Taiyō* 3, no. 6 (1897): 41–46.

———. "Shaka wa ikanaru shuzoku naru ka 釈迦は如何なる種族なるか." *Taiyō* 1, no. 10 (1895): 150–57.

———. *Shakamuni den* 釈迦牟尼伝. Reprint ed. Tokyo: Bunmeidō, 1902.

———. "To What Race Does Buddha Belong?." *Taiyō* 1, no. 12 (1895): 3–4.

Inoue Toshio 井上敏夫, ed. *Kyōkasho shi* 教科書史. Kokugo kyōiku shi shiryō, vol. 2. Tokyo: Tōkyō Hōrei Shuppan Kabushiki Kaisha, 1981.

Iriya Yoshitaka 入矢義高, ed. *Bukkyō bungaku shū* 仏教文学集. Chūgoku koten bungaku taikei, vol. 60. Tokyo: Heibonsha, 1975.

Ishida Ichirō 石田一良. "Hayashi Razan no shisō 林羅山の思想." In *Fujiwara Seika, Hayashi Razan*, edited by Ishida Ichirō and Kataya Osamu. Nihon shisō taikei, vol. 28, 471–89. Tokyo: Iwanami Shoten, 1975.

Ishizawa Yoshiaki 石澤良昭. "Rakugaki to rekishi: 17-seiki ni Ankōru Watto ni sankei shita Nihonjin 落書きと歴史—17世紀にアンコール・ワットに参詣した日本人," *Bunkachō geppō* 309 (1994): 20–21.

Itō Shundō 伊藤俊道. *Shaka jitsu denki* 釈迦実伝記. Tokyo: Morie Shoten, 1902.

Itō Yuishin 伊藤唯真. "Kanbutsu-e to kuge 灌仏会と供花." In *Bukkyō nenjū gyōji*, edited by Itō Yuishin. Bukkyō minzokugaku taikei, vol. 6, 79–96. Tokyo: Meicho Shuppan, 1986.

Iwamoto Yutaka 岩本裕. "Tonkō ni okeru Butsuden, honshōtan 敦煌における仏伝・本生譚." In *Tonkō no bungaku bunken*. Vol. 9, Kōza Tonkō, edited by Kanaoka Shōkō, 429–58. Tokyo: Daitō Shuppansha, 1990.

Iyanaga, Nobumi. "Medieval Shintō as a Form of 'Japanese Hinduism': An Attempt at Understanding Early Medieval Shintō." *Cahiers d'Extrême-Asie* 16 (2006–2007): 263–304.

——— 彌永信美. "Yuiitsu no kami to hitotsu no sekai: Kindai shoki Nihon to Furansu ni okeru hikaku shinwagaku no hajimari 唯一の神と一つの世界." In *"Hitotsu no sekai" no seiritsu to sono jōken*, edited by Nakagawa Hisayasu, 165–240. Kizugawa: Kokusai Kōtō Kenkyūjo, 2007.

Izumi Takeo 泉武夫. "Kojin zō Shaka hassō zu 個人藏釈迦八相図." *Kokka*, no. 1263 (2001): 49–50.

Izumoji Osamu 出雲路修. "Gōtama Budda no tanjō: Butsuden no hen'yō o megutte ゴータマ·ブッダの誕生: 仏伝の変容をめぐって." *Setsuwa denshōgaku*, no. 7 (1999): 1–10.

Jaffe, Richard M. "Seeing Śākyamuni: Travel and the Reconstruction of Japanese Buddhism." *Journal of Japanese Studies* 30, no. 1 (2004): 65–96.

Jichōshi [Ryōgetsu] 治鳥子［良月］. "Tsuiyō harae 追蝿払." In *Nihon shisō tōsō shiryo*, edited by Washio Junkyō, vol. 8, 299–426. Tokyo: Meicho Kankōkai, 1975.

Jin Taikuan 金泰寬. "Dunhuang bianwen *Taizi chengdao jing, Baxiang bianwen, Po mo bianwen, Xiang mo bian* yu Fojing bijiao yanjiu 敦煌變文「太子成道經」、「八相變」、「破魔變文」、「降魔變文」與佛經比較研究." Master's thesis, Guoli Zhengzhi Daxue, 1984.

Jin Weinuo 金维诺. *Shuanglinsi caisu* 双林寺彩塑. 2nd ed. Tianjin: Tianjin Renmin Chubanshe, 2007.

Jiun Sonja 200-kai Onki no Kai 慈雲尊者二百回遠忌の会, ed. *Shinjitsu no hito Jiun Sonja: Shakuson hitosuji no shōgai to sono oshie* 真実の人慈雲尊者: 釈尊ひとすじの生涯とその教え. Tokyo: Daihōrinkaku, 2004.

Jōdoshū Daijiten Hensan Iinkai 浄土宗大辞典編纂委員会, ed. *Jōdoshū daijiten* 浄土宗大辞典. Vol. 3. Tokyo: Jōdoshū Daijiten Kankōkai, 1974.

Kabushiki Kaisha G. B. 株式会社 G. B. et al., eds. *Budda no kotoba: Budda to Nihonjin* ブッダの言葉 仏陀と日本人. Tokyo: Tokuma Shoten, 2012.

Kajitani Ryōji 梶谷亮治. "Butsudenzu no tenkai: Bukkyō setsuwa-e no hyōgen to tekisuto 仏伝図の展開: 仏教説話絵の表現とテキスト." In *Engi-e to nise-e*, edited by Nakano Masaki, 158–68. Tokyo: Kōdansha, 1993.

Kamens, Edward. *The Three Jewels: A Study and Translation of Minamoto Tamenori's Sanbōe*. Ann Arbor: Center for Japanese Studies, University of Michigan, 1988.

Kaminishi, Ikumi. *Explaining Pictures: Buddhist Propaganda and Etoki Storytelling in Japan*. Honolulu: University of Hawaii Press, 2006.

"'Kanazōshi' 'otogizōshi' hangi hatsu hakken: Kyōto no tera, danka e no seppō ni shiyō? 「仮名草子」「御伽草子」版木初発見: 京都の寺、檀家への説法に使用? " *Sankei shinbun*, October 12, 2003, 29.

Kanmuri Ken'ichi 冠賢一. *Kinsei Nichirenshū shuppanshi kenkyū* 近世日蓮宗出版史研究. Kyoto: Heirakuji Shoten, 1983.

Kanno Hiroshi 菅野博史. "Hirata Atsutane no *Indo zōshi* to Bukkyō kenkyū no igi 平田篤胤の『印度蔵志』と仏教研究の意義." In *Kinsei no seishin seikatsu*, edited by Ōkura Seishin Bunka Kenkyūjo, 697–734. Tokyo: Zoku Gunsho Ruijū Kanseikai, 1996.

Kansai Daigaku Toshokan 関西大学図書館, ed. *Aohon kurohon shū* 青本黒本集. Kansai Daigaku Toshokan eiin sōsho Dai 1-ki, vol. 7. Suita: Kansai Daigaku Shuppanbu, 1997.

Karetzky, Patricia Eichenbaum. "A Chinese Illustration of the *Guoqu xianzai yinguo jing* at Dunhuang." *Journal of Chinese Religions*, no. 16 (1988): 55–72.

———. *Early Buddhist Narrative Art: Illustrations of the Life of the Buddha from Central Asia to China, Korea, and Japan*. Lanham, MD: University Press of America, 2000.

Kashiwahara Yūsen 柏原祐泉. "Hirata Atsutane ni okeru hai-Butsu ron no honshitsu ni tsuite 平田篤胤における排仏論の本質について." *Ōtani shigaku* 4 (1955): 1–13.

———, ed. *Ishinki no Shinshū* 維新期の真宗. Shinshū shiryō shūsei, vol. 11. Kyoto: Dōhōsha Shuppan, 1983.

———. "Kinsei hai-Butsu no shisō 近世排仏の思想." In *Kinsei Bukkyō no shisō*, edited by Kashiwahara Yūsen and Fujii Manabu, 517–32. Tokyo: Iwanami Shoten, 1973.

Kashiwahara Yūsen 柏原祐泉 and Fujii Manabu 藤井学, eds. *Kinsei Bukkyō no shisō* 近世仏教の思想. Nihon shisō taikei, vol. 57. Tokyo: Iwanami Shoten, 1973.

Kasugai Shin'ya 春日井真也. "Indo to Nihon (4): Hori Shitoku no shisō to shōgai (1) インドと日本 (四) : 堀至徳の思想と生涯 (一) ." *Bukkyō Daigaku kenkyū kiyō*, no. 55 (1971): 63–132.

———. "Indo to Nihon (5): Hori Shitoku no shisō to shōgai (2) インドと日本 (五) : 堀至徳の思想と生涯 (二) ." *Bukkyō Daigaku kenkyū kiyō*, no. 56 (1972): 59–118.

———. *Indo: Kinkei to enkei* インド・近景と遠景. Kyoto: Dōhōsha Shuppan, 1981.

———. "Ōnishi Ryōkei to Hori Shitoku: Ōnishi Ryōkei shokan o chūshin to shite 大西良慶と堀至徳—大西良慶書簡を中心として." *Kōnan Joshi Daigaku kenkyū kiyō*, no. 11/12 (1975): 443–58.

Katō Jun 加藤諄. *Bussokuseki no tame ni: Nihon kenzai bussokuseki yōran* 仏足石のために: 日本見在仏足石要覧. Tokyo: Tsukiji Shokan, 1980.

Katō, Shūichi. "Tominaga Nakamoto, 1715–46: A Tokugawa Iconoclast." *Monumenta Nipponica* 22, no. 1/2 (1967): 177–93.

——— 加藤周一, ed. *Tominaga Nakamoto, Ishida Baigan* 富永仲基　石田梅岩. Vol. 18, *Nihon no meicho*. Tokyo: Chūō Kōronsha, 1978.

Katō Totsudō 加藤咄堂. *Daishō shaka* 大聖釈迦. Tokyo: Katō Kumaichirō, 1891.

Katsuo Kin'ya 勝尾金弥. *Denki jidō bungaku no ayumi: 1891 kara 1945-nen* 伝記児童文学のあゆみ: 1891から1945年. Kyoto: Mineruva Shobō, 1999.

Kawabata Yasunari 川端康成 et al., eds. *Kyōto jiten* 京都事典. Tokyo: Jinbutsu Ōraisha, 1967.

Kawaguchi Ekai 河口慧海. *Upāsaka Bukkyō* 在家仏教. *Kawaguchi Ekai chosaku senshū*, vol. 1. Tokyo: Keibunsha, 2009.

Kawaguchi Kōfū 川口高風. *Meiji zenki Sōtōshū no kenkyū* 明治前期曹洞宗の研究. Kyoto: Hōzōkan, 2002.

Kawano Satoshi 河野訓. *Kan'yaku Butsuden kenkyū* 漢訳仏伝研究. Ise: Kōgakkan Daigaku Shuppanbu, 2007.

———. "Shoki Chūgoku Bukkyō no Butsuden o meguru sho mondai: *Shugyō hongikyō* ni kanren shite 初期中国仏教の仏伝をめぐる諸問題: 『修行本起経』に関連して." *Tōyō Bunka Kenkyūsho kiyō*, no. 113 (1991): 127–76.

Kawato Michiaki 川戸道昭. "Tomasu Kārairu to Meiji no chishikijin: *Eiyū sūhairon* no juyō o megutte トマス·カ-ライルと明治の知識人:「英雄崇拝論」の受容をめぐって." *Eigo Ei-Bei bungaku*, no. 35 (1995): 389–415.

Keene, Donald. "Hirata Atsutane and Western Learning." *T'oung Pao* 42, no. 5 (1954): 353–80.

Ketelaar, James Edward. "The Non-Modern Confronts the Modern: Dating the Buddha in Japan." *History and Theory*, no. 45 (2006): 62–79.

———. *Of Heretics and Martyrs in Meiji Japan: Buddhism and Its Persecution*. Princeton, NJ: Princeton University Press, 1990.

Kikutake Jun'ichi 菊竹淳一. "Kōrai jidai no Nehan hensōzu: Kagawa Jōtokuji o chūshin ni 高麗時代の涅槃変相図: 香川·常徳寺本を中心に." *Yamato bunka*, no. 80 (1988): 17–35.

Kimbrough, R. Keller, and Satoko Shimazaki, eds. *Publishing the Stage: Print and Performance in Early Modern Japan*. Boulder: Center for Asian Studies, University of Colorado, Boulder, 2011.

Kimura Ki 木村毅. "'Mono no aware' to tōzai Shakaden: Sekaiteki shiya ni oite no Meiji bungaku kōsatsu shiron 「物のあはれ」と東西釈迦伝: 世界的視野においての明治文学考察試論." *Bunrin*, no. 10 (1976): 1–28.

Kinami Takuichi 木南卓一, ed. *Miyo no hikari: Shakuson den* 三世の光: 釈尊伝. Osaka: Kinami Takuichi, 1980.

Kinnard, Jacob N. "Reevaluating the Eighth-Ninth Century Pāla Milieu: Icono-Conservatism and the Persistence of Śākyamuni." *Journal of the International Association of Buddhist Studies* 19, no. 2 (1996): 281–300.

Klautau, Orion. "Between Essence and Manifestation: Shōtoku Taishi and Shinran during the Fifteen-Year War (1931–1945)." *Ryūkoku Daigaku Ajia Bukkyō Bunka Kenkyū Sentā Wākingu Pēpā* 12, no. 5 (2013): 279–94.

Kobayashi Tatsurō 小林達朗. *Shinran Shōnin eden* 親鸞聖人絵伝. Nihon no bijutsu, vol. 415. Tokyo: Shibundō, 2000.

Kodaigaku Kyōkai 古代學協會, ed. *Rihō Ō ki* 李部王記. Shiryō shūi, vol. 3. Kyoto: Rinsen Shoten, 1969.

Kōfūkan Henshūsho 光風館編輯所, ed. *Shihan kokubun: Daiichi buyō kyōju bikō* 師範国文: 第一部用教授備考. 3rd revised ed. Vol. 8. Tokyo: Kōfūkan Shoten, 1935.

Kohn, Livia. *Laughing at the Tao: Debates among Buddhists and Taoists in Medieval China*. Princeton, NJ: Princeton University Press, 1995.

Koizumi Hiroshi 小泉弘 et al. *Sanbō-e shūsei: Shohon taishō* 三宝絵集成: 諸本対照. Tokyo: Kasama Shoin, 1980.

Kokubungaku Kenkyū Shiryōkan 国文学研究資料館, ed. *Chūsei butsuden shū* 中世仏伝集. Shinpukuji zenpon sōkan, vol. 5. Kyoto: Rinsen Shoten, 2000.

Kokuritsu Gekijō Chōsa Yōseibu Geinō Chōsashitsu 国立劇場調査養成部芸能調査室 and Kindai Kabuki Nenpyō Hensanshitsu 近代歌舞伎年表編纂室, eds. *Kindai kabuki nenpyō Kyōto hen* 近代歌舞伎年表　京都篇. Vol. 4. Tokyo: Yagi Shoten, 1998.

Komine Kazuaki 小峯和明. "Butsuden to etoki II: Chūsei Butsuden no yōsō 仏伝と絵解きII: 中世仏伝の様相." *Etoki kenkyū*, no. 9 (1991): 17–29.

———. "Higashi Ajia no Butsuden bungaku/Budda no monogatari to kaiga o yomu: Nihon no *Shaka no honji* to Chūgoku no *Shakushi genryū* o chūshin ni 東アジアの仏伝文学·ブッダの物語と絵画を読む: 日本の『釈迦の本地』と中国の『釈氏源流』を中心に." *Ronshō kokugo kyōiku gaku* 3 (2012): 120–28.

———. "Higashi Ajia no Butsuden o tadoru: Hikaku setsuwagaku no kiten 東アジアの仏伝をたどる: 比較説話学の起点." *Bungaku* 6, no. 6 (2005): 30–41.

———. "Imēji no kairō (6): *Shakushi genryū* o yomu イメージの回廊(6): 『釈氏源流』を読む." *Tosho*, no. 760 (2012): 52–57.

———. "Nihon to Higashi Ajia no 'Bukkyō bungaku': *Shakushi genryū* o chūshin ni 日本と東アジアの〈仏伝文学〉: 『釈氏源流』を中心に." *Bukkyō bungaku*, no. 39 (2014): 18–32.

———. "Shinpukuji zō *Shaka nyorai hassō shidai* ni tsuite: Chūsei Butsuden no shin shiryō 真福寺蔵『釈迦如来八相次第』について: 中世仏伝の新資料." *Kokubungaku Kenkyū Shiryōkan kiyō*, no. 17 (1991): 107–28.

Kōyasan Shōmyō no Kai 高野山声明の会. *Jōrakue: Kōyasan no shōmyō* 常楽会: 高野山の声明. Bikutā Dentō Bunka Shinkō Zaidan VZCG-346, 2004. Recorded June 22–23, 2004.

Kubota Jun 久保田淳 and Yamaguchi Akiho 山口明穂, eds. *Myōe Shōnin shū* 明恵上人集. Tokyo: Iwanami Shoten, 1981.

Kujirai Kiyotaka 鯨井清隆. "Kamakura jidai ni okeru Nehan hensōzu no tenkai ni tsuite: Jishōin, An'yōin bon to *Shiza kōshiki* no kanren o chūshin ni 鎌倉時代における涅槃変相図の展開について: 自性院·安養院本と『四座講式』の関連を中心に." *Bukkyō bijutsu*, no. 323 (2012): 36–58.

Kurobe Michiyoshi 黒部通善. *Nihon Butsuden bungaku no kenkyū* 日本仏伝文学の研究. Osaka: Izumi Shoin, 1989.

———. "Shaka ichidai denki kosui kan 3 (honkoku) 釈迦一代伝記鼓吹(巻三) <翻刻>." *Aichi Gakuin Daigaku Kyōyōbu kiyō* 43, no. 1 (1995): 190–74 [reverse pagination].

———. "Shaka ichidai denki kosui kan 7 (honkoku) 釈迦一代伝記鼓吹(巻七) <翻刻> ." *Aichi Gakuin Daigaku Kyōyōbu kiyō* 44, no. 3 (1995): 140–25 [reverse pagination].

Kyoto Kokuritsu Hakubutsukan 京都国立博物館, ed. *Nehanzu no meisaku: Tokubetsu chinretsu* 涅槃図の名作: 特別陳列. Kyoto: Seifūkai, 1978.

———. *Shaka shinkō to Seiryōji: Tokubetsu tenrankai* 釈迦信仰と清凉寺: 特別展覧会. Kyoto: Kyoto Shinbunsha, 1982.

Kyōto-shi 京都市. *Ukyō-ku* 右京区. Shiryō Kyōto no rekishi, vol. 14. Tokyo: Heibonsha, 1994.

Ladda, Kaewrithidej. "*Shaka nyorai tanjō-e*: Jōruriteki shukō ni yoru Shaka denki no hen'yō 『釈迦如来誕生会』: 浄瑠璃的趣向による釈迦伝記の変容." *Kokugo kokubun* 72, no. 2 (2003): 161–83.

Lamotte, Étienne, trans. *Le traité de la grande vertu de sagesse de Nāgārjuna (Mahā prajñāpāramitāśāstra)*. Vol. 1. Louvain: Bibliothèque du Muséon, 1944.

Lee, Kenneth Doo. *The Prince and the Monk: Shōtoku Worship in Shinran's Buddhism*. Albany: State University of New York Press, 2007.

Lei Yuhua 雷玉华. "Kezier 110 ku Fozhuan bihua de yiyi 克孜尔110窟佛传壁画的意义." *Sichuan Daxue xuebao (Zhexue shehui kexue ban)*, no. 142 (2006): 101–5.

Leoshko, Janice. "Scenes of the Buddha's Life in Pāla-Period Art." *Silk Road Art and Archaeology*, no. 3 (1993–1994): 251–76.

Lesbre, Emmanuelle. "Une vie illustrée du Buddha (Shishi yuanliu, 1425), modèle pour les peintures murales d'un monastère du XVe s. (Jueyuan si, Sichuan oriental)." *Arts asiatiques* 57 (2002): 69–101.

Li Jingde 黎靖德 and Wang Xingxian 王星賢, eds. *Zhuzi yulei* 朱子語類. Lixue congshu, vol. 8. Beijing: Zhonghua Shuju, 1986.

Li Ru 李茹. "Dunhuang Mogaoku di-290 ku Fozhuan gushihua de tushi yishu ji qi yuanliu shishi 敦煌莫高窟第290窟佛传故事画的图式艺术及其源流试释." *Dunhuangxue jikan*, no. 3 (2009): 77–83.

Liang Weiying 梁尉英. "Dunhuang Fozhuan gaiguan ji qi Zhongguohua zhi tedian 敦煌佛傳概觀及其中國化之特點." In *1990 Dunhuangxue guoji yantaohui wenji: Shiku kaogu bian*, edited by Duan Wenjie, Lin Yingshan, and Liang Weiying, 319–54. Shenyang: Liaoning Renmin Chubanshe, 1995.

LoBreglio, John S. "Uniting Buddhism: The Varities of *Tsūbukkyō* in Meiji-Taishō Japan and the Case of Takada Dōken." *Eastern Buddhist* 37, no. 1/2 (2005): 39–76.

Lokesh, Chandra, and Sushama Lohia. *Life of Lord Buddha: Compiled by Monk Pao-ch'eng from Chinese Sutras and Illustrated in Woodcuts in the Ming Period*. New Delhi: International Academy of Indian Culture and Aditya Prakashan, 2010.

Lopez, Donald S., Jr. *From Stone to Flesh: A Short History of the Buddha*. Chicago: University of Chicago Press, 2013.

Lupton, Julia Reinhard. *Afterlives of the Saints: Hagiography, Typology, and Renaissance Literature*. Stanford: Stanford University Press, 1996.

Machida Kōichi 町田幸一. "Kaisetsu: Gojū no tō tōhon sozō 解説: 五重塔塔本塑像." In *Hōryūji*, edited by Nara Rokudaiji Taikan Kankōkai. Nara Rokudaiji Taikan, vol. 3, 5–45. Tokyo: Iwanami Shoten, 2000.

Machimoto Tonkū 町元呑空. *Gōtō jūnishū kōyō: Ichimei Tōyō tetsugaku hikkei* 鼇頭十二宗綱要: 一名東洋哲學必携. Kyoto: Nagata Bunshōdō, 1887.

Maeda Eun 前田慧雲. "Shakuson ni tai suru yo no kansō 釈尊に対する余の感想." *Keisei* 160 (1909): 5–7.

Mair, Victor H. *T'ang Transformation Texts: A Study of the Buddhist Contribution to the Rise of Vernacular Fiction and Drama in China*. Cambridge, MA: Harvard University Press, 1989.

Mannami Hisako 万波寿子. "Edo jidai no Nishi Honganji to shuppan 江戸時代の西本願寺と出版." *Ajia yūgaku*, no. 155 (2012): 154–63.

Masuda Katsumi 益田勝美. "Budda no kuni Tenjiku e no gongu: Sono keifu ブッダの国·天竺への欣求: その系譜." *Kokubungaku kaishaku to kyōzai no kenkyū* 28, no. 4 (1983): 19–26.

Masuzawa, Tomoko. *The Invention of World Religions: Or, How European Univer-*

salism Was Preserved in the Language of Pluralism. Chicago: University of Chicago Press, 2005.

Matsuda, Yūko. "Chinese Versions of the Buddha's Biography." *Indogaku Bukkyōgaku kenkyū* 37, no. 1 (1988): 24–33.

Matsunaga Motoki 松永材. *Hirata Atsutane no Bukkyō-kan* 平田篤胤の仏教観. Tokyo: Kazama Shobō, 1944.

Matsunaga Yūkei 松長有慶. *Kōyasan no inori* 高野山の祈り. Vol. 3, *Kōyasan Kōbō Daishi Kūkai no mandara sekai*. Kyoto: Dōhōsha Media Puran, 2005.

Mayeda, Sengaku. "Nanjō Bunyū." In *Encyclopedia of Religion*, edited by Lindsay Jones, Mircea Eliade, and Charles J. Adams, 6414. Detroit: Macmillan Reference USA, 2005.

McCallum, Donald F. "The Replication of Miraculous Icons: The Zenkoji Amida and the Seiryoji Shaka." In *Images, Miracles, and Authority in Asian Religious Traditions*, edited by Richard H. Davis. Boulder: Westview Press, 1988: 207–26.

———. "The Saidaiji Lineage of the Seiryōji Shaka Tradition." *Archives of Asian Art* 49 (1996): 51–67.

McCullough, William H., and Helen Craig McCullough, trans. *A Tale of Flowering Fortunes: Annals of Japanese Aristocratic Life in the Heian Period*. 2 vols. Stanford, CA: Stanford University Press, 1980.

McNally, Mark. *Proving the Way: Conflict and Practice in the History of Japanese Nativism*. Cambridge, MA: Harvard University Asia Center, 2005.

Migita Yūji 右田雄二. "Shaka no shōgai sōdai ni: Chōkokuka Nakamura Shin'ya san ga 'Hassō zuzō': Nara Yakushiji e 18-nendo hōnō 釈迦の生涯、壮大に／彫刻家・中村晋也さんが「八相図像」＝奈良県・薬師寺へ１８年度奉納." *Minami Nihon Shinbun*, January 5, 2014, 2.

Miki Shōtarō 三木正太郎. "Hirata Atsutane no Bukkyō kenkyū 平田篤胤の仏教研究." *Kōgakukan Daigaku kiyō* 6 (1968): 248–87.

Miura Shū 三浦周. "Bukkyō kindaika no ichi sokumen: *Shakkyō shōmu shoha narabi ni saiha* o chūshin ni 仏教近代化の一側面:『釈教正謬初破並再破』を中心に." *Taishō Daigaku Daigakuin kenkyū ronshū*, no. 27 (2003): 39–48.

Miyagawa Yasuko 宮川康子. *Tominaga Nakamoto to Kaitokudō: Shisōshi no zenshō* 富永仲基と懐徳堂: 思想史の前哨. Tokyo: Perikansha, 1998.

Miyakawa Ikkyō 宮川一敬. "Udana Nichiki ni okeru hai-Butsu ron ni tai suru shisei 優陀那日輝における排仏論に対する姿勢." *Indogaku Bukkyōgaku kenkyū* 21, no. 2 (1973): 192–93.

Miya, Tsugio 宮次男 et al., eds. *Kadokawa emakimono sōran* 角川絵巻物総覧. Tokyo: Kadokawa Shoten, 1995.

Miyazaki Kenji 宮崎健司. *Nihon kodai no shakyō to shakai* 日本古代の写経と社会. Tokyo: Hanawa Shobō, 2006.

Miyoshi Aikichi 三好愛吉. "Daishō Kangiten kō 大聖歓喜天考." *Bukkyō shirin* 2, no. 22 (1896): 26–35.

Mizuno Katsuhiko 水野克比古. *Sekihōji: Jakuchū 500 rakan* 石峰寺 SEKIHOJI Temple: 若冲五百羅漢. Kyoto: Unsōdō, 2013.

Mizuno Seiichi 水野清一 and Nagahiro Toshio 長廣敏雄. *Dai 10-dō* 第十洞. *Unkō sekkutsu: Seireki go-seiki ni okeru Chūgoku hokubu Bukkyō kutsuin no kōkogakuteki chōsa hōkoku*, vol. 7. Kyoto: Kyōto Daigaku Jinbun Kagaku Kenkyūjo, 1952.

Mizuta Norihisa 水田紀久, ed. *Tominaka Nakamoto, Yamagata Bantō* 富永仲基・山片蟠桃. Nihon shisō taikei, vol. 43. Tokyo: Iwanami Shoten, 1976.

Mochizuki Shigeru 望月茂. *Sakura Azumao* 佐久良東雄. Tokyo: Dai Nihon Yūbenkai Kōdansha, 1943.

Mochizuki Shinkō 望月信亨 and Tsukamoto Zenryū 塚本善隆. *Mochizuki Bukkyō daijiten* 望月仏教大辞典. Tokyo: Sekai Seiten Kankō Kyōkai, 1954.

Mohr, Michel. *Buddhism, Unitarianism, and the Meiji Competition for Universality*. Cambridge, MA: Harvard University Asia Center, 2014.

Mori Kazuya 森和也. "Kindai Bukkyō no jigazō to shite no gohōron 近代仏教の自画像としての護法論." *Shūkyō kenkyū* 81, no. 2 (2007): 411–36.

Morrell, Robert E. *Early Kamakura Buddhism: A Minority Report*. Berkeley: Asian Humanities Press, 1987.

Motoi Makiko 本井牧子. "*Shaka no honji* to sono engen: *Hokekyō* no sennin kyūshi o meguru 『釈迦の本地』とその淵源:『法華経』の仙人給仕をめぐる." In *Chūsei no monogatari to kaiga*, edited by Ishikawa Tōru, 215–43. Tokyo: Chikurinsha, 2013.

"Mozaiku モザイク." *Bijutsu shukan*, no. 80 (1915): 5.

"Mr. Takahashi Goro." *The Churchman*, September 6, 1896, 290–91.

Murakami Senshō 村上専精. *Daijō Bussetsu ron hihan* 大乗仏説論批判. Tokyo: Kōyūkan, 1903.

———. "Shakamuni Butsu shuttan nyūmetsu no gappi kō 釈迦牟尼仏出誕入滅ノ月日考." *Bukkyō shirin* 1, no. 4: 303–17.

Murase, Miyeko. *Emaki: Narrative Scrolls from Japan*. New York: Asia Society, 1983.

Murphy, Regan Eileen. "The Urgency of History: Language and Ritual in Japanese Buddhism and Kokugaku." PhD diss., Harvard University, 2010.

Murray, Juila K. "The Childhood of Gods and Sages." In *Children in Chinese Art*, edited by Ann Barrott Wicks, 108–32. Honolulu: University of Hawaii Press, 2002.

Nagai Kazuaki 永井一彰. *Hangi wa kataru* 板木は語る. Tokyo: Kasama Shoin, 2014.

Naitō Tōichirō 内藤藤一郎. *Nihon Bukkyō kaiga shi: Nara chō honki hen* 日本仏教絵画史: 奈良朝本期編. Kyoto: Seikei Shoin, 1934.

Najita, Tetsuo. *Visions of Virtue in Tokugawa Japan: The Kaitokudō Merchant Academy of Osaka*. Chicago: University of Chicago Press, 1987.

Naka Michiyo 那珂通世. "Shakashu no setsu ni tsukite Inoue Bungaku Hakushi ni shissu 釈迦種説に就きて井上博士に質す." *Taiyō* 2, no. 2 (1896): 184–87.

———. "Shakashu no setsu ni tsukite Inoue Bungaku Hakushi ni shissu 釈迦種説に就きて井上博士に質す." *Shigaku zasshi* 6, no. 11 (1895): 58–68.

Nakada Norio 中田祝夫, ed. *Tōdai-ji fujumonkō no kokugogakuteki kenkyū* 東大寺諷誦文稿の国語学的研究. Tokyo: Kazama Shobō, 1969.

Nakajima Takeshi 中島岳志. "Hori Shitoku: 20-seiki shotō no Indo netsu 堀至徳: 20世紀初頭のインド熱." In *Kindai Nihon no Bukkyōsha: Ajia taiken to shisō no hen'yō*, edited by Ogawara Masamichi, 313–45. Tokyo: Keiō Gijuku Daigaku Shuppankai, 2010.

Nakamura, Hajime. "The Aṣṭāmahāsthānacaityastotra and the Chinese and Tibetan Versions of a Text Similar to It." In *Indianisme et bouddhisme: Mélanges offerts à Mgr Étienne Lamotte*, 259–65. Louvain: Institut Orientaliste, 1980.

Nakanishi Naoki 中西直樹 and Yoshinaga Shin'ichi 吉永進一. *Bukkyō kokusai nettowāku no genryū: Kaigai Senkyōkai (1888-nen—1893-nen) no hikari to kage* 仏教国際ネットワークの源流: 海外宣教会 (1888年~1893年) の光と影. Kyoto: Sanninsha, 2015.

Nakano Genzō 中野玄三. *Nehanzu* 涅槃図. Nihon no bijutsu, vol. 268. Tokyo: Shibundō, 1988.

Namiki Seishi 並木誠士. "Shakadō engi: Shaka shinkō no zōfuku 釈迦堂縁起: 釈迦信仰の増幅." *Bijutsu fōramu 21*, no. 15 (2007): 124–27.

Nanjio, Bunyiu [Nanjō, Bun'yū]. *A Catalogue of the Chinese Translation of the Buddhist Tripitaka: The Sacred Canon of the Buddhists in China and Japan.* Oxford: Clarendon Press, 1883.

——— 南条文雄. "Hassō jōdō 八相成道." *Tōyō tetsugaku* 3, no. 7 (1896): 345–49.

———. "Indo kodai chiri 印度古代地理." *Bukkyō shirin* 1, no. 1 (1894): 36–47.

———. *Kaikyūroku* 懐旧録. Tokyo: Daiyūkaku Shobō, 1927.

Nara Kokuritsu Bunkazai Kenkyūjo 奈良国立文化財研究所, ed. *Shichidaiji junrei shiki: Nara Kokuritsu Bunkazai Kenkyūjo sōritsu sanjisshūnen kinen* 七大寺巡礼私記: 奈良国立文化財研究所創立三十周年記念 Nara: Nara Kokuritsu Bunkazai Kenkyūjo, 1982.

Nara Kokuritsu Hakubutsukan 奈良国立博物館, ed. *Budda Shakuson: Sono shōgai to zōkei* ブッダ釈尊: その生涯と造形. Nara: Nara Kokuritsu Hakubutsukan, 1984.

———, ed. *Shaji engi e* 社寺縁起絵. Tokyo: Kadokawa Shoten, 1975.

———, ed. *Yakushiji saitō ato shutsudo sozōgun* 薬師寺西塔跡出土塑像群. Nara: Nara Kokuritsu Hakubutsukan, 1981.

Nara Kokuritsu Hakubutsukan 奈良国立博物館 and Bukkyō Bijutsu Kyōkai 仏教美術協会, eds. *Oshakasama tanjō* お釈迦さま誕生. Nara: Bukkyō Bijutsu Kyōkai, 2000.

Narihara Yuki 成原有貴. "Katsuta Shōkin 'Shutsujo Shaka' no tokushitsu to imi ni kan-suru kōsatsu 勝田蕉琴「出城釈迦」の特質と意味に関する考察." In *Bukkyō bijutsu to rekishi bunka*, edited by Manabe Shunshō, 549–69. Kyoto: Hōzōkan, 2005.

Nattier, Jan. *A Guide to the Earliest Chinese Buddhist Translations: Texts from the Eastern Han and Three Kingdoms Periods*. Tokyo: International Research Institute for Advanced Buddhology, Soka University, 2008.

Nenzi, Laura. *Excursions in Identity: Travel and the Intersection of Place, Gender, and Status in Edo Japan*. Honolulu: University of Hawaii Press, 2008.

Ng, Wai-ming. "The Shintoization of the *Yijing* in Hirata Atsutane's *Kokugaku*." *Sino-Japanese Studies* 19 (2012): 32–47.

Nihon Bijutsuin Hyakunenshi Henshūshitsu 日本美術院百年史編集室, ed. *Nihon Bijutsuin hyakunenshi 1-kan jō (zuhan hen)* 日本美術院百年史　一巻上（図版編）. Tokyo: Nihon Bijutsuin, 1989.

———, ed. *Nihon Bijutsuin hyakunenshi 2-kan jō (zuhan hen)* 日本美術院百年史　二巻上（図版編）. Tokyo: Nihon Bijutsuin, 1990.

———, ed. *Nihon Bijutsuin hyakunenshi 3-kan jō (zuhan hen)* 日本美術院百年史　三巻上（図版編）. Tokyo: Nihon Bijutsuin, 1992.

Nihon Geijutsuin Jimukyoku 日本芸術院事務局, ed. *Nihon Geijutsuin shi* 日本芸術院史. Tokyo: Nihon Geijutsuin Jimukyoku, 1963.

Nishida Nagao 西田長男. "Hirata Atsutane no gakumon: Jihitsubon *Daibibasha-ron bassui* o chūshin to suru sono Indogaku/Bukkyōgaku kenkyū o tsūjite 平田篤胤の学問: 自筆本「大毘婆沙論抜翠」を中心とするその印度学・仏教学研究を通じて." *Kokugakuin zasshi* 64, no. 11/12 (1963): 1–53.

Nishikawa Kyōtarō 西川杏太郎, ed. *Chōkoku* 彫刻. Vol. 2, *Kokuhō daijiten*. Tokyo: Kōdansha, 1985.

Nishimura, Ryō. "The Intellectual Development of the Cult of Śākyamuni: What Is 'Modern' about the Proposition That the Buddha Did Not Preach the Mahāyāna?" Trans. Micah Auerback. *Eastern Buddhist* 42, no. 1 (2011): 9–29.

Nitten Shi Hensan Iinkai 日展史編纂委員会, ed. *Bunten hen* 文展編. Vol. 1, *Nitten shi*. Tokyo: Nitten, 1980.

Nobuko, Ishi. "Sekkyō-bushi." *Monumenta Nipponica* 44, no. 3 (1989): 283–307.

Noma Seiroku 野間清六. "Busshō-e to tanjō-Butsu 仏生会と誕生仏." *Myūjiamu*, no. 61 (1956): 2–6.

Nōnin Hakugan 能仁柏巌. "Mukai nanshin 霧海南針." In *Kyōgihen: Tai-gairai shisō*, Sōtōshū sensho, vol. 6, edited by Ishikawa Rikizan, 89–188. Kyoto: Dōhōsha, 1981.

Novetzke, Christian Lee. *Religion and Public Memory: A Cultural History of Saint Namdev in India*. New York: Columbia University Press, 2008.

Ōguri Dōei 大栗道栄 and Kindaichi Haruhiko 金田一春彦. *Shiza kōshiki: Shōmyō de katarareta Shaka no monogatari* 四座講式: 声明で語られた釈迦の物語. Tokyo: Shinchōsha, 1992.

Okada, Tetsuzō. "The Department of Philosophy in the Imperial University of Tokyo." *The Japan Evangelist* 5, no. 9 (September 1898): 273–80.

Ōkuwa Hitoshi 大桑斉 and Maeda Ichirō 前田一郎, eds. *Razan, Teitoku Ju-Butsu mondō: Chūkai to kenkyū* 羅山・貞徳『儒仏問答』: 注解と研究. Tokyo: Perikansha, 2006.

Okuyama Naoji 奥山直司. *Hyōden Kawaguchi Ekai* 評伝河口慧海. Tokyo: Chūō Kōron Shinsha, 2003.

Olof, A. M. "Sŏkka Yŏrae Sipchi Haengnok: An Attempt to Find Its Place in Buddhist Literature." In *Twenty Papers on Korean Studies Offered to Professor W. E. Skillend*, edited by Daniel Bouchez, Robert C. Provine, and Roderick Whitfield, 203–17. Paris: Collège de France, Centre d'études coréennes, 1989.

Ōmi Toshihiro 碧海寿広. *Kindai Bukkyō no naka no Shinshū: Chikazumi Jōkan to gudōshatachi* 近代仏教のなかの真宗: 近角常観と求道者たち. Kyoto: Hōzōkan, 2014.

Ōmiya Kōnin 大宮孝潤. "Shakamuni den 釈迦牟尼伝." *Shimei yoka* 22, no. 1 (1909): 1–14.

———. "Shakamuni den 釈迦牟尼伝." *Shimei yoka* 22, no. 4 (1909): 4–9.

"Ōmiya Kōnin Bonji ten/Nichi-In kokkyō juritsu 60-shūnen, Ōmiya Kōnin seitan 140-nen 大宮孝潤梵字展／日印国交樹立六十周年·大宮孝潤生誕百四十年記念." http://www.buddha-world.jp/file/pickup/vol012/index.html.

Ono Bunkō 小野文珖. "Udana Nichiki: Kindai Nichirenshū no senkakusha 優陀那日輝: 近代日蓮宗の先覚者." In *Kindai Nichiren kyōgaku no shisōka: Kindai Nichiren kyōdan, kyōgaku-shi shiron*, edited by Nakano Kyōtoku, 23–69. Tokyo: Kokusho Kankōkai, 1977.

Otani Daigaku Shinshū Sōgō Kenkyujo Daigakushi Hensan Kenkyūshitsu 大谷大学真宗総合研究所大学史編纂研究室, ed. *Ōtani Daigaku kindai 100-nen no ayumi* 大谷大学近代 100年のあゆみ. Kyoto: Ōtani Daigaku, 1997.

Pak Pyŏngdong. *Pulgyŏng chŏllae sŏrhwa ŭi sosŏljŏk pyŏnmo yangsang: Pyŏnmunjip Sŏkka Yŏrae sipchi suhaenggi yŏn'gu*. Seoul: Yŏngnak, 2003.

Pak Soyŏng 朴昭映. "Koryŏ hugi Unmuk ŭi *Sŏkka yŏrae haengjŏk song* yŏn'gu 高麗後期 雲默의 『釋迦如來行蹟頌』 研究." PhD diss., Tongguk Taehakkyo, 2011.

———. "*Shaka nyorai gyōseki ju* ni mirareru Shaka nyorai ichidaiki: Tendai kyōgaku no shiten kara no kōsatsu 『釈迦如来行跡頌』に見られる釈迦如米一代記." *Eizan Gakuin kenkyū kiyō*, no. 30 (2008): 140–18 [reverse pagination].

———. "Unmoku sen *Shaka nyorai gyōseki ju* ni mirareru Tendai kyōhan ni tsuite no ichi kōsatsu 雲默撰『釈迦如来行跡頌』に見られる天台教判についての一考察." *Indogaku Bukkyōgaku kenkyū* 58, no. 1 (2009): 164–68.

———. "Unmoku sen *Shaka nyorai gyōseki ju* no 'Kegon Agon ichiji' setsu ni tsuite 雲默撰『釈迦如来跡頌』の「華厳阿含一時」説について." *Tendai gakuhō*, no. 50 (2007): 118–28.

Pan Fu'en 潘富恩, ed. *Er Cheng yishu* 二程遗书. Tiandiren congshu. Shanghai: Shanghai Guji Chubanshe, 2000.

Parkes, Graham. "The Early Reception of Nietzsche's Philosophy in Japan." In *Nietzsche and Asian Thought*, edited by Graham Parkes, 177–99. Chicago: University of Chicago Press, 1991.

Peers, Glenn. *Sacred Shock: Framing Visual Experience in Byzantium*. University Park: Pennsylvania State University Press, 2004.

Petralia, Randolph Spencer. "Nietzsche in Meiji Japan: Culture Criticism, Individualism and Reaction in the 'Aesthetic Life' Debate of 1901–1903." PhD diss., Washington University in St. Louis, 1981.

Phillips, Quitman Eugene. "Kano Motonobu and Early Kano Narrative Painting." PhD diss., University of California at Berkeley, 1992.

Picco, Mark. "A Critical Exegesis and Translation of Zhu Xi's Critique of Buddhism, as Found in the 126th Chapter of the 'Zhuzi Yulei.'" Master's thesis, University of Calgary, 2005.

Pye, Michael. *Emerging from Meditation*. Honolulu: University of Hawaii Press, 1990.

Radich, Michael. *How Ajātaśatru Was Reformed: The Domestication of "Ajase" and Stories in Buddhist History*. Tokyo: International Institute for Buddhist Studies of the International College for Postgraduate Buddhist Studies, 2011.

Reitei [Umebori] Kokuga 鈴亭[梅暮里]谷峨. *Hasshū kigen Shaka jitsuroku* 八宗起原釈迦実録. Tokyo: Seiundō, 1854.

"Review: Chinese Buddhism: A Volume of Sketches." *The North China Herald and South China & Consular Gazette*, December 2, 1880, 512–13.

Ruppert, Brian Douglas. *Jewel in the Ashes: Buddha Relics and Power in Early Medieval Japan*. Cambridge, MA: Harvard University Asia Center, 2000.

Ryu Sŭngjin 柳承珍. "Hōkei sanzon senbutsu to Einga kyō: Kodai Nihon ni okeru sokujiin zazō no fuzai o kangaeru tegakari to shite 方形三尊せん仏と絵因果経: 古代日本における触地印坐像の不在を考える手掛かりとして." *Kyoto bigaku bijutsu shigaku* 9 (2010): 35–69.

Ryūkoku Daigaku Ryūkoku Myūjiamu 龍谷大学龍谷ミュージアム, ed. *Shakuson to Shinran: Indo kara Nihon e no kiseki* 釈尊と親鸞: インドから日本への軌跡. Kyoto: Hōzōkan, 2011.

Saji Jitsunen 佐治実然. "Shakamuni Butsu ryakuden gairon 釈迦牟尼仏略伝概論." *Shūkyō*, no. 19 (1893): 14–18.

Sakado Hiromu 沙加戸弘. *Shinshū kankei jōruri tenkaishi josetsu: Sozai no jidai* 真宗関係浄瑠璃展開史序説: 素材の時代. Kyoto: Hōzōkan, 2008.

Sakaino Kōyō 境野黄洋. "Rekishiteki Bukkyō 歴史的仏教." *Bukkyō shirin* 1, no. 8 (1894): 503–14.

Santorī Bijutsukan サントリー美術館 et al., eds. *Kōdaiji no meihō: Hideyoshi to Nene no tera* 高台寺の名宝: 秀吉とねねの寺. Kyoto: Jubusen Kōdaiji and Asahi Shinbunsha, 1995.

Sasaki, Ruth Fuller, trans., and Thomas Kirchner, ed. *The Record of Linji*. Honolulu: University of Hawaii Press, 2009.

Satō Ryōyū 佐藤亮雄, ed. *Hyakuza hōdan kikigaki shō* 百座法談聞書抄. Tokyo: Nan'undō Ōfūsha, 1963.

Satō Shino 佐藤志乃. "Shaka to Sujātā 釈迦とスジャーター." *Ajia yūgaku*, no. 21 (1999): 47–58.

———. "Yokoyama Taikan to Ajantā hekiga: 1903-nen saku *Shaka chichi ni au* o chūshin ni 横山大観とアジャンター壁画: 1903年作《釈迦父に逢う》を中心に." *Indo kōko kenkyū*, no. 32 (2010–2011): 57–70.

Satow, Ernest Mason, and A. G. S. Hawes. *A Handbook for Travellers in Central & Northern Japan, Being a Guide to Tōkiō, Kiōto, Ōzaka* [*sic*], *Hakodate, Nagasaki, and Other Cities; the Most Interesting Parts of the Main Island; Ascents of the Principal Mountains; Descriptions of Temples; and Historical Notes and Legends*. Murray's Hand-book, Japan. 2nd ed. London: Murray, 1884.

Sawa Ryūken 佐和隆研 et al. *Kyōto daijiten* 京都大事典. Kyoto: Tankōsha, 1984.

Sawada Atsuko 沢田篤子. "Kōshiki 講式." In *Nihon ongaku daijiten*, edited by Hirano Kenji, Kamisangō Yūkō and Gamō Satoaki, 439–40. Tokyo: Heibonsha, 1989.

Sawada, Janine Anderson. *Confucian Values and Popular Zen: Sekimon Shingaku in Eighteenth-Century Japan*. Honolulu: University of Hawaii Press, 1993.

Schmid, D. Neil. "*Yuanqi*: Medieval Buddhist Narratives from Dunhuang." PhD diss., University of Pennsylvania, 2002.

Seiiki Bunka Kenkyūkai 西域文化研究会, ed. *Tonkō Bukkyō shiryō* 敦煌仏教資料. Seiiki bunka kenkyū, vol. 1. Kyoto: Hōzōkan, 1958.

Sekiguchi Masayuki 関口正之. "Onomichi-shi Jikōji shozō Shaka hassō zu ni tsuite (1) 尾道市持光寺所蔵釈迦八相図について (一) ." *Bijutsu kenkyū*, no. 317 (1981): 21–32.

———. "Onomichi-shi Jikōji shozō Shaka hassō zu ni tsuite (2) 尾道市持光寺所蔵釈迦八相図について (二) ." *Bijutsu kenkyū*, no. 319 (1982): 23–31.

———. "Onomichi-shi Jikōji shozō Shaka hassō zu ni tsuite (3) 尾道市持光寺所蔵釈迦八相図について (三) ." *Bijutsu kenkyū*, no. 321 (1984): 15–24.

———. "Onomichi-shi Jikōji shozō Shaka hassō zu ni tsuite (4) 尾道市持光寺所蔵釈迦八相図について (四) ." *Bijutsu kenkyū*, no. 333 (1985): 11–19.

———. "Onomichi-shi Jikōji shozō Shaka hassō zu ni tsuite (5) 尾道市持光寺所蔵釈迦八相図について (五) ." *Bijutsu kenkyū*, no. 344 (1989): 13–18.

Sen, Tansen. *Buddhism, Diplomacy, and Trade: The Realignment of Sino-Indian Relations, 600–1400*. Honolulu: University of Hawaii Press, 2003.

"Shaka hassô zoku Yamato bunko." Museum of Fine Arts, Boston. Last modified May 14, 2015. http://educators.mfa.org/shaka-hassô-zoku-yamato-bunko-162518.

"Shaka monogatari (Keichō 16-nen shahon) 釈迦物語 (慶長十六年写本) ." In *Muromachi jidai monogatarishū*, edited by Yokoyama Shigeru and Ōta Takeo, vol. 4, 23–52. Tokyo: Inoue Shobō, 1962.

"Shaka no gohonji しゃかの御本地." In *Sekkyōbushi shōhon shū*, edited by Yokoyama Shigeru and Fujiwara Hiroshi, vol. 1, 180–95. Tokyo: Ōokayama Shoten, 1936.

"Shaka no honji (Kan'ei 20-nen kanpon) 釈迦の本地 (寛永二十年刊本) ." In *Muromachi jidai monogatari taisei*, edited by Yokoyama Shigeru and Matsumoto Ryūshin, vol. 7, 118–62. Tokyo: Kadokawa Shoten, 1979.

"Shakkyō shōmu tenda 釈数正謬天唖." In *Nihon shisō tōsō shiryō*, edited by Washio Junkyō, vol. 10, 195–280. Tokyo: Meicho Kankōkai, 1969.

Sharf, Robert H. "The Scripture in Forty-Two Sections." In *Religions of China in Practice*, edited by Donald S. Lopez Jr., 360–71. Princeton, NJ: Princeton University Press, 1996.

Sharf, Robert H., and Elizabeth Sharf, eds. *Living Images: Japanese Buddhist Icons in Context*. Palo Alto, CA: Stanford University Press, 2002.

Shibata Mitsuhiko 柴田光彦. *Honbun hen* 本文篇. *Daisō zōsho mokuroku to kenkyū: Kashihon Ōnoya Sōbē kyūzō shomoku*, vol. 1. Musashimurayama: Seishōdō Shoten, 1983.

Shigeki Denhachirō 茂木傳八郎. "Hirara Sensei no Indo zōshi o yomite Hirata Atsutane o ronzu 平田先生の印度藏志を読みて平田篤胤を論ず." *Myōkōge* 161, no. 10 (1916): 15–30.

Shimaji Daitō 島地大等, ed. *Aibai zenshū* 愛楳全集. Tokyo: Morie Shoten, 1906.

Shimaji Morkuai 島地黙雷. "Busshiki konrei 仏式婚礼." In *Shimaji Mokurai zenshū*, edited by Futaba Kenkō and Fukushima Kanryū, vol. 4, 158–62. Kyoto: Honganji Shuppanbu, 1976.

Shimazaki Tōson 島崎藤村. "Yashi no hakage 椰子の葉陰." In *Tōson zenshū*, vol. 2, 455–67. Tokyo: Chikuma Shobō, 1966.

Shimizu, Yoshiaki. "On Spirituality in the Work of Itō Jakuchū (1716–1800)." In *Homage to All Creatures Great and Small: The Visionary World of Itō Jakuchū (1716–1800)*, edited by United States-Japan Foundation, 68–81. New York: United States-Japan Foundation, 2009.

Shinbo Tōru 真保亨. *Butsudenzu* 仏伝図. Tokyo: Mainichi Shinbunsha, 1978.

Shinkai Taketarō 新海竹太郎. "Genkon no chōkoku ni tsuite 現今の彫刻に就て." *Bijutsu shinpō*, January 5, 1903. 3.

———. "Rerīfu (Taiheiyō Kaiga Tsukinamikai nite) shōzen れりーふ (太平洋絵画月次会にて) 承前." *Bijutsu Shinpō* 3, no. 2 (1905): 2.

———. "Shaka hassō 釈迦八相." *Chūō bijutsu* 1, no. 1 (1915): 34–35.

Shinran. *The Kyogyoshinsho, or the "Teaching, Practice, Faith, and Attainment."* Translated by Yamamoto Kosho. Tokyo: Karin Bunko, 1958.

"Shiryūgoto しりうごと." In *Kinsei zuisō shū*, edited by Odaka Michiko and Suzuki Makoto, Shinpen Nihon koten bungaku zenshū, vol. 82, 405–79. Tokyo: Shōgakukan, 2000.

"Shiryūgoto しりうごと." Edited by Sekine Masanao, Wada Hidematsu, and Tanabe Katsuya, Nihon zuihitsu taisei dai 3-ki, vol. 11, 406–48. Tokyo: Yoshikawa Kōbunkan, 1976.

Schopenhauer, Arthur. *The World as Will and Representation*, translated by E. F. J. Payne. Vol. 1. New York: Dover Publications, 1966.

Silk, Jonathan A., ed. *Buddhism in China: Collected Papers of Erik Zürcher.* Leiden: Brill, 2013.

Skilling, Peter. "Dharma, Dhāraṇī, Abhidharma, Avadāna: What Was Taught in Trayastriṃśa?" *Sōka Daigaku Kokusai Bukkyōgaku Kōtō Kenkyūsho nenpō*, no. 11 (2007): 37–60.

Sng, S. A. "This 'Buddha' Should Be Forgotten." *The Daily Enlightenment.* Last modified December 3, 2014. http://thedailyenlightenment.com/2014/12/this-buddha-should-be-forgotten/comment-page-1/.

Snodgrass, Judith. "*Budda no fukuin*: The Deployment of Paul Carus's *Gospel of Buddha* in Meiji Japan." *Japanese Journal of Religious Studies* 25, no. 3/4 (1998): 319–44.

———. "Defining Modern Buddhism: Mr. and Mrs. Rhys Davids and the Pāli Text Society." *Comparative Studies of South Asia, Africa and the Middle East* 27, no. 1 (2007): 186–202.

Spae, Joseph. "Buddhism as Viewed by Two Tokugawa Confucianists: Itô Jinsai's Letter to Dôkô and Its Refutation by Satô Naokata." *Monumenta Nipponica* 5, no. 1 (1942): 167–87.

Staggs, Kathleen M. "In Defense of Japanese Buddhism: Essays from the Meiji Period by Inoue Enryō and Murakami Senshō." PhD diss., Princeton University, 1979.

Stone, Jacqueline. “A Vast and Grave Task: Interwar Buddhist Studies as an Expression of Japan’s Envisioned Global Role.” In *Culture and Identity: Japanese Intellectuals during the Interwar Years*, edited by J. Thomas Rimer, 217–33. Princeton, NJ: Princeton University Press, 1990.

———. *Original Enlightenment and the Transformation of Medieval Japanese Buddhism*. Honolulu: University of Hawaii Press, 1999.

Strong, John S. *The Buddha: A Short Biography*. Oxford: Oneworld, 2001.

———. “A Family Quest: The Buddha, Yaśodharā, and Rāhula in the Mūlasarvāstivāda Vinaya.” In *Sacred Biography in the Buddhist Traditions of South and Southeast Asia*, edited by Juliane Schober, 113–28. Honolulu: University of Hawaii Press, 1997.

Sueki Fumihiko 末木文美士. *Kindai Nihon to Bukkyō* 近代日本と仏教. Tokyo: Toransubyū, 2004.

T’ongdosa Sŏngbo Pangmulgwan 通度寺聖寶博物館. *T’ongdosa Sŏngbo Pangmulgwan myŏngp’um torok: T’ongdosa Sŏngbo Pangmulgwan kaegwan kinyŏm* 通度寺聖寶博物館 名品圖錄: 通度寺聖寶博物館開館紀念. Yangsan: T’ongdosa Sŏngbo Pangmulgwan, 1999.

Tachibana Shundō 立花俊道. “Kan’yaku sho Butsuden to kakugo kakkoku shoden no Butsuden 漢訳諸仏伝と各語各国所伝の仏伝.” In *Bukkyōgaku no sho mondai*, edited by Buttan Nisen Gohyaku-nen Kinen Gakkai, 253–63. Tokyo: Iwanami Shoten, 1935.

Tahara Tsuguo 田原嗣郎. *Hirata Atsutane* 平田篤胤. Jinbutsu sōsho, vol. 111. Tokyo: Yoshikawa Kōbunkan, 1963.

Tajihi Ikuo 多治比郁夫 and Nakano Mitsutoshi 中野三敏, eds. *Kinsei katsujiban mokuroku* 近世活字版目録. Nihon shoshigaku taikei, vol. 50. Musashi Murayama: Seishōdō, 1990.

Takagi Yutaka 高木豊. “Sōden 僧伝.” In *Nihon Bukkyōshi jiten*, edited by Imaizumi Yoshio, 621–22. Tokyo: Yoshikawa Kōbunkan, 1999.

Takahashi Gorō 高橋五郎. “Butsudō shinron 仏道真論.” In *Kyōgihen: Tai-gairai shisō*, edited by Ishikawa Rikizan, Sōtōshū sensho, vol. 6. Kyoto: Dōhōsha, 1981.

———. “Tetsugakkan no kaikōshiki ni nozomite kanzuru tokoro ari isasaka sho shite kōko ni shisshi, awasete sokusei tetsugaku no ikan o ronben su 哲学館ノ開校式ニ臨ミテ感ズル所アリ聊カ書シテ江湖ニ質シ、併セテ速成哲学ノ如何ヲ論弁ス.” *Rikugō zasshi*, no. 81 (1886).

Takano Masami 高野正巳. “Shaka Nyorai tanjō-e 釈迦如来誕生会.” In *Nihon bungaku daijiten*, edited by Fujimura Tsukuru, 445–47. Tokyo: Shinchōsha, 1950.

Takashima Beihō 高島米峰. “Chōkokukai no senkusha 彫刻界の先駆者.” *Chūō bijutsu* 13, no. 4 (1927): 218–20.

Takayama Chogyū 高山樗牛. *Shaka* 釈迦. Tokyo: Hakubunkan, 1899.

Takeda Kazuaki 武田和昭. “Kagawa Jōtokuji no Nehan hensōzu ni tsuite: Sono seiritsu to Chōfukuji Nehanzu to no kankei o chūshin to shite 香川·常徳寺の涅槃変相図について: その成立と長福寺·涅槃図との関係を中心として.” *Bukkyō geijutsu*, no. 196 (1991): 11–36.

Takemura Shinji 竹村信治. "Shakuson den 釈尊伝." *Kokubungaku kaishaku to kanshō* 51, no. 9 (1986): 70–75.

Taki Seiichi [Setsuan] 滝精一［節庵］. "Tenrankai shokan (chū) 展覧会所感（中）." *Tōkyō Asahi shinbun*, October 27, 1915, 6.

Tamamuro Fumio 圭室文雄. "Hirata Atsutane no hai-Butsu ron ni tsuite 平田篤胤の排仏論について." In *Hirata Atsutane no gakumon to shisō*, vol. 5, *Haga Noboru chosaku senshū*, 355–64. Tokyo: Yūzankaku, 2002.

Tamura Maiko 田村眞依子. "Kinsei/Kindai ni okeru 'Nichiren-ki mono' no ichi kōsatsu 近世・近代における「日蓮記物」の一考察." *Nichiren kyōgaku kenkyūsho kiyō*, no. 31 (2004): 121–28.

Tanaka Ichimatsu 田中一松. "Chūsei ni okeru Eingakyō no sho sakuhin 中世における絵因果経の諸作品." In *Eingakyō*, edited by Kadokawa Shoten Henshūbu, Nihon emakimono zenshū, vol. 6, 55–65. Tokyo: Kadokawa Shoten, 1969.

Tanaka Shūji 田中修二. *Chōkokuka Shinkai Taketarō ron* 彫刻家・新海竹太郎論. Tsuruoka: Tōhoku Shuppan Kikaku, 2002.

Tanaka Yoshiyasu 田中義恭. *Tanjōbutsu* 誕生仏. Nihon no bijutsu, vol. 159. Tokyo: Shibundō, 1979.

Tezuka Osamu 手塚治虫. *Budda 4* ブッダ4. Tezuka Osamu bunko zenshū, vol. BT-111. Tokyo: Kōdansha, 2011.

———. *Buddha 4: The Forest of Uruvela*. New York: Vertical, 2006.

Thelle, Notto R. *Buddhism and Christianity in Japan: From Conflict to Dialogue, 1854–1899*. Honolulu: University of Hawaii Press, 1987.

Thomas, Julia Adeney. *Reconfiguring Modernity: Concepts of Nature in Japanese Political Ideology*. Berkeley: University of California Press, 2001.

Tōbu Bijutsukan 東武美術館 et al., eds. *Budda ten: Ōinaru tabiji* ブッダ展: 大いなる旅路. Tokyo: NHK Promōshon, 1998.

Tōhō Shoin 東方書院, ed. *Nihon emaki zenshū* 日本絵巻全集, vol. 1. Tokyo: Tōhō Shoin, 1928.

Tokiwa Daijō 常盤大定. "Kako genzai ingakyō kaidai 過去現在因果経解題." In *Hon'enbu 4*, Kokuyaku issaikyō, vol. 32, 1–10. Tokyo: Daitō Shuppansha, 1929.

———. "Kanishika-ō 迦膩色迦王." *Bukkyō shirin* 3, no. 26 (1896): 1–22.

Tokumitsu Shōryū 徳光松隆. *Shakuson shinjitsu denki* 釈尊真実伝記. Nagasaki: Hōtokukai, 1882.

Tōkyō Ongaku Gakkō 東京音楽学校, ed. *Kinsei hōgaku nenpyō: Gidayū bushi no bu* 近世邦楽年表: 義太夫節之部. Tokyo: Rikugōkan, 1927.

Tomimura Takafumi 冨村孝文. "Gedatsu Shōnin Jōkei no Shaka shinkō ni tsuite 解脱上人貞慶の釈迦信仰について." *Ryūkyū Daigaku Hōbungakubu kiyō: Shigaku, chirigaku hen* 32 (1989): 139–48.

Tominaga Nakamoto 富永仲基. *Shutsujō kōgo* 出定後語. Tokyo: Ryūbunkan, 1982.

Tomomatsu Entai 友松円諦. *Bukkyō no mirai o hiraku: Shakai to mukiau Bukkyō to wa* 仏教の未来をひらく: 社会と向き合う仏教とは. Tokyo: Suzuki Shuppan, 2002.

Tongguk Taehakkyo Han'guk Pulgyo Chŏnsŏ P'yŏnch'an Wiwŏn 東國大學校韓國佛敎全書編纂委員, ed. *Koryŏ sidae pyŏn 3* 高麗時代篇 3. Han'guk Pulgyo chŏnsŏ, vol. 6. Seoul: Tongguk Taehakkyo Ch'ulp'anbu, 1994.

Tsai, Suey-Ling. *The Life of the Buddha: Woodblock Illustrated Books in China and Korea*. Wiesbaden: Harrassowitz, 2012.

Tsuboya Zenshirō 坪谷善四郎. *Hakubunkan gojū-nen shi* 博文館五十年史. Tokyo: Hakubunkan, 1937.

Tsuchiya Hiromasa 土屋博政. "Naze Nihon Yuniterian Misshon wa shinten shinakatta no ka: Kurei Makōrī to Nihon Yuniterian Misshon (1) なぜ日本ユニテリアン·ミッションは伸展しなかったのか: クレイ·マコーリィと日本ユニテリアン·ミッション(I)." *Keiō Gijuku Daigaku hiyoshi kiyō: Eigo Ei-Bei bungaku* 39, no. 2001 (2001): 27–141.

Tsuchiya Maki 土屋真紀. "*Shakadō engi emaki* o meguru ichi kōsatsu 「釈迦堂縁起絵巻」をめぐる一考察." *Bijutsushi* 57, no. 1 (2007): 90–107.

Tsukishima Hiroshi 築島裕. "*Tōdaiji fujumon kō* shōkō 「東大寺諷誦文稿」小考." *Kokugo kokubun* 21, no. 5 (1952): 341–49.

Tsukuba Daigaku Toshokan 筑波大学図書館, ed. *Jiun Sonja to Shittan gaku: Jihitsubon Hokke darani ryakuge to Bongaku shinryō no sekai* 慈雲尊者と悉雲学: 自筆本『法華陀羅尼略解』と「梵学津梁」の世界. Ibaraki: Tsukuba Daigaku Fuzoku Toshokan, 2010.

Tsutsumi Kunihiko 堤邦彦. *Edo no kōsō densetsu* 江戸の高僧伝説. Tokyo: Miyai Shoten, 2008.

Uchimura Katsushi 内村和至. "Hagiwara Otohiko no gesaku rui ni tsuite 萩原乙彦の戯作類について." *Bungei kenkyū*, no. 116 (2012): 1–31.

Ueda Kazutoshi 上田万年 and Higuchi Yoshichiyo 樋口慶千代. *Chikamatsu goi* 近松語彙. Tokyo: Fuzanbō, 1930.

Ueyama Shigeru 植山茂, and Ōtsuka Katsumi 大塚活美, eds. *Mibudera ten: Dainenbutsu kyōshin to Jizō shinkō no tera, sōken 1000-nen kinen* 壬生寺展: 大念仏狂言と地蔵信仰の寺　創建1000年記念. Kyoto: Kyōto Bunka Hakubutsukan, 1992.

Umehara Sueji 梅原末治. "Oshidashi Shaka tanjō Maya bunin oyobi suinyo zō 押出釈迦誕生摩耶夫人綏女像." *Shiseki to bijutsu*, no. 389 (1968): 322–26.

Umezu Jirō 梅津次郎. "Emakimono zanketsu aiseki no fu 11: Eingakyō 絵巻物残欠愛惜の譜<11>: 絵因果経." *Nihon bijutsu kōgei*, January 1966, 104–10.

Vermeersch, Sem. "An Early Korean Version of the Buddha's Biography." *Journal of the Oxford Centre for Buddhist Studies* 1 (2011): 197–211.

Visser, Marinus Willem de. *Ancient Buddhism in Japan: Sūtras and Ceremonies in Use in the Seventh and Eighth Centuries A.D. and Their History in Later Times*. Leiden: E. J. Brill, 1935.

Wakabayashi, Bob Tadashi. "Katō Hiroyuki and Confucian Natural Rights, 1861–1870." *Harvard Journal of Asiatic Studies* 44, no. 2 (1984): 469–92.

Waley, Arthur. *Ballads and Stories from Tun-huang: An Anthology*. New York: Macmillan, 1960.

Walthall, Anne. *The Weak Body of a Useless Woman: Matsuo Taseko and the Meiji Restoration*. Chicago: University of Chicago Press, 1998.

Wang, Eugene Yuejin. *Shaping the Lotus Sutra: Buddhist Visual Culture in Medieval China*. Seattle: University of Washington Press, 2005.

Wasaki Kōtarō 和崎光太郎. "Shoki Teiyū Rinrikai ni okeru rinriteki 'shūyō': Anesaki Masaharu to Ukita Kazutami ni chakumoku shite 初期丁酉倫理会における倫理的<修養>: 姉崎正治と浮田和民に着目して." *Kyōikushi fōramu*, no. 7 (2012): 3–17.

Washizuka, Hiromitsu, et al., eds. *Transmitting the Forms of Divinity: Early Buddhist Art from Korea and Japan*. New York: Japan Society, 2003.

Watanabe Kinzō 渡邊金造. *Hirata Atsutane kenkyū* 平田篤胤研究. Tokyo: Rokkō Shobō, 1942.

Watanabe Masako 渡辺雅子. "Nihon chūsei Butsudenzu no hen'yō: Shimon shutsuyū o chūshin ni shite 日本中世仏伝図の変容: 四門出遊を中心にして." In *Bukkyō bijutsu to rekishi bunka*, edited by Manabe Shunshō, 481–507. Kyoto: Hōzōkan, 2005.

———. "A Preliminary Study of 'Life of the Buddha' in Mediaeval Japan: The Metropolitan Museum Paintings." *Orientations* 27, no. 8 (1996): 46–56.

Watanabe Satoshi 渡邉里志. *Butsudenzu ronkō* 仏伝図論考. Tokyo: Chūō Kōron Bijutsu Shuppan, 2012.

———. "Eingakyō Butsudenzu no zuzōteki kenkyū shiron: Kyōto Jōbonrendaiji bon o chūshin ni 絵因果経仏伝図の図像的研究試論: 京都·上品蓮台寺本を中心に." In *Bijutsushika, ōi ni warau: Kōno Motoaki sensei no tame no Nihon bijutsushi ronshū*, edited by Kōno Motoaki Sensei Taikan Kinen Ronbunshu Henshu Iinkai, 199–220. Kunitachi: Buryukke, 2006.

———. "Nihon no butsuden bijutsu (Muromachi jidai made) 日本の仏伝美術（室町時代まで）." In *Butsuden bijutsu no denpan to hen'yō: Shiruku Rōdo ni sotte*, edited by Shiruku Rōdo Gaku Kenkyū Sentā, 84–95. Nara: Shiruku Rōdo Gaku Kinen Kokusai Kōryū Zaidan, 1997.

Watanabe Shōgo 渡邉昭五. "Shūso kakefuku eden etokishi no shoron 宗僧掛幅絵伝絵解き史の緒論." *Ōtsuma kokubun*, no. 30 (1999): 109–43.

Watt, Paul. "Body, Gender, and Society in Jiun Sonja's (1718–1804) Buddhism." In *Engendering Faith: Women and Buddhism in Premodern Japan*, edited by Barbara Ruch, 325–40. Ann Arbor: Center for Japanese Studies, University of Michigan, 2002.

———. "Jiun Sonja (1718–1804): Life and Thought." PhD diss., Columbia University, 1982.

Weston, Victoria Louise. *Japanese Painting and National Identity: Okakura Tenshin and His Circle*. Ann Arbor: Center for Japanese Studies, University of Michigan, 2004.

Willemen, Charles. "Selected Materials for the Study of the Life of Buddha Śākyamuni." *Pacific World*, no. 13 (2011): 67–80.

Woodcock, Matthew. "Crossovers and Afterlife." In *A Companion to Middle English Hagiography*, edited by Sarah Salih, 141–57. Woodbridge: D. S. Brewer, 2006.

Xing Lili 邢莉莉. *Mingdai Fozhuan gushihua yanjiu* 明代佛传故事画研究. Beijing: Xianzhuang Shuju, 2010.

Yamada, Keichyu [Keichū]. *Scenes from the Life of Buddha*. Chicago: Open Court, 1898.

Yamada Yoshio 山田孝雄, ed. *Konjaku monogatari shū 1* 今昔物語集1. Vol. 22, *Nihon koten bungaku taikei*. Tokyo: Iwanami Shoten, 1959.

Yamagata Genjō 山県玄浄. *Hyakuren no tetchō* 百錬之鉄腸. Kyoto: Dentōsha, 1897.

Yamagishi Kōki 山岸公基. "Hōryūji saiken o meguru seiji jōkyō to gojū no tō tōhon shimengu 法隆寺再建をめぐる政治情況と五重塔塔本四面具." *Mikkyō zuzō* 26 (2007): 1–16.

Yamaguchi Seiichi 山口静一, ed. *Kawanabe Kyōsai sashie 1: Shōsetsu, kokkei fūshibon yori* 鍋暁斎挿絵 1: 小説、滑稽風刺本より. Kyōsai shiryō, vol. 7. Warabi: Kyōsai Kinenkan, 1985.

Yamamoto Shindō 山本晋道. "Hirata Atsutane no Bukkyō-kan 平田篤胤の仏教観." *Kenshin gakuhō* 32 (1941): 17–40.

Yamamuro Shin'ichi 山室信一. "Nihon gakumon no jizoku to tenkai 日本学問の持続と転回." In *Gakumon to chishikijin*, edited by Matsumoto Sannosuke and Yamamuro Shin'ichi, Nihon kindai shisō taikei, vol. 10, 455–98. Tokyo: Iwanami Shoten, 1988.

Yamanaka Yutaka 山中裕, ed. *Eiga monogatari* 栄花物語. Shinpen Nihon koten bungaku zenshū, vol. 32. Tokyo: Shōgakkan, 1995.

———. *Heianchō no nenjū gyōji* 平安朝の年中行事. Tokyo: Hanawa Shobō, 1972.

Yamanashi Toshio 山梨俊夫. *Egakareta rekishi: Nihon kindai to "rekishiga" no jiba* 描かれた歴史: 日本近代と「歴史画」の磁場. Kunitachi: Buryukke, 2005.

Yamauchi Susumu [Shinkyō] 山内晋［晋卿］. "Kyōso Shaka ni tai-suru kodai Bukkyōto no shisō 教祖釈迦に対する古代仏教徒の思想." *Taiyō* 3, no. 2 (1897): 439–46.

Yamabe, Nobuyoshi. "*The Sūtra on the Ocean-Like Samādhi of the Visualization of the Buddha*: The Interfusion of the Chinese and Indian Cultures in Central Asia as Reflected in a Fifth Century Apocryphal Sūtra." PhD diss., Yale University, 1999.

Yang Ungi. "T'ongdosa p'alsangdo wa *Sŏkssi wŏllyu* ŭi kwangye pigyo 通度寺 八相圖와 『釋氏源流』의 관계 비교." *Pulgyo misul sahak*, no. 3 (2005): 214–36.

Yi Yŏngja 李永子. "Mugi ŭi Ch'ŏnt'ae sasang: Sŏkka yŏrae haengjŏk song ŭl chungsim ŭro 無寄의 天台思想: 釋迦如來行蹟頌을 中心으로." *Han'guk Pulgyohak* 3 (1977): 77–103.

Yi Yŏngjong 李英宗. "Chosŏn sidae p'alsangdo tosang ŭi yŏnwŏn gwa chŏngae 朝鮮時代八相圖 圖像의 淵源과 展開." *Misul sahak yon'gu*, no. 215 (1997): 27–56.

———. "T'ongdosa Yongsanjŏn ŭi *Sŏkssi wŏllyu ŭnghwa sajŏk* pyŏk'hwa yŏn'gu 通度寺 靈山殿의 『釋氏源流應化事蹟』벽화 연구." *Misul sahak yon'gu*, no. 250–51 (2006): 253–85.

Yifa. *The Origins of Buddhist Monastic Codes in China: An Annotated Translation and Study of the Chanyuan qinggui*. Honolulu: University of Hawaii Press, 2002.

Yomota Inuhiko 四方田犬彦. "Genzai shakai ni motomerareru *Budda* no sekaikan 現在社会に求められる『ブッダ』の世界観." *Ushio*, June 2011, 224–29.

Yoshida Asako 吉田麻子. *Chi no kyōmei: Hirata Atsutane o meguru shomotsu no shakaishi* 知の共鳴: 平田篤胤をめぐる書物の社会史. Tokyo: Perikansha, 2012.

Yoshida Masaki 吉田真樹. "Kinsei shomin Bukkyō to *Shutsujō shōgo* 近世庶民仏教と『出定笑語』." In *Hirata Atsutane: Reikon no yukue*, 131–49. Tokyo: Kōdansha, 2009.

Young, John. *The Christ of History: An Argument Grounded in the Facts of His Life on Earth*. London: Longman, Brown, Green, and Longmans, 1855.

Yūda Yoshio 祐田善雄. "Chikamatsu nenpu 近松年譜." *Kokubungaku kaishaku to kanshō* 30, no. 3 (1965): 112–21.

Zhao, Ng Xin. "Review of Osamu Tezuka's 'Buddha 1 & 2.'" *The Daily Enlightenment*. Last modified December 1, 2014. http://thedailyenlightenment.com/2014/12/review-of-osamu-tezukas-buddha-1-2/.

Finding Aid for Names and Terms

Conventions: Proper nouns referring to Chinese or Korean individuals, or to the titles of scriptures or other works originally inscribed in China or Korea, are given in standard (full) Chinese script. Other proper nouns, titles of paintings or writings composed in Japanese, and Japanese terms are generally given using standard Japanese *shinjitai*, the "new character forms" which are now current. Titles of scriptures or other works are listed under the English translation used in this text. The appearance of an asterisk before a Sanskrit title indicates that the title is a hypothetical reconstruction. For the sake of easy recognition, the Chinese titles of Buddhist scriptures are typically given in their abbreviated forms. As elsewhere in this study, an italicized letter *T* before a number refers to the sutra number in the Taishō Tripiṭaka.

Acalanātha (Jpn. Fudō Myōō 不動明王)
Acts of the Buddha (Aśvaghoṣa). See *Praise of the Deeds of the Buddha*
Ajātaśatru (Jpn. Ajase 阿闍世)
Akegarasu Haya 暁烏敏
amacha 甘茶
Amaterasu Ōmikami 天照大神
Amitābha (Jpn. Amida 阿弥陀)
Ānanda (Jpn. Ananda 阿難陀, abbr. Anan 阿難)
Anesaki Masaharu 姉崎正治
Aṅgulimāla (Jpn. Ōkutsumara 央掘摩羅)

Anthology from the Patriarchal Hall (*Zu tang ji* 祖堂集)
An'yōin 安養院
Ārāḍa (Jpn. Arara 阿羅羅, alt. Arara あらら)
Ārāḍa Kālāma (Jpn. Arara Karan 阿羅邏迦蘭)
Arai Kanpō 荒井寛方
Arakida Reijo 荒木田麗女
Art News (*Bijutsu shinpō* 美術新報)
Asita (Jpn. Ashida 阿私陀)
aśoka tree (Jpn. *mu'uju* 無憂樹)
Aśvaghoṣa (Jpn. Memyō 馬鳴)
Avadāna [*i.e., Tale*] *of the Practice* [*of the Bodhisattva*] (Ch. *Xiuxing benqi jing*, Jpn. *Shugyō hongi kyō* 修行本起經, *T* 184)
Avalokiteśvara (Jpn. Kanzeon 観世音 or Kannon 観音)

Ba, General (Jpn. Ba Shōgun 馬将軍)
baku 獏
Baocheng 寶成
bhikṣu precepts (Jpn. *gusokukai* 具足戒)
Bimbisāra (Jpn. Binbashara 頻婆娑羅)
Biography for the Instruction of Children (Jpn. *Kyōjiden* 教児伝)
Biography of Śākyamuni (*Shakamuni den* 釈迦牟尼伝) (Inoue)
The Biography of the Fundamental Aspiration behind Śākyamuni's Emergence into the World (*Shaka shusse honkai denki* 釈迦出世本懐伝記)
Bira 鞞羅, 84
A Birth Assembly for the Tathāgata Śākyamuni (*Shaka nyorai tanjō-e* 釈迦如来誕生会) (Chikamatsu)
Birth of the Buddha (*Buttan* 仏誕) (Kosaka)
Birth of the Buddha (*Buttan zu* 仏誕図) (Kanzan)
bodhi tree (Jpn. *bodaiju* 菩提樹)
Brahmā (Jpn. Bonten 梵天)
The Buddha and Sujātā (Budda to Sujātā フッダとスジャーター*)*
The Buddha Suffering on This Earth (*Chi ni nayameru Shaka* 地に悩める釈迦) (Tomomatsu)
"Buddha-ancestor" (Jpn. Busso 仏祖)
Bukkyōka 仏教家
Bunten 文展
busshi 仏師
Busshō-e 仏生会

caṇḍāla (Jpn. *sendara* 旃陀羅)
Central Arts Review (*Chūō bijustu* 中央美術)

Ceremonial in Four Sessions (*Shiza kōshiki* 四座講式) (Myōe)
Chan 禪
Channa (Jpn. Shanoku 車匿)
character (*jinkaku* 人格)
Ch'egwan 諦觀
Cheng Yi 程頤
Chikamatsu Monzaemon 近松門左衛門
chōbuku 調伏
Chōfukuji 長福寺
Chōnen 奝然
Chŏng Tojŏn 鄭道傳
Chongshansi 崇善寺
Chosŏn 朝鮮
Chronicle of the Bejeweled Forest (*Bao lin zhuan* 寶林傳)
Chronicle of the Buddhas and Patriarchs (Ch. *Fozu tongji*, Jpn. *Busso tōki* 佛祖統紀, *T* 2035)
A Compass in a Sea of Mist (*Bukai nanshin* 霧海南針) (Hakugan)
Compassion Flower Sutra (Skt. **Karuṇapuṇḍarīka nāmamahāyāna sūtra*, Ch. *Beihua-jing*, Jpn. *Hikekyō* 悲華經, *T* 157)
Compendium of Indian Records (*Indo zōshi* 印度蔵志) (Atsutane)
Confucius (Jpn. Kōshi 孔子)
The Conquest of Māra (Gōma 降魔) (Katsuta)
"conversion of the barbarians" (Ch. *huahu* 化胡)
Correction of the Errors of the Buddhists (Ch. *Shijiao zhengmiu* 釋教正謬) (Edkins)
"Correction of the Errors of the Buddhists" Spits at Heaven (*Shakkyō shōmyū tenda* 釈教正謬天唾)
Cremation (*Jai* 闍維) (Kanzan)
Cūḍapanthaka (Jpn. Shurihantoku 周利槃特, abbr. Hantoku 槃特)

Daifukudenji 大福田寺
Daigakuryō 大学寮
Daigoji 醍醐寺
Daocheng 道誠
Daoxuan 道宣
The Detailed Record of the Life of Śākyamuni (*Sŏkpo sangjŏl* 釋譜詳節)
Devadatta (Buddha's cousin) (Jpn. Daibadatta 提婆達多, abbr. Daiba 提婆)
Dharma Assembly of Permanence and Bliss (*Jōrakue* 常楽会)
dharmakāya (body of truth, Jpn. *hosshin* 法身)
Dharma-meeting of Non-obstruction (Jpn. *Mushae* 無遮会)
Dialogue between a Confucianist and a Buddhist (*Ju-butsu mondō* 儒仏問答)
Dīpaṃkara (Ch. Pugwang, Jpn. Fukō 普光)

Dōshūn 道春
Drafts for a Compendium of Indian Records (*Indo zōshi kō* 印度蔵志稿)
Dunhuang 敦煌

Edo 江戸
Eifukuji 叡福寺
Eight Event–nirvana paintings (*hassō Nehanzu* 八相涅槃図)
Eight Phases (Jpn. *hassō* 八相)
Eight Phases of the Life of Śākyamuni, A Japanese Library (*Shaka hassō Yamato bunko* 釈迦八相倭文庫)
Eisai (a.k.a. Yōsai 栄西)
eiyū 英雄
Eizon (a.k.a. Eison 叡尊)
Emerging from Meditation and Then Speaking (*Shutsujō kōgo/Shutsujō gogo* 出定後語) (Nakamoto)
End of the Dharma (Jpn. *mappō* 末法, alt. *sue no yo* 末の世)
engi hōju 縁起法頌
eraṇḍa tree (Jpn. Iran 伊蘭)
Erin 慧琳
"Essentials of the Moral Way" ("Yuandao" 原道) (Han)
etoki 絵解き
The Evil Elephant Takes Refuge in the Buddha (*Akuzō no ki-Butsu* 悪象の帰仏)
An Explanation of the Way of Awakening (*Godōben* 悟道弁)

Five Periods of the Buddha's preaching (Jpn. *gojikyō* 五時教)
Flower Garland Sutra (Skt. *Avataṃsaka Sūtra*, Ch. *Huayanjing*, Jpn. *Kegonkyō* 華嚴經, *T* 278)
Flowers of Wisdom (*Bodai no hana* 菩提の花)
The Flower-Viewing Hall, a Japanese Library (*Hanamidō Yamato bunko* 花観台大和文庫, alt. 花観堂大和文庫)
Four Encounters (*shimon shutsuyū* 四門出遊)
Four Forces of Evil (Jpn. *shima* 四魔)
"Four Great World Sages" (*Sekai shidai seijin* 世界四大聖人)
Four Noble Truths (Jpn. *Shishōtai* 四聖諦)
"Four Sages of the World" ("Sekai no shisei" 世界の四聖)
Frank Words on Current Issues (*Sōbō kigen* 草茅危言)
fuhenteki 普遍的
Fujii Senshō 藤井宣正
Fujishima Ryōon 藤島了穏
Fujiwara clan 藤原氏
Fujiwara Fuhito 藤原不比等

Fujiwara Seika 藤原惺窩
Fukuda Gyōkai 福田行誡
Fumon Entsū 普門円通
Fundamental Institutions for the Sangha (*Konpon sōsei* 根本僧制)
Furukawa Rōsen 古河老川

Gaṇeśa (Jpn. Kangiten 歓喜天)
Gautamī (Kyōdonmi 憍曇弥)
Genealogy of Śākyamuni (Ch. *Shijia pu* 釋迦譜, *T* 2040) (Sengyou)
Genealogy of the Śākya Clan (Ch. *Shijia shi pu* 釋迦氏譜, *T* 2041) (Daoxuan)
genshiteki Bukkyō 原始的仏教
genshitsu 原質
Gentei 玄貞
gesaku 戯作
gesō 外相
Gikan 義寛
gikobun 擬古文
The Golden Needle of Truth (*Shinri kinshin* 真理金針)
Go-Momozono 後桃園 (emperor)
Gopī (Jpn. Kui 瞿夷)
Go-Sakuramachi 後桜町
gosirsa-candana tree (Jpn. *gozu sendan* 牛頭栴檀)
Gōtan-e 降誕会
Great Exegesis (Skt. **Mahāvibhāṣā*, Ch. *Apidamo da piposha lun*, Jpn. *Abidatsuma dai bibasha ron* 阿毘達磨大毘婆沙論, *T* 1545)
Great Prajñāpāramitā Sūtra (Skt. *Mahāprajñāpāramitā Sūtra*, Ch. *Da bore jing*, Jpn. *Dai hannya kyō* 大般若經, *T* 220)
Grove of Buddhist History (*Bukkyō shirin* 仏教史林)
Guanding 灌頂
Guṇabhadra (Ch. Qiunabatuoluo 求那跋陀羅)
Gyōchi 行智
Gyōki 行基

Hakuryōton 伯了頓
Half the Life of Śākyamuni (*Shaka no hansei* 釈迦の半生)
Hamasaki Ayumi 浜崎あゆみ
Han Yu 韓愈
Hanamatsuri 花祭
Hārītī (Jpn. Kishimojin 鬼子母神)
Hattori Somon (Ten'yū) 服部蘇門 (天游)
Hayakawa Sesshū 早川雪洲

Hayashi Razan 林羅山
Heaven of the Pure Abode (Jpn. Jōgoten 浄居天)
Hermitage of the Twin Dragons (Sōryūan 雙龍庵)
Hiei, Mount (Jpn. Hieizan 比叡山)
Higashi Honganji 東本願寺
Higuchi Ryūon 樋口竜温
hihyōteki geshin 批評的解信
Hiramatsu Shunsei 平松俊正
Hirayama Ikuo 平山郁夫
Hiroyasu Shinzui 広安真随
Hishida Shunsō 菱田春草
historical painting (*rekishiga* 歴史画)
Historical Review 史学雑誌
Hitoyoshi 人吉
Hōkiin 宝亀院
Hōnen 法然
Honganji 本願寺
honji 本地
honjimono 本地物
honzon 本尊 (main image)
Hori Shitoku 堀至徳
Huisi 慧思
Hyech'o 慧超

Ibukinoya 気吹舎
ijin 偉人 (great man)
Ikasuri Shrine (Jpn. Ikasuri Jinja 坐摩神社)
Ikuta Chōkō 生田長江
The Illustrated Sutra of Past and Present Cause and Effect (Jpn. *Kako genzai e-inga kyō* 過去現在絵因果經)
Illustrated Three Jewels (*Sanbōe* 三宝絵)
An Initial Refutation and a Re-Refutation of "Correction of the Errors of Buddhism" (*Shakkyō shōmyū tenda shoha narabi ni saiha* 釈教正謬初破並再破) (Tetsujō)
An Initial Refutation of "Correction of the Errors of Buddhism" (*Shakkyō shōmyū tenda* 釈教正謬天唾) (Tetsujō)
Inoue Enryō 井上円了
Inoue Masu 井上マス
Inoue Tetsujirō 井上哲次郎
Institute for Defense of the Dharma (Gohōjō 護法場)
ippanteki 一般的
Ishikawa Shuntai 石川舜台

Ishiyamadera 石山寺
issai shuchi 一切種智
Itō Chūta 伊東忠太
Itō Jakuchū 伊藤若冲
Itō Jinsai 伊藤仁斎
Itō Shundō 伊藤俊道
Itō Tōgai 伊藤東涯

jakyō 邪教
Japan Art Institute (Jpn. Nihon Bijtusuin 日本美術院)
Japanese Library of the Eight Phases of the Life of Śākyamuni (*Shaka hassō Yamato bunko* 釈迦八相倭文庫)
Japanese Writing in the Divine Script (*Shinji hifumi den* 神字日文伝)
jātaka (Jpn. *honshōtan* 本生譚)
Jikōji 持光寺
jinbutsu 人物
jinkaku 人格
Jishōin 自性院
jitsugyō no yū 実業ノ雄
Jiun Onkō 慈雲飲光
jiyū tōkyū 自由討究
Jōbonrendaiji 上品蓮台寺
Jōdō Shinshū 浄土真宗
Jōganji 貞観寺
Jōkei 貞慶
Jōrakuji 常楽寺
jōroku 丈六
jōruri 浄瑠璃
Jōtokuji 常徳寺
Jueyuansi 覺苑寺
Jusen'in Nissen 寿仙院日篓

kabuki 歌舞伎
Kaidan'in 戒壇院
Kaimeimon'in 開明門院
Kakugan Jitsumyō 覚巌実明
Kālāma (Jpn. Karan 迦蘭, alt. Karara からら)
kalaviṅka (Jpn. Karyōbinga 迦陵頻伽)
kanazōshi 仮名草子
Kanbutsu-e 灌仏会
Kanō Motonobu 狩野元信

Kaṇṭhaka (Jpn. Kondei 犍陟)
Kapilavastu (Jpn. Kabirae 迦毘羅衛)
Kasuga 春日
Kāśyapa brothers (Jpn. San Kashō 三迦葉)
Katō Hiroyuki 加藤弘之
Katō Kiyomasa 加藤清正
Katō Totsudō 加藤咄堂
Katsushika Hokusai 葛飾北斎
Katsuta Shōkin 勝田蕉琴
Kawaguchi Ekai 河口慧海
Kawanabe Kyōsai 河鍋暁斎
kenkyō fukai 牽強付会
Kenshin Daishi 見真大師 [a.k.a. Shinran]
Kichijōnyo 吉祥女
Kiriya Senrin 桐谷洗鱗
Kōbō Daishi 弘法大師 [a.k.a. Kūkai]
koden 古伝
Kōgetsu Sōgi 皓月宗顗 (Nobuko 信子)
kojitsu 故実
Kōkadō Isai 好花堂意齊 (a.k.a. Yamada no Kakashi 山田案山子)
Kokugaku 国学
kōkyō 公共
Koryŏ 高麗
Kōsanji 耕三寺
kōshiki 講式
kōshō 考証
Kosugi Sugimura 小杉榲邨
Kōunbō 香雲房
Kōya, Mount (Jpn. Kōyasan 高野山)
kṣatriya (Jpn. *setteiri* 刹帝利)
Kūkai 空海 (Kōbō Daishi 弘法大師)
Kumārāyana (Jpn. Kumaraen 鳩摩羅琰)
Kuwahara Keiichi 桑原啓一
kyōhō 教法
kyōmon 教門
Kyōraimon'in 恭礼門院 (Fujiwara Tomiko 藤原富子)
kyōsō hanjaku 教相判釈 (abbr. *kyōhan* 教判)

Lamaism (Jpn. *Ramakyō* 喇嘛教)
Laozi 老子

Latter Portion of the Sutra of the Great Parinirvāṇa (Ch. *Da banniepan jing houfen*, Jpn. *Dai hatsunehan gyō gobun* 大般涅槃経後分, *T* 377)
Lectures on Comparative Religion and Eastern Philosophy (*Hikaku shūkyō oyobi Tōyō tetsugaku kōgi* 比較宗教及東洋哲学講義)
Legends from Chinese Antiquity (*Sekiken taikoden* 赤県太古伝)
Liezi 列子
The Light of the Four Seas (*Shikai no hikari* 四海の光) (Hayakawa)
The Light of the Three Ages (*Miyo no hikari* 三世の光) (Kōgetsu)
Lin Xiyi 林希逸, 129
Lotus Sutra (Skt. *Saddharmapuṇḍarīka sūtra*, Ch. *Miaofa lianhua jing*, Jpn. *Myōhō renge kyō* 妙法蓮華經, *T* 262)

Maeda Eun 前田慧雲
Mahābhijñājñānābhibhū (Jpn. Daitsūchishōbustu 大通智勝仏)
Mahākalā (Jpn. Daikoku 大黒)
Mahākāśyapa (Jpn. [Dai] Kasō [大] 迦葉)
Mahāmaya sūtra (Ch. *Mohe Moye jing*, Jpn. *Maka Maya kyō* 摩訶摩耶經, *T* 383)
Mahāprajāpatī Gautamī (Jpn. Makahajahadai Kyōdonmi 摩訶波闍波提憍曇弥)
Mahāvairocana (Jpn. Dainichi 大日)
Mahāyāna Mahāparinirvāṇa Sūtra. See *Sutra of the Great Decease.*
Maheśvara (Jpn. Makeishura-ten 摩醯首羅天)
Maitreya (Jpn. Miroku 弥勒)
Makahajahadai 摩訶波闍波提 (a.k.a. Daiaidō 大愛道)
mandala (Jpn. *mandara* 曼荼羅)
manifest trace (Jpn. *suijaku* 垂迹)
Mañjuśrī (Jpn. Monju 文殊)
Mantei Ōga 万亭応賀
Māra (demon king) (Jpn. Mara 魔羅)
Matsui Shōyō 松居松葉
Matsuyama Matsutarō 松山松太郎
Maudgalyāyana (Jpn. Mokukenren 目犍連, abbr. Mokuren 目連)
Māyā (Jpn. Maya 摩耶)
Meiji 明治
"Memorial on the Bone of Buddha" (*Lun Fogu biao* 論佛骨表)
Michiko 通子 (Erin 慧琳)
Middle Scripture of the Authentic Deeds (Ch. *Zhong benqi jing*, Jpn. *Chū hongi kyō* 中本起經, *T* 196)
Minamoto Tamenori 源為憲
Ming 明
Minor Section of the Monastic Code of the Root Group That Teaches That All Exists

(Skt. *Mūlasarvastivāda vinayakṣudrakavastu,* Ch. *Genben shuoyiqie youbu pinaiye zashi,* Jpn. *Konpon setsuissai ubu binaya zasshi* 根本説一切有部毘奈耶雑事, *T* 1451)
Mitsukuri Rinshō 箕作麟祥
Miyake Setsurei 三宅雪嶺
Miyazaki Kenji 宮崎健司, 34
A Mocking Discourse upon Emerging from Meditation (*Shutsujō shōgo* 出定笑語)
Mogao 莫高
Momozono 桃園
montsui no ge 聞槌偈
The Moon's Reflection and the Life of Śākyamuni (*Wŏrin Sŏkpo* 月印釋譜)
mōsō 妄想
Motoori Norinaga 本居宣長
Murakami Senshō 村上専精
Murasaki Shikibu 紫式部
Muromachi 室町
Mushanokōji Saneatsu 武者小路実篤
Musubi no Ōkami 産霊大神
Myōe 明恵

Nāgārjuna (Jpn. Ryūju 龍樹)
naijitsu 内実
Naitō Tōichirō 内藤藤一郎
Naka Kansuke 中勘助
Naka Michiyo 那珂通世
Nakamura Hajime 中村元
Nakamura Shin'ya 中村晋也
Nanda (Buddha's half-brother) (Jpn. Nanda 難陀)
Nandabalā (Jpn. Nandahara 難陀波羅)
Nanjō Bun'yū 南条文雄
Nara 奈良
nenbutsu 念仏, 74–75
Net of Brahmā Sutra (Ch. *Fanwang jing,* Jpn. *Bonmō kyō* 梵網經, *T* 1484)
New Treatise on Buddhism (*Butsudō shinron* 仏道新論) (Takahashi)
Nichiren 日蓮
Nihonga 日本画
Niiro Chūnosuke 新納忠之介
ningenmi 人間味
nirmāṇakāya (body of transformation) (Jpn. *ōjin* 応身)
nirvana (Jpn. *nehan* 涅槃)
Nirvana Assembly (*Nehan-e* 涅槃会)
Nirvana Ceremonial (*Nehan kōshiki* 涅槃講式)

Nirvana Sutra. See *Sutra of the Great Decease*.
Nobuko 信子
Nōnin Hakugan 能仁柏巌
Notes Taken while Listening to One Hundred Sessions of Sermons (Jpn. *Hyakuza hōdan kikigaki shō* 百座法談聞書抄)
Nousu Kōsetsu 野生司香雪

Oda Tokunō 織田得能
Ode to the Acts of the Tathāgata Śākyamuni (*Sŏkka yŏrae haengjŏk song* 釋迦如來行蹟頌)
The Offering of the Milk Gruel (*Nyūbi kuyō* 乳糜供養)
Office of Translation (Hon'yaku kyoku 翻訳局)
Okakura Kakuzō (Tenshin) 岡倉覚三 (天心)
Okina Kyūin 翁久允
Ōmiya Kōnin 大宮孝潤
On the Race of the Buddha (Jpn. *Shaka shuzoku ron* 釈迦種族論)
Onoe Matsunosuke 尾上松之助
Origin Tale of the Hall of Śākyamuni (*Shakadō engi* 釈迦堂縁起, a.k.a. *Seiryōji engi* 清涼寺縁起)
Original Ground of the Tathāgata Śākyamuni (*Shaka no honji* 釈迦の本地)
Origins and Transmission of the Śākya Clan (*Shishi yuanliu* 釋氏源流)
Orthodox Transmission of the Śākya Clan (Ch. *Shimen zhengtong*, Jpn. *Shakumon shōtō* 釋門正統)
Ōshima Sadamasu 大島貞益
Ōtani Kōei 大谷光瑩 (a.k.a. Gennyo 現如)
Ōtani Kōzui 大谷光瑞 (a.k.a. Kyōnyo 鏡如)
otogizōshi 御伽草子

parinirvāṇa (Jpn. *hatsunehan* 般涅槃)
Pearl Grove of the Dharma Garden (Ch. *Fayuan zhulin*, Jpn. *Hō'onjurin* 法苑珠林, *T* 2122)
A Personal Record of Refutations of Heresy (*Hekija kanken roku* 闢邪管見)
Platform Sutra of the Sixth Patriarch (Ch. *Liuzu tan jing*, Jpn. *Rokuso dan gyō* 六祖壇經, *T* 2008)
Praise of the Deeds of the Buddha (Skt. *Buddhacarita*, Ch. *Fo suo xing zan*, Jpn. *Butsu sho gyō san* 佛所行讃, *T* 192) (Aśvaghoṣa)
Prince Siddhartha beneath the Jambu Tree (*Enbuju ge no Shitta taishi* 閻浮樹下の悉達太子)
Program of the Eight Events of the Life of the Tathāgata Śākyamuni (*Shaka nyorai hassō shidai* 釈迦如来八相次第)
Pūrṇa (Jpn. Furuna 富楼那)

Rāhula (Buddha's son) (Jpn. Ragora 羅睺羅)
rākṣasa (Jpn. *rasetsu* 羅刹)
The Record of the Eight Phases of the Life of Śākyamuni (*Shaka hassō ki* 釈迦八相記)
Record of the Legend of the Yellow Emperor (*Kōtei denki* 黄帝伝記)
Record of the Ten- Stage Practice of the Tathāgata Śākyamuni (Sŏkka yŏrae sipchi suhaenggi 釋迦如來十地修行記)
Record of the Transmission of the Light of the Lamp of the Jingde Era (Ch. *Jingde chuandeng lu,* Jpn. *Keitoku dentō roku* 景徳傳燈録, *T* 2076)
rekishiga 歴史画
Rikugō zasshi 六合雑誌
Rintanshi 林丹子
Risshō Daishi 立正大師 [a.k.a. Nichiren]
Rousing the Record of the Life of Śākyamuni (*Shaka ichidai ki kosui* 釈迦一代記鼓吹)
Rurisennyo 瑠璃仙女
Ryōgen 良源
Ryōgetsu 良月

Sadamochi 貞行
Saian Urin 載庵禹隣
Saichō 最澄
Saikyōji 最教寺
Saishō Shōtai 西笑承兌
Saji Jitsunen 佐治実然
Sakaino Kōyō 境野黄洋
Śakra (Jpn. Taishaku 帝釈)
Sakura Azumao 佐久良東雄
Sakurada Jisuke III 三世桜田治助
Śākya Tribe (Jpn. Shaka zoku 釈迦族)
Śākyamuni (*Shaka* 釈迦) (film)
Śākyamuni (*Shaka* 釈迦) (Takayama)
Śākyamuni and the Demon Women (*Shaka to majo* 釈迦と魔女)
Śākyamuni Departing from the Fortress (*Shaka shutsujo* 釈迦出城) (Katsuta)
Śākyamuni Encounters His Father (*Shaka chichi ni au* 釈迦父に会う) (Yokoyama)
Samantabhadra (Jpn. Fugen bosatsu 普賢菩薩)
saṃsāra (Jpn. *rinne* 輪廻)
Sarasvatī (Jpn. Benzaiten 弁財天)
Śāriputra (Jpn. Sharihotsu 舎利弗)
Satsuma 薩摩
sculpted wall landscapes (*su shanshui bi* 塑山水壁)
Secret Record of Dialogues about the Economy (*Keizai mondō hiroku* 経済問答秘録)

Seiryōji 清涼寺
Seki Nyorai 関如来
Sekihōji 石峰寺
senbutsu 塼仏
Sengyou 僧祐
sermon-ballads (*sekkyōbushi* 説経節)
Shaku Unshō 釈雲照
shamu 社務
Shigeki Denhachirō 茂木傳八郎
Shimazaki Tōson 島崎藤村
Shimizu Mokuji 清水黙爾
Shimomura Kanzan 下村観山
Shingon 真言
Shinkai Taketarō 新海竹太郎
shinkaku 神格
Shinohara Junmei 篠原順明
Shinran 親鸞
Shintō 神道
Shitennōji 四天王寺
shogun 荘厳
shōhon 正本
Shōmu 聖武
A Short History of Buddhism (*Bukkyō shōshi* 仏教小史) (Fujii Senshō)
shōsetsu 小説
Shōtoku, Prince (Jpn. Shōtoku Taishi 聖徳太子)
Shugendō 修験道
Siddhārtha Addresses an Angel (*Shitta go tenshi zu* 悉達語天使図) (Terasaki Kōgyō)
Sōkenji 宗堅寺
Song 宋
Songgwangsa 松廣寺
Sonshi (a.k.a. Takako) 貴子
Sōtō 曹洞
śramaṇa (Jpn. *shamon* 沙門)
Śrāvastī (Jpn. Shaejō 舎衛城)
Ssangyesa 雙磎寺
Strange Tidings from the Realm of Immortals (*Senkyō ibun* 仙境異聞)
Su Ziyou 蘇子由
Sudatta (Jpn. Shudatsu 須達)
Śuddhodana (Buddha's father) (Jpn. Jōbon 浄飯)
Sugimoto Tetsuo 杉本哲郎

Sujātā (Jpn. Zenshō 善生, alt. Shujata 須闍多)
Sumedha (Jpn. Zen'e 善慧)
Summary of Vulgar Shintō (*Zoku Shintō taii* 俗神道大意)
"superhuman powers" (Skt. *abhijñā*, Jpn. *jinzū* 神通)
Sutra in Forty-Two Sections (Ch. *Shishierzhang jing*, Jpn. *Shijūnishō kyō* 四十二章經, *T* 748)
Sutra of Cosmology (Skt. **Lokasthāna*, Ch. *Da loutan jing*, Jpn. *Dai rōtan kyō* 大樓炭經, *T* 23)
Sutra of Past and Present Cause and Effect (Chinese *Guoqu xianzai yinguo jing*, Jpn. *Kako genzai inga kyō* 過去現在因果經, *T* 189)
Sutra of the Authentic Deeds of the Buddha (Ch. *Fo benxing jing*, Jpn. *Butsu hongyō kyō* 佛本行經, *T* 193)
Sutra of the Collection of Authentic Deeds of the Buddha (Ch. *Fo benxing ji jing*, Jpn. *Butsu hongyō jikkyō* 佛本行集經, *T* 190)
Sutra of the Display of the Deeds of the Buddha (Skt. *Lalitavistara*, Ch. *Puyao jing*, Jpn. *Fuyō kyō* 普曜經, *T* 186)
Sutra of the Great Decease (Ch. *Da banniepan jing*, Jpn *Dai hatsunehan gyō* 大般涅槃經 *T* 374, *T* 375)
Sutra of the Great Foundation (Pāli *Mahāpadānasuttanta*, Ch. *Dabenjing*, Jpn. *Daihon-kyō* 大本經, *T* 1)
Sutra of the Great Sammata King (Ch. *Zhongxu mohedi jing*, Jpn. *Shuko makadai kyō* 衆許摩訶帝經, *T* 191)
Sutra of the Heroic March (Skt. **Śūraṃgamasūtra*, Ch. *Shoulengyanlang jing*, Jpn. *Shuryōgon kyō* 首楞嚴經, *T* 945)
Sutra of the Liberation Blood Bowl (Ch. *Xiepen jing*, Jpn. *Ketsubon kyō* 血盆經)
Sutra of the Titles of the Eight Great Numinous Stupas (Ch. *Bada lingta minghao jing* , Jpn. *Hachidai ryōtō myōgō kyō* 八大靈塔名號經, *T* 1685)
Sutra of the Wise and the Foolish (Skt. *Damamūkanidāna Sūtra*, Ch. *Xianyu jing*, Jpn. *Gengukyō* 賢愚經, *T* 202)
Sutra of Vimalakīrti (Skt. *Vimalakīrtinirdeśasūtra*, Ch. *Weimojing*, Jpn. *Yuimagyō* 維摩經, *T* 475)
Sutra on the Achievement of the Way by the Prince [i.e., *Siddhartha*] (Ch. *Taizi cheng-dao jing* 太子成道經)
Sutra on the Descent into Laṅka (Skt. *Laṅkāvatārasūtra*, Ch. *Leng qie jing*, Jpn. *Ryōga kyō* 楞伽經, *T* 671)
Sutra on the Ocean-Like Samādhi of the Visualization of the Buddha (Ch. *Guanfo san-mei hai jing*, Jpn. *Kanbutsu sanmai kai kyō* 觀佛三昧海經, *T* 643)
Suzuki Shōsan 鈴木正三

Taigaku 大壑
Takada Dōken 高田道見
Takahashi Gorō 高橋五郎

Takakusu Junjirō 高楠順次郎
Takashima Beihō 高嶋米峰
Takayama Chogyū 高山樗牛
Taki Seiichi 滝精一
Tale of Flowering Fortunes (*Eiga monogatari* 栄花物語)
Tale of Genji (*Genji monogatari* 源氏物語)
Tale of Śākyamuni (*Shaka monogatari* 釈迦物語)
Tale of Śākyamuni (*Shakuson monogatari* 釈尊物語) (A. Christina Albers)
Tale of Śākyamuni in Eight Phases (*Shaka hassō monogatari* 釈迦八相物語)
Tales of the Three Lands (*Sangoku denki* 三国伝記)
Tales of Times Now Past (*Konjaku monogatarishū* 今昔物語集)
Tang 唐
Teitoku 貞徳
Tempō Reforms (Jpn. Tenpō kaikaku 天保改革)
Tendai (Ch. Tendai) 天台
Tetsugakukan 哲学館
Terasaki Kōgyō 寺崎広業
Tezuka Osamu 手塚治虫
Theory of the Revitalization of Buddhism (*Bukkyō katsuron* 仏教活論)
The Three Jewels (Jpn. *Sanbōe* 三宝絵)
Tōdaiji Notes for Sermons (*Tōdaiji fujumon kō* 東大寺諷誦文稿)
Tokugawa Ieyasu 徳川家康
Tokugawa Nariaki 徳川斉昭
Tokumitsu Shōryū 徳光松隆
Tokyo School of Fine Arts (Tōkyō Bijutsu Gakkō 東京美術学校)
Tominaga Nakamoto/Tominaga Chūki 富永仲基
Tomomatsu Entai 友松円諦
T'ongdosa 通度寺
transformation texts (Ch. *bianwen* 變文)
Trāyastriṃśa heaven (Jpn. Tōriten 忉利天, alt. Sanjūsanten 三十三天)
"[Treasure] Hall of the Great Hero" (Ch. *Daxiong [bao]dian*, Kor. *Taeŭng [po]jŏn* 大雄［寶］殿)
Treatise on the Great Perfection of Wisdom (Skt. * *Mahāprajñāpāramitāśastra*, Ch. *Dazhidu lun*, Jpn. *Daichido ron* 大智度論, *T* 1509) (Nāgārjuna)
True Biography of Śākyamuni (*Shaka jitsu denki* 釈迦実伝記) (Itō Shundō)
True Biography of the Venerable Śākyamuni (*Shakuson shinjitsu denki* 釈尊真実伝記) (Tokumitsu Shōryū)
"true texts" (Jpn. *shōhon* 正本)
Tsurugi Shrine (Jpn. Tsurugi Jinja 劔神社)
Twelve Gate Treatise (Skt. **Dvādaśamukha Śāstra*, Ch. *Shi'er menlun*, Jpn. *Jūni monron* 十二門論, *T* 1568) (Nāgārjuna)

Udana-in Nichiki 優陀那院日輝
Udāyana (a.k.a. Rudrāyana; Jpn. Uden 優塡)
Udāyin (Jpn. Udai 優陀夷)
Udraka Rāmaputra (Jpn. Utsuranhotsu, alt. Utsuzuranhotsu 鬱頭藍弗)
Ugai Tetsujō/Ukai Tetsujō 養鸕徹定
Umebori Kokuga II 二世梅暮里谷峨 (a.k.a. Reitei Kokuga 鈴亭谷峨, Hagiwara Otohiko 萩原乙彦, etc.)
ūrṇā (Jpn. *byakugō* 白毫)
Uruvilvā Kāśyapa (Jpn. Urubinra Kashō 優楼頻螺迦葉)

Vairocana (Jpn. Birushana 毘盧遮那)
Vaiśravaṇa (Jpn. Bishamonten 毘沙門天)
Vimalakīrti (Jpn. Yuima 維摩)
Vipaśyin (Jpn. Bibashi 毘婆尸)
Virūḍhaka (Jpn. Ruri 瑠璃)

Wang Bo 王勃
warigaki 割書
The Way and Its Power (*Daode jing* 道德經)
A Whisk for Swatting Away a Fly (*Tsuiyō barae* 追蠅払) (Ryōgetsu)
"worldling" (Skt. *pṛthagjana*, Jpn. *bonjin* 凡人, *bonbu* 凡夫)
Wuzong 武宗 (emperor)

Xuanzang 玄奘

Yanshansi 岩山寺
Yakushi Nyorai 薬師如来
Yakushiji 薬師寺
Yamada Keichū 山田敬中
Yamagata Bantō 山片蟠桃
Yamagata Genjō 山県玄浄
Yaśas (Jpn. Yasha 耶舎)
Yaśodharā (wife of Buddha) (Jpn. Yashudara 耶輸陀羅, abbr. Yashu 耶輸)
Yijing 義淨
yinyuan 因緣
yojana (Jpn. *yujun* 由旬)
Yokoyama Taikan 横山大観
Yongsanjŏn 靈山殿
Yōzan Gimon 葉山義文
Yuan 元
Yungang 雲崗

Zama-ban 坐摩版
zange 懺悔 (confession)
zasu 座主
Zen 禅
Zetsugaku 絶学
Zhanran 湛然
Zhen Luan 甄鸞
Zhiyi 智顗
Zhu Xi 朱熹
zokusan hendo 粟散辺土

Index

Page numbers in italic refer to figures.